# Queenship and Power

Series Editors
Charles Beem
University of North Carolina, Pembroke
Pembroke, NC, USA

Carole Levin
University of Nebraska-Lincoln
Lincoln, NE, USA

This series focuses on works specializing in gender analysis, women's studies, literary interpretation, and cultural, political, constitutional, and diplomatic history. It aims to broaden our understanding of the strategies that queens—both consorts and regnants, as well as female regents—pursued in order to wield political power within the structures of male-dominant societies. The works describe queenship in Europe as well as many other parts of the world, including East Asia, Sub-Saharan Africa, and Islamic civilization.

More information about this series at
http://www.palgrave.com/gp/series/14523

Janice North · Karl C. Alvestad
Elena Woodacre
Editors

# Premodern Rulers and Postmodern Viewers

Gender, Sex, and Power in Popular Culture

palgrave
macmillan

*Editors*
Janice North
Altoona, PA, USA

Karl C. Alvestad
Department of History
University of Winchester
Winchester, UK

Elena Woodacre
Department of History
University of Winchester
Winchester, UK

Queenship and Power
ISBN 978-3-319-68770-4      ISBN 978-3-319-68771-1   (eBook)
https://doi.org/10.1007/978-3-319-68771-1

Library of Congress Control Number: 2017957840

Cover credit: Vladimir Pomortzeff/Alamy Stock Photo

Printed on acid-free paper

This Palgrave Macmillan imprint is published by Springer Nature
The registered company is Springer International Publishing AG
The registered company address is: Gewerbestrasse 11, 6330 Cham, Switzerland

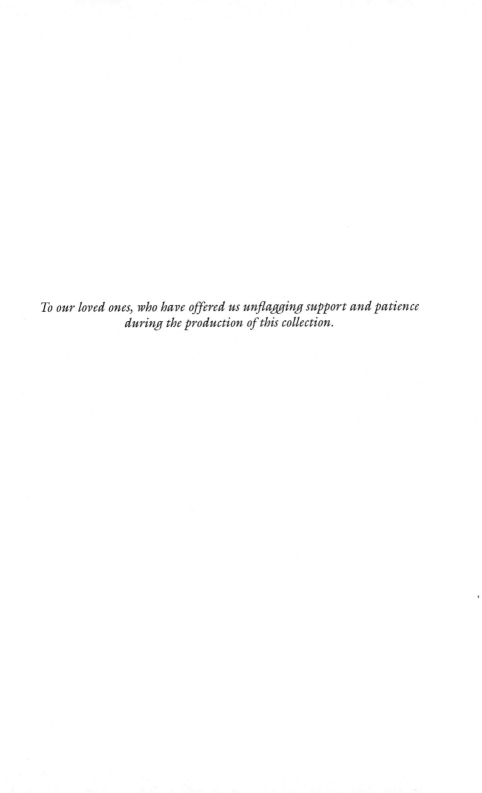

*To our loved ones, who have offered us unflagging support and patience during the production of this collection.*

# ACKNOWLEDGEMENTS

The editors would like to thank Christine Pardue at Palgrave Macmillan for her assistance throughout the process, which has been invaluable. We would also like to thank Timothy McCallister and Kavita Mudan Finn for their helpful comments on the introduction and Daniel Delgado Díaz for his assistance with formatting the images in the book for production.

# CONTENTS

# EDITORS AND CONTRIBUTORS

## About the Editors

**Janice North** is an independent scholar and a specialist in medieval and Golden Age Iberian literatures, who previously taught at the University of Arkansas and the University of Virginia. She received her Ph.D. from the University of Virginia in 2013, after defending her thesis on Queen María de Molina of Castile (1284–1321) and her influence on thirteenth- and fourteenth-century literature and historiography. Her publications *include "El Caballero de Dios y la muy noble reina*: María de Molina's Patronage of the *Libro del Caballero Zifar" (Romance Quarterly* 63:3, 2016), "Queen Mother Knows Best: María de Molina and the Vestiges of Medieval Politics in Modern Historiography" (*Royal Mothers and Their Ruling Children*, Palgrave Macmillan, 2015), and a forthcoming article in the *Bulletin of Spanish Studies*, "Three Queens for the Same Throne: Politics, Sex, and Disorder in TVE's *Isabel"* (2018).

**Karl C. Alvestad** is a specialist on Norwegian medievalism and early medieval and Viking age Scandinavia, and is currently a lecturer in history at the University of Winchester. His thesis *Kings, Heroes and Ships: The Use of Historical Characters in Nineteenth- and Twentieth- Century Perceptions of the Early Medieval Scandinavian Past* explored elements of Norwegian medievalism in the nineteenth and twentieth century with a focus on the use of Vikings as part of Norwegian nation building. He has also published: "Den Nasjonale Olav: Bruk og Misbruk av Helgenkongens Bilde mellom 1920 og 1945" [The National Olaf: The Use and Abuse of St Olaf's image between 1920 and 1945] a chapter in a volume on the image of St Olaf through the ages.

**Elena Woodacre** is a specialist in medieval and early modern queenship and Senior Lecturer in Early Modern European History at the University of Winchester. Her publications include her monograph *The Queens Regnant of Navarre; Succession, Politics and Partnership* (Palgrave Macmillan, 2013) and she has edited/co-edited several collections on queenship and monarchy. Elena is the lead organizer of the 'Kings & Queens' conference series and the founder of the international Royal Studies Network, a resource that aims to bring together scholars who work on monarchical topics. She is also the Editor-in-Chief of the *Royal Studies Journal*.

## Contributors

**Emily S. Beck** is Associate Professor of Early Modern Hispanic Studies and Affiliate Professor in the Comparative Literature and Women and Gender Studies Programs at the College of Charleston. Her primary research interests concern the court of Queen Isabel I of Castile and works that attempt to define and impose idealized behaviors for members of medieval and early modern Iberian society. She has published articles reexamining ways that works from the period subtly communicate broader signs of social acceptance and norms for acceptability, which have particularly important effects on those at the margins of society, including ethnic and religious minorities and women. Her research interests include diverse genres of texts, including popular literary fiction, religious treatises, legal texts, historical chronicles, theatrical interludes, epistles, and manuals of courtesy and etiquette.

**Elizabeth Drayson** is Senior College Lecturer in Spanish at Murray Edwards College and Peterhouse, and member of the department of Spanish and Portuguese of the University of Cambridge. She specializes in medieval and early modern literature and cultural history and her monograph *The Lead Books of Granada* was published by Palgrave

Macmillan in 2013. Her latest book *The Moor's Last Stand: How Seven Centuries of Muslim Rule in Spain Came to an End* was published by Profile Books in 2017.

**Armel Dubois-Nayt** lectures as an associate professor at the University of Versailles-Saint-Quentin. She specializes in the history of ideas in the sixteenth century in Scotland, England, and France with special emphasis on the gender controversy. She has published several articles on John Knox, George Buchanan, and Mary Queen of Scots and co-edited several volumes on the *querelle des femmes* in Europe and early modern women as history writers. She has also co-written a book on women, power, and nation in Scotland. She is currently preparing a book on Mary Queen of Scots in the querelle des femmes.

**Michael R. Evans** is an instructor in history at Delta College, Michigan. He is the author of The *Death of Kings: Royal Deaths in Medieval England* (Continuum, 2003) and *Inventing Eleanor: The Medieval and Post-Medieval Image of Eleanor of Aquitaine* (Bloomsbury, 2014).

**Kavita Mudan Finn** is an independent scholar who previously taught medieval and early modern literature at Georgetown University, George Washington University, Simmons College, Southern New Hampshire University, and the University of Maryland, College Park. She earned her Ph.D. from the University of Oxford in 2010 and published her first book, *The Last Plantagenet Consorts: Gender, Genre, and Historiography 1440–1627*, in 2012. Her work has also appeared in *Shakespeare, Viator, Critical Survey*, and *Medieval and Renaissance Drama in England*, and she has edited several collections, most recently *Fan Phenomena: Game of Thrones* (Intellect, 2017). She is currently working on her second book, which looks at representations of and fan responses to premodern women in television drama, and her chapter in this volume comes from that project.

**Carey Fleiner** is Senior Lecturer in Classical and Early Medieval History and Programme Leader in Classical Studies at the University of Winchester in Great Britain. Her recent publications include "*Optima Mater*: Power, Influence, and the Maternal Bonds between Agrippina the Younger (AD 15–59) and Nero, Emperor of Rome (AD 54–68)" in *Royal Mothers and their Ruling Children: Wielding Political Authority from Antiquity to the Early Modern Era, Vol. 1*, eds. Elena Woodacre and

Carey Fleiner (Palgrave, 2015): 149–170; and *The Kinks: A Thoroughly English Phenomenon* (Rowman, 2017). She lives on the south coast of England.

**Emily C. Francomano** is Associate Professor in the Department of Spanish and Portuguese at Georgetown University, where she is also a core faculty member in the Comparative Literature and Medieval Studies Programs. She is the author of *Wisdom and Her Lovers in Medieval and Early Modern Hispanic Literature* (Palgrave, 2008) and *The Prison of Love: Romance Translation, and the Book in the Sixteenth Century* (University of Toronto Press, 2017), as well as articles on medieval poetry and romance. Her current research revolves around adaptation and how certain narratives, particularly those about gender identities, are told and re-told in many different literary and material forms, from medieval manuscripts to film and digital environments.

**Séverine Genieys-Kirk** is a lecturer in French at the University of Edinburgh. Her main area of research focuses on the history of feminism, and more specifically on early modern women as agents of cultural transactions through literary and artistic production, translation and historiography. She is is currently preparing a monograph arising from an AHRC project award: *Women's Bodies, Spaces and Voices in Early Modern Fiction.* She is also chief editor of SIEFAR' s online dictionary of French women writers (http://siefar.org/), and is a member of the Center for the New Historia Scholars Council (The New School, New York).

**April Harper** is an associate professor of medieval history at the State University of New York, Oneonta. Her research and teaching interests include the history of medicine and sexuality. More specifically, her work examines the idexical signs of gender in medieval medical and legal texts.

**Aidan Norrie** is a historian of monarchy. He is a Chancellor's International Scholar in the Centre for the Study of the Renaissance at The University of Warwick, and Honorary Associate of the Department of English and Linguistics at the University of Otago. Aidan is the editor of *Women on the Edge in Early Modern Europe* (with Lisa Hopkins), and of *From Medievalism to Early Modernism: Adapting the English Past* (with Marina Gerzic). He is currently researching the use of biblical figures in Elizabethan royal iconography, with a focus on Elizabeth I's conflation with Deborah the Judge to create the 'English Deborah.'

**Misty Urban** holds an MFA in fiction and a Ph.D. in Old and Middle English Literature from Cornell University and has published articles on medieval history and literature, teaching medieval literature, and medieval film. She is the author of *Monstrous Women in Middle English Romance*, winner of the D. Simon Evans Dissertation Prize for Medieval Studies, and co-editor of *Melusine's Footprint: Tracing the Legacy of a Medieval Myth*, published in the Explorations in Medieval Culture series by Brill. She teaches and coordinates the Writing Center at Muscatine Community College in Muscatine, Iowa.

**Katherine Weikert** is Lecturer in Early Medieval European History at the University of Winchester. Her areas of interest include gender and authority in the central middle ages, medieval hostageship, and the political use of the medieval in modern society.

# LIST OF FIGURES

# CHAPTER 1

# Introduction—Getting Modern: Depicting Premodern Power and Sexuality in Popular Media

*Janice North, Elena Woodacre, and Karl C. Alvestad*

History is re-constructed through popular media—in novels, films, and television shows—to be more digestible for audiences, many of whom are draw to these narratives by a desire to know more about historical figures and how they negotiated the patriarchy of the past. Yet there is a constant tension between attempting to reconstruct the premodern past in what we believe to be an authentic or accurate way on the page and screen and portraying the past in a way that is most likely to resonate with modern audiences. This tension can also be seen between academics and the writers and producers of popular media, captured humorously in *La Reina de España* (*The Queen of Spain*) where the historical adviser to the movie-within-a-movie is carried off the set whilst raging loudly against the inauthenticity of its portrayal of Isabel I of Castile.

J. North (✉)
Altoona, PA, USA

E. Woodacre · K. C. Alvestad
Department of History, University of Winchester,
Winchester, UK

© The Author(s) 2018
J. North et al. (eds.), *Premodern Rulers and Postmodern Viewers*,
Queenship and Power, https://doi.org/10.1007/978-3-319-68771-1_1

1

This collection features a wide-ranging series of case studies of the treatment of premodern rulers in popular media. Though written by academics, these case studies aim to analyze and understand the motivations behind popular culture portrayals of these important historical figures and how they engage modern audiences, rather than criticize them for a lack of authenticity. The case studies in this volume focus on novels, television series, and film, particularly the strand that has been categorized alternatively as historical/period/costume drama or heritage/post-heritage film and most specifically as a sub-genre known as monarchy films or royal biopics. This introductory chapter will engage with several key themes of the volume and how these case studies connect with them, including the interpretation of history in modern media, the repetition of stories, the intertemporal nature of historical film and fiction, the creation of connections and borders between past and present, and the dangers of presentism.

The sheer volume of productions depicting European monarchs has led us to focus this volume on Western productions. With a few exceptions, the case studies that follow focus on European and Christian monarchs of both genders, which provides a useful opportunity for a comparative analysis of the depictions of premodern rulers in the Western tradition. While our case studies are not exhaustive, they provide a fresh perspective on the depiction of premodern rulers in modern media that adds to wider discussions in the fields of gender in film and literature studies, medievalism, and historical research. Furthermore, although our conclusions should not be applied uncritically to case studies outside of these specific Western contexts, we hope that the ideas and discussions put forth in this collection provide an inspiration for further comparative work on non-Western productions depicting premodern monarchs beyond Europe.

## History and Historical Drama

While modern media aims to represent the premodern past, historical fidelity and edification of the audience are not the primary concerns of the creators who adapt these histories to the page or screen. As Kathleen Coyne Kelly and Tison Pugh observe: 'The artistic forces behind the medieval film genre ... are not as concerned with constructing a historically accurate past as much as they are attempting to make an artistic piece of entertainment (within the financial restraints of the profit-driven economy of most cinemas).'[1] It is this monetary consideration that leads filmmakers and television producers (as well as novelists) to choose stories that they think will draw the largest audience, and to fit them out with the trappings of romance, sex, violence, and political intrigue.

This is not to say, however, that historical accuracy is not a consideration in creating these narratives, as this too draws audiences.[2] When the credits roll, viewers are often left with the impression that they have learned something about history. What they see on the screen may influence or distort what they already knew about the period or person. They may even come to believe that they know the historical protagonists on a personal level, since these are invariably personal stories about relatable people. Moreover, the audience's perception that they are learning about the past can be reinforced by the addition of historical extras or documentary shorts with supplementary material, which can form part of the content on a DVD version or can be placed on an accompanying website. For example, the television series *Versailles* and *Isabel* feature these historical extras; episodes of *Versailles* were immediately followed by an 'Inside Versailles' extra on air and on the BBC iPlayer internet service, and RTVE's *Isabel* includes featurettes on their website.[3] These short videos and articles include interviews with historians that expound upon the factual basis for (or the creative license taken in) a given episode or storyline. In the end, this appearance of concern for historical accuracy enhances the audience's enjoyment, as well as the sense that they have learned something about the past.

When re-telling a story from history—whether it be fictional or historical—the creators (writers, directors, showrunners, and the like) are engaged in interpreting history. In this, they are like historians. Some writers of historical fiction, such as the popular novelist Philippa Gregory, whose work is discussed in this volume by Kavita Mudan Finn, perceive what they do as a form of history writing. However, they do not share the same perspective as historians, who seek a factually accurate and objective representation of events and a deeper understanding of the material and cultural conditions in which those events took place. In order to entertain, these narratives must be subjective (typically taking the perspective of a hero or victim) and merely need to *feel* authentic. They also need to offer relatable characters, who may (and often do) take on contemporary values. In short, although historical credibility is desirable, it is often sacrificed to the demands of entertainment.[4]

Thus, it is tempting to classify the type of history that is produced for popular media as 'history for entertainment' and serious historiography as 'history for edification'. However, the chapters that follow suggest that for many fans and creators, the goal of these media productions is twofold: entertainment and edification. For example, Finn demonstrates how fans of *The White Queen* use the growing number of open-source projects available online to do their own research, and both Finn and Aidan Norrie observe in their respective chapters how popular media's representation of the past often mirrors the debates of historians. Furthermore, films like *The Queen of Spain*—a historical film about making a historical film—and the popular time-traveling series *El Ministerio del Tiempo* (*The Ministry of Time*), examined in Emily C. Francomano's essay, suggest a growing awareness among audience members and creators that the past that we see on the screen is mediated through the present in which it is created.

Lest we come away from this discussion with an aggrandized notion of the superior work of historians in terms of 'edification,' we should consider that historiography has similar limits. Andrew Elliot has demonstrated that, far from being a transparent window onto the past, modern historiography has 'been undermined, and replaced by an acknowledgement of those same distortions of which "filmic history" stands accused'.[5] He cites the lack of objectivity in the source material, competing versions of events, and 'the influence of the present' as factors that destabilize 'the tacit assumption that there is somehow a single version of events from which these films are deviating; an assumption which is no longer afforded even to written History as a discipline'.[6] Robert A. Rosenstone addresses this from a postmodernist perspective, challenging the notion that films should or even can work to portray an 'accurate' version of past events:

> The history film [can be seen] as part of a separate realm of representation and discourse, one not meant to provide literal truths about the past (as if our written history can provide literal truths) but metaphoric truths which work, to a large degree, as a kind of commentary on, and challenge to, traditional historical discourse.[7]

Again, the contributors to this volume do not look to these films, television series, and novels merely to pass judgment on the 'accuracy' of their representation or their value in terms of historical edification. Rather, they do so with the recognition of the limits of our own craft, and with the purpose of discovering the 'cultural work' realized by these histories, with their anachronisms and inaccuracies.[8]

## POPULARITY STAKES AND THE REPETITION OF STORIES

Beyond the issue of historical accuracy, it is necessary to consider the popularity of the genre and unpick the motivations behind it. The sheer number of novels, television series, and films that feature or focus on monarchs are a testament to the public's enduring fascination with premodern rulers. Julianne Pidduck argues that the interest in modern royal families as well as the winning combination of both mythologizing and humanizing premodern rulers on screen are key factors in the popularity of monarchy films or royal biopics.[9] Another important aspect to consider is why particular monarchs are chosen to be protagonists by novelists and filmmakers, while other premodern rulers and consorts are rarely, if ever, featured. For example, in terms of films based on the lives of the queens of the early modern period, which Elena Woodacre evaluates in her chapter, there is a clear dominance in terms of the sheer number of films made about the five most popular screen queens: Anne Boleyn, Elizabeth I, Mary Queen of Scots, Catherine II 'the Great' of Russia, and Marie Antoinette. There are several common factors that may have driven the plethora of movies focused on each: all were controversial in various respects, each faced challenging political circumstances either in their accession or the termination of their reign (or arguably both in the case of Anne Boleyn), all had colorful and complicated love lives that involved difficult husbands and/or lovers (either rumored or openly flaunted in the case of Catherine), and three of these women met their death by execution. These elements, representative of the trappings of a good historical drama, make for memorable lives and dramatic, watchable movies that have the potential to do well at the box office, a key motivation for producers and writers, as discussed earlier. Moreover, Elizabeth I and Catherine II wielded sole power for lengthy and successful reigns, becoming arguably two of the greatest rulers of their particular realms.

This leads to a second rationale for choosing particular monarchs—that viewers favor stories of famous rulers who define key moments of a nation's past. Indeed, Belén Vidal has argued that monarchy films play a key role in the national psyche, acting as 'narratives of history and nation' that serve multiple functions.[10] Vidal notes they can serve both as vehicles for 'tradition and nostalgia for the (imperial) past' and 'explorations of moments of political crisis'.[11] Examples of premodern rulers who are inexorably linked to key moments of national history include Elizabeth I of England, Olaf II of Norway, or Isabel I of Castile—analysis of films and television series that feature all three of these rulers can be found in this collection from Norrie's focus on the gendered representation of Elizabeth, to Karl C. Alvestad's discussion of the changing depiction of Olaf, and multiple chapters that examine Isabel I, including Emily S. Beck and Francomano's studies of the complex relationship that Spanish popular culture has with Isabel I.

This desire to re-view moments of national crisis or glory and familiar faces links to another rationale for the popularity of certain rulers, since viewers and creators are more interested in histories of which they already have some knowledge. It is the same reason that audiences flock to prequels, sequels, and reboots of old series like *Star Trek* or adaptations of comic book series—the comforting familiarity of a known story. If viewers have enjoyed a previous film on Elizabeth I, they are more likely to watch another rather than choose a film about a historical figure that they know nothing about. There is a parallel between Anne Boleyn's life and the blockbuster *Titanic* (1997); the audience knows that Anne will die at the end or that the boat will sink but the anticipation of the tragic ending and the curiosity of how the lead up will be portrayed draws the viewer in.

On the other hand, there are deeper cultural implications to consider in the repetition of stories. If we accept J. Hillis Miller's affirmation that 'we need the "same" stories over and over ... as one of the most powerful, perhaps the most powerful, of ways to assert the basic ideology of our culture,'[12] then what does this repetition say about ideologies of gender and sexuality in our (post)modern social milieu? Have the terms changed significantly from the premodern period, or are there areas of continuity, attitudes that have remained fixed across the centuries? These are some of the questions examined by the case studies in this collection.

## The Intertemporal Nature of Historical Fiction and Period Dramas

The choices made by creators in terms of which premodern figures they decide to focus on and how to portray their lives are all the more important, as historical fiction can be viewed as 'a kind of document chronicling the way that man understands his own history'.[13] For this reason, we argue that what is at stake in these portrayals is contemporary culture's understanding of premodern historical figures, and consequently, the gender and sexual ideologies that they navigated during their lifetime. And yet, there is more than just our understanding of the past at stake here. In scholarship on historical film, television, and novels, it has become an accepted truth that—in the words of Arthur Lindley—'the subject is the present, not the past'.[14] Thus, what is happening on the screen or page is not 'merely a reconstruction or a reconstitution' of the past, 'but really an original contribution to the understanding of past phenomena and their relation to the present'.[15] Accordingly, Claire Monk has argued that the heritage genre of film evolved in the 1990s to produce 'post-heritage' films, notable for modern concerns about gender and sexuality foregrounded against a portrayal of the premodern past.[16]

Historical dramas have much to tell us about the present in which they are created because we define our present by comparison to our past, and vice versa. Modern attitudes and practices are 'modern' because they are perceived as being different from premodern attitudes and practices. In this, art imitates historiography, since modernity has always been defined in contrast to the past. The term 'modernity' has a long history and its use extends further into the past than its current temporal demarcations suggest.[17] Particularly useful to the present study is the definition offered by Coyne Kelly and Pugh:

> Modernity—and its hyperbolic epiphenomenon that we sometimes call postmodernity—might be said to manifest itself as a relation to the past. Modernity, in spite of those moderns who phantasize otherwise, does not necessitate a break with the past; rather, it expresses itself through quotation, imitation, invocation, and allusion to the past. Modernity represents a kind of temporal hybridity, as it were.[18]

Therefore, we might conclude that historical fiction chronicles both the way that we understand our history and our present, which are defined in relation to one another.

For the purposes of this volume, modernity and postmodernity (not to be confused with modern*ism* and postmodern*ism*) are terms used to designate the present in which these historical dramas are created and consumed, and simultaneously that present's relationship with the pre-modern past in which these narratives are set. In this sense, the terms may seem interchangeable. However, the distinctions between modern and postmodern philosophy are relevant to the present study, and we will return to this topic later.

In her 2006 landmark study, Linda Hutcheon observes that when stories are adapted across time and space, this creates 'a kind of dialogue between the society in which the works, both the adapted text and the adaptation, are produced and that in which they are received, and both are in dialogue with the works themselves'.[19] Historical dramas bring the past into dialogue with the present through the creation, in the present, of an imagined past. This imagined past coexists with the present in an intertemporal space, which Coyne Kelly and Pugh identify as 'an important, if not primary site for culturally productive and serious, phantastical play'.[20] And—in line with what Monk has observed about post-heritage film—they contend that: 'The Middle Ages provides an imaginary space far enough removed from the present day to allow for critical analysis of contemporary gender and sexuality.'[21] Typically, the premodern past (in our case medieval and early modern) is used in one of two ways. It is either portrayed as a backward place 'of barbarism and ignorance, brutality and superstition, dungeons, disease and dirt' from which we have progressed or an idealized place 'of young knights in shining armour rescuing beautiful damsels in distress' to which we long to return.[22]

## CREATING COMMUNITIES AND DRAWING BORDERS

Given the inevitable gap between the present and the past, whether it is portrayed as a backward or idealized place, media producers have to adopt strategies in order to reconcile the difference between premodern and (post)modern societal values. In historical drama, the gender and sexual ideologies of the past and present are defined in contrast to one another, either by creating distinctions or connections. There are three ways that this typically plays out. In some cases it involves projecting homophobia or misogyny into the distant past and trying to contain it there, portraying these as attitudes that society has left behind and the past as a foreign country. In other cases, it takes the form of extending feminism or homosexual subjectivity and tolerance into the distant past in order to make connections and create a sense of community. In addition, communities can be created in historical drama by drawing connections between misogynist or homophobic beliefs and practices in the past and the present. As the following examples demonstrate, these three categories of projection (which draw borders between time periods), extension, and connection (which create communities of inclusion or exclusion across time) are better understood as techniques, since they are not hermetic, and in fact are often combined in a variety of ways, such that each novel, film, or television series constitutes a unique statement about both eras.

### *This Is Not Us: Drawing Borders Between Past and Present*

The first technique portrays homophobia and misogyny as 'medieval' practices that are incompatible with modern precepts. Here we might locate twenty-first century stories about 'victim' queens and kings, such as Juana I of Castile and  Mohammad XII of Granada, examined in this volume by Janice North and Elizabeth Drayson. In the film *Juana la Loca* (*Mad Love*), Juana is portrayed as a 'modern' woman inserted into a medieval context, with disastrous consequences. Her desire for personal fulfilment through love and sexual pleasure is incompatible with a world of political marriages and patriarchal family structure, and she ends her life locked away in a prison for her 'madness'. In the case of Mohammad XII—or Boabdil, as he is called in the television series *Isabel*—a gentle prince loses his inheritance because he is 'not man enough' to defend it and, as Drayson explains, because of the decidedly Western and Christian perspective of the television series. In these twenty-first century historical dramas, 'feminine' rulers are removed from power by the restrictive culture of premodern patriarchy, which is largely condemned, while these characters are portrayed with sympathy and understanding. Such a contrast between the backward patriarchy of the past and the compassionate portrayal of these men and women who are victimized for their 'modernity' reflects a desire to contain misogyny— which can be used against women and 'feminine' men[23]—in the distant past. They also show how the dichotomy between past and present can be used to reinforce present values through both drama and comedy; Sophie Mayer laments that 'too often, historical dramas make a mockery of past attitudes for easy laughs … while presenting present audiences as inevitably superior'.[24]

### Premodern Role Models: Extending Modern Concepts and Identities into the Past

*The Girl King*—a 2015 royal biopic of Queen Christina of Sweden analyzed in Séverine Genieys-Kirk's essay—could be located in the second group, which includes dramas that extend the modern concept of homosexual subjectivity into the distant past. While Christina's sexual preferences are unknown to us, the creators chose to portray Christina as a lesbian, extrapolating this possibility from the historical realities of her desire not to marry, her closeness to Ebba Sparre, and her cross-dressing tendencies. As it is still largely accepted that the modern sexual categories of 'homosexual' and 'bisexual' did not exist in the premodern era,[25] this story participates in Caroline Dinshaw's concept of 'affective history,' which she describes as

> an impulse toward making connections across time between, on the one hand, lives, texts, and other cultural phenomena left out of sexual categories back then and, on the other, those left out of current sexual categories now. Such an impulse extends the resources for self- and community building into even the distant past.[26]

Portraying historical figures as gay, bisexual, or transgender—even if we can never be completely certain of their own sexual preferences or gender identities—has the power to create historical models and to write a history in which members of the LGBT community can recognize themselves.

Similarly, as will be discussed further in the introduction to the first section of this volume, feminism is perhaps the modern concept most commonly inserted into historical dramas. In her chapter, Katherine Weikert explains that 'powerful queens give historical examples of strong women that modern women can look to not only as exemplars but also for … a feeling of a connection to the past'.[27] The integration of feminism into a premodern context is accomplished successfully in the television series *Isabel*, which Beck argues uses feminism to cover up a religious devotion that the postmodern audience would likely view as fanaticism, making this controversial ruler more palatable to their secularized and inclusive sense of religion. However, other historical series have been less successful in creating narratives of female empowerment. Such is the case with the miniseries *The White Queen*—which, as Finn and Misty Urban demonstrate—largely failed in its bid to create a narrative of female empowerment due to a reliance on tropes of female rivalry that are popular in reality TV.

In spite of the creators' attempts to invest these histories with feminism, female power is more often than not portrayed as underhanded, inimical, and connected to liberated sexual desires. For example, April Harper demonstrates that in medieval film the forms of power traditionally available to queens—such as family influence, patronage, and diplomacy—have been tainted by an association with 'unmanly' villains and come across as manipulative and dishonest. In her essay, Urban explores how Elizabeth Woodville's transformation into a gifted witch reproduces medieval misogynist stereotypes of female power and how the efforts of ambitious women to gain access to power in *The White Queen* often result in harm to their families. Michael R. Evans and Armel Dubois-Nayt observe a conflation of female sexual drive and political ambition in their respective chapters, and the tragic ends of Mary Queen of Scots and Juana of Castile suggest a persistent belief that lust in a woman leads to destruction.

### *Troubling Masculinity: Connecting Values Past and Present*

Finally, we have films such as Derek Jarman's *Edward II*, examined by Evans, which bridges past and present by transposing the story of a reputedly homosexual king from the fourteenth century into the administration of Margaret Thatcher and the context of anti-gay legislation in 1980s England. This film equates medieval anti-sodomy with twentieth-century homophobia, condemning the latter as 'medieval' and therefore backward and uncivilized. Also analyzed by Evans is the 1995 film *Braveheart*, which demonstrates an opposing tendency, which is to exult 'medieval' gender categories, such as the hypermasculine William Wallace character. *Braveheart* is an apt example of how the Middle Ages can be held up as an idealized time of 'natural' heteronormativity to which the creators and viewers may long to return.[28]

Connected to both the difficulty of portraying premodern masculinity and (post)modern feminist ideas, a common theme in the case studies that follow is that weak men breed strong women, a combination that can be dangerous. Typically what we see is that if a queen is strong, it is because her husband or son is weak. Such is the case with the dominated Boabdil, the ousted Edward II, and the Viking king Olaf in Prima Vera's *Sagaen om Olav den Hellige* (*The Saga of Saint Olaf*). Boabdil and Edward are despised by their fathers as weaklings—Edward is portrayed as a foppish homosexual, disinterested in the responsibilities of kingship in *Braveheart* and Boabdil as a peaceable poet controlled by his mother in *Isabel*. These men are excluded from power because of their femininity; and yet, as Drayson argues, these historical characters have the potential to disrupt traditional models of masculinity and to 'hint at the idea of a new, more forgiving model of the patriarchal monarch'.[29] However, even as the audience is invited to sympathize with these kings in *Isabel* and *World without End*, their female co-rulers are villainized as power-hungry troublemakers, a topic explored by Evans in his chapter on Isabella of France. In Prima Vera's satirical film, the opposite occurs, and the audience is distanced from the 'Eternal King of Norway' because he is portrayed as feminine, bungling, and dominated by his less-than-sympathetic wife.

Despite their differences, what these stories have in common is that when the traditional gender roles are reversed, they have dire consequences: a king's death, the interruption of the lawful succession, or the loss of a kingdom. This tracks with modern notions of premodern power structures, as many find it hard to reconcile the evidence that so many women held significant authority in the premodern period with an understanding that it was an intensively patriarchal time when most women had few of the legal rights and political opportunities that they do today. In spite of advances in academic historiography, popular culture continues to view the premodern era as a 'man's world,' in which women and effeminate men were effectively barred from power. At best, such depictions point to a general lack of understanding about the ways in which premodern women and men cultivated and wielded power; at worst (given that the real subject of these narratives is arguably the present, not the past), they suggest that gender equality has not progressed as far as we may like to believe.

## (Post)Modernity and Narratives of Progress

This brings us to the distinction between modern and postmodern philosophy, and more specifically, to Jean-François Lyotard's theory of the postmodern collapse of the grand narrative of emancipation— or in other words, the 'modern' belief that societal progress, achieved through knowledge, will lead to 'the emancipation of humanity'.[30] While the term 'postmodern viewer' has been used here to denote a consumer of popular culture who, as a product of the time in which she lives, holds a political worldview of pluralism, equality, and tolerance, and who may or may not espouse this 'master narrative of emancipation,' according to Lyotard the philosophical shifts associated with postmodernity have brought about a breakdown in the belief in societal progress.[31]

In the simplest terms, what we see in these case studies is that some of these media show an affinity to either modern or postmodern philosophies about the feasibility of societal progress towards the goal of universal equality for all genders and sexualities. Historical dramas that fall under the first category of drawing borders typically advance the narrative of societal progress. By showing us a dark and exclusionary past in contrast to our bright and inclusive present, they affirm that we have, and that we are still, progressing toward the modernist goal of emancipation. On the other hand, films like Jarman's *Edward II* explicitly and intentionally highlight a lack of progress by establishing a parity between discriminatory beliefs and practices in the past and present, while other media—such as *The White Queen* or *Mary, Queen of Scots*—reveal that same parity, but unintentionally. In addition, nostalgia films, like *Braveheart*, seem to argue in support of universal truths about gender that, while they fly in the face of the modern project of equality for all, are modern in their privileging of the universal and timeless over the particular and timely. Therefore, there is no hard-and-fast answer, no universal truth that we can observe about how the genre of historical drama engages in this epistemological debate. The messages about sex, gender, equality, and essentialism that these popular media transmit are as varied as the political worldviews espoused by the audience and creators.

## Conclusion: Getting Modern? The Consequences of Presentism

Ultimately, these media are grappling (unconsciously perhaps) with the question of whether or not our gendered power structures bear similarities to those of the past. Some films affirm a correspondence; others deny it. Few, however, seem to be conscious of the dangers of presentism as they attempt to 'update' these premodern histories.

According to Coyne Kelly and Pugh, one consequence of collapsing time in historical drama is that 'it strips away foundational arguments of gender and sexuality as embodied in time,' making these conditions and concepts appear transhistorical. They contend 'that the seamlessness of such unions between present and past proclaims a normativity phantastically and historically implausible yet nonetheless stunningly persuasive'.[32] This issue is compounded by the fact that audiences often look to historical drama to learn about the past, and as Dubois-Nayt argues in her chapter, this can result in the historical conditions of masculine domination becoming ingrained in the audience's unconscious.

In short, despite the efforts of some filmmakers, authors, and show-runners to 'modernize' medieval and early modern histories, the stories they produce are in constant tension between the (post)modern attitudes and expectations of filmmakers and audiences on the one hand, and the realities and perceptions of the premodern past on the other. While many of these narratives do push back against normative discourses of gender and sexuality, they continue to reproduce those discourses, in part because they are adaptations of stories rooted in the past. Conversely, as some cases in this volume demonstrate, misogyny or homophobia can be introduced into these stories from the present through the choices made in adaptation, such as the silencing of medieval queens in Hollywood films, discussed in Harper's essay, or the presentation of Edward II as a stereotypical gay man barred from power, in Evan's chapter. This, along with audiences' enthusiasm for the repetition of these 'old' narratives, begs several questions that will be explored in the following chapters. The essays in this volume ask how entrenched 'old' ideas about gender and sexuality are in the present, whether these premodern histories can ever be truly 'modernized,' and what the failure to modernize these histories and historical persons can tell us of dominant ideas about gender and power in popular culture in the present.

The chapters in this volume are organized thematically into three sections that reflect the key themes and ideas that have been introduced here in terms of the representation of gender, sexuality, and power and the ways in which the lives of premodern rulers have been adapted to the modern page and screen. Since the case studies in this volume touch on similar issues, there will inevitably be some overlap between sections; however, the organization has been chosen to highlight common themes, based on what each essay adds to the overall discussion. While each section and its contents will be introduced at length in three separate pieces, which can be found at the outset of each section, a brief summary follows here.

Part one, "Reappraising Female Rulers in Light of Modern Feminism(s)," opens with two essays that expound on commonalities and typologies in the representation of medieval and early modern queens on film. The remaining chapters in this section address the myriad ways in which distinct waves and brands of feminism have influenced representations of medieval and early modern women in popular media. Part two, "Questions of Adaptation: Bringing Premodern Queens to the Page and Screen," addresses how history and historical fiction are adapted into compelling narratives that are designed to appeal to modern and postmodern audiences and how those narratives help shape popular understandings of gender and power. The essays in the third and final section, "Undermining Authority: Rulers With Conflicted Gender and Sexual Identities," include case studies of male and female rulers that are depicted in popular media as having conflicted gender or sexual identities, which are often tied to the gender or sexual identities of their spouses or parents. Taken together, these case studies demonstrate that the lives of premodern rulers have been continually reimagined by generations of writers and filmmakers who each apply ever-changing societal values to their interpretation of the past. More fundamentally perhaps, these case studies also demonstrate that the lives of premodern rulers still resonate with modern viewers.

## NOTES

1. Kathleen Coyne Kelly and Tison Pugh, "Introduction: Queer History, Cinematic Medievalism, and the Impossibility of Sexuality," in *Queer Movie Medievalisms*, ed. Kathleen Coyne Kelly and Tison Pugh (Farnham: Ashgate, 2009), 8.

2. Bettina Bildhauer, *Filming the Middle Ages* (London: Reaktion Books, 2011), 20. According to Bildhauer: 'Historical accuracy is a production value, something that adds credibility to a film. … Audiences will enjoy a film more if it looks authentic to them, if they can imagine the stories told to have really happened; and especially if they can have this confirmed by experts.'

3. "Inside Versailles," BBC, accessed July 14, 2017. http://www.bbc.co.uk/programmes/b08ndt2b/episodes/guide; See for example: "Curiosidades de la Historia: la inseminación artificial, los orígenes de la Beltraneja y la locura de la madre de Isabel," *RTVE*, September 10, 2012. http://www.rtve.es/alacarta/videos/isabel/isabel-curiosidades-historia-inseminacion-artificial-origenes-beltraneja-locura-madre-isabel/1308334/.

4. For an extended discussion of this premise see Chap. 2 "Detail, authenticity and the uses of the past" in Andrew Stubbs, *Historical Film: A Critical Introduction* (New York: Bloomsbury, 2013), 37–60.

5. Andrew B. R. Elliot, *Remaking the Middle Ages: The methods of cinema and history in portraying the medieval world* (Jefferson, NC: McFarland & Co., 2011), 28.

6. Elliot, *Remaking the Middle Ages*, 28, 11.

7. Robert A. Rosenstone, *History on Film: Film on History*, 3rd ed. (London: Routledge, 2018), 7.

8. The term is Coyne Kelly and Pugh's, "Queer History," 4.

9. Julianne Pidduck, *Contemporary Costume Film* (London: BFI, 2004), 169. The tone of royal biopics on premodern rulers can also be driven by the current mood or feeling towards modern royal families, see Belén Vidal, *Heritage Film: Nation, Genre and Representation* (London: Wallflower, 2012), 37.

10. Vidal, *Heritage Film*, 37.

11. Vidal, *Heritage Film*, 36.

12. J. Hillis Miller, "Narrative," in *Critical Terms for Literary Study*, ed. Frank Lentricchia and Thomas McLaughlin (Chicago: University of Chicago Press, 1995), retrieved from http://www.credoreference.com/entry/uchicagols/narrative.

13. Elliot, *Remaking the Middle Ages*, 11. Here, Elliot is making reference to Marc Ferro's *Cinema and History*.

14. Arthur Lindley, "The Ahistoricsm of Medieval Film," *Screening the Past* 3 (1998). http://www.screeningthepast.com/2014/12/the-ahistoricism-of-medieval-film/.

15. Marc Ferro, *Cinema and History*, trans. Naomi Greene (Detroit, MI: Wayne State University Press, 1998), 163.

16. Claire Monk, *Heritage Film Audiences: Period Films and Contemporary Audiences in the UK* (Edinburgh: Edinburgh University Press, 2011), 23.

17. Currently, historians date the beginnings of modernity to the end of the fifteenth century, although admittedly the distinction of the 'medieval' from the 'early modern' is fuzzy at best. See Jürgen Habermas, "Modernity versus Postmodernity," in *A Postmodern Reader*, ed. Joseph Natoli and Linda Hutcheon (Albany, NY: State University of New York Press, 1993), 92–93 for a discussion of the origins and uses of the word 'modern.'
18. Coyne Kelly and Pugh, "Queer History," 2.
19. Linda Hutcheon, *A Theory of Adaptation* (New York: Routledge, 2006), 149.
20. Coyne Kelly and Pugh, "Queer History," 10.
21. Coyne Kelly and Pugh, "Queer History," 10.
22. Bidhauer, *Filming the Middle Ages*, 8, 9.
23. See Eve Sedgwick, *Between Men: English Literature and Male Homosocial Desire* (New York: Columbia University Press, 1985), 20 and Barbara Weissberger, *Isabel Rules: Constructing Queenship, Wielding Power* (Minneapolis, MN: University of Minnesota Press, 2004), 72.
24. Sophie Mayer, *Political Animals: The New Feminist Cinema* (London: I.B. Tauris, 2016), 117.
25. See Michel Foucault, *The History of Sexuality: Volume 1, An Introduction*, trans. Robert Hurley (New York: Vintage, 1990), 43; C.f. Karma Lochrie, introduction to *Heterosyncrasies: Female Sexuality When Normal Wasn't* (Minneapolis, MN: University of Minnesota Press, 2005) and Coyne Kelly and Pugh, "Queer History," 2–3.
26. Caroline Dinshaw, *Getting Medieval: Sexualities and Communities, Pre- and Postmodern* (Durham, NC: Duke University Press, 1999), 47.
27. Katherine Weikert, "Feminism, Fiction, and the Empress Matilda," in *Premodern Rulers and Postmodern Viewers: Gender, Sex, and Power in Popular Culture*, ed. Janice North, Karl C. Alvestad, and Elena Woodacre (New York: Palgrave Macmillan, 2018), 69.
28. This tendency to look to the Middle Ages for models of 'natural' masculinity links to the current controversy over the weaponization of medievalism by white supremacist groups and other terrorist organizations. See for example Dorothy Kim, "Teaching Medieval Studies in a Time of White Supremacy," *In the Middle*, August 28, 2017. http://www.inthemedievalmiddle.com/2017/08/teaching-medieval-studies-in-time-of.html. For further reading on the topic of race in medievalisms and medieval studies, see Jonathan Hsy, "#More Voices: Citation, Inclusion, and Working Together," *In the Middle*, June 13, 2017. http://www.inthemedievalmiddle.com/2017/06/morevoices-citation-inclusion-and.html.
29. Elizabeth Drayson, "Televising Boabdil, last Muslim king of Granada," in *Premodern Rulers and Postmodern Viewers: Gender, Sex, and Power in Popular Culture*, ed. Janice North, Karl Alvestad and Elena Woodacre, 303.

30. Jean-François Lyotard, *The Postmodern Condition: A Report on Knowledge*, trans. Geoff Bennington and Brian Massumi (Minneapolis, MN: University of Minnesota Press, 1984), 60.
31. Lyotard, *The Postmodern Condition*, 31–41, 48–49; For a discussion of the intersections of postmodernity and feminism in popular culture, see Barbara Creed "From Here to Modernity: Feminism and Postmodernism," in *A Postmodern Reader*, ed. Joseph Natoli and Linda Hutcheon (New York: State University of New York Press, 1993), 398–418.
32. Coyne Kelly and Pugh, "Queer History," 3, 4.

## BIBLIOGRAPHY

BBC (British Broadcasting Company). "Inside Versailles." Accessed July 14, 2017. http://www.bbc.co.uk/programmes/b08ndt2b/episodes/guide.
Bildhauer, Bettina. *Filming the Middle Ages*. London: Reaktion Books, 2011.
Coyne Kelly, Kathleen and Tison Pugh. "Introduction: Queer History, Cinematic Medievalism, and the Impossibility of Sexuality." In *Queer Movie Medievalisms*, edited by Kathleen Coyne Kelly and Tison Pugh, 1–18. Farnham: Ashgate, 2009.
Creed, Barbara. "From Here to Modernity: Feminism and Postmodernism." In *A Postmodern Reader*, edited by Joseph Natoli and Linda Hutcheon, 398–418. New York, State University of New York Press, 1993.
Dinshaw, Caroline. *Getting Medieval: Sexualities and Communities, Pre- and Postmodern*. Durham, NC: Duke University Press, 1999.
Elliot, Andrew B. R. *Remaking the Middle Ages: The Methods of Cinema and History in Portraying the Medieval World*. Jefferson, NC: McFarland & Co., 2011.
Ferro, Marc. *Cinema and History*. Translated by Naomi Greene. Detroit, MI: Wayne State University Press, 1998.
Foucault, Michel. *The History of Sexuality: Volume 1, An Introduction*. Translated by Robert Hurley. New York: Vintage, 1990.
Habermas, Jürgen. "Modernity versus Postmodernity." In *A Postmodern Reader*, edited by Joseph Natoli and Linda Hutcheon, 91–104. Albany, NY: State University of New York Press, 1993.
Hillis Miller, J. "Narrative." In *Critical Terms for Literary Study*, edited by Frank Lentricchia and Thomas McLaughlin, 66–79. Chicago: University of Chicago Press, 1995. Retrieved from http://www.credoreference.com/entry/uchicagols/narrative.
Hutcheon, Linda. *A Theory of Adaptation*. New York: Routledge, 2006.
Hsy, Jonathan. "#More Voices: Citation, Inclusion, and Working Together." *In the Middle*, June 13, 2017. http://www.inthemedievalmiddle.com/2017/06/morevoices-citation-inclusion-and.html.

Kim, Dorothy. "Teaching Medieval Studies in a Time of White Supremacy." *In the Middle*, August 28, 2017. http://www.inthemedievalmiddle. com/2017/08/teaching-medieval-studies-in-time-of.html.

Lindley, Arthur. "The Ahistoricsm of Medieval Film," *Screening the Past* 3 (1998), unpaginated. http://www.screeningthepast.com/2014/12/the-ahistoricism-of-medieval-film/.

Lochrie, Karma. Introduction to *Heterosyncrasies: Female Sexuality When Normal Wasn't*. Minneapolis, MN: University of Minnesota Press, 2005.

Lyotard, Jean-François. *The Postmodern Condition: A Report on Knowledge*. Translated by Geoff Bennington and Brian Massumi. Minneapolis, MN: University of Minnesota Press, 1984.

Mayer, Sophie. *Political Animals: The New Feminist Cinema*. London: I.B. Tauris, 2016.

Monk, Claire. *Heritage Film Audiences: Period Films and Contemporary Audiences in the UK*. Edinburgh: Edinburgh University Press, 2011.

Pidduck, Julianne. *Contemporary Costume Film*. London: BFI, 2004.

Rosenstone, Robert A. *History on Film: Film on History*. 3rd ed. London: Routledge, 2018.

RTVE (Radio Televisión Española). "Curiosidades de la Historia: la inseminación artificial, los orígenes de la Beltraneja y la locura de la madre de Isabel." Accessed September 10, 2012. http://www.rtve.es/alacarta/videos/isabel/isabel-curiosidades-historia-inseminacion-artificial-origenes-beltraneja-locura-madre-isabel/1308334/.

Sedgwick, Eve. *Between Men: English Literature and Male Homosocial Desire*. New York: Columbia University Press, 1985.

Stubbs, Andrew. *Historical Film: A Critical Introduction*. New York: Bloomsbury, 2013.

Vidal, Belén. *Heritage Film: Nation, Genre and Representation*. London: Wallflower, 2012.

Weissberger, Barbara. *Isabel Rules: Constructing Queenship, Wielding Power*. Minneapolis, MN: University of Minnesota Press, 2004.

# PART I

# Reappraising Female Rulers in the Light of Modern Feminism(s)

## INTRODUCTION

### *Elena Woodacre*

Feminism has, without doubt, saturated the popular consciousness since the middle of the twentieth century. Whether one supports it or abhors it, whether we are influenced by the first, second, or third waves of the movement or even post or anti-feminism, it is a product of the modern era that is implicitly or explicitly part of our lives and, more importantly for our discussion here, an influence on popular culture.

Popular culture has had an ambivalent relationship with feminism, being both a vehicle to promote it and an instrument to 'undo' it as Angela McRobbie has argued.[1] Indeed Stephanie Genz had noted that popular culture and the media fuelled a backlash against feminism in the 1980s and Penny Griffin has gone so far as to ask whether anti-feminism is more commercially viable than feminism itself.[2] Yet at the same time popular culture has recently been seen as a champion for feminism; 2014 was noted as being a particular high point for feminism with many high-profile female musicians and actresses visibly promoting the movement in their work.[3] The question for us is how these shifts in society towards and away from feminist ideas and indeed the changes in the movement itself are reflected in the films and novels examined in our collection and their portrayals of premodern rulers, particularly the female ones.

As discussed in the general introduction to the volume, our cinema-based studies examine a particular strand of film, which has been given various monikers including 'costume drama' or more recently 'heritage film'. This type of film is often associated with or considered to be particularly appealing to women; however, while these works are set in the recent or distant past, it does not necessarily mean that these films represents stories or characters that reject or do not reflect the feminist-influenced present. Sophie Mayer argues instead that, 'Historical drama is, of course, a powerful site for feminist genealogy, for making visible connections ... It often shows women joining together, even if this begins in conversations about men and matrimony, to create the changes that still resonate today.'[4] Pidduck has noted that modern audiences can identify with (proto-)feminist characters in period films even when they are visibly or even physically struggling with the patriarchal constraints of their setting in the past.[5] Indeed, a recent survey of the audiences of heritage films picked up on the appreciation of the 'strong female characters' in these works—a factor that again may make these films appealing to women in particular.[6] Queens, female rulers, and consorts at the epicenter of power in medieval and early modern realms clearly make for potentially strong female characters to whom modern feminist audiences can relate. Pidduck notes that the marketing campaign for Kapur's *Elizabeth* (1998) played on the premise of '"girl power"—the struggles of a woman trying to make it in a man's world'.[7] However, is it anachronistic to make feminists out of premodern female rulers and attempt to equate them to the women who are political, cultural, and business leaders today?

Another question to ask is whether today's feminist-influenced environment always results in powerful female characters on screen or ones with empowering messages for audiences. Janet Thumim has argued that cinema has 'acted as a brake' on female empowerment and could even be a means to 'enforce patriarchal order's requirements of its female subjects'.[8] While Thumim's argument was geared towards films produced between 1945–1965, Belén Vidal has argued that recent films may be undermining feminism in a different way. Vidal notes that while films made in the 1990s and even earlier were in tune with a wider movement in women's history to retrieve or recover the lives of historical figures, post-millennial heritage films such as *Marie Antoinette* (2006) engage in the 'commodification of feminism... [These films] celebrate versions of femininity empowered by consumer and celebrity cultures'.[9]

The chapters in this section wrestle with these questions and more generally with the ways in which modern feminist-influenced culture has shaped the representation of premodern queens on screen and on the page. Woodacre's chapter examines the typologies that early modern queens have been 'boxed' into when their lives have been portrayed on screen, arguing that these typologies tell us much more about feminist-influenced modern culture than they do about the realities of early modern queenship. In the following study, April Harper argues that medieval queens are 'silenced' on screen, given fleeting appearances in which they are robbed of both agency and voice—in both the political and physical sense. This would appear to concur with Thumim's arguments that cinematic portrayals of female characters are a means of reinforcing patriarchal ideals and disempowering historic royal women. Weikert's chapter, which follows, engages firmly and directly with feminist ideas and their impact on the portrayal of the Empress Matilda in historical fiction. Weikert traces the evolving representation of the Empress, noting the impact of both second- and third-wave feminist ideas. Like Woodacre's chapter, Weikert argues that the portrayals of Matilda reveal more about the present than the reality of the Empress' life—that novels about the historical figure serve as a 'blank slate on which modern writers and readers view feminism' (82). In the next chapter, Carey Fleiner notes, in a similar vein to Harper, the extremely brief film time given to Isabella d'Angoulême in cinematic depictions. Once again, these depictions tell us little about the historical figure herself, reducing Isabella to a foil for her husband John—a means to disparage him and his kingship rather than highlight her own agency as a queen consort and wealthy heiress in her own right.

The final two chapters in this section relate to the television series *The White Queen*, based on the popular novel by Philippa Gregory. Both Misty Urban and Kavita Mudan Finn begin their chapters by noting that the idea of female power was explicitly foregrounded in the publicity materials as the key theme of the *White Queen* series. Yet Urban argues that instead of truly heralding and displaying female power, the characters are depicted with limited agency, working behind the scenes and through covert, even suspect means to achieve their goals of self and familial advancement. This depiction both reinforces medieval ideas about female agency and undermines modern values of female equality and opportunity by insinuating that women can only achieve their aims through subterfuge and 'back-door' tactics, such as influencing their menfolk through sexual or even occult means. Finn examines the fan response to the series—noting that the audience used social media channels to challenge the portrayal of women and female power in the series, often using historical evidence to counter the ahistorical representation of the *White Queen*'s characters.

In summary, these case studies give a mixed view of the impact of feminism on the portrayal of premodern queens on page and screen. Far from ensuring that the women of the medieval and early modern periods were represented as empowered proto-feminists who displayed and espoused values of female equality and empowerment, many of the studies in this collection argue that instead, the queens in these films seem to support patriarchal norms and are portrayed in a way that minimizes their agency and activity. Perhaps one could argue that this might be a more accurate reflection of the premodern period itself where the modern construct of feminism had no place—yet as Finn argues, even fans of *The White Queen* series could recognize that the historical characters in the show had more varied and positive means at their disposal to achieve political success in the fifteenth century than they were displayed as possessing on screen in the twenty-first century. Clearly we should not assume that because a woman possessed title, power, and authority in the premodern world that her agency will be accurately reflected or celebrated in today's feminist-influenced postmodern culture.

## NOTES

1. Angela McRobbie, *The Aftermath of Feminism: Gender, Culture and Social Change* (Los Angeles: Sage Publications, 2009), 16.
2. Stéphanie Genz, *Postfeminities in Popular Culture* (New York: Palgrave Macmillan, 2009), 69 and *Penny Griffin, Popular Culture, Political Economy and the Death of Feminism* (London: Routledge, 2015), see particularly Chap. 6
3. Alice Vincent, "How Feminism conquered pop culture," The Guardian, December 30, 2014, http://www.telegraph.co.uk/culture/culturenews/11310119/feminism-pop-culture-2014.html
4. Sophie Mayer, *Political Animals: The New Feminist Cinema* (London: I.B. Tauris, 2016), 98.
5. Julianne Pidduck, *Contemporary Costume Film* (London: BFI, 2004), 72.
6. Claire Monk, *Heritage Film Audiences: Period Films and Contemporary Audiences in the UK* (Edinburgh: Edinburgh University Press, 2011), 134.
7. Pidduck, Costume, 170.
8. Janet Thumim, *Celluloid Sisters: Women and Popular Cinema* (New York, Palgrave Macmillan, 1992), 211–212
9. Belén Vidal, *Heritage Film: Nation, Genre and Representation* (London: Wallflower, 2012), 110.

# BIBLIOGRAPHY

Genz, Stéphanie. *Postfeminities in Popular Culture*. New York: Palgrave Macmillan, 2009.

Griffin, Penny. *Popular Culture, Political Economy and the Death of Feminism*. London: Routledge, 2015.

Mayer, Sophie. *Political Animals: The New Feminist Cinema*. London: I.B. Tauris, 2016.

McRobbie, Angela. *The Aftermath of Feminism: Gender, Culture and Social Change*. Los Angeles: Sage Publications, 2009.

Monk, Claire. *Heritage Film Audiences: Period Films and Contemporary Audiences in the UK*. Edinburgh: Edinburgh University Press, 2011.

Pidduck, Julianne. *Contemporary Costume Film*. London: BFI, 2004.

Thumim, Janet. *Celluloid Sisters: Women and Popular Cinema*. New York, Palgrave Macmillan, 1992.

Vidal, Belén. *Heritage Film: Nation, Genre and Representation*. London: Wallflower, 2012.

Vincent, Alice. "How Feminism conquered pop culture," *The Guardian*, December 30, 2014, http://www.telegraph.co.uk/culture/culturenews/11310119/feminism-pop-culture-2014.html.

# CHAPTER 2

# Early Modern Queens on Screen: Victors, Victims, Villains, Virgins, and Viragoes

*Elena Woodacre*

Queens have been a seemingly never-ending source of fascination across a variety of media, in contemporary accounts, biography and prosopography, historiography, fiction, and film. In terms of academia, this same fascination, coupled with the rise of women's history and gender studies, has resulted in the advent of queenship studies, a rich vein of scholarship that has brought new layers of analysis and understanding to the lives and roles of queens across the centuries. In terms of popular culture, each generation has overlaid its own interests and values on the lives of queens, reinterpreting them to fit in with the societal values and preoccupations of their era. Indeed, as noted in the section introduction, in the current era we are all influenced, directly or indirectly, by the progression of feminism and a plethora of female politicians and leaders, which have affected the way that we view queens both past and present. This modern rise of female leaders has perhaps increased our fascination with the 'Monstrous Regiment' of regnant, regent, and powerful consort queens of the early modern era but has also encouraged us to make 'proto-feminists' out of these premodern women, looking for harbingers

E. Woodacre (✉)
University of Winchester, Winchester, UK

© The Author(s) 2018                                                         27
J. North et al. (eds.), *Premodern Rulers and Postmodern Viewers*,
Queenship and Power, https://doi.org/10.1007/978-3-319-68771-1_2

of our own age of female politicians from these intriguing royal women of the past. While we do have to be careful of present-centeredness or 'Whig history' on screen in our interpretation of queens, an analysis of the representation of early modern queens on film can tell us a great deal about our own society and how we view women today by how we present and categorize these historical figures.

This chapter will give a wide-ranging overview of the representation of early modern queens on film and television, focusing on the typologies that the queens of this period have been grouped into by modern media. While it must be noted that there are also excellent representations of medieval queens, such as the renowned performance of Katherine Hepburn in *The Lion in Winter* and non-European contemporaries of the 'Monstrous Regiment,' such as the fascinating examination of the Sultanate of Women period in the Ottoman Empire in the Turkish television series *The Magnificent Century*, this chapter will focus on European queens from the sixteenth to the eighteenth centuries, primarily, though not exclusively, in English-language modern media formats.[1] It is hoped that further research might take the categories suggested in this paper for the representation of queens in the early modern era and analyze how readily they map to women beyond the confines of Europe and/or this particular period of the 'Monstrous Regiment'.

## Typologies of Queens on Screen: Victors, Victims, Villains, Virgins, and Viragoes

To understand how these historical figures have been classified and interpreted by (post)modern viewers and producers, this study proposes five major categories of representation, which have been labelled as 'Victors, Victims, Villains, Virgins, and Viragoes'. Exploring each one in turn will give a greater understanding of the ways in which filmmakers and television producers have depicted these royal women on screen and how these queens have been continually reshaped by the interests of successive generations of viewers.

It is only natural to assume that the ever-increasing emphasis on female equality that has run alongside the development of film and television would have an impact on the representation of the queens of the 'Monstrous Regiment' era as victors—strong rulers and 'proto-feminists'. While representations of queens as victors certainly exist, as will be discussed shortly, this category is not as popular as one might imagine—indeed this paper will argue that filmmakers, by and large, have been more concerned with the love lives, rather than the political agency, of queens.

One of the ways in which the queens of this period are most clearly shown as political actors is at the moment of their coronation when they are assuming power. It is indeed coronations that define a queen's position and thus form key scenes for any biopic, particularly those of a female ruler. Examples include the deliberate references to Elizabeth I's coronation portrait in Kapur's *Elizabeth* (1998) or, beyond the early modern period, depictions of the coronations of Victoria and Elizabeth II in their respective 2016 television series.[2] All three feature young, beautiful queens (nervously perhaps) assuming the weight of office in ceremonial garb in packed cathedrals against a score of choristers.

A coronation can be seen as a triumphal moment when a queen had to overcome considerable obstacles to claim a throne. An excellent example is the RTVE miniseries *Isabel*; the entire first series is dedicated to the Infanta's difficult position in the fractured court of her half-brother Enrique IV and her contested position as heir.[3] Isabel's coronation forms the climax of the first series—it is foreshadowed in the opening scene of the series, but it is only in the final episode, after the trials that she had to endure to secure her throne that we see the full coronation scene where Isabel is finally crowned in front of a cathedral and a crowd of supporters, looking majestic and ethereal in a long white gown. Yet it is in the scene immediately after the coronation where the steel of the young queen and her determination to rule is shown. Isabel declares to her councillors that she will not be a weak ruler like her brother Enrique and that 'Everyone in this realm must understand one thing very clearly: that I, Isabel, am the Queen of Castile. And only God can remove me from this throne.'[4]

Catherine the Great's coronation, after her coup against her husband Peter in 1762, was another triumphal moment. Indeed, the critical events of 1762 are often the climax and ending of films of the Empress' life, with the exception of the 1995 series that continued to explore her reign and affair with Potemkin. Yet, this pivotal moment in Catherine's life is not always portrayed as one of complete triumph or a celebration of female rule. The 2014 Russian series *Ekaterina* is perhaps the most understated example of her victory, with the first series ending with Catherine's march to the throne in full ceremonial garb while a herald announces the incredibly long list of her subsidiary titles—at the final moment, the Empress turns with an expression of quiet triumph and satisfaction.[5] Catherine's coup and coronation are sometimes portrayed on film as triumph spliced with tragedy. In *Young Catherine*, Julia Ormond gives a rousing speech to her troops on horseback that incites them to support her bid for the throne.[6] Her subsequent coronation juxtaposes the ceremony with images of her brooding lover Orlov who salutes her almost wistfully with his sword though he cannot be by her side as her consort, and it is insinuated, as the father of her child. In the final scenes of 1934's *The Rise of Catherine the Great*, Catherine receives the adoration of a cheering crowd below from a balcony and claims, 'This is the happiest day of my life! And I always believed nobody cared for me—and suddenly I'm loved. I'm loved by so many!'[7] She thanks the nobles who have supported her coup and heads to her room with her lover who has the unenviable task of telling the Empress of her husband's death. Catherine, aghast and angry, returns to the nobles asking, 'Who was it? Who killed him? Who spoilt my victory?' Her anger builds to hysterics, shouting, 'I'll punish all of you if you don't show me the one [who killed him]!' and ordering them to get out before sinking into a chair to bemoan her husband's death. Her counsellor tells Catherine that, 'Everything has a price, Your Majesty. And the crown has the highest price of all ... Russia wanted you at any price.' The Empress stares into space, tearfully claiming, 'He always called me Little Catherine...' and the picture fades to black, reducing Catherine from a triumphant Empress to a grieving widow—insinuating that a crown is less important than love and demonstrating the high price a woman can pay for power.

Coronations are not the only way to show a queen as a triumphant and savvy political leader—speeches are another excellent way to demonstrate her agency and leadership on screen. In Kapur's *Elizabeth the Golden Age*, Cate Blanchett delivers several speeches that emphasize her strength as a ruler.[8] In one scathing interchange with the Spanish ambassador, she tells him, 'Go back to your rathole sir. Tell Philip I fear neither him, nor his priests, nor his armies. Tell him if he wants to shake his fist at us, we'll give him such a bite he'll wish he kept his hands in his pockets!' The ambassador responds by warning her that, 'There is a wind coming madam, which will sweep away your pride' and turns to leave. Elizabeth shouts after him, shaking with anger: 'I too can command the wind, sir! I have a hurricane in me that will strip Spain bare if you dare to try me!'

The Tilbury speech is perhaps Elizabeth I's most well-known proc-
lamation, and though historians are still divided on the most accurate version of the speech, or indeed if it was ever given, it continues
to be frequently represented on screen.[9] It is a rousing monologue
than any actress would relish delivering and indeed many of the most
celebrated women who have taken on the role of Elizabeth I including Flora Robson, Glenda Jackson, Helen Mirren, Cate Blanchett, and
Anne-Marie Duff have all given moving versions of the famous Tilbury
speech.[10] To magnify the militaristic aspect of the speech, as an exhorta-
tion to her troops, Elizabeth is often represented on horseback in some
form of armor, from Glenda Jackson's armored collar, to the breastplate
worn by Mirren, Duff, and Robson, or even Cate Blanchett's improbable
full suit of armor. It is this last costume that shows a modern preoccupa-
tion with gender equality—Elizabeth not only has the 'heart and stomach of a king' but she can wear his armor too.

Yet queens are not always depicted as strong victors, astride horses on
the battlefield—they are also represented as victims and tragic figures.
This can be either of events beyond their control, such as Helen Mirren's
Oscar-nominated portrayal of Queen Charlotte who is struggling with
her husband's deteriorating mental health and interfamily strife in *The
Madness of King George* (1995) or queens who are undone by love. Mary
Queen of Scots is perhaps the classic example of the latter category, a
queen who lost her throne after three marriages ended in tragedy: with
François II's early death, Darnley's murder, and Bothwell's exile and
death in prison. She is repeatedly portrayed as an example of a ruler who
put the woman before the queen 'privileging the idea that a woman's
real happiness lies in the private realm, with a husband and a child'.[11]
Mary is the foil to her rival Elizabeth, who chooses duty and crown over
love and rules from her head, as John Guy argues, while Mary ruled
from the heart.[12] Indeed, as if to stress the differences between the two
queens, they are often portrayed in a meeting on film, in *Mary Queen of
Scots* (1971) or *Mary of Scotland* (1936) for example, although we know
that no such meeting took place.[13] Recent theatrical performances have
taken this duality even further; for example, in the two-woman show
*It's so nice* (2011), Barbara Sylvain and Lula Béry play out a conversa-
tion/confrontation between the two queens, and at the Almeida theatre
in the winter of 2016–2017 Juliet Stevenson and Lia Williams enacted
Fredrick Schiller's *Mary Stuart*, flipping a coin before they took the
stage to see which actress will play which queen.[14] Yet no matter how

the rivalry between Mary Queen of Scots and Elizabeth I is staged or filmed, ultimately Mary remains the victim, losing first her heart, then her crown, and ultimately her head, while Elizabeth emerges the victor from their rivalry.

Mary Queen of Scots is not the only queen who is depicted on film as losing a crown for love. Sophia Dorothea of Celle lost the opportunity to become the first Hanoverian queen of England as her husband George I dissolved their marriage and imprisoned Sophia for over 30 years due to her affair with Count von Königsmarck—her tragic story became the plot for the film *Saraband for Dead Lovers* (1948) . Juana I of Castile is often given the sobriquet of '*la Loca*' ('The Mad') due to the persistent image of her as being mentally unstable, and her fascinating story has been repeatedly filmed—Janice North gives extended consideration to treatments of Juana's life, reign, and relationship with her husband later in this volume. Juana's decline is often represented in film as being due to her tempestuous relationship with her husband, Philip 'the Fair' of Castile. Indeed the English title for the 2001 Spanish film *Juana la Loca* was *Mad Love*, expressing the central role that love played in undoing the queen who was literally driven mad by love for her unfaithful husband in this portrayal.[15] Juana and Philip's relationship is also a feature of the last section of the RTVE series *Isabel* and forms the focus of the follow-on feature film *La corona partida* (The Broken Crown).[16] In the RTVE version, we see Juana's decline from a sharp, intelligent girl before her marriage to a miserable wreck due to the cruel treatment of her ambitious consort. Yet, however much she appears to hate him and rail against his imprisonment of her in the early stages of her reign, once he dies Juana is devoted to him, consulting and even kissing his corpse as she travels with it each night on its way to be interred. Juana appears as a character again in the *Carlos, Rey Emperador* (*Carlos, King Emperor*) series, which RTVE commissioned as a sequel to the popular *Isabel*.[17] Here she is a mercurial figure and poor mother, something that she claims to regret on her deathbed scene with her daughter Leonor, though she argues that Philip was always more important to her than her children and wishes for death so that she might be finally reunited with him.

Anne Boleyn is another queen who is often portrayed as a tragic figure whose rise and fall was tied to the waxing and waning of love. Anne Boleyn is not only a popular figure in historical films, as Susan Bordo's *The Creation of Anne Boleyn* has demonstrated; she is arguably a cultural industry in her own right, with a plethora of novels on her life, popular histories and academic studies as well as websites and blogs that discuss her short but eventful life and reign.[18] Before Anne's first film outing in the 1920 German epic *Anna Boleyn*, she had featured on stage in plays such as Shakespeare's *Henry VIII* and Donizetti's early nineteenth-century opera *Anna Bolena*.[19] The question of Anne's ambition is a recurring theme in popular culture portrayals of the queen and provokes the question of whether she can be classed as a 'victor' or a 'victim'.

Retha Warnicke charts the portrayal of Anne Boleyn in English-language sources, arguing that Anne was largely portrayed as an innocent victim, devoid of ambition until George Boker's mid-nineteenth-century play *Anne Boleyn: A Tragedy*.[20] An increasing emphasis on Anne's ambition can be seen in more recent film portrayals of her life, yet interpretations differ between Anne's slowly developing ambition in *Anne of the Thousand Days* to Anne being supremely ambitious and almost a villain in stage and television adaptations of Hilary Mantel's *Wolf Hall* and *Bring up the Bodies*.[21] In the TV series *The Tudors* and the film adaptation of Philippa Gregory's *The Other Boleyn Girl*, there is more ambiguity as to whether Anne (and her sister Mary) is a victim of her family's ambition or is masterminding her own rise.[22] Anne's increasingly ambitious and hypersexualized portrayal can be seen as a reflection of modern society, reframing Anne as a sexually liberated, proto-feminist figure that twenty-first century women might be able to relate to better than the demure and virtuous figure of John Banks's 1682 Restoration play 'Vertue Betray'd: Or Anna Bullen, a tragedy'.[23] Anne's ambition and drive can also be seen as a precursor to her daughter, the regnant queen, Elizabeth I—echoed in Anne's remark to Henry VIII in *Anne of the Thousand Days* that 'Elizabeth shall be a greater queen than any king of yours!'[24] Just as premodern plays and works such as Foxe's *Book of Martyrs* often portrayed Anne as the genesis of Elizabeth's stewardship of the Reformed religion in England, modern audiences can see an ambitious and bold Anne as a harbinger of a powerful female ruler.[25]

However victorious her production of Elizabeth might appear, Anne's execution groups her with a small but significant group of Victim queens who suffered the same tragic end, including Mary Queen of Scots, Lady Jane Grey, and Marie Antoinette. Like the focus on coronations for the Victor queens, the executions of these 'victims' have often played a dramatic role in the conclusion of films about these royal women. Anne's execution has been captured in generally every major biopic about her including *The Other Boleyn Girl, Anne of the Thousand Days,* and series where she appears, such as Showtime's *The Tudors.* The execution of Lady Jane Grey, so dramatically pictured in Delaroche's famous 1833 painting, is captured at the finish of the 1986 film starring Helena Bonham Carter, who later played another execution scene as Anne Boleyn in the 2003 British television series *Henry VIII.*[26] Jane's actions on screen in *Lady Jane* closely follow the account in Foxe's *Book of Martyrs* in which she fumbled for the block asking plaintively 'Where is it? What do I do?'[27]

The execution of Mary Queen of Scots has also been a feature of most biopics of the Scottish queen as well as a key scene in many films on Elizabeth I due to the pivotal nature of Mary's trial and death in Elizabeth's reign. Indeed, Mary's execution forms arguably the earliest portrayal of queens on film, with the minute-long feature on her death produced in 1895. Jonathan Stubbs notes that while an effort was made to produce the Elizabethan costumes for this short film, 'it seems most likely that the film's attraction was its gruesome content [i.e. Mary's execution] rather than its evocation of the past.'[28] Yet not all of the screen versions of her death capture the many blows that it supposedly took to sever her head from her body, preferring to let their leading actresses make a more dignified end. Marie Antoinette's execution has also been filmed multiple times from the 1938 version with Norma Shearer to the 2001 *Affair of the Necklace.*[29] The English title *Shadow of the Guillotine* for the 1956 French film *Marie Antoinette Reine de France*, demonstrates the continuing fascination with the queen's execution, as does the constant stream of tourists who make a pilgrimage to the Conciergerie in Paris, where an imprisoned Marie Antoinette spent her last days.[30] From the cultural industries and tourist sites connected to these executed women, it is clear that Victim queens leave a long, lasting legacy, which makes them cinematic gold.

Queens can be not only victorious or tragic heroes, but Villains too. Some queens, such as Marie de Medici who appears as a scheming royal mother in the BBC's *The Musketeers,* have an occasional outing as a villainess, while other women like Catherine de Medici or Mary Tudor, seem typecast in the role.[31] Catherine de Medici has a veritable Black Legend, which began in her own period, arguably triggered by those horrified by the St. Bartholomew's Day Massacre and the turbulence of the French Wars of Religion, when Catherine de Medici was at the heart of governance alongside her sons.[32] Malevolent portrayals of this queen are typified in 1994's *La Reine Margot* where Virna Lisi, in her first major scene, is negotiating coolly with a paid assassin.[33] In the CW series *Reign*, Catherine is still a schemer but is oddly cast with the Canadian actress Megan Follows, famous for portraying the Edwardian ingénue Anne of Green Gables. Follows brings not only a note of wry comedy at times but has tried to bring a somewhat nuanced understanding of her character noting that, 'What I like about my character is even if my actions are unsavory or might seem really outrageous ... she's grounded in a motivation that, for her, justifies her actions. They may not justify them for everybody else (laughs), but in her mind they justify her actions.'[34]

Mary Tudor is another queen who is often portrayed or identified as a villain, even though her popular sobriquet of 'Bloody Mary' has been challenged by newer revisionist histories of her reign.[35] She most frequently appears as a villain foil to her sister Elizabeth I; for example, in Joanne Whalley's regal but dark portrayal of Mary in *The Virgin Queen* opposite Anne-Marie Duff in 2005 or Kathy Burke's version in Kapur's 1998 *Elizabeth*. When Mary is not an outright villain, she often becomes a victim of her hopeless love for Philip of Spain. Examples of a victim Mary include Jane Lapotaire's portrayal of a woman who wishes to protect her young cousin in *Lady Jane* but is ultimately forced to send her to the block in order for Mary's marriage to Philip to take place. Another example is Angela Cremonte's beautiful but lovelorn Mary who tries desperately to please her young husband in *Carlos, Rey Emperador* but knows that he will never truly reciprocate her affections. Even Whalley claims in an interview for the BBC that she felt sorry for the queen she portrayed 'because day-to-day life was pretty tough on her. She was very alone and very conflicted about how to deal with things.'[36] While some queens, like Mary Tudor and Catherine de Medici have an international renown as Villain queens, others have a significant place in national memory and popular culture as a villainess. Kataryzna Kosior has profiled the long-term reputation of Bona Sforza, Queen of Poland, who has long been cast as a scheming poisoner, surveying historiography as well as modern portrayals in popular culture from a play in 1914 to a television series on the queen in the 1980s.[37]

An interesting trend can be spotted in the portrayal of Virgin queens, focusing on their younger years or rise to power. This emphasis can be linked to the plethora of teen films, with a first wave in the 1950s followed by another surge in the 1980s, which Timothy Shary argues is connected to the placement of multiplex theatres within or next to malls, a key locus of American teen culture.[38] Finding that teens were a lucrative market of moviegoers, Hollywood began producing increasing numbers of films designed to appeal to their interests. Films on queens can be seen to be capitalizing on this trend, with *Lady Jane* appearing in 1986, the same year that the classic teen flicks *Ferris Bueller's Day Off* and *Pretty in Pink* made their debut.[39] Although *Lady Jane* may not be instantly identified with these more mainstream teen films, the protagonist also struggles with issues that many teens could readily identify with and that form the basis of many teen movies: conflict with parents, social awkwardness, first love, coming of age, and taking on adult responsibilities. The young Helena Bonham Carter makes an engaging ingénue and Cary Elwes an attractive romantic foil as Guildford—he went on to play the dashing lead in *The Princess Bride* the following year.[40]

While again perhaps less obvious as teen films, a renewed focus on the early years of well-known queens made their stories more appealing to a younger audience. In the nineties, multiple movies and miniseries revisited the rise of two famous premodern queens: Elizabeth I and Catherine II 'the Great' of Russia. The latter's early years were the focus of two miniseries, *Young Catherine*, starring Julia Ormond in 1991 and *Catherine the Great*, starring Catherine Zeta-Jones in 1995.[41] *Young Catherine*, as the title suggests, focuses on Catherine's rise to power, culminating in her coup and coronation in 1762. Although Ford and Mitchell argue that Ormond 'neither looks nor acts like a teen,' clearly this coming of age biopic of the beautiful young princess who emerges from the control of the aging Empress Elizabeth, finds love in the form of the gallant Orlov, and ultimately triumphs over her husband to take the crown would appeal to a younger audience as a sort of follow-on from a Disney fairy tale.[42]

The rise of Elizabeth I was also revisited in the nineties in Shekhar Kapur's *Elizabeth*, starring Cate Blanchett. Elizabeth's early years had been portrayed before in *Young Bess*, starring Jean Simmons in 1953, emerging just before the early heyday of teen films in the fifties.[43] Both films have a strong emphasis on a central romance but a very different focus for Elizabeth's affections. In *Young Bess*, the love story is focused on Elizabeth's obsession with Thomas Seymour, played by Simmons' husband Stewart Granger. Simmons' Elizabeth not only deals with first love and heartbreak but plays the rebellious teen in her confrontation with her father Henry VIII.[44] Kapur's *Elizabeth* also struggles with a controversial relationship, but this time with Joseph Fiennes' Robert Dudley. Fiennes was perhaps at his peak as a romantic lead, with the Oscar-winning *Shakespeare in Love* coming out in the same year. However, while both *Young Bess* and *Elizabeth* feature young love, heartbreak, and Elizabeth's precarious transition to adulthood and monarchy, Kapur's 1998 biopic is perhaps slightly too dark to be classified as a teen film—in this case the 1953 treatment is clearly better suited to a younger audience.

Teen queens returned to the screen in the twenty-first century, led by Sofia Coppola's romp *Marie Antoinette*, starring Kirsten Dunst, in 2006.[45] In this film, there is no doubt of the appeal to the teenage audience, with not only romance and coming-of-age struggles but an extended shopping scene, played out against Kevin Shield's remix of the Bow Wow Wow classic from the 1980s 'I want candy'. Robert Rosenstone notes that this version of Marie Antoinette 'in behavior and speech can seem more like a Valley Girl than the rigidly raised daughter of Austrian empress Maria Theresa.'[46] Dunst graced the cover of *Vogue* in September 2006 with the headline, 'Kirsten Dunst is the teen queen who rocked Versailles' and in an article on the life of Marie Antoinette by Kennedy Fraser accompanied by a full photoshoot by famed photographer Annie Leibovitz.[47] Belén Vidal argues *Marie Antoinette* started a trend for 'monarchy films with an emphasis on young women', pairing it in his discussion with 2009's *The Young Victoria*. Belen notes that '*Marie Antoinette* and *The Young Victoria* update the monarchy genre and target it at young female audiences by foregrounding a feminine perspective on teen romance as opposed to a feminist consciousness.'[48] Belén goes further to suggest that these films engage in the 'commodification of feminism', allowing these privileged royal teens to demonstrate 'consumption and self-display' on screen—certainly something that the infamous shopping scene in *Marie Antoinette* appears to demonstrate.[49] The following decade saw the advent of the popular CW series *Reign*, which can best be described as 'Mary Queen of Scots goes to high school.'[50] T. L. Stanley argues that the show's producers aimed to capitalize on the public's fascination with the marriage of William and Kate, the Duke and Duchess of Cambridge, and give viewers a teen-friendly 'sanitized' version of Showtime's *The Tudors*.[51] Like *The Tudors*, *Reign* has been criticized for playing fast and loose with history in its desire to appeal to its core teen audience. The modern soundtrack, hairstyles, and costumes are all designed to appeal to today's teens rather than bearing any resemblance to the historical fashions for example. The first episode features a scene where Mary and her ladies prepare for an event; the sequence of the girls dressing and applying their anachronistic makeup feels almost like a post from a YouTube beauty vlogger. The series' star Adelaide Kane dismissed this criticism with the comment, 'How many teenage girls do you know who are obsessed with history—I wasn't at that age.'[52]

The emphasis on romance, and even sex, in the teen-focused films is part of a wider trend in cinematic depictions of voracious or Virago queens in the twentieth and twenty-first century. There is little doubt that early modern queens have been 'sexed up' on modern screens. Indeed, the explicit nature and the number of sex scenes in the Showtime series *The Tudors* lent it an air of notoriety, not to mention protests from historians regarding the historical inaccuracy of the show.[53] Basil Glynn argues that the series is completely driven by Henry's sexual needs, reducing the agency of the queens in this series to women who are forced to submit to the king's desires in order to have any influence.[54]

Certainly sex itself is not anachronistic, but the emphasis on sexual scenes and the presentation of scantily or provocatively clad queens on screen is a product of modern culture. There has been intensive and prolonged debate about the representation and sexualization of the female body on film by feminist scholars. Laura Mulvey's groundbreaking and controversial piece 'Visual Pleasure and Narrative Cinema' argued that female bodies on screen were objects of pleasure to be ogled by the 'male gaze'.[55] Yet Stacey and others have argued that we need to consider the 'female gaze' on male bodies and women's homoerotic appreciation of the female form on screen as well.[56] Yet whether the body of a queen is (erotically) surveyed by the male or female gaze, it is clear that the inclusion of sex is a key element of modern cinema. This makes Viragoes theoretically more interesting than Virgins to filmgoers; Pidduck notes when discussing portrayals of the love life of Elizabeth I that, 'clearly a queen who is not a virgin makes for more interesting cinema.'[57] Pidduck argues that the portrayal of Elizabeth I in Kapur's 1998 film, which stresses the tension between her sexualized 'body natural' and her increasingly constrained 'body politic' as queen is 'a contemporary protofeminist discourse about women's pleasure, power and right to control their own bodies.'[58] Gill, in her work on postfeminist media culture and the sexualization of modern culture, has argued that a woman's possession of an attractive and highly sexualized body can be seen as both her source of power and a questionable asset that is under constant scrutiny and criticism by others, both male and female—the bodies of queens on screen would appear to be no exception to Gill's arguments.[59] While this emphasis on sex can largely be seen as a reaction to the post-sexual revolution mentality of modern audiences, it is important to note that steamy portrayals of the love lives of queens can predate the 1960s 'Summer of Love'. Indeed, Marlene Dietrich's turn as Catherine the Great in *The Scarlett Empress* (1934) with its emphasis on her supposed legion of lovers risked contravening the recently enacted Hayes censorship code.[60] Even the promotional material was suggestive, with one poster bearing the tagline 'Her whisper was a command to love'. Dietrich's movie contrasted with another 1934 movie on the Russian Empress, *The Rise of Catherine the Great*, which made Catherine more of a spurned wife than a sexual predator. Ford and Mitchell argue that, 'Each of the two 1934 biopics wraps Catherine's marriage and sexuality in a package recognizable to viewers: the faithful wife and the insatiable wanton, opposite stereotypes, but both less risky than presenting Catherine's sexual dilemma [i.e. the need for an heir] to the Hayes office or to viewers.'[61] Zeta-Jones' post-sexual revolution portrayal of Catherine's love life in 1995 takes the innuendo of Dietrich's biopic to another level entirely, 'like *The Scarlett Empress* on steroids, with less artsy presumption and more bare flesh'.[62]

Queens in bed or behaving badly has become a recurring theme in recent movies with several portrayals of adulterous consorts. Anne Boleyn was brought down by accusations of affairs with other men, including her brother George Boleyn. The 2008 film *The Other Boleyn Girl* runs with this allegation, in a scene in which Natalie Portman's Anne tearfully begs her brother to help her conceive a son to maintain her hold on the throne, to the aversion and disgust of their sister Mary and George's wife Jane, who watches their tryst from the shadows. A running plot line in the BBC's *Musketeers* series (2014–2016), which became a favorite of fan wikis and video montages, was the love story between Anne of Austria and the musketeer Aramis. This affair also features in *The Man in the Iron Mask*, which is also based on the novels of Alexandre Dumas, although Roger Macdonald alleges a real-life love affair between Anne and the Duke of Buckingham in his book *The Queen's Diamonds*.[63] A more widely recognized queenly love affair between Caroline Matilda, Queen of Denmark and the physician and royal advisor Struensee forms the basis of the aptly titled 2012 film, *A Royal Affair*.[64] Like Anne of Austria, Caroline Matilda is another neglected royal wife who seeks comfort in the arms of another, but Caroline and Struensee's relationship is redeemed by their efforts to reform the realm with Enlightenment ideas and preserve it from the excesses of an unstable king. Staying with the eighteenth century, in *Marie Antoinette*, Dunst embarks in a steamy love affair with her lover Axel von Fersen, while in 2012's *Les Adieux à la Reine*, the emphasis is on innuendos of a lesbian romance between the queen and at least one of her ladies.[65]

Greater interest in LGBT studies and wider public acceptance of lesbian relationships have not only changed our understanding of the love lives of queens but their portrayal on film. Queen Christina of Sweden is an excellent example of the impact this societal and scholarly shift has had on the cinematic representation of a historical figure, and Séverine Genieys-Kirk's chapter to follow discusses the shifting portrayal of Christina in greater detail. In Greta Garbo's star vehicle *Queen Christina* in 1933, the central plot premise is the queen's love affair with the Spanish ambassador.[66] Garbo's Christina gives up the throne to run away with Don Antonio but he is tragically killed just before the couple are due to embark on a ship, leaving the queen alone and throneless. *The Girl King* was released in 2015, taking a radically different interpretation of Christina's abdication and her sexual preferences.[67] In *The Girl King*, Christina is obsessed with her lady-in-waiting, Ebba Sparre, with whom she shares kisses and an erotic love scene. Christina's sense of betrayal and fury when Ebba marries is demonstrated in a scene where the queen's passion for Ebba makes her seem almost unhinged with love. Interestingly, Garbo's Christina also briefly kisses Ebba and shows anger at Ebba's marriage, but this is portrayed as a jealous friend and mistress, rather than a romantic passion. Ultimately, while both movies engage with Christina's well known cross-dressing tendencies, masculine attitudes, and refusal to marry, they portray her sexuality in very different ways, reflecting the times in which each biopic was produced.

This emphasis on the love lives and sexuality of the queens can be seen as a way of humanizing them for modern viewers, making them less of a historical ruler and more of a relatable woman with recognizable feelings and physical needs. However, does this emphasis on their emotional and physical sides also rob these queens of agency and authority—two areas that queenship scholars are constantly seeking to identify and analyze? Are we more interested in them as women than as queens on screen?

There is also a sense that runs through these films that love and power are incompatible, that queens are doomed to be unhappy in love or must sacrifice one for the other. Indeed, David Grant Moss argues that the predicaments of Elizabeth I, and arguably all of the queens surveyed here, represent the 'postmodern difficulty of a woman "trying to have it all,"' balancing careers, motherhood, and relationships.[68] Yet can we equate these premodern queens and their postmodern viewers so simply, given that their lives were played out in a completely different societal context and that these queens dealt with responsibilities and pressures that most moviegoers could not map to their own day-to-day experience of juggling careers, commuting, and the rest? Perhaps we continually return to the lives of premodern queens because their lives are so different from our own that watching movies about them becomes a kind of escapism from modern life. Emphasizing the love lives of queens is a way to make connections with the audience, reminding us that however different their lives might be, they had to cope with heartbreak and tragedy just like their postmodern viewers. Yet by watching them triumph over the Spanish Armada, as in *Elizabeth the Golden Age*, or claiming a contested throne in *Isabel*, or even in going nobly to their death like Anne Boleyn in *Anne of the Thousand Days*, we find aspirational models, even if we cannot (or would not want to) replicate their exact experiences. Yet, even though the historical queens of the early modern period often wielded considerable power and authority, they would arguably find it hard to empathize with today's feminist values and the lifestyles of the postmodern viewers who enjoy watching films about the lives of queens.

Ultimately, it is important to recognize that these categories of Victors, Victims, Villains, Virgins, and Viragoes are constructs of our modern value system, including the advent of feminism and our modern views of sex and sexuality, rather than any reflection on early modern queenship or the realities of these historical figures' lives. While filmmakers and television producers did not necessarily intend to create these typologies, their formation reveals a perception, even if it is unconscious or inaccurate, of how powerful women and gender roles operate in both the premodern period and in our own.

# NOTES

1. *The Lion in Winter*, Feature Film, directed by Anthony Harvey (Haworth Productions, 1968). *The Magnificent Century (Muhtesem Yüzyil)*, Television Series, directed by Durul and Yagmur Taylan (Tim's Productions, 2011–2014).

2. *Elizabeth*, Feature Film, directed by Shekhar Kapur (Working Title Films, 1998). *The Crown*, Television Series, directed by Peter Morgan (Netflix, 2016–). *Victoria*, Television Series, directed by Daisy Goodwin (Mammoth Screen, 2016–).

3. *Isabel*, Television Series, directed by Jordi Frades (Diagonal TV, 2011–2014).

4. My translation above, the original lines are "Porque todos en este reino tienen que tener algo muy claro: que yo, Isabel, soy la reina de Castilla. Y solo Dios podrá apartarme de este trono." *Isabel*, Episode 13.

5. *Ekaterina*, Television Series, directed by Aleksandr Baranov (Amedia See, 2014).

6. *Young Catherine*, Television Series, directed by Michael Anderson (Consolidated Entertainment, 1991).

7. *The Rise of Catherine the Great*, Feature Film, directed by Paul Czinner (London Film Productions, 1934).

8. *Elizabeth: The Golden Age*, Feature Film, directed by Shekhar Kapur (Universal Pictures, 2007).

9. See Susan Frye, "The Myth of Elizabeth at Tilbury" *The Sixteenth Century Journal* 23, no. 1 (1992): 95–114.

10. *Fire over England*, Feature Film, directed by William K. Howard (London Film Productions, 1937); *Elizabeth: The Golden Age* (2006); *Elizabeth R*, Television Series, directed by Roderick Graham (BBC, 1971); *The Virgin Queen*, Television Series, directed by Coky Giedroyc (BBC, 2005); *Elizabeth I*, Television Series, directed by Tom Hooper (HBO, 2005).

11. Elizabeth A. Ford and Deborah C. Mitchell, *Royal Portraits in Hollywood: Filming the Lives of Queens* (Lexington, KY: The University Press of Kentucky, 2009), 143.

12. John Guy, "Mary Queen of Scots (1971)" in *Tudors and Stuarts on Film*, ed. Susan Doran and Thomas S. Freeman (New York: Palgrave Macmillan, 2009), 149.

13. *Mary Queen of Scots*, Feature Film, directed by Charles Jarrott (Universal Pictures, 1971); *Mary of Scotland*, Feature Film, directed by John Ford (Radio Pictures, 1936).

14. Fredrik Schiller, *Mary Stuart*, Theatrical Performance, directed by Robert Icke. Almeida Theatre, London, 2016–2017; Barbara Sylvain and

Lula Béry, *It's so nice*, Theatrical Performance, directed by Cyril Aribaud and Léonard Clarys, Oh My God Theatre Company, 2011.

15. *Juana la Loca Juana la Loca (Mad Love)*, Feature Film, directed by Vicente Aranda (Canal+, 2001).

16. *La Corona Partida*, Feature Film, directed by Jordi Frades (Diagonal TV, 2016).

17. *Carlos Rey Emperador*, Television Series, directed by Álvaro Cervantes (Diagonal TV, 2015–16).

18. Susan Bordo, *The Creation of Anne Boleyn: A New Look at England's Most Notorious Queen* (Boston: Houghton Mifflin Harcourt, 2013).

19. *Anna Boleyn*, Feature Film, directed by Ernst Lubitsch (Messter Films, 1920). Gaetano Donizetti; *Anna Bolena*, Opera, 1830; William Shakespeare, *Henry VIII*, Play, 1632.

20. Retha Warnicke, "Anne Boleyn in History, Drama and Film" in *High and Mighty Queens of England*, ed. Carole Levin, Debra Barrett-Graves and Jo Eldridge Carney, 239–255. George Boker, "Anne Boleyn: A Tragedy" (Philadelphia: A. Hart, 1850).

21. *Anne of the Thousand Days*, Feature Film, directed by Charles Jarrott (Hal Wallis Productions, 1969); *Wolf Hall*, Television Series, directed by Peter Kosminsky (BBC Productions, 2015); Mike Poulton, *Wolf Hall and Bring up the Bodies: The Stage Adaptation* (New York: Picador, 2014).

22. *The Tudors*, Television Series, created by Michael Hurst (Showtime Networks, 2007–2010); *The Other Boleyn Girl*, Feature Film, directed by Justin Chadwick (Columbia Pictures, 2008).

23. John Banks, "Vertue Betray'd: Or Anna Bullen, a tragedy" (London: R. Bentley and M. Magnes, 1682).

24. *Anne of the Thousand Days*.

25. John Foxe, *The Unabridged Acts and Monuments Online or TAMO* (HRI Online Publications, Sheffield, 2011). http://www.johnfoxe.org.

26. Paul Delaroche, "The Execution of Lady Jane Grey", oil on canvas, National Gallery, London, NG 1909.

27. Foxe, *The Unabridged Acts and Monuments Online* (1583 edition), Book 10, 1446 and *Lady Jane*, Feature Film, directed by Trevor Nunn (Paramount Pictures, 1986).

28. Jonathan Stubbs, *Historical Film: A Critical Introduction* (New York: Bloomsbury, 2013), 62.

29. *Marie Antoinette*, Feature Film, directed by W. S. Van Dyke (MGM, 1938); *The Affair of the Necklace*, Feature Film, directed by Charles Shyer (Warner Bros., 2001).

30. *Marie Antoinette Reine de France (Shadow of the Guillotine)*, Feature Film, directed by Jean Delannoy (Franco-London Films, 1956).

31. *The Musketeers*, Television Series, directed by Adrian Hodges (BBC, 2014–16). See particularly season 1, episode 6 'Mothers, sons and royal scandal'.
32. See N. M. Sutherland, "The Legend of the Wicked Italian Queen," *The Sixteenth Century Journal* 9, no. 2 (1978): 45–56.
33. *La Reine Margot*, Feature Film, directed by Patrice Chéreau (Renn Productions, 1994).
34. Interview with Megan Follows quoted in "The CW's *Reign*: Megan Follows on Catherine's Royal Motivations," *Access Hollywood*, October 24, 2013. https://www.accesshollywood.com/articles/the-cws-reign-megan-follows-on-catherines-royal-motivations-139074/.
35. See Susan Doran and Thomas Freeman, eds., *Mary Tudor: Old and New Perspectives* (New York: Palgrave Macmillan, 2011).
36. *BBC.co.uk*, "The Virgin Queen: Characters, Queen Mary," accessed July 24, 2017. http://www.bbc.co.uk/drama/virginqueen/joanne_whalley.shtml.
37. Kataryzna Kosior, "Outlander, Baby Killer, Poisoner? Rethinking Bona Sforza's Black Legend" in *Virtuous or Villainess? The Image of the Royal Mother from the Early Medieval to the Early Modern Era*, ed. Carey Fleiner and Elena Woodacre (New York: Palgrave Macmillan, 2016), 199–223.
38. Timothy Shary, *Teen Movies: American Youth on Screen* (London: Wallflower Press, 2005), 54.
39. *Ferris Bueller's Day Off*, Feature Film, directed by John Hughes (Paramount Pictures, 1986); *Pretty in Pink*, Feature Film, directed by Howard Deutch (Paramount Pictures, 1986).
40. *The Princess Bride*, Feature Film, directed by Rob Reiner (Act III Communications, 1987).
41. *Catherine the Great*, Television Miniseries, directed by Marvin J. Chomsky (Skylark Cine Inc, 1996).
42. Ford and Mitchell, *Royal Portraits*, 54.
43. *Young Bess*, Feature Film, directed by George Sidney (MGM, 1953).
44. See *Royal Portraits*, 240–241 for a discussion of this scene with Henry VIII.
45. *Marie Antoinette*, Feature Film, directed by Sofia Coppola (Columbia Pictures, 2006).
46. Robert A. Rosenstone, *History on Film: Film on History*, 3rd ed. (London: Routledge, 2018), 150.
47. Kennedy Fraser, "Kirsten Dunst: Teen Queen," *Vogue* (September 2006).
48. Belén Vidal, *Heritage Film: Nation, Genre and Representation* (London: Wallflower, 2012), 109.
49. Vidal, *Heritage Film*, 110.
50. *Reign*, Television Series, directed by Laurie McCarthy (World 2000 Entertainment, 2013–2017).

51. T. L. Stanley, "*Reign* hopes to seduce teens with its tales of Mary Queen of Scots," *Los Angeles Times*, September 13, 2013. http://www.latimes.com/entertainment/tv/showtracker/la-et-st-reign-mary-queen-of-scotts-20130915-story.html.

52. Lisa de Moraes, "CW's first crunchy-gravel drama *Reign* flirts with history," *Deadline Hollywood*, July 30, 2013. http://deadline.com/2013/07/tca-cws-first-crunchy-gravel-drama-flirts-with-history-552425/.

53. For an intensive discussion of the series by historians, see William Robison, ed., *History, Fiction and The Tudors: Sex, Politics, Power and Artistic License in the Showtime Television Series* (New York: Palgrave Macmillan, 2016).

54. Basil Glynn, "The Conquests of Henry VIII: Masculinity, Sex and the National Past" in *Television, Sex and Society: Analyzing Contemporary Representations*, ed. Basil Glynn, James Aston and Beth Johnson (New York: Continuum, 2012), 164–165.

55. Laura Mulvey, "Visual Pleasure and Narrative Cinema," in *Feminism and Film*, ed. E. Ann Kaplan, (Oxford: Oxford University Press, 2000), 34–47.

56. Jackie Stacey, "Desperately Seeking Difference," in *Feminism and Film*, ed. E. Ann Kaplan, (Oxford: Oxford University Press, 2000), 450–465.

57. Julianne Pidduck, *Contemporary Costume Film* (London: BFI, 2004), 170.

58. Pidduck, *Costume Film*, 172.

59. Rosalind Gill, "Postfeminist media culture: elements of a sensibility," *European Journal of Cultural Studies* 10, no. 2: 147–166.

60. *The Scarlett Empress*. Feature Film. Directed by Josef von Sternberg. (Paramount Pictures, 1934).

61. Ford and Mitchell, *Royal Portraits*, 51.

62. Ford and Mitchell, *Royal Portraits*, 63.

63. Roger Macdonald, *The Queen's Diamonds* (Cambridge: Cambridge Academic, 2010); *The Man in the Iron Mask*, Feature Film, directed by Randall Wallace (United Artists, 1998).

64. *A Royal Affair*, Feature Film, directed by Nikolaj Arcel (Zentropa Entertainments, 2012).

65. For continuing popular interest in Marie Antoinette's relationship with Fersen, see Evelyn Farr's collection of their letters in *I love you madly: Marie Antoinette and Count Fersen-The secret letters* (London: Peter Owen, 2016); *Les Adieux à la Reine* was linked to Chantal Thomas' book *The Wicked Queen: The Origins of the Myth of Marie Antoinette* (English version, New York: Zone Books, 2001), which explored the sexual slander directed at the French queen. *Les Adieux à la Reine*, Feature Film, directed by Benoît Jacquot (GMT Productions, 2012).

66. *Queen Christina*, Feature Film, directed by Rouben Mamoulian (MGM, 1933).
67. *The Girl King*, Feature Film, directed by Mika Kaurismäki (Mariana Films, 2015).
68. David Grant Moss, "A Queen for Whose Time? Elizabeth I as Icon for the Twentieth Century" *The Journal of Popular Culture* 39, no. 5 (2006): 800.

## WORKS CITED

### *Films/Television Series*

*The Affair of the Necklace*. Feature Film. Directed by Charles Shyer. Warner Bros., 2001.
*Anna Boleyn*. Feature Film. Directed by Ernst Lubitsch. Messter Films, 1920.
*Anne of the Thousand Days*. Feature Film. Directed by Charles Jarrott. Hal Wallis Productions, 1969.
*Catherine the Great*. Television Miniseries. Directed by Marvin J. Chomsky. Skylark Cine Inc, 1996.
*Carlos, Rey Emperador*. Television Series. Directed by Álvaro Cervantes. Diagonal TV, 2015–2016.
*The Crown*. Television Series. Directed by Peter Morgan. Netflix, 2016–.
*Ekaterina*. Television Series. Directed by Aleksandr Baranov. Amedia See, 2014.
*Elizabeth*. Feature Film. Directed by Shekhar Kapur. Working Title Films, 1998.
*Elizabeth I*. Television Series. Directed by Tom Hooper. HBO, 2005.
*Elizabeth R*. Television Series. Directed by Roderick Graham. BBC, 1971.
*Elizabeth: The Golden Age*. Feature Film. Directed by Shekhar Kapur. Universal Pictures, 2007.
*Ferris Bueller's Day Off*. Feature Film. Directed by John Hughes. Paramount Pictures, 1986.
*Fire over England*. Feature Film. Directed by William K. Howard. London Film Productions, 1937.
*The Girl King*. Feature Film. Directed by Mika Kaurismäki. Mariana Films, 2015.
*Henry VIII*. Television Series. Directed by Pete Travis. PBS, 2003.
*Isabel*. Television Series. Directed by Jordi Frades. RTVE/Diagonal TV, 2011–2014.
*Juana la Loca (Mad Love)*. Feature Film. Directed by Vicente Aranda. Canal+, 2001.
*La Corona Partida*. Feature Film. Directed by Jordi Frades. Diagonal TV, 2016.
*Lady Jane*. Feature Film. Directed by Trevor Nunn. Paramount Pictures, 1986.
*La Reine Margot*. Feature Film. Directed by Patrice Chéreau. Renn Productions, 1994.

*Les Adieux à la Reine*. Feature Film. Directed by Benoît Jacquot. GMT Productions, 2012.

*The Lion in Winter*. Feature Film. Directed by Anthony Harvey. Haworth Productions, 1968.

*The Magnificent Century (Muhtesem Yüzyil)*. Television Series. Directed by Durul and Yagmur Taylan. Tim's Productions, 2011–2014.

*The Man in the Iron Mask*. Feature Film. Directed by Randall Wallace. United Artists, 1998.

*Marie Antoinette*. Feature Film. Directed by W.S. Van Dyke. MGM, 1938.

*Marie Antoinette*. Feature Film. Directed by Sofia Coppola. Columbia Pictures, 2006.

*Marie Antoinette Reine de France (Shadow of the Guillotine)*. Feature Film. Directed by Jean Delannoy. Franco-London Films, 1956.

*Mary of Scotland*. Feature Film. Directed by John Ford. Radio Pictures, 1936.

*Mary Queen of Scots*. Feature Film. Directed by Charles Jarrott. Universal Pictures, 1971.

*The Other Boleyn Girl*. Feature Film. Directed by Justin Chadwick. Columbia Pictures, 2008.

*Pretty in Pink*. Feature Film. Directed by Howard Deutch. Paramount Pictures, 1986.

*The Princess Bride*. Feature Film. Directed by Rob Reiner. Act III Communications, 1987.

*Reign*. Television Series. Directed by Laurie McCarthy. World 2000 Entertainment, 2013–.

*The Rise of Catherine the Great*. Feature Film. Directed by Paul Czinner. London Film Productions, 1934.

*A Royal Affair*. Feature Film. Directed by Nikolaj Arcel. Zentropa Entertainments, 2012.

*The Scarlett Empress*. Feature Film. Directed by Josef von Sternberg. Paramount Pictures, 1934.

*The Tudors*. Television Series. Created by Michael Hurst. Showtime Networks, 2007–2010.

*Queen Christina*. Feature Film. Directed by Rouben Mamoulian. MGM, 1933.

*Victoria*. Television Series. Directed by Daisy Goodwin. Mammoth Screen, 2016–.

*The Virgin Queen*. Television Series. Directed by Coky Giedroyc. BBC, 2005.

*Wolf Hall*. Television Series. Directed by Peter Kosminsky. BBC Productions, 2015.

*Young Bess*. Feature Film. Directed by George Sidney. MGM, 1953.

*Young Catherine*. Television Series. Directed by Michael Anderson. Consolidated Entertainment, 1991.

*The Young Victoria*. Feature Film. Directed by Jean-Marc Vallée. GK Films, 2009.

## Plays/Performances/Paintings

Banks, John. "Vertue Betray'd: Or Anna Bullen, a tragedy." London: R. Bentley and M. Magnes, 1682.

Boker, George. "Anne Boleyn: A Tragedy." Philadelphia: A. Hart, 1850.

Delaroche, Paul. "The Execution of Lady Jane Grey," oil on canvas, National Gallery, London, NG 1909.

Donizetti, Gaetano. *Anna Bolena*. Opera, 1830.

Poulton, Mike. *Wolf Hall and Bring up the Bodies: The Stage Adaptation*. New York: Picador, 2014.

Schiller, Fredrick. *Mary Stuart*. Theatrical Performance. Directed by Robert Icke. Almeida Theatre, London, 2016–17.

Shakespeare, William. *Henry VIII*. Play, (London, 1632).

Sylvain, Barbara and Lula Béry. *It's so nice*. Theatrical Performance. Directed by Cyril Aribaud and Léonard Clarys. Oh My God Theatre Company, 2011.

## Published Works

Bordo, Susan. *The Creation of Anne Boleyn: A New Look at England's Most Notorious Queen*. Boston: Houghton Mifflin Harcourt, 2013.

Doran, Susan and Thomas Freeman, eds. *Mary Tudor: Old and New Perspectives*. New York: Palgrave Macmillan, 2011.

Farr, Evelyn. *I love you madly: Marie Antoinette and Count Fersen-The secret letters*. London: Peter Owen, 2016.

Ford, Elizabeth A. and Deborah C. Mitchell. *Royal Portraits in Hollywood: Filming the Lives of Queens*. Lexington, KY: The University Press of Kentucky, 2009.

Foxe, John. *The Unabridged Acts and Monuments Online or TAMO*. HRI Online Publications, Sheffield, 2011. http://www.johnfoxe.org.

Frye, Susan. "The Myth of Elizabeth at Tilbury." *The Sixteenth Century Journal* 23, no. 1 (1992): 95–114.

Gill, Rosalind. "Postfeminist media culture: elements of a sensibility." *European Journal of Cultural Studies* 10, no. 2: 147–166.

Glynn, Basil. "The Conquests of Henry VIII: Masculinity, Sex and the National Past." In *Television, Sex and Society: Analyzing Contemporary Representations* Edited by Basil Glynn, James Aston and Beth Johnson, 157–174. New York: Continuum, 2012.

Grant Moss, David. "A Queen for Whose Time? Elizabeth I as Icon for the Twentieth Century." *The Journal of Popular Culture* 39, no. 5 (2006): 796–816.

Guy, John. "Mary Queen of Scots (1971)." In *Tudors and Stuarts on Film*, edited by Susan Doran and Thomas S. Freeman, 136–149. New York: Palgrave Macmillan, 2009.

Kosior, Kataryzna. "Outlander, Baby Killer, Poisoner? Rethinking Bona Sforza's Black Legend." In *Virtuous or Villainess? The Image of the Royal Mother from the Early Medieval to the Early Modern Era*, edited by Carey Fleiner and Elena Woodacre, 199–223. New York: Palgrave Macmillan, 2016.

Macdonald, Roger. *The Queen's Diamonds*. Cambridge: Cambridge Academic, 2010.

Mulvey, Laura. "Visual Pleasure and Narrative Cinema." In *Feminism and Film*, edited by E. Ann Kaplan, 34–47. Oxford: Oxford University Press, 2000.

Pidduck, Julianne. *Contemporary Costume Film*. London: BFI, 2004.

Robison, William ed. *History, Fiction and The Tudors: Sex, Politics, Power and Artistic License in the Showtime Television Series*. New York: Palgrave Macmillan, 2016.

Rosenstone, Robert A. *History on Film: Film on History*. 3rd ed. London: Routledge, 2018.

Shary, Timothy. *Teen Movies: American Youth on Screen*. London: Wallflower Press, 2005.

Stacey, Jackie. "Desperately Seeking Difference." In *Feminism and Film*, edited by E. Ann Kaplan, 450–465. Oxford: Oxford University Press, 2000.

Stubbs, Jonathan. *Historical Film: A Critical Introduction*. New York: Bloomsbury, 2013.

Sutherland, N.M. "The Legend of the Wicked Italian Queen." *The Sixteenth Century Journal* 9, no. 2 (1978): 45–56.

Thomas, Chantal. *The Wicked Queen: The Origins of the Myth of Marie Antoinette*. English version, New York: Zone Books, 2001.

Vidal, Belén. *Heritage Film: Nation, Genre and Representation*. London: Wallflower, 2012.

Warnicke, Retha. "Anne Boleyn in History, Drama and Film." In *High and Mighty Queens of England*, edited by Carole Levin, Debra Barrett-Graves and Jo Eldridge Carney, 239–255. New York: Palgrave Macmillan, 2003.

### News Stories/Internet Sources

"The CW's *Reign*: Megan Follows on Catherine's Royal Motivations." *Access Hollywood*, October 24, 2013. https://www.accesshollywood.com/articles/the-cws-reign-megan-follows-on-catherines-royal-motivations-139074/.

BBC "The Virgin Queen: Characters, Queen Mary" http://www.bbc.co.uk/drama/virginqueen/joanne_whalley.shtml.

Lisa de Moraes, "CW's first crunchy-gravel drama *Reign* flirts with history." *Deadline Hollywood*, July 30, 2013. http://deadline.com/2013/07/tca-cws-first-crunchy-gravel-drama-flirts-with-history-552425/.

Kennedy Fraser, "Kirsten Dunst: Teen Queen", *Vogue* (September 2006).

T.L. Stanley, "*Reign* hopes to seduce teens with its tales of Mary Queen of Scots" *Los Angeles Times*, September 13, 2013. http://www.latimes.com/entertainment/tv/showtracker/la-et-st-reign-mary-queen-of-scotts-20130915-story.html.

# CHAPTER 3

# Silencing Queens: The Dominated Discourse of Historical Queens in Film

## *April Harper*

While teaching a course on medievalism, I was delivering a lecture in which I mentioned the *rois fainéants*. A student commented that the 'do nothing' kings of history were well matched to the 'do nothing' queens of film. While the comparison was not meant to be entirely accurate, it did spark a heated discussion and my own interest in the sharp divide between the active, talkative, and often defiant noblewomen and princesses and the inactive, largely absent, and almost always silent queens of medieval film. This distinction is made more apparent when historical queens are examined separately from those of legend. The majority of 'medieval' queens are fictitious: the mothers of fairytale characters or the errant queens of Arthurian romance. Historical queens do not feature commonly in cinema. Princesses and noblewomen are easily found, and interestingly, are also easily heard. These women engage in conversation and banter with other women as well as with male characters. Curiously, however, this is not true of queens. While the student in class commented on the lack of activity in this group of 'do nothing queens,' upon reflection it is not so much that historical queens do nothing in

A. Harper (✉)
State University of New York, Oneonta, USA

© The Author(s) 2018                                                         51
J. North et al. (eds.), *Premodern Rulers and Postmodern Viewers*,
Queenship and Power, https://doi.org/10.1007/978-3-319-68771-1_3

film, as it is they say nothing, or very little. Speech, or lack thereof, is the greatest divide between these groups of women. It is a separation that is inversely associated to the power each woman possesses and is a direct consequence of modern discomfort with female speech and gendered portrayals of power and agency.

In my search for the depiction of historical, medieval queens in English-language, Hollywood productions, I found only five.[1] Of these, four included queens whose on-screen presence was longer than roughly ten minutes and included any speaking. While films depicting the early modern period seem to be fascinated with queens, films depicting the medieval period boast very few queen portrayals: Eleanor of Aquitaine; Sibylla of Jerusalem; Isabella of France, wife of Edward II; and Isabel I of Castile. Eleanor of Aquitaine appears in at least 22 films and television series that portray both historical as well as fictive storylines, most notably her inclusion in the Robin Hood corpus. In his excellent work on the post-medieval image of Eleanor, Michael R. Evans notes that, 'a central element of the myth of Eleanor is that of her exceptionalism ... she is assumed to be a woman out of her time—unique among women ... Amazement at Eleanor's power and independence is born from a presentism that assumes ... medieval women were all downtrodden and marginalized.'[2] Evans' work challenges that belief and proves that Eleanor was far from unique, despite the copious amount of literature, both medieval and modern, scholarly and fictional, that attempts to enforce this image. The Eleanor of film is often likewise depicted as exceptional and this may be one reason why she and she alone among the medieval queens is often given large speaking roles. If Eleanor is unique among queens, it is not in her historical person or power, but in her cinematic representation. For although cinematic depictions of her vary, she is almost exclusively depicted as the dowager queen, in her old age, and it is the relationship with her sons that characterizes her. Very few films, with the exception of *The Lion in Winter* even show her in relation to her husband Henry II; most, like the 2010 *Robin Hood*, prefer to cast her as a rather grumpy and essentially powerless woman in her last years of life, interacting not with her beloved son Richard, but often bickering and fighting with arguably her least favorite child, John. Only one work, and that work a TV series—the 1978 short-lived production: *The Devil's Crown*—depicted her in her prime. However, in this work she has a relatively minimal part and only two episodes portray her outside her role as a queenly mother. The role of a queen mother was one sanctioned for women in the Middle Ages and is perhaps the best understood out of all the possible power outlets available for medieval women as portrayed in modern film.[3] However, this too places Eleanor as an exception to images of medieval queens in film, since historical queens are almost always depicted in the early years of their marriages and/or as childless, regardless of historical fact. Eleanor's exceptionalism in film serves not to challenge the premise of this paper, but provides key evidence that the traditional cinematic medieval queen is not one who wields independent power, functions as part of a monarchy and family, exists in a network of strong women, and speaks, but rather is one who is foreign, isolated, childless, and silent. This convention is most evident in the portrayals of the remaining three queens: Isabella of France from *Braveheart*, Sibylla of Jerusalem from *Kingdom of Heaven*, and Isabel of Spain from *1492: Conquest of Paradise.*

The foreignness of the queen is a key element in the portrayal of each woman's character and has a profound impact on her powerlessness, isolation, and silence. Early studies of queenship argued that these women were commonly 'foreigners in a foreign land, sometimes betrothed in the cradle and sent to the households of their prospective husbands to learn the language and customs which would shape their lives. The isolation and vulnerability produced by this almost universal practice of royal exogamy ... made them easy targets for criticism or attack.'[4] This image is adopted wholesale in film where there is a strong intent to present the queens as 'other.' This is done first by emphasizing their foreignness. Isabella of France, as depicted in *Braveheart*, speaks with a very heavy French accent and is the only character to do so. Although this may be due in part to the casting of the French Actress Sophie Marceau for the role, the accent appears to have been deliberately thickened. While she sometimes speaks to her maid in French as a kind secret language they may engage in and not be overheard or understood, the language functions to separate her from the rest of the English court. Edward I's character constantly berates her for being French and speaks very poorly of her family and the French in general, showing a complete distaste for them and creating a very strong divide between the English and French. While this technique helps to make Isabella a sympathetic character, it is not only out of place in a film centered on the conflict between Scotland and England, but it requires a not-insignificant amount of time to create the image of intense hostility between England and France, not only personally and politically, but culturally. Time is an expensive commodity in filmmaking and this hostility does not further the plot or contribute to the development of the central character of Wallace. It would appear that Gibson deliberately created this hostility to isolate the figure of Isabella.

While the manipulation and disregard for historical accuracy is commonplace throughout *Braveheart*, it is the character of Isabella that is perhaps most distorted.[5] The historical Isabella was only two years old when the events of the film took place. Isabella never traveled to Scotland, never met Edward I or William Wallace, and was never the princess of Wales, as her marriage to Edward II took place several months after his coronation. Isabella gave birth to her first child, the future Edward III, in November of 1312, placing the conception of the heir to the throne in February, when she and her husband were together in York, seven years after Wallace was executed and 13 years before her relationship with Roger Mortimer. In the early years of their marriage, Isabella was a child and seemed to have little interaction with her husband, but by the time she was sixteen, she had begun to take a powerful role in his court, was a loyal supporter of her husband, and the two seemed to have a genuine affection for one another.[6] Most importantly, Isabella was not isolated in the English court. While the position of the foreigner queen could be problematic for some medieval queen consorts of Europe, more recent studies of queenship have begun to challenge this image and assumption by understanding monarchy to be a complex dynastic enterprise in which queens played a crucial part in conjunction with the king.[7] Isabella was already part of the interlocking political, familial, and social structure that formed much of the English monarchy. Far from being a foreigner, Isabella was Edward II's second cousin. Edward was, after all, a Plantagenet King, who traced his lineage and right to rule from both Norman and Angevin ancestry and was related by blood to the royal family of France. Isabella had many other relatives and friends at the English court, including her Aunt Marguerite, who was the dowager queen of England, and her cousins Thomas, earl of Norfolk, and Edmund, the earl of Kent. Edward II's Uncle Edmund, the earl of Lancaster, had married Isabella's widowed grandmother, providing cousins for Edward and uncles for Isabella in the persons of Thomas and Henry of Lancaster. Isabella had a wide variety of friends, family, and eventual political supporters at the English court. The language of the court was Anglo-Norman, a dialect of Old French that was extremely similar to the Francien dialect Isabella most likely spoke. Isabella was hardly foreign or alone in the English court.[8]

In the film, though, this network of friends and family is deliberately absent. Isabella is most often alone. She is the only woman at court and often sits by herself, away from the others. The separation of her from the men physically and socially is echoed in several scenes in which she seeks the solitude of a cloister. Even on diplomatic missions, such as that to broker peace with Wallace, she is sent alone of all the court, with only a single lady in waiting and a lone priest as an interpreter. Unaccompanied, she meets Wallace in a cabin in the woods for their second encounter and ultimately is not seen at all, as her presence in the second half of the film is mainly through the notes her handmaiden brings to Wallace on her behalf. When she informs the dying Edward I she is pregnant with Wallace's child, she describes a future in which Wallace and Edward I will be dead and makes a thinly veiled threat that Edward II will not last long. While the scene is focused on the anger of Edward I as he realizes his line has ended, it is also an image of complete isolation for Isabella, who states Wallace's son will rule, but provides no role or future for herself.

The foreignness and isolation of the queen are likewise integral to the image of Sibylla of Jerusalem in *Kingdom of Heaven* (2005). At the film's outset, she is depicted as sexually forward and exotic, exhibiting all the assumptions of orientalism. She wears heavy makeup, especially dark kohl around her eyes, and reddens her lips in a sexually suggestive fashion; her clothing is most often comprised of silks that are always flowing around her body in a sensual fashion and often expose a bare midriff, a leg, or décolletage. Her appearance marks her as, 'the exoticised Oriental female ... presented as an immodest, active creature of sexual pleasure who held the key to a myriad of mysterious erotic delights'.[9] Sibylla seems almost perversely crafted to support Edward Said's statement that, 'the Orient seems still to suggest not only fecundity but sexual promise (and threat), untiring sensuality, unlimited desire, [and] deep generative energies'.[10] Regardless of the physical heat of the desert, the gravity of a situation, or a need to do work, Sibylla's character prefers to take spontaneous journeys, to play, make love, and enjoy the pleasures of food, humor, and sex. She seems untouched by the travails of the crusaders, or by the gravity of the situation of her kingdom. The oriental image of the queen is reinforced through her language as well. Her first lines of the film are in Arabic and while she speaks English to the Crusaders, she is often depicted speaking in foreign tongues to her subjects and servants.

The only other character to be depicted speaking multiple languages is Saladin, reinforcing Sibylla's image as Eastern, rather than European.

Her foreignness puts her at odds with the crusaders who are presented as Western in their speech, clothing, and mannerisms. In the occasions in which Sibylla joins the men, she is the only woman present. The men occasionally comment as to her behavior and dress, which they find inappropriate, and they actively isolate her further. When talk turns to politics, the men physically turn away from Sibylla to continue their conversation and twice when strategy is discussed, she leaves the room, seemingly out of boredom. While the historic character of Sibylla has been much maligned due to her loyalty to her unlikable husband, and the conquest of her kingdom by Saladin just a year after her coronation, her apathy for and exclusion from power as portrayed in the film cannot be reconciled with reality. Sibylla ruled for a brief period and in a tumultuous time, but was anything but timid or uninterested. She had popular support for becoming queen and had shown great acumen and ability in removing the threat of her step-sister's claim to the throne and securing the support of key nobles. She was crowned alone by the patriarch and only afterwards did she confer the crown on her husband, whose authority was then derived from her own.[11]

Sibylla of *Kingdom of Heaven* is not only rejected from male society, but also from the company of other women. When supposedly travelling to Cana to see where Christ turned water to wine, she brings a single female servant. She roams Jerusalem and the outlying land alone or with few attendants who keep their distance and never interact with the queen.[12] Women are commonly seen in the background of the film; there are occasional scenes of women working in the fields, at the siege a large number of women are hidden in the castle for protection, and afterwards, they make up the largest part of those who flee Jerusalem as refugees. However, the appearance of these women is somewhat surprising as the audience never sees Sibylla interact with these women who must live within her very home. This gendered isolation in the film is also in sharp contrast to the surroundings of the historic Sibylla who was part of a powerful network of queen consorts, queens regent, and ruling queens. Sibylla was the granddaughter of Melisende, a ruling queen of Jerusalem. She was the daughter of Agnes of Courtenay, who was an enormously powerful regent for her son, Baldwin IV. Agnes possessed an extraordinary shrewdness and ability for politics, securing her own nominees to some of the most powerful positions in the land and arranging advantageous marriages for her daughter and step-daughter. In addition, Agnes helped to organize the marriage of the queen dowager, Maria Comnena, to Balian Ibelin in order to stop Maria from possibly acting as queen in Baldwin IV's court. While her son ruled, Agnes acted as the 'virtually uncrowned queen' of Jerusalem.[13] Though Sibylla was raised in the convent of Bethany, her education was one that prepared her to rule, since from an early age, her brother's leprosy was evident and it became apparent that her father's second marriage would not produce a son. Sibylla's great-aunt Ioveta, the sister of Queen Melisende, was abbess of the convent. Sibylla's solitary female figure in *Kingdom of Heaven* is deliberately excluded from this network of powerful, ruling women. Instead, Sibylla functions as 'part of the goods of empire, the living rewards available to men ... exploited without misgiving'.[14] As Sibylla transitions from princess to queen following her brother's death, her isolation is complete, as she, like Isabella in *Braveheart*, becomes almost invisible. Sibylla is seen only as a lone figure on parapets or sitting in the shadows of her room. She finally retreats to the darkness in the innermost part of the castle where she takes on the role of a nun, and although she tends the injured, her new role as an ascetic powerfully conveys the transformation from physical isolation to her emotional and psychological solitude.

While there is very little of Isabel of Castile's character in the film *1492: Conquest of Paradise* (1992), she too is presented through images of foreignness and isolation. Unlike Isabella of France who was a foreign-born queen consort, or even Sibylla who, though part of a second generation born in the Holy Land, was still part of a foreign occupation, Isabel of Castile was in no way a foreigner, but rather queen regnant of a dynasty spanning some 15 generations. While not exotically dressed or behaved as the character of Sibylla in *Kingdom of* Heaven, Isabel's character is similarly introduced in a foreign atmosphere. In the film, Columbus travels to the Alhambra where Isabel is residing after the conquest of Granada. The fortress is barren and devoid of any semblance of a royal court. Outside, Muslim residents engage in daily life and business and children play; the set design is evocative of a medina.[15] Inside, Isabel is alone at a desk. While the room lacks the expected trappings of orientalism—elaborate tapestries, lush carpets, exotic flora and fauna, and the like—the image of Isabel exudes many of the qualities of Romantic Orientalism. She wears an elaborate, richly colored gown, her hair is loose, unruly, and dyed a dark red, giving her a look more akin to a Pre-Raphaelite 'Lady of Shalott,' than the medieval Spanish queen.

The isolation of the queen is common throughout the film. From her first meeting with Columbus in the empty Alhambra, to her last scene granting Columbus' final voyage to the Americas, she always meets with him alone, in large, empty rooms devoid of courtiers, attendants, and often even of furniture. When there is action in a court scene, it is action and/or dialogue between men; the queen hides behind screens and watches, alone or with a single maiden. The influential queen is made a minor character in the film and one that bears no resemblance to the historical queen who waged a five-year war of succession against her niece, chose her own husband, stipulated that he sign a contract limiting his powers in Castile, and later refuted his claim to rule by Salic Law. She, like Sibylla, had powerful role models of queenship in her family, including her grandmother, Catherine of Lancaster, and her aunt Maria, queen of Aragon. While much of her early childhood was spent with her mother in the safety of the countryside, by 1492 she was anything but powerless or isolated in her own court.[16]

In each film, the writer and director have purposely included historic, powerful women in their works, at times grossly manipulating history to do so. There seems to be an underlying acknowledgement that these women were essential to the period and the story. However, their real power is never explored; instead, there is only a pretense of power in the depiction of each of the three queens that quickly dissipates. In *Braveheart*, Isabella finally gets the courage to confront Edward I in front of several of his men, decrying his cowardly treachery, but is incapable of concluding her thoughts and has no planned exit from the scene; she abruptly states that she will return to her needlework and exits by a small side stairway. In *Kingdom of Heaven*, Sibylla plots to assassinate her husband, Guy de Lusignon and save Jerusalem by marrying Balian. But when Balian refuses to kill him, she suddenly abandons her plans, crowns Guy and retreats, rarely to be seen and only heard from twice again—her remaining lines total only four sentences. In *1492*, Columbus reminds Isabel of Castile that she was responsible for ejecting the Muslims from Spain and hails her great victories, her unique world view, and progressive thinking, bolstering her courage to support his voyage. But just as she begins to straighten in her posture and physically rise to that image, Columbus begins to flirt with her and asks her how old she is. Upon finding out she is a year older than he, she turns away in a kind of girlish embarrassment and becomes silent.[17]

The silence of medieval queens in film is perhaps the most notable commonality between these women. Their isolation and their foreignness are much more than merely historical inaccuracies; they function to create a void of communication surrounding the queen.[18] With no family, friends, supporters, and few, if any, servants, these queens are given few opportunities and very little reason to speak. While this may appear to be just another of Hollywood's misogynies, it is curious that silence is not a common characteristic of medieval female figures in cinema. The opposite is often the case; there are innumerable, garrulous peasant women and chatty maids. Noblewomen, including every Maid Marion and a plethora of princesses are commonly loquacious. Female speech is not, however, female power. The misogynous representation of speaking women as inane in their chatter or weak in their verbal posturing is common. Interestingly, in the openings of both Braveheart and *Kingdom of Heaven*, Isabella of France and Sibylla are both introduced as talkative princesses. However, upon becoming queens, or taking of queenly roles, there is a sudden, profound silence from these figures. While the chatter of princesses is depicted as a flaw, there is no strength in a queen's silence.

Isabella of France's silence grows as she moves ever-closer to taking on the role of queen. By the midpoint of the film when she is sent as ambassador to Wallace, she begins by asking if he 'would speak to a woman'. Following this timid beginning, her opening words become confident, but they are the words of King Edward. Later in the conversation, when she is forced to speak of her own volition, her responses are rare and only given in whispers. In this pivotal scene, she attempts to persuade Wallace to surrender and promises that Edward will allow him to go free. It is the longest scene of dialogue in the film, consisting of 17 exchanges between the two. The use of the term 'dialogue' may be misleading, however, as she does not speak. Wallace speaks for almost two full minutes before the camera turns to Isabella for a response, but she only offers a small head tilt. Wallace then further explains his motivations for continued action against the king. The camera turns to the queen, but her response is only another small head tilt, this time to the right. This kind of strange verbal/non-verbal interaction continues between them for 15 more exchanges until he ends his speech by stating she is about to become queen and she must learn how to become one. Her response is to open her mouth, but soundlessly. The scene powerfully demonstrates the connection between queenship and silence. Queenship seems to create a Derridean restriction of possibility in speaking in which 'the necessarily restricted passageway of speech against which all possible meanings push each other, prevent[s] each other's emergence. Speaking frightens me because, by never saying enough, I also say too much.'[19] Throughout the film, there are only four scenes in which Isabella utters a verbal response. Most often she responds with total silence, head tilts or small mouthing motions, unwilling or perhaps unable to engage any man, be it Wallace, Edward I, or his courtiers, with a verbal response.

As soon as Sibylla, once a physically and verbally provocative princess, is crowned queen, she almost entirely ceases speaking and becomes a recluse. While Balian gives a not-entirely inspiring battle speech to the troops who face the might of Saladin's army at the gates, Sibylla is far away on the inner keep's walls, watching in silence. Later, as Balian comes to tell her they have withstood the first assault on the castle, she has a single line to offer and then responds to his almost five minutes of speech and questions with silence. While the men commence battle, she goes into a dark room, cuts off her hair in the style of a nun, and begins to help the wounded in almost total silence. When word reaches her later of Saladin's victory, she has no response. Her last and single line of dialogue is found in the scene when she is given an option to leave Jerusalem with Balian after the city falls. She mentions in a soft, mumbled voice she that she is 'still queen of Tripoli and Acre'. It is an odd scene with a juxtaposition of images: a queen claiming her lands and power, but in a weak voice, with her head shaved, and in the garb of a nun. She joins the refugees, follows Balian to France, and even meets a military group intent on liberating her kingdom through the Third Crusade, all without her uttering a word. She ceases to communicate in anything other than a pensive glare or a sly smile. Sibylla's claim to still be a queen seems to keep her silent as well.[20]

The silence of these historical queens is difficult to understand. It is tempting to try to read power into their motivation. As Nicholas Burbules has argued, 'Silence can ... be a form of protest, willfully withdrawing from a discussion that has become irrelevant or offensive.'[21] Silence, therefore does not have to indicate a powerless state, but could be a strategy. Derrida, Kristeva, and Cixous have all explored the power of gendered language in the construction of identity. Nikita Dhawan has noted that from this gendering:

[H]ierarchies are built into language itself that is structured as feminine 'lack' and masculine 'presence'. Phallologocentrism, i.e., language ordered around an absolute Word (logos) which is 'masculine,' systematically excludes, disqualifies, denigrates, diminishes, silences the 'feminine'.[22]

Dhawan goes on to argue that as, 'subjectivity is constructed through language, thus resistance must arise in language itself, to transform patriarchal language by subverting it from within, to challenge dominant patriarchal discourses'.[23] It is possible that these women are refusing to engage in male discourse and are therefore claiming their own space and power through silence.

However, while the silence of Isabel in *1492* might be understood as her refusal to engage in flirtatious banter with Columbus, the scenes of silence in these films are not scenes of challenge or subversion. Isabel of Castile seems shamed and embarrassed rather than 'willfully withdrawing' from the conversation. Likewise, Isabella seems incapable of retort, gullible in her belief of Edward's honorable intentions, and unprepared for her diplomatic task. Sibylla abandons all control of her kingdom, her person, her future, and even her power of speech to Balian who takes her from Jerusalem, returns to his village in France and, in the face of Sibylla's silence, even greets her cousin Richard I of England as they meet by chance on the king's way to the Third Crusade. Rather than serving as a kind of resistance, the queens' silence seems to echo Heidegger's argument that speech is power and their silence is the marginalizing of their knowledge and ideas, that are simply not worthy of being heard.[24] He maintains that 'silence is an effect ... to create a hierarchy of experience, to differentiate the knowers of truth from the ignorant, who are rendered as "non-players" through silence ... These kinds of discourses not only produce silences, but promote indifference to the voice of the other.'[25] And so perhaps, the silence of these queens serves a more sinister and troubling purpose. Just as the ubiquitous use of rape scenes in television and cinematic productions of 'medieval' stories, such as *Game of Thrones*, have provided a safe and seemingly legitimate way for some to revel in rape culture while safely placing it in a degenerate past that we can verbally condemn, so silencing queens of the past may go some way towards legitimizing attempts to silence women in our present.

This silencing of powerful women, which is at the core of current resistance movements in popular culture and politics, such as the

#ShePersisted and Pantsuit Nation action groups, has long been prevalent in Hollywood's treatment of women on and off the screen. One of the most obvious examples was Seth McFarlane's 2013 Oscar Awards performance in which he composed and sang 'We've Seen Your Boobs' to a slideshow of actresses who were present at the ceremony. He drew attention to some of the most powerful women of Hollywood who have been attacking the patriarchy in interviews, playing strong female characters, and taking on films of social and political importance. As he danced across the stage, laughing and pointing at individual women, he made reference to scenes in which their breasts were exposed, regardless of whether the nudity was part of a rape scene, a scene of domestic violence, or of war crimes. The camera focused on each of the women, including Meryl Streep, Kate Winslet, and Charlize Theron—the queens of Hollywood—as they sat in silence while he and many in the audience laughed. Their silence echoed that of these historic queens, illustrating that the patriarchy in general, and the Hollywood patriarchy specifically, wishes to witness women physically and sexually, but not verbally. The voice of authority has the privilege of whether it chooses to listen to a certain discourse. And it would seem that the filmmakers at least do not choose to listen to women.

Edward Said's criticism of Western men suppressing the voices of Eastern women sheds light on another possible understanding of the silence of these queens. Orientalism produced a double oppression of women, casting them both as victims of their own 'unenlightened' culture and patriarchal ideology as well as the objectification of the colonial power that portrays them as eroticized and licentious.[26] Scholars of medievalism have noted that in cinema, the idea of 'the past as a foreign country' is an almost necessary convention in modern film and literature.[27] That foreignness of the middle ages manifests not only in orientalist physical depictions of these queens, but in their character, speech, and roles. Queens especially suffer from competing ideologies that strive to cast them as powerless, foreign, isolated victims of 'a man's world,' but also revel in portraying them as excessively sexual and promiscuous. Historians of queenship have noted that 'even as women's history, feminism and gender studies have changed society and scholarship in important ways, the demand for historical fiction on queens continues unabated … for example Eleanor Herman's *Sex with the Queen: 900 Years of Vile Kings, Virile Lovers, and Passionate Politics*.[28] Though the study of queenship has been gaining prominence since the 1990s, understanding the role of the queen and the nature of her power has been problematic due in large part to the definition of power. Many medieval and modern texts have ignored a queen's role in government and the power of her agency. Power was too often classified as publicly political and military, and thus queens were 'deemed unimportant to monarchy, meddlers in governance and politics, or dabblers in the patronage of art and literature'.[29] A queen's power was seen as a 'soft power' and largely dismissed. However, as the historiography of queenship has grown; the understanding of a queen's role as sometimes regent and intercessor has improved; and the real power of controlling dynastic concerns, her influence with the Church, and her role within the monarchy itself have begun to be explored, the agency of medieval queens is impossible to ignore.

It seems, however, difficult to convey on screen. Each of these three films opens with a claim of historical veracity. It is difficult to understand, therefore, why the image of the isolated, foreign, silent, powerless queen is portrayed—is it a perceived reality of the power of queens in the Middle Ages by an uninformed audience or a problem with the concepts of power and agency? In interviews following the release of *Kingdom of Heaven*, actress Eva Green stated she was furious with the portrayal of Sibylla and felt the most powerful parts of her character had been cut from the piece.[30] Director Ridley Scott alluded in the director's cut version of the film that it is difficult to portray the kind of power queens often exercised.[31] Such an argument holds very little water in the case of each of these historical queens. Isabella's infamous actions against her husband later in their marriage would lend themselves well to film: betrayal, revolt, a possible affair with Roger Mortimer, the manipulation of the heir to the throne, and the deposition and death of the king. Isabel of Castile's struggle for the throne, her self-arranged marriage to Fernando, and her subsequent conquest of Granada would be a plot akin to many cinematic blockbusters featuring male protagonists. Within *Kingdom of Heaven* itself, the excuse seems weak, since Sibylla and her mother's interaction and manipulation of the Byzantine court and the princes of the Holy Land would make superb cinematic intrigue, yet Ridley Scott deliberately chose to place her sitting in the dark, in silence, while he gave that stratagem to characters such as Guy de Luisignan.

While this paper acknowledges that there may be multiple factors contributing to the silencing of medieval queens in cinema, the transference of a queen's agency to a male antagonist may be one of the most powerful catalysts for the silencing of a queen. Public political or martial power is awarded to heroes in medieval film. It is active and traditionally interpreted as masculine power. Intrigue and subterfuge is often the power of the antagonist who is depicted as secretive, private, and unmanly. In the effort to cast the male protagonist as the embodiment of masculine authority, strength, and honor, screenwriters and directors often showcase these qualities in opposition to those exhibited by the male antagonist who is therefore physically weaker, distrustful, and does not play by the accepted norms of masculine behavior. Unfortunately, many of these attributes of the antagonist—the private use of power, rather than public; personal negotiation, rather than martial display—are the primary powers that a queen wielded through influence, intercession, dynastic control, patronage, and diplomacy. While these vehicles of power are not inherently good or bad, they are deemed to be feminine forms of power and therefore when wielded by men, it is because these antagonists are deemed unworthy or incapable of meeting the hero on the masculine field of honor. These forms of power become equated with the weak and the detestable. When filmmakers assign these forms of agency to men and especially to villains, intercession becomes manipulation, influence transforms into intimidation, dynastic control becomes tyranny, and patronage equates to payoffs. If the queen in these films is to reflect and enhance the qualities of the hero, and eschew the frivolity of femininity, she must surrender her power, her agency, and her voice to the male protagonist.

In the awkward moment of Isabella and Wallace's first meeting, she asks if he 'would speak to a woman'. Wallace shows that he, like most male figures in the films analyzed herein, will not only speak *to* a woman, but largely *at* and *for* a woman, especially if she is a queen. The cinematic portrayal of medieval historical queens and their male protagonists is not unlike that of the nineteenth-century author Flaubert describing his female subject: 'She never spoke of herself, never represented her emotions, presence, or history. He spoke for and represented her.'[32] Often displaced in time and robbed of their historical agency, power, and character, the ruling queens of the cinematic Middle Ages are isolated, objectified as foreign, and silenced by the patriarchy and fragile construction of Hollywood masculinity. The silencing of queens reveals not only a repeated, willful manipulation of women's history that denies historical precedence of female power and agency, but also poses difficult questions regarding the modern treatment of powerful women's voices, and why 'learning to act like a queen,' as Wallace admonishes Isabella, means being seen, but never heard.

# NOTES

1. The selection of films was deliberately narrowed to one language group and one production center in order to compare and analyze the portrayal of these queens. A cross-linguistic or cross-cultural comparison, though beyond the scope of this piece, would be an important continuation of this topic.
2. Michael Evans, *Inventing Eleanor: The Medieval and Post-medieval Image of Eleanor of Aquitaine* (New York: Bloomsbury Academic, 2014), 3.
3. See Tina-Karen Pusse and Katharina Walter, eds., *Precarious Parenthood: Doing Family in Literature and Film*, Cultural Studies, vol. 40. (Berlin: Lit, 2013). For historical texts on mothering and queenship, see John Carmi Parsons, *Medieval Mothering* (New York: Garland Publishing, 1999) and Bonnie Wheeler, *Eleanor of Aquitaine: Lord and Lady* (New York: Palgrave Macmillan, 2008).
4. Anne Duggan, *Queens and Queenship in Medieval Europe* (Woodbridge: The Boydell Press, 1997), xviii.
5. A. E. Christa Canitz, "'Historians ... Will Say I Am a Liar': The Ideology of False Truth Claims in Mel Gibson's Braveheart and Luc Besson's The Messenger," in *Postmodern Medievalisms*, ed. Richard Utz and Jesse G. Swan. *Studies in Medievalism* 13 (Cambridge, 2004), 127–142.
6. Kathryn Warner, *Isabella of France, the Rebel Queen* (Stroud: Amberley Publishing, 2016), 37–63.
7. Anne Duggan's collection and Theresa Earenfight, *Queenship in Medieval Europe* (London: Palgrave Macmillan, 2013), and Lisa St. John, *Three Medieval Queens: Queenship and the Crown in Fourteenth-Century England* (New York: Palgrave Macmillan, 2012).
8. For information on Isabella's relationship to her husband's family, see Warner, *Isabella of France, passim;* W. M. Ormrod, W. M. *Edward III* (New Haven: Yale University Press, 2013), 24; J. R. S. Phillips, *Edward II* (New Haven, Conn.: Yale University Press, 2011); and Sophie *Menache*, "*Isabella of France* Queen of England: A Reconsideration," *Journal of Medieval History* 10 (1984): 107–124.
9. Ensieh Shabanirad and Seyed Mohammad Marandi, "Edward Said's Orientalism and the Representation of Oriental Women in George Orwell's Burmese Days," *International Letters of Social and Humanistic Sciences* vol. 60 (2015): 24.
10. Edward Said, *Orientalism* (New York: Vintage Books, 1978), 188.
11. Bernard Hamilton, "Women in the Crusader States. The Queens of Jerusalem 1100–1190," in Derek Baker, *Medieval Women* (Oxford: Blackwell, 1978), 171.
12. John M. Ganim, "Framing the West, Staging the East: Set Design, Location, and Landscape in Cinematic Medievalism," in *Hollywood in*

*the Holy Land. Essays on Film Depictions of the Crusades and Christian Muslim Clashes*, ed. Nickolas Haydock and E. L. Risden (Jefferson, NC and London, 2009), 31.

13. Bernard Hamilton, "Women in the Crusader States," 168.
14. Shabanirad and Marandi, "Edward Said's Orientalism" 24.
15. John Ganim, *Medievalism and Orientalism: Three Essays on Literature, Architecture and Cultural Identity* (New York: Palgrave, 2005), 4, 102–106.
16. See Barbara Weissberger, *Isabel Rules: Constructing Queenship, Wielding Power* (Minneapolis: University of Minnesota Press, 2004), 28, 43 and Marvin Lunenfeld, "Isabel I of Castile and the Company of Women in Power," *Reflexions Historiques* (Winter) 1977: 222.
17. The myth that Columbus and Isabel were lovers was made popular by Alejo Carpentier's novel *El arpa y la sombra* (1979) and was bolstered by Salman Rushdie's short story, "Christopher Columbus and Queen Isabella of Spain Consummate Their Relationship," *East, West* (New York, Vintage: 1994). See Weissburger, 187–206.
18. Andrew B. R. Elliott, *Remaking the Middle Ages* (Jefferson, NC: McFarland and Company, 1995), 206–208.
19. Jacques Derrida, *Writing and Difference* (Chicago: University of Chicago Press, 1978), 83.
20. After the fall of Jerusalem, Sibylla joined her husband, Guy, and travelled to Tyre, the only Christian city left in the kingdom. However, they were refused entry by Conrad of Montferrat. Sibylla and two of her four daughters died a few months later in Acre.
21. Nicholas Burbules, *Dialogue in Teaching: Theory and Practice* (New York: Teachers College Press, 1993), 156.
22. Nikita Dhawan, *The Power of Silence and the Silence of Power*, accessed May 2, 2017. http://www.gradnet.de/papers/pomo02.papers/power.htm.
23. Dhawan, *Power of Silence*.
24. Martin Heidegger "Prolegomena zur Geschichte des Zeitbegriffs," Gesamtausgabe Bd. 20 (Frankfurt am Main: Vittorio Klostermann, 1979), 376.
25. Dhawan, *Power of Silence*.
26. R. J. C. Young, *Postcolonialism* (London: Blackwell Publishers, 2001).
27. Andrew B. R. Elliott, *Remaking the Middle Ages*, 22–23 and 42–43.
28. Theresa Earenfight, *Queenship in Medieval Europe* (London: Palgrave Macmillan, 2013), 5.
29. Earenfight, *Queenship*, 4.
30. For the interview see http://ohnotheydidnt.livejournal.com/17852896.html.
31. For the interview see https://www.tribute.ca/interviews/ridley-scott-kingdom-of-heaven/director/8632/ and director's cut DVD interview with Scott.
32. Said, *Orientalism*, 6.

## BIBLIOGRAPHY

*1492: Conquest of Paradise.* Feature Film. Directed by Ridley Scott. Gaumont Film Company, 1992.

*Braveheart.* Feature Film. Directed by Mel Gibson. Los Angeles: Icon Productions/The Ladd Company, 1995.

Burbules, Nicholas. *Dialogue in Teaching: Theory and Practice.* New York: Teachers College Press, 1993.

Canitz, A.E. Christa. "'Historians ... Will Say I Am a Liar': The Ideology of False Truth Claims in Mel Gibson's *Braveheart* and Luc Besson's *The Messenger.*" In *Postmodern Medievalisms.* Edited by Richard Utz and Jesse G. Swan. *Studies in Medievalism* 13. Cambridge, 2004: 127–142.

Derrida, Jacques. *Writing and Difference.* Chicago: University of Chicago Press, 1978.

Dhawan, Nikita. *The Power of Silence and the Silence of Power,* accessed May 2, 2017. http://www.gradnet.de/papers/pomo02.papers/power.htm.

Duggan, Anne. *Queens and Queenship in Medieval Europe.* Woodbridge: The Boydell Press, 1997.

Earenfight, Theresa. *Queenship in Medieval Europe.* London: Palgrave Macmillan, 2013.

Elliott, Andrew B.R. *Remaking the Middle Ages.* Jefferson, NC: McFarland and Company, 1995.

Evans, Michael. *Inventing Eleanor: The Medieval and Post-medieval Image of Eleanor of Aquitaine.* New York: Bloomsbury Academic, 2014.

Ganim, John, M. "Framing the West, Staging the East: Set Design, Location, and Landscape in Cinematic Medievalism." In *Hollywood in the Holy Land. Essays on Film Depictions of the Crusades and Christian Muslim Clashes.* Edited by Nickolas Haydock and E.L. Risden. Jefferson, NC and London: McFarland and Company, 2009: 31–45.

Ganim, John, M. *Medievalism and Orientalism: Three Essays on Literature, Architecture and Cultural Identity.* New York: Palgrave, 2005.

Hamilton, Bernard. "Women in the Crusader States. The Queens of Jerusalem 1100–1190." In *Medieval Women.* Edited by Derek Baker. Oxford: Blackwell, 1978: 185–204.

Heidegger, Martin. "Prolegomena zur Geschichte des Zeitbegriffs," Gesamtausgabe Bd. 20. Frankfurt am Main: Vittorio Klostermann, 1979.

*Kingdom of Heaven,* Director's Edition DVD. Feature Film. Directed by Ridley Scott. Twentieth Century Fox, 2005. Beverly Hills, CA: Twentieth Century Fox Home Entertainment, 2005.

Lunenfeld, Marvin. "Isabel I of Castile and the Company of Women in Power." *Reflexions Historiques* (Winter 1977): 207–229.

Rushdie, Salman. "Christopher Columbus and Queen Isabella of Spain Consummate Their Relationship" *East, West*. New York: Vintage, 1994.

Said, Edward. *Orientalism*. New York: Vintage Books, 1978.

Shabanirad, Ensieh and Seyyed Mohammad Marandi. "Edward Said's Orientalism and the Representation of Oriental Women in George Orwell's Burmese Days." *International Letters of Social and Humanistic Sciences* 60 (2015): 22–33.

St. John, Lisa. *Three Medieval Queens: Queenship and the Crown in Fourteenth-Century England*. New York: Palgrave Macmillan, 2012.

Warner, Kathryn. *Isabella of France, the Rebel Queen*. Stroud: Amberley Publishing, 2016.

Weissburger, Barbara. *Isabel Rules: Constructing Queenship, Wielding Power*. Minneapolis: University of Minnesota Press, 2004.

Young, R.J.C. *Postcolonialism*. London: Blackwell Publishers, 2001.

# CHAPTER 4

# Feminism, Fiction, and the Empress Matilda

*Katherine Weikert*

Strong women from the medieval era are written in modern fiction for women contemporary to the writers.[1] This is presentism, and as Chandra L. Power has described it, presentism as a 'twofold concern: *writerly presentism*, e.g., a novelist's imposition of the values, beliefs, and practices of modern times onto a past era; and *readerly presentism*, i.e., a reader's perception that a book written in or about the past is, for example, racist or sexist'.[2] The implication of work on medieval queens in this context is clear: writers of historical fiction, regardless of the level of research that they may put into their work, are liable to imprint their culturally specific beliefs onto the past.[3] Readers of historical fiction, particularly if historical fiction is their only brush with the medieval past, are likely to incorporate pre-existing notions of the medieval world and arrive at an idea of the past that is inherently sexist by nature, seeking validity in the problems of their modern world by finding them in a distant past. This view is further shaped by readers' own horizons of understanding: 'Historical understanding would be impossible, since the past in its otherness may only be grasped in so far as the interpreter is able to separate the alien from his own horizon.'[4] Furthermore, 'the type of literature women read is linked to their wider world-view'.[5] With this social

K. Weikert (✉)
University of Winchester, Winchester, UK

© The Author(s) 2018
J. North et al. (eds.), *Premodern Rulers and Postmodern Viewers*,
Queenship and Power, https://doi.org/10.1007/978-3-319-68771-1_4

and cultural shaping, readers would be highly sensitive to portrayals of gender struggle in the medieval past, and the writers prone to overlay a modern understanding of gender onto the past, without sensing separate horizons of understanding. The reading of women's historical literature and romance in the post-feminist[6] world undousbtedly causes complicated and sometimes conflicting conclusions about its use, purpose, and even benefits or negatives.[7] Regardless, what is clear is the popularity of the genre, particularly for middle-class women. Romance Writers of America state that in 2015, romantic fiction accounted for 34% of total sales of adult fiction in the United States, and 84% of romance readers are women,[8] with an average annual income of US$55,000.[9]

The Empress Matilda, the focus of this chapter, provides a historical character onto which writerly and readerly presentism has been mapped. Historical scholarship has seen multiple works on her: most recently, Marjorie Chibnall's biography (1991), still the standard academic text, alongside popular history books by the Earl of Onslow (1939), Nesta Pain (1978),[10] and Helen Castor (2010). Although it is not unfair to say that Matilda is understudied in current scholarship, particularly in comparison to the wealth of scholarship on medieval English kings, she is certainly not unknown. But the diffusion of information about Empress Matilda into a popular audience has been piecemeal, and she comes to the modern world with a mixed reputation. Marjorie Chibnall describes Matilda in the Oxford Dictionary of National Biography:

> Hostile chroniclers … attacked her as haughty and intractable … when she met opposition … with all the firmness that had been accepted, however reluctantly, from her father, it was regarded as unwomanly, arrogant and obstinate in her.[11]

Chibnall clearly presents that a norm in her father was not perceived as a norm in Matilda. It is not the place of this chapter to debate the character of the historical Matilda; it is generally accepted in modern scholarship that she was probably no more or less wilful or authoritative than her male counterparts, though her gender worked against her on this count. But the popular press has tended to latch onto the words 'arrogant' and 'haughty'[12] and shift the understanding from a *representation* of Matilda into *Matilda*. Matilda thus comes down into modern public history as a maligned queen, ready to be rewritten in terms appropriate for readers' expectations and modern experiences.

In parallel to the last few decades of extensive scholarship in women's history and gender history, historical fiction featuring queens as protagonists has also been popular. This is no surprise; in the view of the Western world post-1960s feminism, powerful queens give historical examples of strong women that modern women can look to not only as exemplars but also for entertainment and a feeling of a connection to the past, despite the presentism of that connection. Popular culture after the advent of second-wave feminism has felt inclined to apply current forms of feminism to Matilda; to some degree, the historiographical disagreements about Matilda created a container that can more easily hold modern ideas.[13] The novels based on Matilda's life, perhaps unsurprisingly, are set around the years of the civil war of the mid-twelfth century, when Matilda was at the highest and lowest points of her power in England. Each novel roughly follows the historical outline of the civil war with fictive liberty taken for dramatic purposes.

Of five novels that I have identified with Matilda as the main protagonist, only three reached a wide readership: Jean Plaidy's *The Passionate Enemies*[14]; Sharon Penman's *When Christ and His Saints Slept*[15]; and Elizabeth Chadwick's *Lady of the English*.[16] These examples of a modern, fictitious Matilda follow the concerns for some women addressed by modern feminism, reflecting a Matilda for the time of her writing. This response to social environment is perhaps unsurprising as the romance genre has demonstrated a 'response to readers' interests and cultural changes in a way that is unmatched by most other types of publishing and popular media'.[17] However, acknowledgement of different experiences and the shift into intersectional feminism has been neglected, reflecting a disjointedness not only between the past and the perception of the past, but also highlighting the fact that these books prioritize the experience and concerns of white, middle-class female readers. Their horizons of understanding have been overlaid on Matilda's medieval experience, rendering others' invisible, and reflecting a writerly presentism that maps onto the readerly presentism of only specific modern women.

The first post-second-wave-feminism Matilda to hit the bookshelves was Plaidy's *The Passionate Enemies* in 1976. The choice of Matilda was perhaps an axiomatic one for Plaidy, who liked to focus on 'women of integrity and strong character' who were also 'struggling for liberation, fighting for their own survival'.[18] Throughout *The Passionate Enemies*, Matilda is certainly portrayed as strong-willed, and working entirely to her own agenda. Characters describe her as a 'fascinating virago,' 'wild, imperious, handsome,' with a 'passionate nature' and 'great spirit' when they are being kind; 'ruthless,' 'arrogant and overbearing,' demanding, exacting, selfish, imperious, a shrew and virago, 'drunk with power,' harsh and without gratitude, and with a 'vindictive nature' when in anger.[19] 'Haughty' is used throughout the novel to describe Matilda in both kinder and more critical moments.[20] Plaidy's Matilda 'wanted power more than she wanted love'.[21]

If love is not an overarching concern for this fictional Matilda, sex clearly is. In fact, Matilda is presented as sexualized—and in control of her sexuality—from the very start of the novel. At her introduction, we see Matilda through the eyes of Stephen, her passionate rival: Stephen dreams of what it would have been like to have married Matilda, or at to have least seduced her. He ruminates on her own willingness to be seduced when they were young together.[22] Our first view of Matilda herself in turn is a presentation of her in her ornate imperial bed, thinking sexy thoughts of Stephen in return.[23] There is very little covert operation here. In fact, the next time the scene returns to Matilda, she is once again in her bed, longing for the days when she and Stephen would tease and torment each other.[24] There is no doubt that this Matilda is not just sexualized, but comfortable with and in control of her sexuality. Insomuch as Plaidy may be considered in the romance genre, this also provides the main tension in which there is a '[disturbance with] the proper mapping of the "machinery of sexuality" onto the "machinery of alliance."'[25]

In fact, Matilda even wields her sexuality as a tool for control against Stephen as the war between them progresses. When Stephen arrives at Arundel to take Matilda prisoner, she uses the memory of sex, the promise of sex, and actual sex to negotiate her release and safe passage to her brother in Bristol—where, Stephen is told, they can meet again for more sex.[26] This is clearly not just a sexually liberated Empress Matilda; this is a woman in charge of her sexuality and making use of it for her personal pleasure as well as her political gain. The mostly-female audience of Plaidy's Matilda would have recognized this drive to power, despite the limitations that society had placed upon her (and their) biological sex; bodily and political freedom were active parts of the 1970s feminism. In alignment with Bridget Fowler's note that 'images of "reformed patriarchy" and formal equality pervade much [historical romance], and this change corresponds to the historical restructuring of relations between men and women around the bourgeois ideals of freedom and equality,'[27] this Matilda reflects a readerly expectation of the changing dynamics between men and women, more reflective of the 1970s and 1980s than the twelfth century. As Diana Wallace has pointed out, the exclusion of women from traditional histories 'offers one particularly crucial reason why women writers have turned to the historical novel as a discourse within which women can be made central'.[28] Here Plaidy, perhaps unknowingly, was following the second-wave feminism tenet of reinserting women back into the histories of the Middle Ages, though perhaps 'playing a part unwittingly in classifying medieval women as conforming (or not) to strict gender roles' since the romance genre conventions were too restrictive for more than that.[29] Plaidy's Matilda was a woman for the 1970s, superimposing the horizon of her readers on the horizon of the historical past, and perhaps Plaidy saw very little difference or no othering of the past in her presentation of a feminist Matilda.

The Matilda of Penman's *When Christ and His Saints Slept* represents a much-altered protagonist from Plaidy's unapologetic Matilda of the 1970s. In fact, the different Matilda is on display almost immediately in the narrative, setting the scene and the personal motivations of this Matilda's drive to power. Our first view of her is again from a second-hand view of two women gossiping about the arrogant and sharp-tongued Countess of Anjou who has rejected her husband Geoffrey. One of the two women indicates in veiled language that Matilda's rejection of Geoffrey has 'goad[ed] him into maltreating her,'[30] suggesting that Geoffrey abuses her both physically and sexually.

This is confirmed not a page later, when we first meet Matilda while she is examining her split lip and bruises and refusing the advice of her trusted maid, who is counseling Matilda to be more submissive and respectful to her husband.[31] But Matilda refuses, stating, 'Pride is the only defence I have.'[32] Immediately we have the *raison d'être* for Matilda's actions in the next several decades, and the explanation of her arrogant demeanor: her acquisition of power was the sole way in which she could be free, the only way she would never again need a husband's consent or a father's permission.[33] We see then a Matilda who is a wronged victim, not in possession of her own power but instead a knowing pawn of the men around her, and one who seeks to avenge her victimhood through freedom and power—hence her initial drive to the throne. Her historical political agency is thus removed by ascribing her political drive to personal motivations.[34]

It is important to point out that Matilda's rapes by Geoffrey do not fit the tropes of rape seen in romance novels particularly in a boom in the 1970s and beyond.[35] In that trope, editorial commentary viewed women's rape in fiction as a part of fulfilling a reader's rape fantasy, and an escape from the responsibility of sex. In addition, the trope would allow characters to 'enjoy sexual pleasure while still maintaining their moral purity'.[36] This is obviously a very controversial topic in romance writing, but Penman's use of rape on Matilda has little to do with a defunct trope. Matilda instead is raped and beaten both to humanize her as well as to give her a reason for her immense desire for power—the same trope we now see a backlash against as shorthand for a vulnerable woman and a hated man.[37]

With a protagonist depicted as a victim comes the inevitable victim-blaming. This, seen from characters who are supporters of Matilda's, compounds the complexity of presenting a twelfth-century female victim to a modern audience: a powerful woman being brought low sings of the repression that a twentieth-century audience would expect in medieval times, a readerly presentism that is deemed authentic as it meets the preconceived notions of its audience. A minor female character speaks outright that Matilda 'brought much of her troubles upon herself. If she'd not been so haughty, if she'd been more tactful, more womanly' in her personality, she would not have had to fight both her husband and father.[38] In a further scene, Matilda's three brothers discuss how they might protect her from Geoffrey, their views are negated by: '[Matilda] is not blameless either. She puts me to mind of a woman who salts a well and complains when the water is not fit to drink.'[39] This is victim-blaming, twelfth-century style, though this woman is also the only one who demonstrates some understanding of gender politics—as perceived in the twentieth century—in a twelfth-century context. In the next breath the woman explains that a woman in their world does not have much at hand to make their place nicer so she might as well use what she has—feminine wiles.[40] Matilda herself tries to believe that if her father knew of her mistreatment at Geoffrey's hands, he would not blame her for the break-up of her marriage, although another character informs her outright that her father believed that she brought Geoffrey's violence to her upon herself.[41] This character, her brother's wife, also blames Matilda for Geoffrey's actions.[42] In fact, despite an insistence that Matilda's lack of feminine wiles makes her culpable for others' actions, her own biological womanliness is at one point blamed for her failures:

one of her own men assumes Matilda is menstruating when she is demanding with the Londoners who were asking for tax relief, although the Londoners call her 'unwomanly'.[43] In this Matilda cannot win: her lack of femininity means she is to blame for her controlling father and the physical harm brought to her by her husband, though her unchangeable biology can be used to equally to blame her for the characteristics that make her 'unwomanly'.

*When Christ and His Saints Slept* also utilizes themes of difference between men and women, although in all scenarios it is to point out how unfair gender difference played out in the twelfth century. Most of this recognition of difference comes from and through Matilda herself, as the stage on which gender difference is sharply noted. Very early in the novel she pulls a knife on Geoffrey to protect herself against his violence, and he notes that she clearly had not been trained to wield one—something that he finds desirable.[44] In fact, her female inability to fight is regularly mentioned. When she holds London but is not yet crowned, Matilda remarks with frustration that if she had bested Stephen in hand-to-hand combat, no one would doubt her right to rule.[45] Stephen himself notes that her claim to the throne 'depended on support from men'.[46] When Matilda flees a desperate situation in Winchester, she envies 'the men their weapons, their male right to self-defence'; her skirts further hamper her riding and leave her with bloody wounds on her inner thighs as she had to ride astride for the sake of speed.[47] In fact, at one point Matilda specifically rages because all of her misfortunes have happened to her because she is a woman.[48]

Sewing is often used as a demonstration Matilda's lack of patience with 'womanly' things. Sewing, needlework, and embroidery are often stereotypically used to denote womanly pastimes and pursuits in most periods in the past despite deconstructions that show this to be historiographically and historically a romantic inconsistence;[49] nonetheless, sewing is still used as shorthand for feminine in historical contexts. At one point Matilda is shown in a group of women who are putting together a stitched wall-hanging and Matilda declines to participate:

> She was a very proficient needle-woman ... for she was that most driven of beings, a perfectionist, compelled to excel even at pastimes that gave her no pleasure. But *she cared little for female companionship and even less for traditional female pursuits*, preferring instead to challenge [her brother] to a game of chess.[50]

Immediately we can see the dichotomy of Matilda's own gender identification in a way that is sympathetic to a late twentieth-century audience: when placed in a world where sewing is a 'traditional female pursuit' she prefers the more masculine pastime of chess, displaying her flouting of the societal regulation of female behavior. This is seen several times through the narrative. When Matilda is relinquishing her claim and sailing away from England, she visits with her stepmother and both sit with sewing, though Matilda's 'lay forgotten in her lap' as they visited.[51] In fact, at one point Matilda is noted as acting oddly because she *was* sewing![52]

The Matilda of *When Christ and His Saints Slept* is a character steeped in third-wave feminism, and very likely a conscious construction as such. This Matilda is a victim of men as well as historical circumstance, concerned about her work–life balance,[53] is far less sexualized, is concerned about her personal relationships with the people in her life, and even sees war as a journey towards self-awareness.[54] The victim Matilda, so desperate for control of her own life, finds a modicum of contentment only for the struggles she had survived; the story, albeit ostensibly about a power-struggle between members of the nobility, is ultimately about Matilda's journey to a greater understanding of herself, a journey to a personal emancipation[55]—an understanding that actually takes away her own historical agency. In establishing her character early in the novel, Matilda notes that she 'has no rights at all, not even over my own body'.[56] She wants no daughters as she does not want them to be used as she is.[57] In fact, overtly feminist statements are indeed made by most of the cast of characters at some point in the novel: Stephen thinks that it is terrible that Matilda's husband and father make plans for her without her input or permission.[58] A secondary female character ruminates that she 'needed to believe that not all the women in her world had their wings clipped; surely there must be a few still able to soar up in the sky, untamed and fearless and free'.[59] Throughout the novel, statements such as these demonstrate an insertion of modern, third-wave feminist thought into the mouths of twelfth-century elites, anachronistic as they may be. In such a way, a period perceived as misogynist becomes more palatable to a third-wave feminist audience; the feminism of the late twentieth century is recognizable in the character, making her both more relatable and more sympathetic. Again, this readerly presentism maps firmly onto a sense of authenticity to the audience, meeting their preconceived expectations of the medieval world and providing no real dialogue with either the text or the past.

Our last Matilda is from Elizabeth Chadwick's 2011 *Lady of the English*. This too is a Matilda steeped in third-wave feminism, though this can be seen in different forms than in Penman's Matilda. This Matilda values her own relationship with the most important woman in her life, her stepmother Adeliza; this Matilda and even Adeliza are also shown with a new level of comfort with and pleasure in their sexuality. This Matilda furthermore continues with the trend of seeing her life as a journey, her war and struggle giving her a better understanding of herself, and highlights the biological and gender differences between her and other leaders of the time, third-wave importance of gender difference.

It is in Adeliza's relationship with Matilda where we see the most important relationship of the novel. Unlike the Matilda of the Penman, they are even represented as sewing together at one point![60] Their first embrace upon Matilda's return from Germany reminds Matilda that her own mother was not soft and motherly, and she nearly cries at Adeliza's touch.[61] When they argue about Geoffrey's treatment of Matilda, Adeliza quickly backs down from her suggestions to Matilda; Adeliza does not want to lose her relationship with Matilda over arguing about a man, as odious as he might be.[62] In fact, Adeliza often intercedes on Matilda's behalf, even when at risk to herself, both with her first husband, Matilda's father, and her second husband, a staunch supporter of Stephen.[63] Their relationship transcends what we might think of as a stereotypical step-relationship to that of a mother–daughter relationship at times, and more like sisters at others. Their bond is represented as one borne of affection, friendship, and kinship. The sisterly bond between them also, at times, interferes with crucial political decisions taken by other characters, such as when Adeliza's husband opts to respect the bond between Adeliza and Matilda rather than his own political alliance with Stephen at the time of Matilda's arrival and sojourn at Arundel.[64] The emotional here trumps the politically logical or even expedient action of handing Matilda over to Stephen.

Both Matilda and Adeliza are also portrayed in sexual terms, with both enjoying their sexual encounters, underlining a new third-wave reclamation of sexual pleasure that may particularly echo trends in feminism beyond the 1990s.[65] Both experience this in separate ways, however. Matilda experiences a healthy amount of sexual pleasure in what is surely, in modern ideas, a very unhealthy relationship. The tension between the desire she and Geoffrey share alongside their hatred of one another sits uncomfortably with modern readers. Although Geoffrey is not portrayed as raping Matilda, as in the Penman, he does cruelly beat her at the beginning of their marriage to the degree that Matilda cannot walk for the pain,[66] and once, after discovering that Matilda was actively working to prevent pregnancy, is portrayed as a sexual predator, although whether or not this is a scene of rape is ambiguous.[67] However, despite this, Matilda acknowledges and enjoys her sexuality. She discovers at their marriage that even though she hates her husband, she enjoys sex with him.[68] When returning from her marital banishment, Matilda ruminates that she still sexually wants Geoffrey, even though she hated him and he beat her.[69] In fact, though the two enter what is essentially a working relationship in seeking the throne for their son, it is only time and distance that weans Matilda from the 'corrosive but compelling' sexual need she felt for Geoffrey.[70]

Matilda's sexuality is also used against her by other characters. In one disturbing passage, a peripheral male character compares Matilda to Stephen's wife Maheut, who is seen as dumpy and motherly, in opposition to Matilda's conflated power and sexuality:

> [Maheut] was utterly loyal to Stephen, and her brisk, motherly manner engendered loyalty in others. When with Stephen in public, she kept her eyes lowered and her mouth closed, cultivating the persona of a modest, submissive wife...
>
> The Empress had no such maternal image to temper her own abrasive nature. If she thought a man was a fool, she said so to his face in front of others, and gave no quarter. She was tall, slender, beautiful, desirable—like a mistress, and while few men would ever strike their mothers [many] would take a fist to a mistress.[71]

Matilda's comparison to being a mistress to Maheut's motherliness is taken to a disturbing conclusion in finding it justification for physical punishment of Matilda. She is 'the potential [victim] of a femininity which … endlessly defin[es her] in terms of sexual status'; this imagined sexual availability is grounds for blame and punishment,[72] from political, to personal, to corporeal.

Adeliza, however, has a different projection in learning about her sexuality. We are introduced to Adeliza within the first few pages of the novel, with her first husband atop of her as she waits through sex patiently but not pleasurably.[73] Sex to Adeliza is a means to an end: her role, as the queen, was to provide the needed male heir. However, in her second marriage, sex is different, and, Adeliza is surprised to discover, enjoyable. On her second marriage night, Adeliza is portrayed as orgasming for probably the first time in her life.[74] In modern romance parlance, this is an example of one of the powers of the Mighty Wang, with a hero's penis restoring a heroine to orgasm and fertility[75]; indeed, she becomes pregnant almost immediately despite years of infertility with her first husband. Adeliza becomes the modern idea of the wholly fulfilled medieval woman, with loving children, wealth, influence, a loving husband (who even builds separate toilets in the castle for her so that he would not splash the seat![76]), and, just as importantly, an active and enjoyable sex life.

Chadwick's Matilda also expresses a third-wave stress on biological and gendered difference. Menstruation in particular is not only discussed frequently but becomes of particular gendered importance in at least one part of the narrative. As one might expect from a woman whose sole job is to produce an heir, Adeliza at a few moments specifically takes note of her 'flux,' once ascribing it as punishment from God for a deed she did not know.[77] But Matilda's 'flux' takes on a form that has just as severe political impacts as Adeliza's lack of heirs for her first husband. At a crucial point in the narrative, when Matilda and her faction have taken London but are waiting for the coronation and negotiating with the people of London, she is noted as being irritable and having a headache due to menstruation.[78] It is well-considered historical fact that Matilda's inability to reach an agreement with the Londoners caused her ultimate loss of the city; here, the author specifically attributes her lack of diplomacy with the Londoners to not only her mood because of menstruation but more specifically because of the author's unsubstantiated suspicion that Matilda suffered from severe premenstrual syndrome.[79]

This Matilda's negotiation of femininity also plays out in the difference of genders, not just different biology. Very early on, Matilda considers the difficulties in having masculine tendencies, such as directness, and thus 'flouting the natural law'.[80] Throughout the novel, Matilda negotiates her gender identity, staying almost on the boundary between what is seen as masculine or feminine. Her role in the Holy Roman Empire is one clearly expressed as queenly and with feminine attributes: being a peacemaker, alleviating suffering, patronizing the arts.[81] Her femininity is played at several points: her power as a woman, even if Empress or queen, is a tool for the power of men[82]; her femininity is 'regulated and expressed through class difference'[83] at the upper echelons of medieval society as a female royal. She is referred to as a vessel for the throne, a particularly female representation.[84] She engages with thinking about her own physical appearance.[85] She is even at one point depicted as sewing, and uses a sewing metaphor! But, on top of this, Matilda more strongly negotiates her position as a woman in a man's world. She recognizes the lives of girls and women as different to those of the men around her.[86]

Overall, these three fictional Matildas show specific responses to feminist movements. This response to social environment is unsurprising in these novels since the genre, as noted, is known to have responded to cultural changes in a usually parallel way.[87] Indeed, the genre of the romance novel itself grew alongside the feminist movement starting in the 1970s.[88] But the three novels also fail to take in account a crucial area of modern feminism: the concept of intersectionality. The concept of intersectionality was first termed by Kimberlé Crenshaw in 1991 in dealing with the combined oppressions of being a woman and a person of color,[89] and has since grown in its definition to more widely accept that differing forms of oppression work together. In this case, the concept was not yet in play at the time of Plaidy's writing, though accepting this as rote negates the strong activity of black feminists in the 1970s, the environment that surrounded Plaidy's work on Matilda. Perhaps unfortunately but unsurprisingly in works that deal with the highest ranks of medieval society, diversity and concepts of intersectionality are also virtually invisible in both post-third-wave works. This is a topic that Chandra L. Power is sensitive to in historical fiction, in the 'lack of alternative voices in any given era [which] serves to deny' alternative experiences, 'conflating the dominant attitudes of an era with all attitudes of an era ... The values of the dominant class are seen as the *only* values of an era.'[90]

The most obvious opportunity for intersectionality in these three novels would be in explorations of medieval class, though this is not generally seen. In fact, the most obvious non-elite characters seen in *When Christ and His Saints Slept* are a mistress of Geoffrey, used to give a negative point of view of Matilda, and an apothecary and his family who lose everything in the destruction of Winchester. This man had his own shop, and the family lived above it; in modern terms, these townspeople would have been probably middle-class and not medieval peasants, though certainly not the royalty seen elsewhere. However, these middle-class townspeople are not formed characters but merely props of the destruction seen in Winchester and a catalyst for Matilda to consider the death and destruction that her war has wrought. Despite the plight of these townspeople bringing her to tears, Matilda ultimately decides that her war is just and is being fought for the rights of her son, that class trumps humanity, and that the invisible lower class members of society are here only collateral damage. The suffering of the middle class that she sees spurs her to charity rather than changing the course of the war. Indeed, in terms of diversity, all characters in all the books presented are white Christians, despite a sizable Jewish population in medieval England before the expulsion in 1290[91] and certainly a visible Jewish population in Winchester, one of the main cities of action in the book. This is hardly the intersectionality one would hope for. With a publication date of the Penman in 1994 and the Crenshaw article in 1991, perhaps the academic ideas had not yet had time to filter into larger awareness by the time of Penman's book, though the same cannot be said for the Chadwick. However, there has been strong recent interest in race, racism, and medievalism by medieval and medievalism scholars,[92] with much of this moving online (following a tenet of fourth-wave feminism) and ergo being freely accessible to a large audience.[93] With this growing availability to access quality work on intersectionalism, race, and the medieval, perhaps this disinterest in intersectionality will see a reversal in future fiction on medieval women.

In conclusion, the study of Matilda in modern fiction reveals much about the friction and intersections between the historical past and the modern reader. At the heart of almost all the modern secondary works on Matilda intended for a public audience is the gendered terminology used to describe her in primary and secondary sources. The pervasiveness of her reputation, and the representation used for her by crucial sources that were not in her favor, have been distilled into public knowledge as the actual Matilda: a haughty virago. The importance of her gendered representation creates a Matilda that is ready for adaptation and appropriation for an audience that has been brought up within second- and third-wave feminism in the West. This should be no surprise; as it has been noted, 'In women's hands, the historical novel has often become a political tool ... offering a critique of the present through their treatment of the past.'[94] The importance of this ready-to-adapt medieval woman, and one in a position of power at that, cannot be underestimated in altering a modern view of a medieval past, and the readerly presentism this presents. As Toby Litt argues, reading historical fiction renders a casual reader of the genre less able to know more about the past by reading these works, since '[w]hat the reader will do is *feel* they know more about the past … [there are] mental slippages required in order to produce and consume historical fiction'.[95] As Jan Nelis has also pointed out, a history 'stripped of most of its content [becomes] a highly abstract feeling rather than a "history"'.[96] The dialogue that exists between the reader and these texts is one that is passive and subconscious, and with the social framework of feminism, the reader may not recognize the different horizons between the past and themselves. Indeed, these novels represent a horizon similar to the readers' own, without an acknowledgement of the otherness of the past itself:

> A dialogue consists of not only two interlocutors, but also of the willingness of one to recognize and accept the other in his otherness … Literary understanding becomes dialogical only when the otherness of the text is sought and recognized from the horizon of our own expectations, when no naïve fusion of horizons is considered, and when one's own expectations are corrected and extended by the experience of the other.[97]

The diversity of representations of Matilda from her contemporary times to our own provide a blank slate on which modern writers and readers view feminism in the past, seeking validation of their own problems and feminist issues through their existence in a long-ago past, refusing a genuinely dialogical understanding of the text or the past. But unfortunately, these viewings of feminist problems via a medieval queen ultimately reflect only one concern, that of the white, middle- or upper-class reader. Unlike Fowler's study of the importance of the romance novel to working-class women readers, without an acknowledgement of intersectionality, these Matildas only give validation to a singular experience and its oppressions, rendering the representations the domain of the white, middle-class reader and their horizons of experience and understanding.

## NOTES

1. My thanks to Andrew Elliott, Carey Fleiner, Carole Levin, Kenneth Longden, and the editors of this volume for thoughtful suggestions and comments on earlier versions of this chapter. All remaining errors are, of course, my own.

2. Chandra L. Power, "Challenging the Pluralism of Our Past: Presentism and the Selective Tradition in Historical Fiction Writing for Young People," *Research in the Teaching of English* 37, no. 4 (May 2003): 426.
3. Toby Litt, "Against Historical Fiction," *Irish Pages* 5, no. 1 (2008): 113–114.
4. Hans Robert Jauss, "The Identity of the Poetic Text in the Changing Horizon of Understanding," in *Reception Study: From Theory to Cultural Studies*, ed. James L. Machor and Philip Goldstein (Abington: Psychology Press, 2001), 7.
5. Bridget Fowler, *The Alienated Reader: Women and Popular Romantic Literature in the Twentieth Century* (Harlow: Prentice-Hall, 1991), 4.
6. Here, and at any point in this chapter, 'post-feminist' is meant in terms of the Western world after the advent of second-wave feminism rather than the current and rather spurious claims of the mid-2010s being a 'post-feminist' climate.
7. For examples of opposing viewpoints, see Litt, "Historical Fiction," and Julie M. Dugger, "'I'm a Feminist, But…' Popular Romance in the Women's Literature Classroom," *Journal of Popular Romance Studies* 4, no. 2 (24 October 2014). http://jprstudies.org/2014/10/im-a-feminist-but-popular-romance-in-the-womens-literature-classroomby-julie-m-dugger/.
8. Romance Writers of America, "Romance Statistics," accessed November 17, 2017. https://www.rwa.org/page/romance-industry-statistics.
9. Romance Writers of America, "Reader Statistics," accessed May 5, 2017. https://www.rwa.org/p/cm/ld/fid=582. The surveying information did not include ethnic identities.
10. Both of which Marjorie Chibnall refers to as "wholly devoid of scholarly apparatus," *The Empress Matilda* (Oxford: Blackwell, 2000, 2nd edition), 2–3.
11. Marjorie Chibnall, "Matilda (1102–1167)," *Oxford Dictionary of National Biography* (Oxford University Press, 2004), accessed May 6, 2017. http://www.oxforddnb.com/view/article/18338.
12. "Matilda was less popular with contemporary chroniclers than Stephen; in many ways she took after her father, being prepared to loudly demand compliance of her court, when necessary issuing threats and generally appearing arrogant. This was felt to be particularly inappropriate since she was a woman." "The Anarchy," Wikipedia, accessed January 22, 2017, www.Wikipedia.org/wiki/The_Anarchy, citing Chibnall 1991; "…her perceived arrogance alienated many of her supporters and she was never crowned." "Matilda (1102–1167)," BBC History, accessed January 22, 2017, http://www.bbc.co.uk/history/historic_figures/matilda_queen.shtml; "…her arrogance and tactless demands for money provoked the

citizens [of London] to chase her away..." "Matilda, Daughter of Henry I," *Encyclopaedia Britannica*, accessed January 22, 2017, https://www.britannica.com/biography/Matilda-daughter-of-Henry-I; "...she had an arrogant and haughty manner and was heartily disliked." Johnson, Ben, "Empress Maud," *History Magazine*, accessed January 22, 2017, http://www.historic-uk.com/HistoryUK/HistoryofEngland/Empress-Maud/.

13. The same can be said about other medieval queens popularized in modern fiction, such as Eleanor of Aquitaine and Anne Boleyn.

14. Jean Plaidy, *The Passionate Enemies* (London: Pan, 1976).

15. Sharon Penman, *When Christ and His Saints Slept* (New York: Henry Holt & Co., 1995).

16. Elizabeth Chadwick, *Lady of the English* (Naperville, IL: Sourcebooks/Landmark, 2011).

17. Linda J. Lee, "Guilty Pleasures: Reading Romance Novels as Reworked Fairy Tales," *Marvels & Tales* 22, no. 1 (2008): 54.

18. Bruce Lambert, "Eleanor Hibbert, Novelist Known as Victoria Holt and Jean Plaidy," *The New York Times*, January 21, 1993. http://www.nytimes.com/1993/01/21/books/eleanor-hibbert-novelist-known-as-victoria-holt-and-jean-plaidy.html.

19. Plaidy, *Enemies*, 14–15, 113, 140, 217, 220, 235, 264, 268, 270, 286.

20. Plaidy, *Enemies*, 101, 120, 130, 231, 235.

21. Plaidy, *Enemies*, 14.

22. Plaidy, *Enemies*, 14.

23. Plaidy, *Enemies*, 28–29.

24. Plaidy, *Enemies*, 57.

25. Fowler, *Alienated*, 8.

26. Plaidy, *Enemies*, 226–229.

27. Fowler, *Alienated*, 9.

28. Diana Wallace, *The Woman's Historical Novel: British Writers, 1900–2000* (Basingstoke: Palgrave Macmillan, 2005), ix.

29. Andrew Elliott, pers. comm.

30. Penman, *Christ*, 33.

31. Penman, *Christ*, 35.

32. Penman, *Christ*, 36.

33. Penman, *Christ*, 99, 279.

34. Andrew Elliott, pers. comm.

35. For a succinct summary, see Kate Ellis, "Gimme Shelter: Feminism, Fantasy, and Women's Popular Fiction," in *American Media and Mass Culture: Left Perspectives*, ed. Donald Lazere (Berkeley: University of California Press, 1987), 217; in more detail and slightly more up to date in Fowler, *Alienated*.

36. Tan, Candy, "Talking About the R Word," *Smart Bitches, Trashy Books*, September 14, 2005. http://smartbitchestrashybooks.com/2005/09/talking_about_the_r_word/.
37. Mary Hamilton, "Does Tomb Raider's Lara Croft Really have to be a Survivor of a Rape Attempt?," *The Guardian*, June 13, 2012, http://www.theguardian.com/commentisfree/2012/jun/13/tomb-raider-lara-croft-rape-attempt; Chris Ostendorf, "TV's Rape Problem is Bigger than 'Game of Thrones,'" *Salon*, April 22, 2014, http://www.salon.com/2014/04/22/tvs_rape_problem_is_bigger_than_game_of_thrones_partner/.
38. Penman, *Christ*, 91.
39. Penman, *Christ*, 182.
40. Penman, *Christ*, 182.
41. Penman, *Christ*, 43–44.
42. Penman, *Christ*, 46.
43. Penman, *Christ*, 313.
44. Penman, *Christ*, 41.
45. Penman, *Christ*, 316.
46. Penman, *Christ*, 333.
47. Penman, *Christ*, 385, 392.
48. Penman, *Christ*, 418.
49. Mary Beaudry, "Stitching Women's Lives: Interpreting the Artifacts of Sewing and Needlework," in *Interpreting the Early Modern World: Transatlantic Perspective*, ed. Mary C. Beaudry and James Symonds (Berlin: Springer, 2011), 143–158.
50. Penman, *Christ*, 172; my italics.
51. Penman, *Christ*, 584.
52. Penman, *Christ*, 457.
53. Katherine Weikert, "The Empress Matilda and Motherhood in Popular Fiction, 1970s to the Present," in *Virtuous or Villainous? The Image of the Royal Mother from the Early Medieval to the Early Modern Eras*, eds. Elena Woodacre and Carey Fleiner (Baskingstoke: Palgrave Macmillan, 2016), 225–245.
54. Penman, *Christ*, 548.
55. Ealasaid Munro, "Feminism: A Fourth Wave?," *Political Insight* 4, no. 2 (September 2013): 22–25.
56. Penman, *Christ*, 36, 39, 38.
57. Penman, *Christ*, 59.
58. Penman, *Christ*, 49–50.
59. Penman, *Christ*, 233.
60. Penman, *Christ*, 54.
61. Penman, *Christ*, 25–26.
62. Penman, *Christ*, 113.

63. Penman, *Christ*, 116, 257, 281, 294.
64. Penman, *Christ*, 280–282; 415–418.
65. R. Clare Snyder, "What is Third-Wave Feminism? A New Directions Essay," *Signs* 34, no. 1 (2008): 175–196.
66. Penman, *Christ*, 94, 104–105, 112.
67. Penman, *Christ*, 143–145.
68. Penman, *Christ*, 92–93.
69. Penman, *Christ*, 137.
70. Penman, *Christ*, 451.
71. Chadwick, *Lady*, 327.
72. Alison Light, "'Returning to Manderley': Romance Fiction, Female Sexuality and Class," *Feminist Review* 16 (Summer 1984): 15–17; quote from 17.
73. Chadwick, *Lady*, 8.
74. Chadwick, *Lady*, 160–163.
75. Sarah Wendell, "The Bitchery Glossary," *Smart Bitches Trashy Books*, November 21, 2011. http://smartbitchestrashybooks.com/2011/11/the-bitchery-glossary/.
76. Chadwick, *Lady*, 466.
77. Chadwick, *Lady*, 32.
78. Chadwick, *Lady*, 366.
79. Chadwick, *Lady*, 523.
80. Chadwick, *Lady*, 40.
81. Chadwick, *Lady*, 55.
82. Chadwick, *Lady*, 129.
83. Light, "Manderley," 9.
84. Chadwick, *Lady*, 36, 148.
85. Chadwick, *Lady*, 194.
86. Chadwick, *Lady*, 148, 150.
87. Lee, "Pleasures," 54.
88. Ibid.
89. Kimberlé Crenshaw, "Mapping the Margins: Intersectionality, Identity Politics, and Violence Against Women of Color," *Stanford Law Review* 43 (1991): 1241–1299.
90. Power, "Challenging the Pluralism," 428–429. Emphasis original.
91. Patricia Skinner, *The Jews in Medieval England* (Woodbridge: Boydell Press, 2003).
92. Katherine Weikert and Elena Woodacre, "Gender and Status in the Medieval World," *Historical Reflections/Reflexions Historique* 42, no. 2 (2016): 3.
93. In The Middle, the blog of the BABEL Working Group, regularly provides posts questioning the academy, medieval studies and racism:

http://www.inthemedievalmiddle.com/, accessed January 22, 2017. In February 2017, The Public Medievalist also instituted a regular series on Race, Racism and the Middle Ages: http://www.publicmedievalist.com/race-racism-middle-ages-toc/, accessed May 6, 2017. See also, amongst others, Helen Young, "Place and Time: Medievalism and Making Race," *The Year's Work in Medievalism* 28 (2013): 2–6; as well as other ways that medieval academics intersect with white nationalism and the alt-right: Eli Saslow, "The white flight of Derek Black," *The Washington Post*, October 15, 2016. https://www.washingtonpost.com/national/the-white-flight-of-derek-black/2016/10/15/ed5f906a-8f3b-11e6-a6a3-d50061aa9fae_story.html?utm_term=.75dc17dbb7bc.
94. Wallace, *Novel*, 2.
95. Litt, "Historical Fiction," 114.
96. Jan Nelis, "Constructing Fascist Identity: Benito Mussolini and the Myth of Romanitá," *The Classical World* 100, no. 4 (2007): 402.
97. Jauss, "Identity," 9.

## Bibliography

### Published Sources

Alan, Richard William, 5th Earl Onslow. *The Empress Maud*. London: J. Clarke, 1939.
Beaudry, Mary. "Stitching Women's Lives: Interpreting the Artifacts of Sewing and Needlework." In *Interpreting the Early Modern World: Transatlantic Perspectives*, edited by Mary C. Beaudry and James Symonds, 143–158. Berlin: Springer, 2011.
Beem, Charles. *The Lioness Roared: The Problems of Female Rule in English History*. Basingstoke: Palgrave Macmillan, 2008.
Chadwick, Elizabeth. *Lady of the English*. Napierville, IL: Sourcebooks/Landmark, 2011.
Chibnall, Marjorie. *The Normans*. Oxford: Blackwell, 2000, 2nd edition 2008.
Crenshaw, Kimberlé. "Mapping the Margins: Intersectionality, Identity Politics, and Violence against Women of Color." *Stanford Law Review* 43 (1991): 1241–1299.
Dugger, Julie M. "'I'm a Feminist, But...' Popular Romance in the Women's Literature Classroom." *Journal of Popular Romance Studies* 4, no. 2 (24 October 2014). http://jprstudies.org/2014/10/im-a-feminist-but-popular-romance-in-the-womens-literature-classroomby-julie-m-dugger/.
Ellis, Kate. "Gimme Shelter: Feminism, Fantasy, and Women's Popular Fiction." In *American Media and Mass Culture: Left Perspectives*, edited by Donald Lazere, 216–232. Berkeley: University of California Press, 1987.

Fowler, Bridget. *The Alienated Reader: Women and Popular Romantic Literature in the Twentieth Century.* Harlow: Prentice-Hall, 1991.

Jauss, Jans Robert. "The Identity of the Poetic Text in the Changing Horizon of Understanding." In *Reception Study: From Theory to Cultural Studies*, edited by James L. Machor and Philip Goldstein, 7–28. Abington: Psychology Press, 2001.

Lee, Linda J. "Guilty Pleasures: Reading Romance Novels as Reworked Fairy Tales." *Marvels & Tales* 22, no. 1 (2008): 52–66.

Light, Allison. "'Returning to Manderley': Romance Fiction, Female Sexuality and Class." *Feminist Review* 16 (Summer 1984): 7–25.

Light, Allison. "'Young Bess': Historical Novels and Growing Up." *Feminist Review* 33 (Autumn 1989): 57–71.

Litt, Toby. "Against Historical Fiction." *Irish Pages* 5, no. 1 (2008): 111–115.

Munro, Ealasaid. "Feminism: A Fourth Wave?" *Political Insight* 4, no. 2 (September 2013): 22–25.

Nelis, Jan. "Constructing Fascist Identity: Benito Mussolini and the Myth of Romanità." *The Classical World* 100, no. 4 (2007): 391–415.

Penman, Sharon. *When Christ and His Saints Slept.* New York: Henry Holt & Co., 1995.

Plaidy, Jean. *The Passionate Enemies.* London: Pan, 1976.

Power, Chandra L. "Challenging the Pluralism of Our Past: Presentism and the Selective Tradition in Historical Fiction Writing for Young People." *Research in the Teaching of English* 37, no. 4 (May 2003): 425–466.

Snyder, R. Clare. "What is Third-Wave Feminism? A New Directions Essay." *Signs* 34, no. 1 (2008): 175–196.

Tolhurst, Fiona. *Geoffrey Monmouth and the Translation of Female Kingship.* New York: Palgrave Macmillan, 2013.

Wallace, Diana. *The Woman's Historical Novel: British Writers, 1900–2000.* Basingstoke: Palgrave Macmillan, 2005.

Weikert, Katherine. "The Empress Matilda and Motherhood in Popular Fiction, 1970s to the Present." In *Virtuous or Villainous? The Image of the Royal Mother from the Early Medieval to the Early Modern Eras*, edited by Elena Woodacre and Carey Fleiner, 225–245. Basingstoke: Palgrave Macmillan, 2016.

Weikert, Katherine, and Elena Woodacre. "Gender and Status in the Medieval World." *Historical Reflections/Reflexions Historique* 42, no. 1 (2016): 1–7.

Young, Helen. "Place and Time: Medievalism and Making Race." *The Year's Work in Medievalism* 28 (2013): 2–6.

## News Articles and Internet Sources

BBC History, "Matilda (1102–1167)." Accessed January 22, 2017. http://www.bbc.co.uk/history/historic_figures/matilda_queen.shtml.

BBC History, "Matilda (1102–1167)." Oxford Dictionary of National Biography, Oxford University Press, 2004. Accessed May 6, 2017. http://www.oxforddnb.com/view/article/18338.

*Encyclopedia Britannica.* "Matilda, Daughter of Henry I." Last modified May 11, 2009. https://www.britannica.com/biography/Matilda-daughter-of-Henry-I.

Hamilton, Mary. "Does Tomb Raider's Lara Croft Really Have to be a Survivor of a Rape Attempt?" *The Guardian,* June 13, 2012. http://www.theguardian.com/commentisfree/2012/jun/13/tomb-raider-lara-croft-rape-attempt.

*In The Middle.* Accessed January 22, 2017. http://www.inthemedievalmiddle.com/.

Johnson, Ben. "Empress Maud." *History Magazine.* Accessed January 22, 2017. http://www.historic-uk.com/HistoryUK/HistoryofEngland/Empress-Maud/.

Lambert, Bruce. "Eleanor Hibbert, Novelist Known as Victoria Holt and Jean Plaidy." *The New York Times,* January 21, 1993. http://www.nytimes.com/1993/01/21/books/eleanor-hibbert-novelist-known-as-victoria-holt-and-jean-plaidy.html.

Ostendorf, Chris. "TV's Rape Problem is Bigger than 'Game of Thrones.'" *Salon,* April 22, 2014. http://www.salon.com/2014/04/22/tvs_rape_problem_is_bigger_than_game_of_thrones_partner/.

Romance Writers of America. "Romance Statistics." Accessed November 17, 2017. https://www.rwa.org/p/cm/ld/fid=580.

Romance Writers of America. "Reader Statistics." Accessed May 6, 2017. https://www.rwa.org/p/cm/ld/fid=582.

Saslow, Eli. "The White Flight of Derek Black." *The Washington Post,* October 15, 2016. https://www.washingtonpost.com/national/the-white-flight-of-derek-black/2016/10/15/ed5f906a-8f3b-11e6-a6a3-d50061aa9fae_story.html?utm_term=.75dc17dbb7bc.

Tan, Candy. "Talking About the R Word." *Smart Bitches, Trashy Books,* September 14, 2005. Accessed January 26, 2017. http://smartbitchestrashybooks.com/2005/09/talking_about_the_r_word/.

The Public Medievalist. "TPM Special Series: Race, Racism and the Middle Ages." May 6, 2017. http://www.publicmedievalist.com/race-racism-middle-ages-toc/.

Wendell, Sarah. "The Bitchery Glossary." *Smart Bitches, Trashy Books,* November 21, 2011. http://smartbitchestrashybooks.com/2011/11/the-bitchery-glossary/.

Wikipedia. "The Anarchy." Last modified February 2, 2017. Accessed January 22, 2017. https://en.wikipedia.org/wiki/The_Anarchy.

# CHAPTER 5

# 'She Is My Eleanor': The Character of Isabella of Angoulême on Film— A Medieval Queen in Modern Media

## Carey Fleiner

### INTRODUCTION[1]

The life of Isabella of Angouleme (c. 1188–1246) is the stuff of fiction: At the age of thirteen, the 'Helen of the Middle Ages,' was heir to important property in France.[2] Supported by her parents, she spurned her fiancé Hugh of Lusignan, Count of La Marche (breaking a legal contract of affiance) in favor of John of England[3] (who divorced his first wife for her—and to acquire said property).[4] When she was perhaps only between nine and fourteen years old, she was sent to be educated at Hugh of Lusignan's estate when John fetched her back to Angouleme for a quick wedding. Although the 35-year-old John seems to have waited a few years before consummating the marriage,[5] the chroniclers note that the pair scandalized the court with their vigorous sex life and extravagant living.[6] Isabella persuaded first John; then her second husband, Hugh, the son of the original fiancé Hugh of Lusignan,[7] who was a powerful castellan (whom she stole from her own preteen daughter,

C. Fleiner (✉)
University of Winchester, Winchester, UK

© The Author(s) 2018                                                                 91
J. North et al. (eds.), *Premodern Rulers and Postmodern Viewers*,
Queenship and Power, https://doi.org/10.1007/978-3-319-68771-1_5

whom she then kidnapped);[8] and finally her son Henry III to pursue useless wars against the French—wars that they lost[9] when promised Lusignan support failed to show up.[10] Isabella declared herself a queen until the day she died,[11] refusing to pay homage to her French overlord (the count of Poitou)[12]—appearing instead with her family at his home at Christmas in 1242 to beg forgiveness for her and Hugh's transgressions against his authority;[13] after a suitably humble display of obeisance, they withdrew and set the place on fire on the way out. Isabella's final (alleged) act of infamy was a plot to poison King Louis IX in 1243,[14] whereupon she fled to the abbey at Fontevraut. According to legend, she finished her life living in a bricked up secret room (*secretissima camera*) in the abbey.[15]

This paper focuses primarily on Isabella's two main big screen appearances, 1977's *Robin and Marian* (directed by Richard Lester) and 2010's *Robin Hood* (directed by Ridley Scott). It will survey, against the relevant historical context of Isabella's life and career, how these two cinematic Isabellas reflect the image of the queen as a royal wife as recorded by contemporary literature, if not subsequently shaped by nineteenth-century cultural expectations for acceptable feminine behavior. Isabella has a richly developed character in modern popular fiction, especially historical romances, for example, where she comes across as an ambitious, aggressively sexual woman limited by contemporary expectations of appropriate female roles. As a royal wife and mother, Isabella was expected to be a model of the domestic helpmeet and counterpart to her husband's public responsibilities, but her forward behavior was seen as a sign that her menfolk were ineffective, especially the 'wicked' John. On film, however, she has very limited screen time: perhaps, between the two films, a grand total of about twenty minutes. However, in that short amount of time and with limited dialogue she becomes a powerful symbol representing John's failings as a leader and king.

## Looking for the Historic Isabella

Only recently has English scholarship focused on Isabella and a re-examination of her life. Her earliest modern biographies are French, Castaigne in 1836 and Surin in 1846, followed by Agnes Strickland's English biography in 1854. At first in modern scholarship, she appears as a secondary character: mid-twentieth-century scholarship focuses on her Lusignan husband and brood,[16] and of course she makes an appearance in scholarship on John of England. Recent scholarship on John, like other maligned 'historical villains,' re-examines the nature of his rule and the sources that recount it, and these studies have brought Isabella herself into the spotlight,[17] especially from the 1990s. She has been the topic of dedicated studies[18] that examine her actions in light of the growing trend on medieval queen consorts and queens who wielded authority behind the throne.[19] Despite such ongoing scholarship, however, Agnes Strickland's biography—errors, sentimentality, and all—often remains the first, if not last stop for those authors who craft the fictional Isabella as they fold into their dramas Strickland's innovative but uncritical reading of primary sources and her own Victorian morality.[20]

Primary sources for Isabella include the ruins of Fontevraud castle, her sarcophagus, and her seal. Written sources include royal records, Isabella's own letters and charters, royal financial records, and charters such as those found in the Close Rolls, Charter Rolls, and Pipe Rolls, and contemporary chronicles and accounts including papal and English monastic chronicles.[21] The latter sources tend to be brief if not synoptic, and, despite the variety of surviving sources that mention Isabella, it is these monastic chronicles that primarily shape the image of the queen that we see on the big screen. These chroniclers are not particularly sympathetic towards Isabella, least of all Matthew Paris.[22] Matthew was a monk at St. Albans and a prolific writer and illustrator best known for his *Chronica Maiora* and *Historia Anglorum*.[23] No mere cloistered churchman, it seems he was well-acquainted with the movers and shakers at the English court, and he shows no inhibition when criticizing the nobility—John's military incompetence, for example, and Henry III's inability to control neither his Savoyard in-laws nor his Poitevin half-siblings.[24] Roger of Wendover's contemporary account of Isabella, folded into Matthew's *Historia Anglorum*, is a principle source of the best-known anecdotes—sleeping in with John until 11 am every day, the extravagant spending, her beauty, greed, and ambition, and the subsequent shenanigans of her French children as they ran roughshod over their half-brother Henry's hospitality. Matthew's information on Isabella and John comes down to him second hand, and Weiler notes that while Matthew was scrupulous in naming his sources, he inserted his own views and criticisms into the narrative.[25] That said, it does not mean that Matthew is necessarily inaccurate; rather, one must keep in mind Matthew's purpose for writing history and his idea of historical accountancy. The idea of history as a source of moral exempla predates Matthew by centuries, being entrenched in the Roman and Greek biographical and historical writing of authors such as Sallust or Plutarch. For Matthew Paris, as again with Strickland, Matthew took seriously his duty to provide moral guidance and instruction.[26] He makes no attempt to delve into Isabella's motivations, although his bile for Isabella takes on a different character than his usual dismissal of ambitious women as 'viragoes.' Medieval authors called a woman a virago if she did not follow the passive or domestic role expected of her and demonstrated more political ambition (or competency) than the men around her.[27] Instead, Matthew comments that the French described Isabella as 'more Jezebel than Isabella,' that is, her sexuality and 'feminine wiles' weakened, influenced and manipulated the men in her life.[28]

## ISABELLA ON FILM

Isabella's literary character reflects a complicated scenario in the eras of women's liberation and post-feminism. She is presented as a strong woman who elicits sympathy because she is oppressed by the men around her; however, she still needs men (and her beauty) for fulfillment. Strickland's biography remains a profound influence on creators of historical fiction as they dramatize Isabella's story and adapt her circumstances to their contemporary audiences. Thus, Isabella's character has been fitted into different eras. For example, the frustrated Victorian housewife might readily relate to Strickland's nineteenth-century, ambitious, but suppressed medieval queen. Likewise, in the feminist 1970s, the Isabella of historical romance appears as a liberated, but frustrated political superwoman. Finally, in the post-feminist, politically correct new millennium, Isabella is recast yet again as a woman who relies on her sex as a means to enthrall the men around her, but at the same time, needs a man to tame her passions and remind her that she is a woman. Isabella is most fully fleshed out in modern historical fiction from the 1970s onwards.[29] Recent examples of the literary Isabella include Erica Laine's *Isabella* (2015) where Isabella's relationship with John is set out as the origins of the Hundred Years' War, Jean Plaidy's *The Prince of Darkness* (1978) in which Isabella is carried off by a John who is in league with Satan himself, and Lisa Hilton's *The Stolen Queen* (2011) where young Isabella is held captive by a cult 'of the old religion' who plan to use her to overthrow Christianity in England. Rachael Bard's *Isabella: Queen without a Conscience* (2006) relates Isabella's story from multiple first-person points of view to present more sympathy for Isabella than found in previous versions of the story; Bard's Isabella is driven to use her sexuality and ambition less selfishly and more as a means of survival. No matter what the framework of these stories is, the character of Isabella still reflects Strickland's portrayal of an ambitious woman trying to fulfill her expected role against the restrictions placed upon her by social expectations on the one hand, and the repression of the menfolk around her on the other hand.

Novels allow for extensive storytelling, but unless it is a multi-part television series, historical films rely on shortcuts and assumed audience knowledge in place of deep character development. Isabella's celluloid characterizations are very brief, and yet they nevertheless indicate her passion, her influence on politics, and the weakness and folly of the men around her. The two films in which Isabella appears are both revisions of the tale of Robin Hood, a character who himself carries about 110 years' worth of cinematic baggage.[30] Recent depictions of Robin revisit his heroism and his relationship with Maid Marian. Isabella appears only tangentially—she should not be in these films, since Robin's king is Richard I, and John is but a prince, but 1977s *Robin and Marian* sets the story late in Robin's career, and 2010s *Robin Hood* fiddles a bit with the timeframe.[31] John is still a prince at the start of the film and becomes king early on; Isabella is, in the film, the niece (in real life, first cousin, once removed) of the king of France, with whom John plans to replace his wife.

*Robin and Marian* (directed by Richard Lester) depicts the title characters in their middle age, as author James Goldman was inspired to reflect on the lack of strong heroes in popular culture in the mid-1970s, and, in particular, the evolution of Robin Hood as a cinematic hero over the course of the twentieth century.[32] Noting that Robin's adventures always depict him in his prime, and that all that was ever noted about his death was that he was struck down 'by treachery,' Goldman decided to present Robin as a middle-aged man and to give him a death connected to his 'character and intentions'.[33] Robin (Sean Connery)'s acceptance of his reputation and the difficult relationship between Robin and Marian (if not Robin and Little John, played by Ronnie Corbett) are the principle focus of Lester's intriguing film.[34] Lester's plan was to put on the screen 'historical truth' and to ratchet down the myth and to make Robin a more realistic character.[35] As a consequence, *Robin and Marian* is a 'lived-in' film[36] and is meant to reflect the bitter cynicism and deep disillusionment of 1970s' America.[37] John himself has only about ten minutes' screen time, and Isabella perhaps less than five minutes, although she warrants mention early on in the film. When catching up on the news of the past twenty years, Robin (Sean Connery) learns from Will Scarlet (Denholm Elliott) that Robin has become a legend, and that the king (Ian Holm) is now married to and besotted with a twelve-year-old girl and lies in bed all day with her. The sarcastic tone in which Will tells the story and Robin's look of distaste tell us all we need to know about King John current reputation as a dirty old man who is neglecting his royal duties.

When we finally see John at nearly halfway through the film, he is sat before a splendid tent overlooking a sea cliff and shouting at a papal legate; he is a man, according to Goldman's script 'given to fits of uncontrollable rage'.[38] From behind him appears Isabella (Victoria Abril) wrapped only in a fur duvet. Very young, 'an adorable girl, who looked every day of twelve,'[39] speaking stilted English, she begs him petulantly to come back to bed. Seeing her, John instantly loses his anger and becomes a soppy schoolboy; they cannot keep their hands off each other. She asks him to return to bed, informing him that '[she's] clean all over'.[40] His eyes wander to her breasts, but when Isabella offers to drop her furs, John becomes self-conscious and nods awkwardly towards his men (who have been watching in disgust). She chirps, 'I don't mind; I think you're pretty! You're pretty every place!'[41] She settles for a kiss as John sends her back to the tent, but not without a lot of backwards glances and a little wave from the king. He then turns back to the business at hand and to shout at his chancellor. In only a few minutes, actor Ian Holm conveys a man in the middle of a mid-life crisis; lust, shame, and longing cross quickly over his features at the sight of his queen; Abril's Isabella—a pouty pre-teen, beautiful and empty-headed—is here interested only in luring the king back into her bed. Women's liberation may have come to Lester's Sherwood Forest in the form of an embittered Maid Marian, but it has not reached the king's bedroom. This Isabella represents John's corruption, weakness, and consequent lack of respect from his own men.

Ridley Scott also chose to depict Isabella in his 2010 reimagining of the Robin Hood story written by Brian Helgeland, Ethan Reiff, and Cyrus Voris (screenplay by Helgeland)—in this case a 'prequel' of how Robin became an outlaw, and a film affected by modern feminism and late twentieth-century political correctness. Here, too, Isabella has very little screen time in the film's theatrical release of 140 minutes—the longer director's cut is well worth a look, at least for us, since otherwise trimmed dialogue that establishes Isabella's role is restored. In the film, Isabella herself is nearly lost between the two better-known women in the film, each of whom are familiar to cinematic and literary audiences: Cate Blachett's Maid Marian and Eileen Atkins' Eleanor of Aquitaine. Blanchett's Maid Marian reflects the influence of strong, independent post-modern feminism on popular culture, and modern Marian is worth a longer discussion than can be allowed here. More important for us, and the consideration of these two films, Eleanor reminds us of when she dominated the stage and screen on the first wave of feminism in 1968s *Lion in Winter*. Isabella has been connected to and compared with Eleanor since Strickland's account, and in Scott's *Robin Hood* (especially in the director's cut and David Coe's novelization of Brian Helgeland's screenplay), the parallel between Isabella and Eleanor is established at Isabella's introduction in the film. Eleanor has just berated her son for romping with 'the niece' of the king of France (i.e., Isabella). John retorts that his own wife is 'barren as a brick' and he plans to appeal to the Pope for an annulment. He then reminds his mother that she gave Henry eight children and he, 'the runt of the litter,' is the hope for the kingdom; he says that not only will Isabella provide him with the heirs that he needs, but that 'she is *my* Eleanor.'[42]

## 'SHE IS MY ELEANOR'

Half way through Strickland's biography of Isabella, there is a break in the narrative of Isabella and John as Strickland focuses on the death of Eleanor of Aquitaine. She tells the reader that Eleanor had been willful, lusty, and independent but that 'adversity ... improved [her] character' as a young woman—rather reminiscent of Isabella—but as she grew older, she learned 'a stern lesson of life' and that 'power, beauty, and royalty are but vanity'.[43] Eleanor, unfortunately, learned that lesson too late for it to have full effect on her life.[44] Similarly, Strickland notes that the same misfortunes plagued Isabella, because her own pride and willfulness were similar to the problems faced by Eleanor, as even this great queen failed to tame her own 'restless spirit'.[45]

The screenwriter for *Robin and Marian* was James Goldman who won a Tony in 1966 for his play *Lion in Winter.* He wrote the screenplay for the film in which Eleanor is brought to life by Katharine Hepburn

Audiences of the film generally do not know the historical Eleanor; they know Hepburn (who stepped into the role following the portrayal of the queen by the then-unknown Sian Phillips in 1964s *Becket*).[46] *Becket*'s Eleanor is a passive character, helpless and restricted by domestic roles; as Finke notes, the character is restricted by the very clothes she wears and often remains static in scenes where Peter O'Toole's Henry chews up the scenery around her.[47] *Lion in Winter*'s Eleanor, by contrast, is a formidable dame; Goldman's stage directions describe her as truly handsome, authoritative, with great presence; she is 'a genuinely feminine woman thoroughly capable of holding her own in a man's world' in contrast to the king's cynical use of marriage to Alais as a token of exchange, nothing more.[48] Hepburn's regal presence makes the queen a powerful royal equal in the domestic sphere,[49] and she stands firm against O'Toole's ranting and raving. Her conflict with Henry over their sons is central to the plot, and she displays the political influence a queen could wield behind the scenes in her domestic capacity.[50] In Act 1, scene 1 of *Lion in Winter*, Henry tells his lover (and fiancée to his son) Alais not to be 'jealous of the gorgon; she is not among the things I love'; she is 'the new Medusa' and 'the great bitch'.[51] He reminds the young woman that he has not kept Eleanor imprisoned at Chignon 'out of passionate attachment'. In *Robin and Marian*, Goldman has Richard I refer to his mother Eleanor, again, as 'the bitch'.[52] Eleanor is never seen in the film, as we glimpse only her baggage train, but surely 1976 audiences anticipated a cameo by Hepburn and may well have recalled at that moment her strong characterization, and thus be reminded of this formidable queen in comparison to John's current consort.

Unlike Goldman and Lester's film, Scott's film includes an interaction between Eleanor and Isabella. The comparison between Isabella and Eleanor arguably plays a significant role, especially if she is meant to be *John*'s Eleanor. Isabella (Sophie Marceau) is introduced as an empty-headed sex toy, romping about with John in his bed whilst his cast-aside wife watches them through the keyhole. Isabella scornfully dismisses criticism from her mother-in-law Eleanor who catches them between the sheets—and Eleanor significantly throws the sheet over Isabella's face because on the one hand, she wants Isabella to hear what she has to say to John, but does not want to look at her. Certainly, in *Robin and Marian* Isabella represents nothing more than a sexual cipher (much like *Becket*'s Alais), and she initially fills this role in the modern film. She certainly reveals John's lust (if not his need for an heir), but she also shows that she is not going to take dismissal from her political role (literally) lying down. She jumps out of bed to stand beside John and to speak for herself as he explains to his mother his importance to the future of the crown, and Isabella's role in his plans.

What is Isabella of Angouleme's role as the Eleanor of the Next Generation? One might argue that she reminds the viewer that she has the potential to become the strong Eleanor depicted in *Lion in Winter* and John another Henry II. In Scott's story, Eleanor is initially the strongest, most decisive woman in John's household. She scolds John's first wife for moping and spying on John and Isabella in bed ('An English princess shut out of her husband's bedchamber by a piece of French pastry!').[53] Ultimately, however, Isabella impresses Eleanor as having 'spirit' when Isabella defends herself as John's choice, and that she will provide John with the heir that Richard has not given to Eleanor.[54] Eleanor is also the one who crowns John and declares him king when Robin delivers to Eleanor the news and the crown of the dead Richard I. In this scene at the gate of the Tower of London, augmented in the director's cut of the film, John follows Eleanor down to the platform where Robin's boat has landed, looking dismayed, if not terrified, on hearing the news of his brother's death. The camera focuses on Isabella as she slips her hand into John's, and after a moment he squeezes and grips hers tightly in his own. The director's cut of the film restores critical lines in another scene that reveals Isabella's partnership with John: at 51 minutes, she speaks up to query William Marshal when he advises John on dealing with the remains of Richard I's army— Marshal gives Isabella a strange look, but John reaches out again to take and squeeze her hand.[55] Meanwhile, in this same scene, Eleanor watches on and is dismissed by John when she offers him advice about taxation—he reveals more of his insecurity by informing his mother that her bad advice and Richard's loyalty to her led to 'the wreckage that is my inheritance'—a remark that earns him a stinging slap from his mother.[56] Eleanor later meets with William who informs her that John is about to be betrayed by a man he believes to be his closest advisor; Eleanor remarks that 'it's up to the King's mother to scold him like a child and point him to his duty' and here she transfers her role of advisor and helpmeet to Isabella. This scene appears in both the uncut and theatrical version; Eleanor approaches Isabella and explains not only the situation to the young queen, but how exactly to tell John of the situation.[57] Isabella is baffled that she is not to tell John the honest truth, but Eleanor rebukes her, saying, 'If *you* wish to be queen, *you* must save John … and England'[58]; Coe extends the scene in his novelization, describing Eleanor's dismay that she had 'fallen, and how desperate matters had grown that she should be so dependent on … this child.'[59] On screen, although frightened, Isabella does as Eleanor asks and stands fast as John whirls about in anger, tearing up the scenery—not unlike the passion and fury exhibited by Henry II in *Lion in Winter* John pulls up only when he sees the stoic Isabella stood firm and holding a dagger at her breast—he puts his hand over hers on the hilt as they both cry. The knife falls away; they clinch and exchange the royal tongue, 'her ardour a match for his' notes Coe in the novelization.[60] Thus, these short scenes onscreen complete Isabella's transformation from mere adornment and heir-factory to that of political helpmeet. Later, we see her accompanying him when he receives a proto-Magna Carta from his nobles.[61] She is also is shown seated in a throne next to him while he hears official business— as he berates his nobles, he silences their protests as well as hers. He sets the charter on fire, declares Robin Hood an outlaw from that day forward, then retreats inside his palace with his queen.

Despite the time constraints of the medium (and trims to the runtime of the theatrical release), Scott's Isabella parallels the Isabella of the historical romances if not the Isabella of history, a bit more closely than Lester's. It is all still flashpoints: first the teenaged sex toy, but even then (in the director's cut) she is seen as an opinionated woman from her introduction. Even without the complete scene of John explaining to his mother Isabella's importance to him, the 'Eleanor' line explicates that her role in Scott's film is shorthand for her potential to influence John with similar competence as Eleanor (as Henry II's wife, then John's mother). Coe's novelization augments this scenario with additional dialogue and description, especially strengthening Isabella's transformation from 'a mere French pastry' to someone who is equal to John in his passions in the scene where she brings him news of William Marshall's treachery. In Scott's film and Helgeland's story, Isabella represents that John has the *potential* to be another Henry II—which of course emphasizes all the more his *failure*, since the audience is assumed to be familiar with the powerful cinematic Eleanor and the long folk-tradition of John I as a miserable loser. *Robin Hood* does not delve this deeply into the story: John is a weakling, and his insecurity (and desires to remedy this) are indicated in his comments to Eleanor that now 'the runt of the litter' has become king. Although the main story here belongs to Robin and Marian, Isabella and John's relationship is a neat little subplot with subtext that rewards the more critical viewers.

## CONCLUSION

To conclude, one must note that since the 1970s and again from the 1990s, there is an increasing body of scholarship devoted to finding 'women's voices' in history, a search made difficult as ancient and medieval sources come through the filter of elite male perception of standards of behavior. Literary history of course can take liberties that scholarship cannot; moralizing biographies, historical fiction, and film fill in gaps in the sparse historical record, recreating the personalities of such powerful women by hanging contemporary attitudes, cultural mores, and experience on the skeleton of intriguing facts provided by the original sources. Time constraints restrict this liberty for cinematic Isabellas; they remain signposts to illustrate the weakness of King John whether besotted by his own lust, and unable to find himself a helpmeet as respected and well-regarded—in popular culture at least—as Eleanor of Aquitaine. The Isabellas in both media remain pawns against the actions of the men (and women) in their stories; historical revisionism has not yet reached this particular corner of popular fiction. The queen receives only the briefest of screen time in both of these films, and ultimately how she behaves and is judged is within the context set for her by John. One awaits cinematic depiction of Isabella that takes advantage of recent trends in the evaluation of royal women's lives, circumstances, and consequent behavior in the context of contemporary sources to see how she fares, perhaps at last on her own terms.

## NOTES

1. The seeds of this chapter were sown in my undergraduate dissertation at the University of Delaware in 1987, when I wrote about Isabella's son William de Valence. Many thanks to Elena Woodacre and other Winchester colleagues for their feedback on earlier versions of this paper, and to Kevin Harty who heard a version of this chapter at MAMO in Lincoln in 2015. Many thanks go also to Kathy Cephas.
2. On Isabella's family holdings, see S. Fougere, *Isabelle d'Angouleme, reine d'Angleterre* (Payre: Edit-France, 1998), 13–26.

# 102   C. FLEINER

3. Matthew Paris, *Matthaei Parisiensis, Monachi Sancti Albani, Chronica Majora*, ed. H. R. Luard, 7 vols. (London: Rolls Series, 1872–1883), ii, 462; Matthew Paris, *Matthaei Parisiensis, Monachi Sancti Albani, Historia Anglorum*, ed. F. Madden, 3 vols. (London: Rolls Series, 1866), ii, 86; Roger de Hoveden, *Chronica Magistri Rogeri de Houedene*, ed. W. Stubbs, 4 vols. (London: Rolls Series, 1868–1871) iv, 119; Roger of Wendover, *Rogeri de Wendover Liber qui dicitur Flores Historiarum*, ed. H. G. Hewlett, 3 vols. (London: Rolls Series, 1886–1889), iii, 148.
4. See *Annales Monastici*, "Annales de Burton," ed. H. R. Luard, 5 vols. (London: The Rolls Series, 1864–1869), i, 202; cf. Matthew Paris, *Historia Anglorum* ii, 86; Roger de Hoveden iv, 119. See also Fougere, *Isabelle d'Angouleme*, 27–31.
5. Roger de Hoveden ii, *Chronica Magistri Rogeri*, 483; N. Vincent, "Isabella of Angoulême: John's Jezebel," in *King John: New Interpretations*, ed. S. D. Church (Woodbridge: Boydell Press, 1999), 173–175.
6. Matthew Paris, *Historia Anglorum* ii, 96. "cum regina epulabatur cotidie splendidissime, usque ad horam prandii sompnos protrahens matutinales."; Roger de Hoveden iii, 171. On Isabella's inheritance and the consequences of breaking the contract with Hugh and her subsequent marriage to John, see Vincent, "John's Jezebel," especially 166–170 and 177–182.
7. "Annales monasterii de Waverlei," in *Annales Monastici*, ed. H. R. Luard, 5 vols. (London: Rolls Series, 1864–1849), ii, 291; "Annales Prioratus de Wigornia," in *Annales Monastici*, iv, 412. See note 16 for scholarship on the identity of Isabella's second husband.
8. "Annales Prioratus de Dunstaplia," in *Annales Monastici*, iii, 57; *Royal and Other Historical Letters Illustrative of the Reign of Henry III*, 2 vols. (London: Rolls Series, 1862), i, Appendix 5, no. 11, 536–537.
9. *Matthew Paris, Chronica Majora* iv, 179, 210–212. *Royal and Other Historical Letters*, i, 22, no. xvii 22, i, 114–115, no. xcvi. Honorius warned Isabella to stop annoying Henry (i, 536, x; Dunstable, iii, 75).
10. *Royal and Other Historical Letters*, ii, 25–27, no. xlxxxiv.
11. On Isabella's coronation, see *Chronica Majora*, ii, 467, Hoveden, *Chronica Magistri Rogeri*, iv, 139, and *Historia Angloroum*, ii, 88. The couple were, in fact, crowned thrice, first at Westminster in October 1200, at Canterbury in early 1201 (*Historia Anglorum* ii, 89), and in 1202 at Canterbury (ii, 96). Isabella's seal, used for personal and official business on her return home to Angouleme, and her tomb effigy depict her crowned and enrobed.
12. Matthew Paris, *Chronica Majora*, iv, 178.
13. Matthew Paris, *Chronica Majora*, iv, 178.

14. Matthew Paris, *Chronica Majora*, iv, 253; Roger of Wendover, *Rogeri de Wendover*, ii, 251.
15. Matthew Paris, *Chronica Majora*, iv, 253.
16. On the Lusignan Hughs and the identity of Isabella's second husband, see H. G. Richardson, "The Marriage and Coronation of Isabella of Angouleme," *English Historical Review* 241 (1946): 289–311 and Sidney Painter "The Houses of Lusignan and the Chatellerault," *Speculum* 30 (1955): 374–384; see also H. Snellgrove, *The Lusignans in England 1247–1258* (Albuquerque: The University of New Mexico Press, 1950) for Isabella's relationship with Henry III.
17. Whilst there is a vast scholarship on John, good starting places include Painter's seminal monograph *The Reign of King John* (Baltimore: Johns Hopkins University Press, 1949); W. L. Warren, *King John* (London: Eyre and Spottiswoode, 1978); S. D. Church, *King John: New Interpretations* (Woodbridge: Boydell Press, 1999); and F. McLynn, *Richard and John: Kings at War* (Cambridge, MA: Da Capo Press, 2007).
18. Fougere, *Isabelle d'Angouleme* and G. Bianciotto, et al.'s *Isabelle d'Angouleme, comtesse-reine et son temps (1186–1246): actes du colloque tenu a Lusignan du 8 au 10 novembre 1996* (Poitiers: Universite de Poitiers, 1999).
19. P. Cook, *Queens Consort of England: The Power behind the Throne* (New York, 1993); John Carmi Parsons, "Piety, Power, and the Reputations of Two Thirteenth-Century English Queens," in *Queens, Regents, and Potentates*, ed. Theresa M Vann (Dallas: Academia, 1993): 107–123; Vincent, "John's Jezebel"; Douglas C. Jansen, "Women and Public Authority in the Thirteenth Century," in *Queens, Regents, and Potentates*, ed. Theresa M. Vann (Dallas: Academia, 1993): 91–105; Charles Beem, *The Lioness Roared: The Problems of Female Rule in English History* (New York: Palgrave Macmillan, 2006); Lisa Hilton, *Queens Consort: England's Medieval Queens from Eleanor of Aquitaine to Elizabeth of York* (New York: Pegasus Books, 2010); Louise J. Wilkinson, "Maternal Abandonment and Surrogate Caregivers: Isabella of Angouleme and her Children," in *Virtuous or Villainess? The Image of the Royal Mother from the Early Medieval to the Early Modern Era*, C. Fleiner and E. Woodacre (New York: Palgrave, 2016): 101–124.
20. M. E. Burstein, "'The Reduced Pretensions of the Historic Muse': Agnes Strickland and the Commerce of Women's History," *The Journal of Narrative Technique* 28, no. 3 (1998): 469–500. Burstein discusses the place of Strickland amongst nineteenth-century historians. See also A. Laurence, "Women Historians and Documentary Research: Lucy Aiken, Agnes Strickland, Mary Everett Green, and Lucy Toulmin Smith,"

in *Women Scholarship and Criticism*, ed. J. Bellamy, A. Laurence, and G. Perry (Manchester: University of Manchester Press, 2000): 130; on Strickland's dependence on sources that had been edited by others, see Christine L. Krueger, "Why She Lived at the PRO: Mary Anne Everett Green and the Profession of History," *Journal of British Studies* 42, no. 1 (January 2003): 65–90. Kruger considers the issue of gender and the nineteenth-century professionalization of history writing; see also R. Maitzen, "This Feminine Preserve: Historical Biographies by Victorian Women." *Victorian Studies* 38, no. 3 (1995): 371–393 on the approaches of Strickland and Everett Green to their sources, subjects, and audience, and B. Dabby, "Hannah Lawrance and the Claims of Women's History In Nineteenth-Century England," *The Historical Journal* 53, no. 3 (2010): 699–722, who compares Strickland and Everett Green's work with journalist Hannah Lawrance (especially 706–807).

21. Many of the Rolls Series volumes are now available online as scanned texts via a project hosted by Stanford University. Matthew Paris's *Historia Anglorum* has been scanned by the British Library, which holds a unique, complete copy.

22. Cf. Vincent, "John's Jezebel," 200–201, 203–204; Wilkinson, "Maternal Abandonment."

23. See R. Vaughan, *Matthew Paris* (Cambridge Studies in Medieval Life and Thought, New Series) (Cambridge, 1979) and B. Weiler, "Matthew Paris on the Writing of History," *Journal of Medieval History* 35, no. 3 (2009): 254–278. Weiler considers Vaughan and Gransden (268–269) and investigates Matthew's approach to history. See Weiler (262–263) for recent discussion of Matthew's sources.

24. Weiler, "Matthew Paris," 269–270 on Matthew Paris's interests in English politics and well-being of the kingdom.

25. Weiler, "Matthew Paris," 274–275.

26. Weiler, "Matthew Paris," 275.

27. Rebecca Reader, "Matthew Paris and Women," in *Thirteenth-Century England VII: The Proceedings of the Durham Conference*, ed. M. Prestone, R. Britnell, and R. Frame (Woodbridge: The Boydell Press, 1997): 153–159. She also considers Matthew's interpretation of female sexuality and its power (157–159); she notes that Matthew's more prurient passages were left untranslated 'unsuitable' for Victorian readership (158).

28. Matthew Paris, *Chronica Majora*, iv, 253—not in reference to her relationship with John, but rather her command of her husband Hugh, in the context of his entanglement in a duel with "a French knight." Cf. Roger of Wendover, *Rogeri de Wendover*, ii, 251, who repeats the same line in the same context—whereas Strickland has Matthew himself offer the opinion (44).

29. See Jerome de Groot, *The Historical Novel* (London: Routledge, 2009) for a survey of scholarship on the historical novel and medievalism, especially 11–50 on the history of the historical novel. On the modern historical romance in the twentieth century, see 52–69, and then in the post-modern era, 97–103.

30. Robin first appears on film in Britain in 1908 (*Robin Hood and his Merry Men*) and 1912 in the USA (David Williams, "Medieval Movies," *The Yearbook of English Studies, Literature in the Modern Media: Radio, Film, and Television Special* 20, no. 5 (1990): 26). On Robin Hood in film in general, see, for example, J. Richards, "Robin Hood on the Screen," in *Robin Hood: An Anthology of Scholarship and Criticism*, ed. Steven Knight (Woodbridge: D. S. Brewer, 1999); Kevin Harty, "Robin Hood on Film: Moving beyond a Swashbuckling Stereotype," in *Robin Hood in Popular Culture: Violence, Transgression, and Justice*, ed. Thomas Hahn (Woodbridge: D. S. Brewer, 2000): 87–99; and Steven Knight, *Robin Hood: A Complete Study of the English Outlaw* (Oxford: Blackwell, 1994), 218–261.

31. See, for example, Leitch, "Adaptations without Sources," on the malleability of Robin Hood's story. He notes that for the past century Robin Hood films freely plunder the various aspects of the Robin Hood myth. See also Stapleford "Contemporary Idea of the Hero," on *Robin and Marian*; he also notes that critics of Lester's film compare Robin not to the original literary sources but rather 1938s *Adventures of Robin Hood* as their point of departure.

32. James Goldman, *Robin and Marian* (New York: Bantam Books, 1976), 6–13; 16–17. Goldman wrote both the screenplay and novelization of *Robin and Marian*; the latter combines script with prose, and is preceded by an essay on his thoughts on traditional heroes in the wake of American disillusionment with and distrust of authority and government after the Vietnam war and other contemporary crises. On *Robin and Marian*, see Harty, "Robin Hood on Film," 94–97 and Stapleford, "Contemporary Idea of the Hero," 182–187; the latter looks at Sean Connery's Robin as a case study of a contemporary hero.

33. Goldman, *Robin and Marian*, 17.

34. John Aberth, *A Knight at the Movies: Medieval History on Film* (New York and London: Routledge, 2003), 177–187.

35. Aberth, *A Knight*, 181.

36. Aberth, *A Knight*, 184–185; Knight, *Robin Hood*, 237–138.

37. Aberth, *A Knight*, 185; Harty, "Robin Hood on Film," 97–98; Richards 436–437.

38. Goldman, *Robin and Marian*, 146.

39. Goldman, *Robin and Marian*, 146.

40. Goldman, *Robin and Marian*, 146.
41. Goldman, *Robin and Marian*, 147.
42. David Coe, *Robin Hood: The Story Behind the Legend* (New York: Tor Books, 2010), 13–15.
43. Strickland, *Lives of the Queens of England*, 34–35.
44. Strickland, *Lives of the Queens of England*, 34–35.
45. Strickland, *Lives of the Queens of England*, 34.
46. See Michael Evans, "A Remarkable Woman?: Popular Historians and the Image of Eleanor of Aquitaine," in *Studies in Medievalism XVIII: Defining Medievalism(s) II*, ed. Karl Fugelso (Boydell and Brewer, 2009): 244–264.
47. Laurie A. Finke and Martin B. Shichtman, *Cinematic Illuminations: The Middle Ages on Film* (Baltimore: The Johns Hopkins Press, 2010): 97–98.
48. Finke and Shichtman, *Cinematic Illuminations*, 94.
49. Finke and Shichtman, *Cinematic Illuminations*, 103.
50. Finke and Shichtman, *Cinematic Illuminations*, 99.
51. Finke and Shichtman, *Cinematic Illuminations*, 102; James Goldman, *The Lion in Winter* (London: Samuel French, 1966), 2.
52. Finke and Shichtman, *Cinematic Illuminations*, 97.
53. See Vincent, "John's Jezebel," 196–197, on a brief discussion of the possible arrangement between John and his two queens. Although John cast aside his first wife on the grounds that she was too closely related (see note 3 above), he provided her with rooms in his household and maintained her upkeep; she and Isabella seemed to reside in at least one palace together.
54. Coe, *Robin Hood*, 15.
55. Cf. Coe, *Robin Hood*, 92–99.
56. Coe, *Robin Hood*, 92–99.
57. In Coe, *Robin Hood*, 182–187.
58. Coe, *Robin Hood*, 185.
59. Coe, *Robin Hood*, 183.
60. Coe, *Robin Hood*, 187.
61. Coe, *Robin Hood*, 291–294. Coe's novelization makes it very clear, without actually saying "Magna Carta," that it was Scott and Helgeland's intention that the audience assume this was meant to be seen as John facing down and rejecting a version of the baronial charter at the start of his reign (1199). To be fair, this scene takes dramatic licence with the facts, the episode roughly matches the historical record (see Matthew Paris, *Historia Anglorum* ii, 96–97), as John was met with complaints in early 1203 from his nobles for his spending sprees and inattention to affairs

of state. He dismissed their complaints, and, according to Matthew, continued to live in lazy luxury whilst roistering with his friends.

## BIBLIOGRAPHY

### Primary Sources

*Annales Monastici.* "Annales de Burton." Edited by H. R. Luard. 5 vols. London: The Rolls Series, 1864–1869.
Hoveden, Roger de, *Chronica Magistri Rogeri de Houedene.* Edited by W. Stubbs, 4 vols. London: Rolls Series, 1868–1871.
Paris, Matthew. *Matthaei Parisiensis, Monachi Sancti Albani, Chronica Majora.* Edited by H. R. Luard, 7 vols. London: Rolls Series, 1872–1883.
Paris, Matthew. *Matthaei Parisiensis, Monachi Sancti Albani, Historia Anglorum.* Edited by F. Madden, 3 vols. London: Rolls Series, 1866.
*The Chronicle of the Reigns of Henry II and Richard I, 1169–1192.* Edited by W. Stubbs, 2 vols. Rolls Series, 1867.
Wendover, Roger. *Rogeri de Wendover Liber qui dicitur Flores Historiarum.* Edited by H. G. Hewlett, 3 vols. London: Rolls Series, 1886–1889.

### Films

*Becket.* Feature Film. Directed by Peter Glenville. 1964. Orlando Park, IL: MPI Home Video, 2007. DVD.
*Robin and Marian.* Feature Film. Directed by Richard Lester. 1976. Culver City, CA: Sony Pictures Home Entertainment, 2002. DVD.
*Robin Hood.* Feature Film. Directed by Ridley Scott. Extended Director's Cut. London: Universal Pictures UK, 2010. DVD.
*The Lion in Winter.* Feature Film. Directed by Anthony Harvey. 1968. London: Studio Canal, 2008. DVD.

### Secondary Sources

Aberth, John. *A Knight at the Movies: Medieval History on Film.* New York and London: Routledge, 2003.
Beem, Charles. *The Lioness Roared: The Problems of Female Rule in English History.* New York: Palgrave Macmillan, 2006.
Bianciotto, Gabriel, et al (eds.). *Isabelle d'Angoulême: comtesse-reine et son temps (1186–1246).* Actes du colloque tenu à Lusignan du 8 au 10 novembre 1996. Poitiers: Universite du Poitiers, 1999.

Burstein, Miriam E. "The Reduced Pretensions of the Historic Muse": Agnes Strickland and the Commerce of Women's History." *The Journal of Narrative Technique* 28, no. 3 (1998): 219–242.

———. "From Good Looks to Good Thoughts: Popular Women's History and the Invention of Modernity, ca. 1839–1870," *Modern Philology* 97, no. 1 (1999): 46–75.

———. "'Unstoried in History'? Early Histories of Women (1652–1902) in the Huntington Library Collections." *Huntington Library Quarterly* 64, no. 3/4 (2001): 469–500.

Church, S. D. *King John: New Interpretations.* Woodbridge: Boydell Press, 1999.

Coe, David. *Robin Hood: The Story Behind the Legend.* New York: Tor Books, 2010.

Cook, Petronelle. *Queens Consort of England: The Power behind the Throne.* New York, 1993.

Curran, Cynthia. "Private Women, Public Needs: Middle-Class Widows in Victorian England." *Albion: A Quarterly Journal Concerned with British Studies* 25, no. 2 (1993): 217–236.

Dabby, Benjamin. "Hannah Lawrance and the Claims Of Women's History in Nineteenth-Century England." *The Historical Journal* 53, no. 3 (2010): 699–722.

De Groot, Jerome. *The Historical Novel.* London: Routledge, 2009.

De Saint Surin, Madame. *Isabelle d'Angoulême.* Paris, 1846.

Evans, Michael. "A Remarkable Woman? Popular Historians and the Image of Eleanor of Aquitaine." In *Studies in Medievalism XVIII: Defining Medievalism(s) II,* edited by Karl Fugelso, 244–264. Boydell and Brewer, 2009.

Finke, Laurie A. and Martin B. Shichtman. *Cinematic Illuminations: The Middle Ages on Film.* Baltimore: The Johns Hopkins Press, 2010.

Flori, Jean. *Eleanor of Aquitaine: Queen and Rebel,* Edinburgh University Press, 2008.

Fougère, Sophie. *Isabelle d'Angoulême, reine d'Angleterre.* Payre: Edit-France, 1998.

Goldman, J. *Robin and Marian: An Original Screenplay.* New York: Bantam Books, 1976.

———. *The Lion in Winter.* London: Samuel French, 1966.

Green, Mary Anne Everett. *Lives of the Princesses of England from the Norman Conquest.* London: Longman, 1857.

Hahn, Thomas, ed. *Robin Hood in Popular Culture: Violence, Transgression, and Justice.* Cambridge: D. S. Brewer, 2000.

Harty, Kevin. "Robin Hood on Film: Moving Beyond a Swashbuckling Stereotype." In *Robin Hood in Popular Culture: Violence, Transgression, and Justice,* edited by T. Hahn, 87–99. Cambridge: D. S. Brewer, 2000.

————. *The Reel Middle Ages: American, Western and Eastern European, Middle Eastern and Asian Films about Medieval Europe*. Jefferson, NC: McFarland, 2006.

Hilton, Lisa. *Queens Consort: England's Medieval Queens from Eleanor of Aquitaine to Elizabeth of York*. New York: Pegasus Books, 2010.

Jansen, Douglas C. "Women and Public Authority in the Thirteenth Century." In *Queens Regents, and Potentates*, edited by Theresa M. Vann, 91–105. Dallas: Academia, 1993.

Knight, Steven. *Robin Hood: A Complete Study of the English Outlaw*. Oxford: Blackwell, 1994.

————. ed. *Robin Hood: An Anthology of Scholarship and Criticism*. Woodbridge: D. S. Brewer, 1999.

Krueger, Christine L. "Why She Lived at the PRO: Mary Anne Everett Green and the Profession of History," *Journal of British Studies* 42, no. 1 (2003): 65–90.

Laurence, A. "Women Historians and Documentary Research: Lucy Aiken, Agnes Strickland, Mary Everett Green, and Lucy Toulmin Smith." In *Women Scholarship and Criticism*, edited by J. Bellamy, A. Laurence, and G. Perry, 125–142. Manchester: University of Manchester Press, 2000.

Leitch, Thomas. "Adaptations without Sources: The Adventures of Robin Hood," *Literature/Film Quarterly*. 36, no. 1 (2008): 21–30.

Lifshitz, Felice. "Destructive Dominae: Women and Vengeance in Medievalist Films." In *Studies in Medievalism XXI: Corporate Medievalism*, edited by Karl Fugelso. 1611–1690. Boydell and Brewer, 2012.

Maitzen, Rohan. "This Feminine Preserve: Historical Biographies by Victorian Women." *Victorian Studies* 38, no. 3 (1995): 371–393.

McLynn, Frank. *Richard and John: Kings at War*. Cambridge, MA: Da Capo Press, 2007.

Painter, Sidney. "The Houses of Lusignan and the Chatellerault," *Speculum* 30 (1955): 374–384.

Painter, Sidney. *The Reign of King John*. Baltimore: Johns Hopkins University Press, 1949.

Parsons, John Carmi. "Piety, Power, and the Reputations of Two Thirteenth-Century English Queens." In *Queens, Regents, and Potentates*, edited by Theresa M. Vann, 107–123. Dallas: Academia, 1993.

Pollard, A. J. *Imagining Robin Hood: The Late-Medieval Stories in Historical Context*. London: Routledge, 2004.

Reader, Rebecca. "Matthew Paris and Women." In *Thirteenth-Century England VII: The Proceedings of the Durham Conference*, edited by M. Prestone, R. Britnell, and R. Frame, 153–159. Woodbridge: The Boydell Press, 1997.

Richards, Jeffrey. "Robin Hood on the Screen." In *Robin Hood: Anthology of Scholarship and Criticism*, edited by Steven Knight, 429–467. Woodbridge: D. S. Brewer, 1999.

————. "Sir Ridley Scott and the Rebirth of the Historical Epic." In *The Return of the Epic Film: Genre, Aesthetics and History in the 21st Century*, edited by Andrew B. R. Elliott. 19–35. Edinburgh: Edinburgh University Press, 2014.

Richardson, H. G. "The Marriage and Coronation of Isabella of Angouleme," *English Historical Review* 241 (1946): 289–311.

Snellgrove, Harold. *The Lusignans in England 1247–1258*. Albuquerque: The University of New Mexico Press, 1950.

Stafford, Pauline. *Queens, Concubines, and Dowagers: The King's Wife in the Early Middle Ages*. Athens: University of Georgia Press, 1983.

Stapleford, Richard. "Robin Hood and the Contemporary Idea of the Hero." *Literature/Film Quarterly* 8, no. 3 (1980): 182–187.

Strickland, Agnes. 1850. *Lives of the Queens of England*. Philadelphia: Lea and Blanchard.

————. *Lives of the Queens of England* (preface by Antonia Fraser). London: Continuum, 2011.

Vaughan, Richard. *Matthew Paris*. Cambridge Studies in Medieval Life and Thought, New Series. Cambridge: Cambridge University Press, 1979.

Vincent, Nicholas. "Isabelle of Angoulême: John's Jezebel." In *King John: New Interpretations*, edited by S. D. Church Suffolk: The Boydell Press, 1999.

Warren, W. L. *King John*. London: Eyre and Spottiswoode, 1978.

Weiler, Björn. "Matthew Paris on the Writing of History," *Journal of Medieval History* 35, no. 3 (2009): 254–178.

Wilkinson, Louise J. "Maternal Abandonment and Surrogate Caregivers: Isabella of Angouleme and her Children," In *Virtuous or Villainous? The Image of the Royal Mother from the Early Medieval to the Early Modern Era*, edited by Carey Fleiner and Elena Woodacre, 101–24. New York: Palgrave, 2016.

Williams, David. "Medieval Movies," *The Yearbook of English Studies*, Vol. 20, Literature in the Modern Media: Radio, Film, and Television Special. 5, 1990: 1–32.

# CHAPTER 6

# Women's Weapons in *The White Queen*

## *Misty Urban*

From its inception, the ten-part TV series *The White Queen* took as its subject the theme of women's power and the strategies by which medieval women procured and preserved ruling power. Advertising itself as 'a riveting portrayal of one of the most dramatic and turbulent times in English history,' *The White Queen*, created and aired in 2013 by the BBC in Britain and in the USA by the cable channel Starz, tells the story of the Wars of the Roses through 'the perspective of three different, yet equally relentless women—Elizabeth Woodville, Margaret Beaufort and Anne Neville'—who, in 'their quest for power ... will scheme, manipulate and seduce their way onto the English throne'.[1] Underlining the promise of 'love and lust, seduction and deception, betrayal and murder,'[2] the cover art depicts the actress who plays Elizabeth Woodville, the titular White Queen, giving the viewer a sultry stare while clenching a sword in her bleeding fingers. The tagline asserts the primacy and power of women in this historical narrative by declaring: men go to battle, women wage war.

This *Desperate Housewives*–meets-*The Tudors* concept of medieval history bases its interpretation of this fourteenth-century English conflict on the bestselling Cousins' War series of historical novels by Philippa

M. Urban (✉)
Muscatine Community College, Muscatine, IA, USA

© The Author(s) 2018                                                                          111
J. North et al. (eds.), *Premodern Rulers and Postmodern Viewers*,
Queenship and Power, https://doi.org/10.1007/978-3-319-68771-1_6

Gregory, which focus on the lives of the ruling women of the time. But these advertising markers also illustrate an understanding of the medieval period that preserves nearly intact the set of assumptions about women's influence, women's agency, and women's tactics that primarily masculine, clerically trained medieval authors in fourteenth-century England most feared and railed against. By imagining that women exerted their power through select and suspect channels—and did so subtly, by manipulating men through sexual or maternal relationships, or by employing gossip or magic—the producers and writers of *The White Queen* capture a version of medieval history that reveals how limited—and how similar—the modern lexicon for understanding women's power is to medieval attitudes that viewed women's bodies and women's speech as weapons that could be used against male-authored structures of power, governance, and control.

That women would have had to work behind the scenes to influence events during the Wars of the Roses is a fact of the historical record, for women, as Gregory writes in the preface to *The Women of the Cousins' War*, 'were not seen as having a public nature; they were not often observed performing visible, significant, and historical acts'.[3] *The White Queen* makes some effort to capture the reality that medieval law made women dependent on their fathers, husbands, or male relatives; only a widow was a *femme sole* under the law. The limited scope given to women in the public realm led medieval chroniclers to regard the events of war, politics, and government as the activities of great men, while the doings of women were typically cast in one of two available female stereotypes, Mary or Eve.[4] One of Elizabeth Woodville's brief appearances in the historical record, in *Arrivall of Edward IV in England* (1471), describes her Marian-like suffering during her time in sanctuary at Westminster as 'right great trowble, sorow, and hevines, whiche she sustayned with all manner pacience that belonged to eny creature,' though she still managed to produce 'to the Kyngs greatyste joy, a fayre son, a prince'.[5] Margaret of Anjou, called a 'virago with the spirit of a man' in the *Great Chronicle of London* and 'mannish' by Polydore Vergil in his *Historia,* demonstrates how women who presumed to influence political events were viewed as usurping male authority.[6]

Yet despite decades of excellent feminist research that continues to explore the many roles women played in medieval history, modern makers and viewers of medieval film continue to believe that the scant public records and conventionalized appearances indicate that medieval women had no role at all beyond being 'victims or wives or mothers'.[7] As historian Jennifer Ward observes, 'When the sources are assessed and examined, there proves to be a wide range of evidence to show that noblewomen could and did play a vital role in late medieval society.'[8] But the understanding of medieval women among general modern audiences is much more limited. Actress Rebecca Ferguson distinguished her character, Elizabeth Woodville, from typical medieval noblewomen, expected to 'just sit back, do needlework and have babies,' and Brian Lowry, TV critic for *Variety*, wrote that medieval women 'are essentially ... props in the wars that men fight, there to be bartered, bedded and bred'.[9]

Emma Frost, the lead writer on the show, noted in an interview how she had to work against this assumption, insisting, 'It's tremendously important to actually excavate those stories and to recognize that these women were real players. They weren't just passive, faceless, voiceless women who didn't do anything.'[10] But *The White Queen*, following Gregory's mission to rescue the women 'hidden from history,'[11] reduces the range of medieval noblewomen's duties and experiences to strictly domestic and sexual roles, turning complex political events into a drama of the royal household. *USA Today* critic Maria Puente notes, 'Even royal women were constrained in the 15th century, so *The White Queen* tries to illuminate for a modern audience how they might have exerted their influence under these conditions.' What results is a narrative of 'royals behaving badly ... lying and scheming, stealing and torturing, loving and hating ... all in the same family'.[12] The spectacle of royal women behaving badly, said executive producer Colin Callendar in not so many words, was what made *The White Queen* an attractive project for Starz.[13]

It is not only modern audiences who enjoy the spectacle of women behaving outrageously, of course. Eve is of universal interest to medieval authors,[14] and narratives of destructive women populated Boccaccio's *De mulieribus claris* (*On Famous Women*, c.1361–1374) well before Joan of Arc (1412–1431) offered a contemporary example of a shocking, tragic life. Shakespeare's first tetralogy, *Henry VI Parts One* through *Three* and *Richard III* (c.1590–1593), gives the female characters active and varied roles in between long orations and battles waged by the men.[15] But literature of the subsequent centuries tends to perpetuate flattened portraits of the key women of the War of the Roses; Margaret of Anjou remains the 'she-wolf' Shakespeare called her, Elizabeth Woodville is a vain and grasping parvenu, and Margaret Beaufort remains the near-saint sketched by Tudor propagandists.[16] Gregory is praised by critics for 'breathing passionate, independent life into the historical noblewomen whose personalities had previously lain flat on family trees, remembered only as diplomatic currency and brood mares'.[17] The questions of vital concern, then as now, were how women exerted influence and to what end. It is in this discussion that the vocabulary of medieval women's power in *The White Queen* becomes confused with, and limited by, modern beliefs.

Part of *The White Queen*'s appeal is the subversion of accepted scripts about gendered power. As the tagline suggests, the TV series grants men the active, public, but limited field of battle, while women plot the deeper strategies of war. Actor David Oakes, who plays George, Duke of Clarence, observes that in *The White Queen*, 'The women are the movers and shakers—they're the strong ones. The men are at their whim.'[18] Gregory, herself a historian, admits that medieval women exercise power in 'individual and subtle ways,'[19] and Ward likewise suggests that a more delicate 'persuasion was the acceptable way for women of all social groups to take action'.[20] Even for the woman at the pinnacle of the political structure, the queen, Ward admits that 'her authority and influence stemmed from her roles as wife and mother'.[21] To wield their will, Ward says, women 'might use stratagem, open conflict, or siege in their attempts to achieve their ends'.[22]

*The White Queen* shows its specific brand of gendered movie medievalism in assuming that these subtler weapons are the more effective ones. Groomed on an ethos of individual achievement and the primacy of the will, post-feminist audiences expect women to make their own choices about their career and their sexual partner—to behave as 'strong, determined women who take their fate into their own hands'.[23] There is also a strong history of TV viewership for soapy melodramas and their 'intense, competitive, woman-on-woman psychodramas'.[24] Modern audiences expect that medieval women shared their same motives and desires, and would use their presumably far more limited means to achieve the familiar purposes of partner selection, acquisition of personal influence, and material security, as well as preservation of their loved ones. Exerting their will in limited circumstances becomes a point of admiration; Gregory says of her heroines that they were 'courageous and determined and went through extraordinary danger ... They conquered the circumstances they were born into and made a life for themselves, which is a very modern and quite feminist theme.'[25]

That its focus on women's agency made it a particularly 'feminist' series surrounded press on *The White Queen*, with critics describing it as a 'fun period piece ... with a feminist slant,'[26] as having a 'sexy, feminist spin' in its focus on 'three kickass women and their fight for power in the court,'[27] or offering a 'decidedly feminine perspective'[28] along with a 'feminine take on history ... about a fight for survival and power'.[29] This language reveals how Western audiences use 'feminist' and 'feminine' interchangeably to indicate 'features or is about women,' and the confusion, particularly about what constitutes the 'feminine,' seems lifted directly from the oft-rehearsed medieval misogyny enshrined in works like Chaucer's *Wife of Bath's Tale* describing women's interests, power, and tactics. Critic Alison Willmore observes that the 'weapons' allowed *The White Queen*'s women are 'ones of words, court politics, alliances, seduction and manipulation,' echoing the assessment by the series' lead writer, Emma Frost, that 'the women have a different arsenal of weapons'. While 'the men go out on a field and whack at each other with a sword, very testosterone-fueled and immediate ... the women, as now, have to find a more subtle way of pulling the strings and getting what they want,' Frost says. In the same interview, Frost elaborates on the female 'arsenal': 'through wit and a better psychological understanding the women have ... they think several steps ahead. There's a network of language and gossip and rumor that they manipulate, and when appropriate, they manipulate the men sexually.'[30] Modern writers attribute the same weapons to women that medieval authors did; they simply imagine a reception by the audience that is delighted rather than horrified.

In celebrating this type of power, *The White Queen* betrays another signature move in the movie medievalism repertoire, and that is to firmly limit what agency women might have to interior, personal, and domestic venues. The gendering of public and private realms was in its nascent stages in the later European Middle Ages,[31] and the modern distinction between the private and public, male and female, is a residue of the highly articulated nineteenth-century separate spheres ideology with its domesticated angel of the house, perpetuated in the pearl-wearing suburban housewife of 1950s America. Ward acknowledges that in England, after the rebellions of Eleanor of Aquitaine and Isabella of France, even queens were 'rarely active in politics,' their position mostly 'ceremonial'.[32] But medieval noblewomen were accustomed to overseeing their properties and running households; queens had a council, officers, and servants including personal attendants, knights, grooms, and

116    M. URBAN

pages on their payroll. Noblewomen could be feoffees of their own or their children's estates and arbitrate disputes; Elizabeth Woodville had a place on her son Edward's council, and Margaret Beaufort, after her son's ascension, owned property in her own name.[33] J. L. Laynesmith notes that while duties of intercession had declined in the later Middle Ages, queens still had a deeply symbolic role and the 'power to complement, legitimize, and enrich her husband's kingship'.[34] Margaret of Anjou, Elizabeth Woodville, and Margaret Beaufort all served as benefactors of chapels and colleges and as patronesses of religious organizations and artistic endeavors like the new printing press.[35] None of this plays a role in the portrayal of these women either in Gregory's novels or the TV series, which instead focus on their function as wives and mothers. In *The White Queen*, even the women at the peak of the social hierarchy, who would have had the largest public responsibilities, are limited in their power plays to the strategies of sex, manipulation, gossip, magic, and maternity.

This compression of character serves a narrative purpose in eliciting identification from the audience, certainly; series writer Emma Frost thinks that the interest 'does come down to the personal details of these women's lives, which are about love and loss and betrayal and having kids and losing a parent and all of those kinds of things'.[36] But in employing this dramatic lens, *The White Queen* perpetuates a limited understanding among modern viewers about the roles and function of medieval noblewomen and the kind of thinking that makes 'feminine' a synonym for 'nefarious' or 'underhanded'. In imagining that the 'real' action behind historical events is orchestrated behind the scenes by powerful and ruthless women, works like *The White Queen* do not extend the modern imagination of women's power beyond the terminus of medieval misogyny, which is to blame women, starting with Eve, for all the bloodshed and mayhem.

The only real difference, as noted, is one of reception. While premodern audiences were presumably horrified by Margaret of Anjou's daring to lead an army, modern audiences are invited to cheer bloodthirsty behavior from their female leads. Following the story told in Antonio Cornazzano in *De mulieribus admirandis* (c.1468),[37] Elizabeth, in episode one of the series, refuses to let Edward rape her and holds his own dagger to her throat, threatening to kill herself, Lucretia-like, if he does not desist. 'Don't doubt my courage, your Grace,' she challenges him. 'I am a match for any man.'[38] The scene signals to modern viewers that

Elizabeth possesses an independent mind and sees herself the equal of any man, even the king, just as the modern female viewer would.

The same marital spirit is expressed by Margaret Beaufort, who wishes she could join in an upcoming battle like her heroine, Joan of Arc. 'I wish I could ride beside you and fight myself,' Margaret says to Jasper Tudor when Warwick's rebellion is forming. Jasper, in what modern audiences would take for a compliment, replies, 'You have the courage of any man. You are a soldier.'[39] This expression of gender equality, at least in fierceness, is not exclusively a modern move; one need only recall Beatrice's passionate outburst in *Much Ado about Nothing*: 'O God that I were a man! I would eat his heart in the market place.'[40] But in picturing its female leads as gifted with masculine courage, the series' writers demonstrate the medieval thinking that named Margaret of Anjou a 'virago' because she did not behave as a suitably helpless, beset-upon female.

This presumed medieval ideology is best communicated by Margaret Beaufort's mother, Lady Beauchamp, who chides Margaret when she mutters about her arranged marriage: 'You are a girl. You do not choose. You live the live your mother chooses for you, or your husband.'[41] The Neville women share this helplessness. 'We are their pieces on a board,' Isabel Neville laments to Anne.[42] As Warwick plots his rebellion, the Countess of Warwick acknowledges the vulnerable situation in which his actions put his womenfolk: 'We must all of us support him and just pray to God that he is successful in this venture. God help us all if he is not.'[43] When Anne is promised to Edward of Lancaster as the next step in her father's scheme, her mother reminds her, 'What we want, what we need is of no importance. The sooner you understand that and realize that your fate will always be in the hands of others, the better.' She counsels her daughter, upon her marriage, 'Play your part, Anne. Please your husband and your new queen.'[44]

Such depictions play to the understanding of medieval women among general audiences, as expressed by TV critic Mary McNamara, that 'a woman's body was both her greatest tool and her inevitable prison'; while 'a man could control his fate by mind or sword, a woman can do it only by proxy'.[45] This assumption allows the female leads to demonstrate their character and invite audience sympathy by employing tactics of self-assertion, part of the celebrated 'feminist' ethos. Anne Neville, newly widowed, tells Richard of Gloucester, 'I have learned to rely only on myself,' despite being imprisoned by George and Isabel.[46] This independence makes the women desirable both to modern viewers and to their historical spouses. Richard proposes directly after Anne's declaration of self-reliance; Edward decides he must have Elizabeth through marriage once his assault is unsuccessful; and Margaret Beaufort, widowed by Warwick's rebellion, negotiates her next marriage with Thomas Stanley on her own.[47]

In the face of female self-assertion, the men convey a sense of being managed and often flounder to exert their presumed authority. Richard Woodville, Baron Rivers, admits that his wife, the formidable Jacquetta, sometimes scares him,[48] while poor, henpecked Henry Stafford begs his wife, Margaret Beaufort, to obey: 'For once, for once please do as I ask.'[49] When evidence emerges that Margaret was involved in planning the Duke of Buckingham's rebellion, her third husband, Stanley, says with a shrug to King Richard, 'I must reprimand my wife. I thought she'd respond to my authority, but...'[50] Further, the male characters who do not understand that the women are truly in charge come to bad ends. Warwick establishes his antipathy to female influence early, when he snarls upon sight of a portrait of Margaret of Anjou: 'Burn it. I will have no truck with a queen who thought to rule her husband, and rule England through him.'[51] George, Duke of Clarence, who complains that his brother is ruled by his wife—'Edward simply does what she tells him,' he complains; 'She has England's high command'[52]—meets his end in a vat of malmsey wine. Both men, in resisting Elizabeth's influence, find themselves undone by her greater power and strategic ability.

This primacy of the individual will is a motif of the series, and is pitched as a woman's particular struggle against a culture that seeks to constrain her. Quite in opposition to the Countess of Warwick's counsel to her daughters, Jacquetta Woodville advises her daughter Elizabeth, 'You may have whatever you want *if* you will take the consequences.'[53] Margaret Beaufort shows the same implacable spirit when she tells her son, 'Never give up' as she sends him to his years of exile in Brittany. 'I won't,' she vows.[54] But while valorizing this modern brand of self-assertion, The White Queen still retains the stereotyped evaluations of its sources. Margaret of Anjou, the most daring of all the women depicted in the series, receives no applause for her courage. Other characters call her a 'whore,' a 'she-devil,' and 'the bad queen,' little better than Vergil's 'pseudo-man' or Shakespeare's 'she-wolf of France'.[55] She is costumed in red, wears a breastplate while her army is on the march, and, in her entrances on-screen, the camera captures first the snake-like hiss of her skirts across the floor. Though she exhibits a refusal to surrender at Tewkesbury and her aspiration is no different than that of the other three female leads—she wishes to put her son on the throne, and rule through him—Margaret alone is both defeated and reviled for her ambition. The only explanation seems to be that she chose the masculine, marital approach to power rather than adhering to the traditional women's weapons—seduction, manipulation, lies, and secret murder—which, in the hands of the other female protagonists, are far more successful means to accomplishing their will.

Sexual expression is another point through which modern audiences are expected to enjoy the transgression of norms on the part of their characters. But while the 'sexiness' and nudity were presumably one of the selling points of *The White Queen*, according to the press,[56] the show itself preserves a pit-and-pedestal thinking about sex that betrays a medieval inheritance. Directors of the frequent and varied sex scenes use the woman-on-top position to demonstrate their characters' confidence in their sexual relations, yet overall there is far less sexual manipulation going on than the promotional copy suggests, and far more adherence to modern conventions surrounding sex and romance. The clearest example of this is Elizabeth and Edward's marriage. Rather than portraying Elizabeth as a scheming widow who seduced a randy and impetuous young man, episode one pictures an instant and mutual sexual attraction between the two. Pressed to fight off the king with a dagger, Elizabeth is more seduced than seducer, while Edward proposes with the declaration 'I *must* have you … I am mad for you.' Chosen, pursued, and vindicated when Edward announces their marriage to the court, Elizabeth plays the receptive role in their courtship and is rewarded with a queenship, plenty of enthusiastic sex, the kind of companionate marriage imagined as the modern ideal, and deathbed declarations that theirs was 'true love'.[57] This is not seduction or manipulation but consenting and mutually pleasurable relations between mature adults.

The other women desire a similar version of modern romance. Despite her mother's description of marriage as a duty to benefit the family, Isabel Neville hopes to love and be loved by her husband, George. Anne experiences marital rape on her wedding night with Edward of Lancaster, but is later rewarded with Richard, who offers her both love and fidelity: 'I will be a true husband, because I love you,' he vows. Even Margaret Beaufort, who insists that her third marriage be chaste, bows to the modern viewer's incredulity that any healthy woman would want to avoid sex and presents herself, nightgowned and loose-haired, to her new husband on their wedding night. Stanley, to her evident embarrassment, heeds their agreement.[58]

Previously, Margaret was more successful in her seduction tactics when she offered sex to her husband, Stafford, so that he would escort her to visit her mother, whereupon she manipulates her half-brother into joining Warwick's rebellion and thereby shortens his life. In a different seduction, Princess Elizabeth visits Richard III in his tent the night before the Battle of Bosworth, offering herself to him out of love, despite the fact that he is her uncle. Elizabeth imagines that if Richard is successful, he will marry her, never mind the difficulties of securing a papal dispensation for incest. The scene seems designed to affirm Elizabeth's agency and independence, but it plays to the modern belief that sexual forwardness is licensed by love but not by ambition. At any rate, both seductions lead to a death, in keeping with medieval warnings against promiscuity.

One weapon available to the women of *The White Queen* that is not familiar to the modern viewer is the use of magic. Like sexuality, this weapon is depicted with an attitude that uncomfortably balances modern skepticism with medieval belief. Gregory sees a belief in magic as key to the medieval mindset,[59] and her characters use it as a form of female manipulation. There is one small and early gesture toward acknowledging medieval apprehensions about this particular tactic: 'Magic!' Elizabeth Woodville scolds her mother in episode one. 'Do you want to be drowned on a ducking stool? It is forbidden!'[60] But elsewhere, magic is regarded as a sort of divine inheritance for the Woodville women: 'We are descended from the river goddess Melusina,' Jacquetta tells her daughter. 'Magic is in our blood.'[61] The viewer is not expected to know the distinctions between the kinds of white magic Jacquetta employs— love charms or divination, like scrying in a mirror—and *maleficium*, magic considered to work by diabolical agency, which was punishable under fifteenth-century law.[62] Rather, the magic is treated as a metaphor for and extension of female will, and the consequence of its use in *The White Queen* is to imply, as medieval authors feared, that unrestrained female power is an inimical force.

Denied access to the traditional weapons of war, the women use magic as a means for furthering their ends. In a chilling scene, Margaret Beaufort, alone at prayer, blows out five burning candles that represent the five lives standing between her son Henry and the throne. Two of the candles signify the princes in the tower. Throughout the series,

Jacquetta, Elizabeth Woodville, and the young Princess Elizabeth influence the weather as a means of self-protection. The women blow up a storm to hinder Warwick from gaining access to Calais and raising a rebellion against Edward; they raise a mist at Barnet so Warwick's forces will be confused and overcome; and they cause the rains that flood the rivers, spoiling the Duke of Buckingham's rebellion and keeping Henry Tudor offshore. Deaths result, but the only harm to the spell-casters is Elizabeth's guilt when she learns that Isabel Neville was on the ship to Calais and the storm caused the stillbirth of her child.

The spells she undertakes out of vengeance are the ones Elizabeth is warned will rebound on her, and they do. When Warwick executes her father and brother, Elizabeth writes two names in blood and puts the paper in a charm she wears around her neck. The curse works; Warwick dies at Barnet, and George is executed for a traitor. A later curse on Richard is more instantly efficacious: his sword arm pains him; his child dies; his wife fades away. But her conviction that Elizabeth is a powerful witch leads Anne to urge Richard to depose Edward V, seize the throne himself, and execute Anthony Woodville and Elizabeth's son Richard Grey. The wish for death produces more death; reaping what one sows is a Christian proverb as familiar to modern audiences as medieval ones.

The darkest statement on female power and weapons seems made by the insinuation that Elizabeth's most powerful curse hurts her own family the most. Alone at night by the river, Elizabeth and her eldest daughter ask their ancestress Melusina to curse the murderer of Edward V with the loss of his firstborn son, and that son's firstborn, until the line dies out—the desperate plea of trapped, grieving women. But in this version of events, Margaret Beaufort is to blame for the death of the princes, and Elizabeth of York was promised to Henry Tudor when the two former enemies joined forces against Richard. Elizabeth does not seem to foresee this connection, though her daughter does.[63] Magic, as a metaphor for female power, is regarded as treacherous, fearful, limitless, and undefeatable—the Neville girls continually fear what the 'witch' will do to their children—but Elizabeth's magic is never offered as a convincing explanation for events. It is just as likely that Edward marries her at his own initiative, keeps the throne through his own prowess, and would have sired an heir eventually. After his death, Elizabeth best protects her family through shrewd negotiation and bargaining tactics. Among the traditional women's weapons, magic does as little good as seduction. Of the women supposedly controlling events, only Margaret Beaufort ends up with what she wants—to put her son on the throne and become

Margaret Regina—and her repertoire includes alliances, subterfuge, trea-
son, rebellion, and murder.

The most direct route to power for the women of *The White Queen*
is through childbirth. The most potent weapon in the female arsenal,
by far, is maternal blood. In episode after episode, *The White Queen*
obsesses on the need for noblewomen to have sons. Production of a
male heir is regarded as a medieval woman's highest achievement, and
his succession secures her material preservation and political influence.
Elizabeth best articulates this logic; when she sees court factions forming against her, she turns to Jacquetta with the desperate plea, 'I must
have a son,' hoping her mother's magic will help her secure Edward's
kingship from threat.[64] When Edward dies, Elizabeth tells her brother
Anthony, 'I must have my son the king to protect me.'[65] And when her
daughter accuses her of cold-hearted ambition, Elizabeth explains the
rules of succession: 'If you have the heirs, you hold all the power.'[66]
In their competition to put their sons on the throne, the female leads of
*The White Queen* condense modern understandings of medieval women
to a single role: that of mother.

Historically, a noblewoman's chief function *was* to bear heirs, and
the stakes were doubled for a queen, since 'heirs were perceived to be
signs of divine approval of their kingship'.[67] The series' writers trans-
late this into the idea that manufacturing an heir makes a royal couple
'safe' on the throne—that is, secure from threat of rebellion or deposition. When Edward first brings his new bride to court, he takes her to
bed with the racy suggestion, 'Let's start our dynasty. Let us make a
son to scotch the Lancastrian threat.'[68] 'Shall we be safe, you and I,
on the throne?' Elizabeth asks, aware of what happened to her predecessor. 'When we have a son,' Edward assures her, 'we will be safe.'
Jacquetta confirms this, warning Elizabeth, 'You must have sons to
protect yourself from Warwick.'[69] Warwick himself, though without
his own male issue, subscribes to the same logic; plotting his rebellion, he complains of Elizabeth to his wife: 'She has no son yet! She
will *not* win.'[70] And Edward, captured by Warwick, writes to his wife,
'If George has a son, we are lost,'[71] for presumably the signal of divine
favor would shift all loyalty to him—never mind the fact that, previously, Margaret of Anjou's son did not stop the Yorks from challenging
Henry VI.

This extremely simplified but dramatically focused view that who-
ever has the heirs wins in the great chess game of king-making leads to

competitive birthing between the female leads and, when the writers feel
it necessary, changes to the historical record. Isabel Neville's firstborn
was a short-lived girl named Anne, but in the film the child is a still-
born son, killed by the storm Elizabeth magically raised. George coldly
informs his bleeding and devastated wife, 'The queen is pregnant again.
We must have a son before she does.'[72] Keeping the competition lively,
the end of episode four juxtaposes scenes of Elizabeth giving birth to
Prince Edward with Margaret Beaufort presenting her son to the read-
epted Henry VI, suggesting that the real battle for royal power lies not
between kings but between the women bringing forth kings.

This emphasis that it is mothers who put sons on the throne both
heightens the theme of female power and contradicts the presumed reality that women are pawns in a larger game. Perhaps unmarried girls are
pieces on a board, but reproductive women are a formidable force. In
disapproving of Edward's marriage to a commoner, his mother, Duchess
Cecily, threatens Elizabeth: 'I could disown him. I could put his brother
George on the throne in his place.'[73] This seems a curious threat considering it was not descent but a series of battles that gained Edward IV the
throne. Likewise, Margaret Beaufort insists throughout the series that
her son is 'direct Lancastrian heir,'[74] even though the historical Henry's
claim was somewhat tangled; the Beauforts had been barred from succession by Henry V, so Henry's claim on the Tudor side was through
Henry V's widow, Catherine of Valois.[75] Nevertheless, *The White Queen*
insists that the woman, the mother, confers the legitimacy of the son and
his claim to kingship.

There is something cruel in this craving for sons considering how very
many of these women watch their sons die. Losing her son John is the
blow that breaks Jacquetta's heart and leads to her death. The loss of her
Prince Edward crushes Margaret of Anjou's ambitions, and she stum-
bles from Tewkesbury Abbey howling in pain. Duchess Cecily sees two
sons on the throne, but is not able to save her favorite even though she
pleads on her knees to Edward for George's life. 'I am your mother!'
she shouts at him. 'I am the king!' Edward shouts back.[76] Poor Anne
Neville, already ill from watching her husband flirt with his niece, lives to
see the death of the prized boy she thought would secure Richard's kingship by becoming Prince of Wales. And Elizabeth, after losing her son
Richard Grey and seeing Edward V imprisoned, only manages to save
the life of Prince Richard by sending him off to Flanders to become
Perkin Warbeck. Among these powerful and relentlessly scheming

women, Margaret Beaufort's son achieves the throne only at the cost of all these other young lives, so many snuffed candles.

Yet, for all the focus on their sons, the series ends as it began, with the hint that queenship is the primary ambition of these highborn women. Margaret wants to enthrone her son not because God wills it, as she claims, but because she wants to become My Lady the King's Mother, Margaret Regina. The series closes on the scene of the Dowager Queen Elizabeth regarding her eldest daughter and realizing, 'You will marry Henry Tudor, and you will be Queen of England, as I once was.'[77] (Gregory's version of the reign of Elizabeth of York is the subject of Starz's *The White Princess*, which premiered in April 2017.) The story's central question of who will get to be queen next gives the series dramatic unity, but while it flattens modern understandings of medieval women to purely sexual and maternal roles, it likewise reduces medieval queenship to the wearing of pretty gowns and scheming against rivals rather than an office of dignity, responsibility, and great influence.

*The White Queen* attempts a convincing and appealing vision of intelligent, resourceful women using the means available to them to protect themselves and their families in turbulent times. But it limits its vocabulary for women's power by falling into the public/private, masculine/feminine divide in which modern audiences live. In restricting women to purely domestic, behind-the-scenes roles, reducing what power they did have then or now to their influence over men through sex or maternity or magic, the modern conception of the medieval gives less latitude to women than the medieval period did. This emphasis on sexuality and maternity as a medieval woman's only means of agency panders to modern conundrums that cannot reconcile the public and the domestic and, furthermore, demonstrates our modern fidelity to deeply held premodern suspicions about the dangers of female bodies and speech. The message of *The White Queen* that female ambition is manifestly destructive makes all its lead characters into a type of Eve, pursuing their own and their family's advancement at the cost of bloodshed and mayhem. In this light, the terms for conceptualizing and evaluating women's power have not shifted significantly from the premodern to the present. The depictions in *The White Queen* rather demonstrate how familiar these literary and historical stereotypes about women are to modern audiences. Only when our own lexicon of women's power expands will modern audiences be able to truly appreciate the complexity of medieval women's lives and accede women real equality in our own historical moment.

## NOTES

1. *Starz Entertainment LLC*, "The White Queen: Series Info," accessed 28 April 2017. https://www.starz.com/series/thewhitequeen/episodes/info.
2. *IMDb.com*, "The White Queen," accessed 29 January 2017. http://www. imdb.com/title/tt2372220/.
3. Philippa Gregory, David Baldwin, and Michael Jones, *Women of the Cousins' War: The Duchess, the Queen, and the King's Mother* (New York: Simon & Schuster, 2011), 24.
4. Jennifer C. Ward, *English Noblewomen in the Later Middle Ages* (New York: Longman, 1992), 2–3, 34; Gregory, *Women of the Cousins' War*, 19–20; see also Gregory, "History vs. Herstory," author website, last modified September 30, 2013. http://www.philippagregory.com/news/news/217.
5. David Baldwin, *Elizabeth Woodville: Mother of the Princes in the Tower* (Stroud: Sutton Publishing, 2002), 50.
6. Kavita Mudan Finn, *The Last Plantagenet Consorts: Gender, Genre, and Historiography, 1440–1627*, Queenship and Power (New York: Palgrave Macmillan, 2012), 36, 54.
7. Jolie Lash, "Starz Announces Premiere Date for The White Queen," *Access Hollywood*, May 23, 2013. https://www.accesshollywood.com/articles/starz-announces-premiere-date-for-the-white-queen-133107/.
8. Ward, *English Noblewomen*, 3.
9. Ferguson quoted in Michael Logan, "Starz's *The White Queen* Puts a Sexy, Feminist Spin on England's Wars of the Roses," *TV Guide*, last modified August 5, 2013, http://www.tvguide.com/news/starz-white-queen-1068891/; Brian Lowry, "Review: The White Queen," *Variety*, last modified August 5, 2013, http://variety.com/2013/tv/reviews/the-white-queen-review-starz-1200573007/.
10. Tierney Sneed, "With 'The White Queen,' Starz Bets on a Woman's Point of View," *US News*, August 7, 2013. http://www.usnews.com/news/articles/2013/08/07/with-the-white-queen-starz-bets-on-a-womans-point-of-view.
11. Gregory, *Cousin's War*, 4, 32.
12. Puente, "The White Queen."
13. Sneed, "Woman's Point of View."
14. John Flood, *Representations of Eve in Antiquity and the English Middle Ages* (New York: Routledge, 2011).
15. Tina Packer, *Women of Will: The Remarkable Evolution of Shakespeare's Female Characters* (New York: Vintage Books, 2015), 48.
16. See, for example, Agnes and Elizabeth Strickland, *Lives of the Queens of England* (London: H. Colburn, 1854); Charlotte Yonge, *Biographies*

*of Good Women*, Second Series (London: J. and C. Mozley, 1865); and Mary Shelley, *The Fortunes of Perkin Warbeck* (London: H. Colburn and R. Bentley, 1830).

17. Helen Brown, "The White Princess, by Philippa Gregory, review," *The Telegraph*, last modified August 1, 2013. http://www.telegraph.co.uk/culture/books/10209224/The-White-Princess-by-Philippa-Gregory-review.html.
18. "Bonus: Series Overview," *The White Queen*. (Meridian, CO: Starz, 2014).
19. Puente, "The White Queen."
20. Ward, *Women in England in the Middle Ages* (New York: Continuum, 2006), 120
21. Ward, *Women in England*, 119.
22. Ward, *Women in England*, 112.
23. Kate Mosse writing in *The Financial Times*, review excerpted on Gregory's website, accessed January 29 2017. http://www.philippagregory.com/books/the-white-queen/reviews.
24. Camille Paglia, *Free Women, Free Men: Sex, Gender, Feminism* (NY: Pantheon, 2017), 263.
25. Lash, "Premiere Date for White Queen."
26. Joanne Ostrow, "'The White Queen' Review: Starz Series is Sexy, Empowering, and Violent," *The Denver Post*, last modified August 8, 2013. http://www.denverpost.com/2013/08/08/the-white-queen-review-starz-series-is-sexy-empowering-and-violent/.
27. Logan, "Starz's The White Queen."
28. Lowry, "Review: The White Queen."
29. Alison Willmore, "'The White Queen' Writer Emma Frost on Sex, Historical Accuracy and Making the Real 'Game of Thrones,'" *IndieWire*, last modified August 9, 2013. http://www.indiewire.com/2013/08/the-white-queen-writer-emma-frost-on-sex-historical-accuracy-and-making-the-real-game-of-thrones-35943/.
30. Willmore, "Writer Emma Frost."
31. Misty Schieberle, *Feminized Counsel and the Literature of Advice in England, 1380–1500* (Turnhout, Belgium: Brepols, 2014), 9.
32. Ward, *Women in England*, 133.
33. See J. L. Laynesmith, *The Last Medieval Queens: English Queenship, 1445–1503* (New York: Oxford University Press, 2004) for an exploration of a queen's public and private duties; Gregory, *The Women of the Cousins' War*, for public roles of these featured women; and David Baldwin, *Elizabeth Woodville*, for Elizabeth's public duties.
34. Laynesmith, *Last Medieval Queens*, 139, 74.
35. Jones, *Women of the Cousins' War*, 314.

36. Willmore, "Writer Emma Frost."
37. Finn, *Last Plantagenet Consorts*, 20.
38. Emma Frost, "In Love with the King," *The White Queen* (hereafter *TWQ*), episode 1, directed by James Kent, BBC/Starz, aired August 10, 2013 on Starz.
39. Emma Frost, "The Storm," *TWQ*, episode 3, directed by James Kent, BBC/Starz, aired August 24, 2013 on Starz.
40. *Much Ado About Nothing*, in *The Norton Shakespeare*, ed. Stephen Greenblatt et al. (New York: W.W. Norton, 1997), 4.1.303–304.
41. Emma Frost, "The Price of Power," *TWQ*, episode 2, directed by James Kent, BBC/Starz, aired August 17, 2013 on Starz.
42. *TWQ*, episode 3.
43. *TWQ*, episode 3.
44. Lisa McGee, "The Bad Queen," *TWQ*, episode 4, directed by Jamie Payne, BBC/Starz, aired September 7, 2013 on Starz.
45. Mary McNamara, "'The White Queen' Courts Confusion," *Los Angeles Times*, August 10, 2013. http://articles.latimes.com/2013/aug/10/ entertainment/la-et-st-white-queen-review-20130810.
46. Nicole Taylor, "Love and Death," *TWQ*, episode 6, directed by Jamie Payne, BBC/Starz, aired September 21, 2013 on Starz.
47. *TWQ*, episode 6.
48. Emma Frost, "In Love with the King," *TWQ*, episode 1, directed by James Kent, BBC/Starz, aired August 10, 2013 on Starz.
49. Malcolm Campbell, "War at First Hand," *TWQ*, episode 5, directed by Jamie Payne, BBC/Starz, aired September 14, 2013 on Starz.
50. Emma Frost, "The Princes in the Tower," *TWQ*, episode 9, directed by Colin Teague, BBC/Starz, aired October 19, 2013 on Starz.
51. *TWQ*, episode 2.
52. Emma Frost, "Poison and Malmsey," *TWQ*, episode 7, directed by Colin Teague, BBC/Starz, aired September 28, 2013 on Starz.
53. *TWQ*, episode 1.
54. *TWQ*, episode 5.
55. Gregory, *Women of the Cousin's War*, 25 and on her website, "Margaret d'Anjou," accessed January 31, 2017. http://www.philippagregory.com/family-tree/margaret-d-anjou.
56. Logan, "Sexy, Feminist Spin."
57. Malcolm Campbell, "Long Live the King," *TWQ*, episode 8, directed by Colin Teague, BBC/Starz, aired October 5, 2013 on Starz.
58. *TWQ*, episode 6.
59. Logan, "Sexy, Feminist Spin."
60. *TWQ*, episode 1.
61. *TWQ*, episode 1.

62. Gary K. Waite, *Heresy, Magic, and Witchcraft in Early Modern Europe* (New York: Palgrave Macmillan, 2003), 16, 12.
63. Emma Frost, "The Final Battle," *TWQ*, episode 10, directed by Colin Teague, BBC/Starz, aired October 19, 2013 on Starz. This is the titular curse of Gregory's *The King's Curse* (New York: Simon & Schuster, 2014).
64. *TWQ*, episode 3.
65. *TWQ*, episode 8.
66. *TWQ*, episode 8.
67. Ward, *Women in England*, throughout; Laynesmith, *Last Medieval Queens*, 110.
68. *TWQ*, episode 1.
69. *TWQ*, episode 2.
70. *TWQ*, episode 2.
71. *TWQ*, episode 2.
72. *TWQ*, episode 3.
73. *TWQ*, episode 1.
74. *TWQ*, episode 9.
75. Jones, *Women of the Cousins' War*, 253–254.
76. *TWQ*, episode 7.
77. *TWQ*, episode 10.

## BIBLIOGRAPHY

Baldwin, David. *Elizabeth Woodville: Mother of the Princes in the Tower*. Stroud, Gloucestershire: Sutton Publishing, 2002.

"Bonus: Series Overview." *The White Queen*. Meridian, CO: Starz, 2014. *The White Queen*. Season 1. Directed by James Kent, Jamie Payne, and Colin Teague. Meridian, CO: Starz Entertainment LLC, 2013.

Finn, Kavita Mudan. *The Last Plantagenet Consorts: Gender, Genre, and Historiography, 1440–1627*. Queenship and Power. New York: Palgrave Macmillan, 2012.

Gregory, Philippa. *The King's Curse*. New York: Simon & Schuster, 2014.

———. *The Kingmaker's Daughter*. New York: Simon & Schuster, 2012.

———. *The Lady of the Rivers*. New York: Simon & Schuster, 2011.

———. *The Red Queen*. New York: Simon & Schuster, 2010.

———. *The White Princess*. New York: Simon & Schuster, 2013.

———. *The White Queen*. New York: Simon & Schuster, 2009.

———, David Baldwin, and Michael Jones. *The Women of the Cousins' War: The Duchess, the Queen, and the King's Mother*. New York: Simon & Schuster, 2011.

Jones, Michael K. and Malcolm Underwood. *The King's Mother: Lady Margaret Beaufort, Countess of Richmond and Derby.* New York: Cambridge University Press, 1992.

Laynesmith, J. L. *The Last Medieval Queens: English Queenship, 1445–1503.* New York: Oxford University Press, 2004.

Schieberle, Misty. *Feminized Counsel and the Literature of Advice in England, 1380–1500.* Turnhout: Brepols, 2014.

Waite, Gary K. *Heresy, Magic, and Witchcraft in Early Modern Europe.* New York: Palgrave Macmillan, 2003.

Ward, Jennifer C. *English Noblewomen in the Later Middle Ages.* New York: Longman, 1992.

———. *Women in England in the Middle Ages.* New York: Continuum, 2006.

# CHAPTER 7

# 'Men Go to Battle, Women Wage War': Gender Politics in *The White Queen* and Its Fandom

## Kavita Mudan Finn

From its first trailers onward, the 2013 joint BBC/Starz miniseries *The White Queen* was very clear about one thing: girl power would be front and center. The initial teaser trailer began with three knights in armor striding in slow motion toward the camera. As they drew nearer, they stripped off the armor, piece by piece, to reveal themselves as the series' three female leads: Rebecca Ferguson as Elizabeth Woodville, Faye Marsay as Anne Neville, and Amanda Hale as Margaret Beaufort. Promotional posters similarly foregrounded the stark dichotomy between men's conflicts on the battlefield and women's conflicts, which took place elsewhere—presumably, in order to find out where, one needed to watch the series. But the prevailing point was that this was not your run-of-the-mill, swords-out medieval drama. Men may go to battle, but *women wage war.*

*The White Queen* presents the fifteenth-century English Wars of the Roses through the eyes of prominent royal and aristocratic women.

K. M. Finn (✉)
Manchester, NH, USA

© The Author(s) 2018
J. North et al. (eds.), *Premodern Rulers and Postmodern Viewers*,
Queenship and Power, https://doi.org/10.1007/978-3-319-68771-1_7

Billed as a feminist reinterpretation of medieval history and based on the bestselling novels by Philippa Gregory, it was clearly aimed at a female audience. Despite its youthful cast, sexual content, and high production values, the series met with ridicule on social media and, after a strong start, viewer enthusiasm waned by the final episodes. This disenchantment stems in part from the writers' emphasis on rivalries rather than alliances between women and the show's insistence that queenship is little more than the exchange of sex for influence, rather than an institution with power in its own right. The addition of witchcraft and incest to the plot further undermined any claims to historical accuracy. In 2017, Starz (without the BBC's involvement or cast members from the 2013 series) produced a follow-up series based on Gregory's sequel *The White Princess*, but it had not finished airing at the time of writing and is thus beyond the scope of this analysis.

Misty Urban's chapter in this volume focuses on motherhood in *The White Queen*, so I will provide a little bit of background before devoting this chapter to several case studies that illustrate the intersection between fan response, historical research, and literary criticism that can be found in discussions of gendered storytelling within this often flawed series. Urban argues that the supposedly 'feminist' interpretation of the fifteenth century at work in *The White Queen* shows not how far we have come, but how deeply we are still tied to old, tired stereotypes about how women exercise power. The women in the series lie, scheme, seduce, and dabble in witchcraft to achieve their ends, while the men seem both clueless and incompetent in comparison. While this makes a nice change from the usual pattern of women existing as plot points in male-centric storylines (I'm looking at you, *Game of Thrones*), it comes with its own problems.

In his landmark 2015 study *Complex TV*, Jason Mittell urges scholars to 'look beyond what appears on a single screen to explore the range of sites where such texts are constituted and serially reconstituted, through practices of cultural engagement'.[1] Later, he specifies that 'the behaviors exhibited by small groups of active online fans are indicative of broader tendencies among many less participatory television viewers, on the basis of how they fit with poetic textual strategies and broader cultural trends, making such fans an important and influential minority viewership'.[2] What is striking about the conversations *The White Queen* generates amongst its fans is how often they mirror contentious arguments between academics. With the rise of digitization projects spearheaded by academic institutions, libraries, scholarly organizations, and Google Books, as well as the growing trend of open-access academic publishing, a determined fan of the show can gain access to a wide variety of fifteenth- and early sixteenth-century source material to support their side or to refute the other side. Indeed, some fan discussions demonstrate a greater understanding of the historical period than the series itself, suggesting that even a subpar representation of queenship can inspire a wide spectrum of audience engagement.[3]

## A WOMAN'S WAR

*The White Queen* is a ten-episode series that aired during the summer of 2013, first on BBC1 and, several weeks later, on the US-based premium network Starz.[4] Covering a roughly 20-year period from 1464 to 1485, the episodes stick to a traditional chronological structure and interweave the storylines of three women: Elizabeth Woodville, wife to King Edward IV (r. 1461–1470; 1471–1483); Anne Neville, wife to King Richard III (r. 1483–1485); and Margaret Beaufort, mother to King Henry VII (r. 1485–1509). Each woman's story is based on a novel by Philippa Gregory in her Cousins' War series—*The White Queen* (2009) about Elizabeth, *The Red Queen* (2010) about Margaret, and *The Kingmaker's Daughter* (2012) about Anne. Unsurprisingly in light of the title, Elizabeth takes precedence, and while the other two women have their own complex lives and challenges, Emma Frost's script constantly pits them against one another while privileging Elizabeth's perspective.

If that were not enough, Elizabeth has one other thing going for her that the other characters do not: *magic*. In the words of one blog commenter shortly after the release of Gregory's novel, making a pithy reference to Shakespeare's *Henry IV*, 'You mean she calls spirits from the vasty deep AND THEY ANSWER?'[5] The short answer is yes.

Perhaps in an attempt to capitalize on the popularity of *Game of Thrones*, or perhaps because Philippa Gregory's *modus operandi* seems to be to take whatever subject matter she's working with and add witchcraft and incest to the mix, *The White Queen* shows characters practicing witchcraft with an actual impact on historical events. Drawing on the supposed connection between Elizabeth Woodville's mother, Jacquetta, and the house of Lusignan, who claimed descent from the fairy Mélusine, the series imbues both women (and eventually Elizabeth's daughter) with magical powers.

The legend of Mélusine is almost certainly older than its written incarnation, but our earliest extant source is Jean d'Arras' *Le Roman de Mélusine* (1393). The prose romance was written at the behest of the powerful duke of Berry, a famous patron of the arts in the French court who also sought to lay claim to the Lusignan inheritance. The *Tres Riches Heures*, a famous book of hours commissioned by the duke of Berry, even includes an image of Mélusine in the illumination for the month of March. In its simplest form—which does a disservice to the romance's interlocking, parallel stories—*Le Roman de Mélusine* is about the daughter of a mortal king and a fairy who is cursed by her mother to transform into a serpent every Saturday. The curse cannot be broken, but Mélusine is told that if she can find a man 'who wishes to marry you and will promise never to look upon you or seek you out on Saturday and never to speak of this to anyone, you shall live out your life as a mortal woman and die naturally'.[6] A young man named Raymond falls in love with her and agrees to the condition that he never enter her room on Saturdays. After they marry, most of the romance concerns itself with the exploits of their sons, but Mélusine's magic is always in the background—she transforms Raymond from a penniless younger son into a powerful magnate, literally building castles from the ground up—and also writ large in the figures of her sons, all of whom share her supernatural bloodline. Eventually, as all readers of fairy tales can predict, Raymond breaks his promise, discovers the truth about his wife, and reveals Mélusine's true nature to the world. Although they forgive one another and make practical provision for their two youngest children, the curse that binds Mélusine also specifies that she cannot remain with Raymond after he has betrayed her. Thus, after their farewells, she transforms into a dragon and bursts forth from one of the castle's windows. She only reappears when the castle of Lusignan is changing hands, violently or otherwise, and operates as a sign of dynastic change. The romance of Jean d'Arras, as well as a later verse rendition by Coudrette (c. 1400), remained popular well into the sixteenth century, appearing in 22 printed editions between 1467 and 1521.[7]

Given what is known about Elizabeth Woodville's own tumultuous life, the parallels and potential symbolism of the Mélusine story make perfect sense. Elizabeth too married for love—or at least is supposed to have done—and became queen of England, no small feat for the widow of a knight. She reigned beside Edward IV over a splendid and fashionable court from 1465 to 1470, and again from 1471 until his unexpected death early in 1483. His younger brother Richard, named Lord Protector in Edward's will, proceeded to claim the throne for himself on the pretext that Edward and Elizabeth's marriage was invalid and their children therefore illegitimate. This reversal of fortune—pinned, like Raymond's betrayal of Mélusine, on a deception at the heart of her marriage—saw Elizabeth lose not only her throne but her brother Anthony and three of her children: her eldest son Richard Grey, executed in June 1483, and her two sons by Edward IV, who disappeared from the Tower of London later that year and were presumed to have been murdered.

In spite of these striking parallels between Elizabeth's life and the story of Mélusine, *The White Queen* retains little of the legend other than Mélusine's name and the broadest outlines of her story. In the first episode, Jacquetta Woodville (Janet McTeer) drags her daughter to the banks of the river near their home and pronounces, 'We are descended from the river goddess Melusina. Magic is in our blood, Elizabeth.'[8] On her instruction, Elizabeth chooses one of three strings dangling in the river and discovers a ring shaped like a crown. The Mélusine of this universe is no longer a powerful and skilled fairy tied to the house of Lusignan, but some sort of aquatic deity whose descendants can communicate with and, to some extent, control bodies of water.[9] This comes up for a variety of plot-contingent purposes ranging from prophecies to conveniently placed fogs to curses upon one's enemies that always, *always* come true. As Genevieve Valentine remarked in a review for the *A.V. Club*, 'there are no coincidences and no caprices, only spells and plot points'.[10]

Jean d'Arras gives his heroine the gift of foresight, suggesting on several occasions that Mélusine predicted her marriage and Raymond's betrayal, as she was well prepared for both. Elizabeth's Sight (the capital letter is implied in the dialogue) is not so predictable, coming to her when she least expects it and rarely telling her what she wants to hear. All the same, Elizabeth's witchy powers give her a clear edge over the other women in the narrative, who are either unaware of them or regard them with what appears to be justifiable fear. In this version of the story, an actual historical event—Isabel suffering a stillbirth while trapped on a ship in the port of Calais after the governor refused entry to her father, the earl of Warwick—is recontextualised as the direct result of a spell cast by Elizabeth and her mother to raise a storm in the English Channel.[11] Their intent is to harm Warwick and Isabel's husband George of Clarence, but instead it is Isabel who suffers most.

Although *The White Queen* does not go so far as to make Elizabeth worship the 'river goddess' Melusina, she wears various charms—including the crown-shaped ring that becomes her wedding ring—over the course of the series that are unquestionably linked to certain characters' lives and deaths and therefore given real power within the universe. This is in contrast to the near-complete absence of the Catholic Church from the series as a whole, with the exception of Margaret Beaufort's storyline, which—as I will discuss in detail later—offers a parallel trajectory to Elizabeth's witchcraft while also framing Margaret as an antagonist and more than a little mad. Indeed, many modern dramas based on premodern subjects tend to sidestep the issue of religion as much as possible—no small feat on a show like *The Borgias*, which takes place in the Vatican, or *The Tudors*, where much of the driving conflict revolves around the English Reformation.[12] No such immediacy exists in *The White Queen*, and thus one can count on the fingers of one hand the number of churchmen in the cast as a whole. Given the historical Elizabeth Woodville's extensive patronage of different saints and mystics, as well as the fact that she ended her life in seclusion at Bermondsey Abbey, it is a strange lacuna, but perhaps not altogether surprising knowing the secular (or, at the very least, non-Catholic) leanings of the show's projected audience.

Both critics and fans found the insertion of magical elements into what purported to be a straightforward historical drama a bit perplexing, but assumed it was a marketing ploy to appeal to fans of *Game of Thrones*. *Variety* called it a 'less elaborate game of thrones' while *The Independent* panned it as 'less historically plausible than *Game of Thrones*, despite being based on real events'.[13]

Posts on the Tumblr blog *The White Queen Confessions* (see Fig. 7.1) serve as useful shorthand for the kinds of conversations the series generated amongst fans. Fans anonymously submit their 'confessions' to the blog, and the blog's moderator pairs those confessions with an image from the series to create a meme-like effect. The image is posted, and thus the conversation begins.

Unlike a typical blogging platform and more akin to Twitter, Tumblr:

> privilege[s] shorter, pithier communication and function[s] primarily by tagging and reposting content. There are no privacy settings, no specific community lanes; only posts and tweets potentially being shared, seen,

liked, argued with, expanded, and commented on by anyone who encounters them.[14]

According to the blog's moderator, the confessions that received the biggest response tend to focus on romantic relationships, and these posts often develop into heated arguments over the course of multiple reblogs. A glance through the archive also reveals that the show's tendency to focus on rivalries rather than alliances between women inspires plenty of posts lauding one character at another's expense. They range in length from a single short sentence ('I don't like Anne.') to multiple lines, nearly enough to obscure the entire image, as in Fig. 7.1. Part of the appeal is anonymity: 'A confession blog is a good place for [fans] to express their opinions without being made to feel foolish.'[15] Through a discussion of several specific interpretive choices in *The White Queen*, I will consider audience reactions, particularly with regard to romantic relationships, which, despite all the political machinations at work, still managed to remain the central focus of this supposedly feminist show.

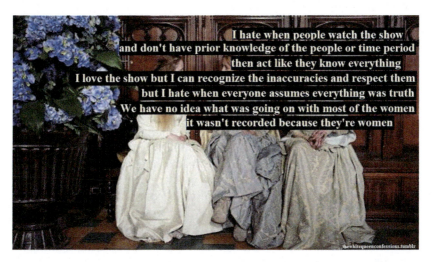

**Fig. 7.1** A post on *The White Queen Confessions*, dated 22 July 2014 (Tumblr)

## EDWARD/ELIZABETH: ROMANCE OR RAPE?

Alongside the introduction of witchcraft, another element in the first episode that distressed fans was the use of rape—or, in this case, near-rape—as a plot device. Drawing on a story which appears independently in two Italian texts—Antonio Cornazzano's 1468 verse collection *De mulieribus admirandis* and Dominic Mancini's 1483 memorandum *The Usurpation of King Richard III*—King Edward IV's 'courtship' of Elizabeth Woodville culminates in his attempt to rape her. According to Mancini,

> When Edward placed a dagger at her throat, to make her submit to his passion, she remained unperturbed and determined to die rather than live unchastely with the king. Whereupon Edward coveted her much the more, and he judged the lady worthy to be a royal spouse, who could not be overcome in her constancy even by an infatuated king.[16]

In Cornazzano's poem, the unnamed lady holds her own dagger to her throat and threatens to kill herself if the king makes good on his threat.[17] The Roman noblewoman Lucretia, who stabbed herself after being raped by Sextus Tarquin, was a well-known medieval example of female virtue, and Cornazzano's heroine demonstrates what such an act would make the king, a role he proves loath to play.

Viewers of *The White Queen*, were clearly meant to applaud Elizabeth's choice to grab Edward's dagger, hold it to her throat, and threaten to kill herself if he went forward, declaring 'I am a match for any man' as she did so. In the context of Cornazzano and Mancini, the anecdote was meant to illustrate Elizabeth's quick wits as well as her virtue, but while other elements of Cornazzano make their way into Thomas More's *History of King Richard III* (c. 1513) and thence to Shakespeare—most notably the line 'she wist herself to simple to be his wife, so thought she her self to good to be his concubine'—the dagger and the explicit threat of rape do not.[18] What fans took issue with in *The White Queen* was not the inclusion of a rape threat, as sadly that is far too common in contemporary television—period, prestige or otherwise. It was the fact that neither character ever brought this moment up again, even as they became romantically involved, were secretly married, and Elizabeth became queen of England.

i really dont like edward as he just comes of [*sic*] a lusty perv

he almost rapes elizabeth, and then marries her to bed her,

and I can tell that shit is gonna go down

when their marriage doesnt work out.

also max's acting is pretty off[19]

In her recap of the episode for *Den of Geek*, Louisa Mellor observes that while the book's first-person narration makes it 'possible to read the attempted rape scene and maintain a belief in Elizabeth's control,' the filmed version 'paints one as a victim and the other as an unforgiveable aggressor'.[20] No matter what the passionate love scenes later in the episode try to convey, it provide difficult for some fans to shake off the memory of that initial encounter, and it is perhaps unsurprising that the scene does not appear in recap montages for later episodes.

Other fans were willing to accept that Elizabeth had evidently moved on, and were enthusiastic about the love story at least until the sixth episode, when Edward begins an affair with Jane Shore. The historical Edward IV was notorious for his promiscuity both before and during his marriage, and Mistress Shore captured the fifteenth- and sixteenth-century imagination, beginning with a brief tangent in Thomas More's *History of King Richard III* (who calls her Edward's 'merriest' harlot) and flourishing in poetry and drama thereafter.[21] *The White Queen*, conversely, frames the affair with Shore as a shocking moment for both Elizabeth and the viewer. Elizabeth has just told her mother that she thinks she's pregnant and is searching for Edward to give him the good news when she walks in on him in bed with Jane.[22] Although there is a throwaway line in the first episode about Edward's reputation with women (and, of course, his flirtation with Elizabeth in the first place), up to the moment that Jane Shore is introduced, his only romantic scenes are with Elizabeth, thus giving viewers the illusion of fidelity.

Fans reacted accordingly. As one White Queen Confession put it, 'Edward won my resentment when he was unfaithful to Elizabeth.'[23] By that point, Edward and Elizabeth had become an accepted couple, and the fact—however historically accurate—that Edward cheated on his wife became a point of contention. A number of other posted confessions go back and forth on Shore's culpability as well as Edward's, particularly after Shore is forced to endure a public shaming in the penultimate episode. Some take the view that she deserved to be shamed for sleeping with a married man, while others defend Shore against what they saw as slut-shaming, pointing out the power imbalance at work.

> A couple of confessions on here talk about Jane Shore and her status as a whore
>
> Now people are entitled to those opinions but
>
> they forget that back then women had no rights whatsoever
>
> Becoming a mistress of a King was seen as a great opportunity for a woman
>
> because it would advance her family's position
>
> Most often the women weren't given a choice, it was decided by the men
>
> So if you want to call Jane a whore,
>
> ask yourself what was her alternative?[24]

As any medievalist could tell you, this is an oversimplification of a complex issue, but there is some truth at its heart, particularly the last two lines. The culture surrounding Tumblr as a social media space encourages awareness of social justice issues, particularly those dealing with representation of marginalized groups. It is worth noting, furthermore, that Shore's contemporaries and those who came after her viewed her as a cautionary tale of the dangers women faced from powerful men. For instance, in the anonymous *True Tragedy of Richard the Third* (printed 1594), Shore's penance and misfortune inspire another character to 'set downe in heroicall verse, the shameful end of a Kings Concubin [*sic*],' while Thomas Heywood's two-part play *Edward the Fourth* (c. 1599) is, despite its title, a tragedy focused on Shore and even includes a sympathetic scene between her and Queen Elizabeth.[25]

*The White Queen* pitted these women against one another—even when they were briefly working together—and, to a degree, encouraged the same arguments in its female fans through its depiction of women competing over a man.

## SHIP WARS: RICHARD/ANNE VS. RICHARD/ELIZABETH

The same episode that revealed Edward's infidelity introduced a second major romantic pairing to the plot: Richard of Gloucester and Lady Anne Neville. Viewers familiar with Shakespeare's version of events probably found this baffling, but *The White Queen* manages, at least over the space of the first seven episodes, to construct a convincing romance between these two characters. Anne's storyline also includes the old Philippa Gregory standby—that her first marriage to Prince Edward of Lancaster was forced upon her and that she was raped on her wedding night.[26] As one recap of the episode on Tumblr put it, 'Anyway, PGregs, rape is not the answer. Stop it or I'm revoking your historical feminist card. Not that you deserve it anyway.'[27] Anne's relatively light-hearted romance with Richard—which fulfills the first half of the sixth episode's title *Love and Death*—therefore, comes as a breath of fresh air for a character who is otherwise relegated to a role of forced subservience, first to her father, then to her mother-in-law (the redoubtable Margaret of Anjou), and finally to her sister and Queen Elizabeth after the final destruction of the Lancastrian line.

Anne is constantly pitted against other women. Her initially close relationship with her sister Isabel disappears in the sixth episode, where Isabel treats her with scorn and disdain and, for reasons unknown, attempts to thwart her budding romance with Richard. Once it is no longer required by the plot, the antagonism between the sisters vanishes with no explanation. Queen Elizabeth's poor treatment of Anne at least makes sense, given that Anne's father the earl of Warwick had Elizabeth's father and brother executed and openly rebelled against Edward IV. However, the viewer is invited to sympathize with Anne, who had no control over her father's actions and is nonetheless being blamed for them. The happy consummation of her relationship with Richard, at the end of the episode, can be seen as the high point in her storyline. Things only get worse from there.

Fans of Richard and Anne's relationship praised the slow-burn quality of the romance. Although the two characters had been seen side by side from the first episode onward, they developed individually and finally came together after a series of missed opportunities and complications. More importantly for fans, after the trauma of the first five episodes, it was a relief to see Anne in what seemed to be a loving and reliable relationship. However, Philippa Gregory's *other* standby plot device soon made its appearance, and sent the fandom into an uproar.

The concept of *shipping* is, in its simplest sense, derived from romantic relationships. To ship two characters together means the fan either believes them to be in a romantic relationship or wants that relationship to happen. Within the *Harry Potter* and *Twilight* franchises, for instance, there was disagreement amongst fans as to whether Harry Potter should have ended up with Hermione Granger rather than with Ginny Weasley, or whether Bella Swan should have ended up with Jacob Black instead of Edward Cullen (in fact, the *Twilight* franchise encouraged this rivalry through their marketing of 'Team Edward' and 'Team Jacob' merchandise). In the case of *The White Queen*, fans who shipped Anne with Richard found themselves in staunch opposition to the introduction of a romantic rival in the form of Elizabeth Woodville's daughter, Elizabeth of York.

Fans acknowledge that there is something odd in shipping historical figures, but, as Melanie Piper argues, fannish interpretation is not especially different from historical drama itself: 'The textual process of fictionalizing a public figure into a character that blends the known public self with an unknown, speculated, or fantasized private self are quite similar in both.'[28] Furthermore, *The White Queen* diverges substantially from anything resembling the historical record in its three final episodes, so it seems unfair to criticize fans for doing exactly what professional adaptations do.

Although almost certainly not based in fact, rumors of a proposed marriage between Richard III and his niece Elizabeth of York after the death of Queen Anne in March 1485 were sufficient that sixteenth-century historians included lusting after his niece as one among Richard's many alleged crimes. Philippa Gregory makes that lust mutual—Elizabeth of York not only pines for her uncle Richard, but, in a scene that notably did *not* make it into the BBC cut and only appeared in the 'sexier' Starz version, consummates a physical relationship with him. Richard openly scorns his wife Anne, publicly humiliates her, and abandons her to die of a mysterious wasting illness—although, unlike in Shakespeare's version, he doesn't appear to have murdered her. Elizabeth in the series has no desire to marry the future Henry VII and is in fact heartbroken when Richard III is killed at the battle of Bosworth Field (which, incidentally, takes place in the dead of winter despite having historically occurred in August).

The fans, perhaps predictably, exploded over this plotline. Some of them enjoyed the edginess of the incestuous and forbidden relationship between uncle and niece while others found it disgusting. It is worth noting that incest had at this point become *de rigueur* in prestige historical (and historical-inspired) television drama, making appearances on *Game of Thrones* and *The Borgias* prior to its introduction in *The White Queen*. And Philippa Gregory has a long history of including it in her novels, as far back as *Wideacre* in 1987 and perhaps most notoriously in *The Other Boleyn Girl*, where she proposes that Anne Boleyn was in fact sleeping with her brother George. This interpretation also spills into the subsequent marriage of Elizabeth of York and King Henry VII, whom Gregory depicts in her novel *The White Princess* as—you guessed it—a serial rapist. Thus, what on the television series is a love triangle becomes a far more complicated quadrangle when Henry enters the picture, and thus begins a whole new ship war, one that Philippa Gregory herself waded into on Twitter.

What interests me most as a scholar of both literature and history of this period is how these two groups of shippers use historical evidence as a tool to advance their opposing arguments. Their conflict in many ways parallels the quarrel between pro- and anti-Richard III historians that has raged since the publication of Horace Walpole's *Historic Doubts on the Life and Reign of Richard III* in 1768. A glance through the 'Richard III,' 'Elizabeth of York,' 'Anne Neville,' and 'Henry VII' tags on Tumblr reveals page after page of long, detailed, serious (and sometimes not-so-serious) arguments about the purported relationships between these four individuals. Some of the people involved are scholars themselves, while others are simply devoted fans, but in both cases, they often use resources provided by organizations like the Richard III Society to bolster their arguments. The society has made a staggering amount of primary material about the fifteenth century freely available on their website, and while it may seem strange to see this kind of information deployed as ammunition for a shipping war, as a teacher, I enjoy it.

To all of the people saying Richard/Elizabeth didn't happen

There is evidence of Elizabeth writing letters about how she loved him

Also, are you forgetting that marriage wasn't about love

it was about assets and marrying to your benefit?

Also, Anne Neville was Richard's Cousin's daughter

The idea of them being in love is naïve

People are confusing fiction for fact[29]

The confession above references a letter allegedly written by Elizabeth of York to the duke of Norfolk in 1485, where she expresses enthusiasm for *either* marriage to her uncle *or* a marriage that her uncle is arranging for her—the wording is unclear. The latter reading is supported by archival evidence of discussions with the kingdom of Portugal for an alliance between Elizabeth of York and the duke of Beja, a marriage that would have placed her and any potential children in the line of succession for the Portuguese throne. More importantly, however, the letter may or may not exist. The earliest reference to it appears in Sir George Buck's *History of the Life and Reigne of Richard the Third* (1646), where he describes its contents and claims it is 'in the magnificent Cabinet of *Thomas* Earl of Arundel and Surrey,' but nobody in the nearly four intervening centuries has unearthed either the actual letter or a reliable copy of it.[30] This hasn't stopped it from persisting as a linchpin for arguments that Richard III wasn't as bad as those nasty sixteenth-century historians made him out to be, and that Henry VII is the real villain of the piece. Here, of course, it is used to justify the claim that Richard was carrying on a consensual love affair with his niece.

On the opposing side, I have to admit that I have not seen more frequent quotation of the poem attributed to Elizabeth of York that includes the line 'My heart is set upon a lusty pin' than in arguments claiming that her marriage to Henry VII was in fact a happy one and that Richard/Elizabeth shippers need to shut it. The most recent biographies of both Elizabeth and Henry emphasize their closeness, particularly linked to the change in Henry's behavior after Elizabeth's death in 1503.[31] It is perhaps not surprising that these arguments often dovetail with the never-ending debate over whether Richard III was Shakespeare's Machiavellian extraordinaire, a Lovely Man Really, or—as most scholars believe—something in between. Figure 7.2.

And, yes, Philippa Gregory *did* wade into this argument and make a truly stupid contribution. It's clear which side of the ship war she's on.

**Fig. 7.2**  Tweet from Philippa Gregory (@PhilippaGBooks) on 19 October 2013

It is worth keeping in mind that ship wars generally exist at the fringes of the fandom, although some have become associated with bullying and other toxic behaviors. There are plenty of fans who follow *The White Queen* or who use Tumblr to discuss actual fifteenth-century history without devolving into arguments about who was sleeping with whom. What does not help is Gregory's own interjections, where she sets forth her interpretations not as interpretations but as facts. Gregory's status as 'historian' has less to do with any academic qualification and more to do with her repeated insistence that what she writes is history, as well as her frequent, bewildering, appearances on documentaries. She has some true believers who are willing to take at face value anything she includes in her novels, but the majority of fans are smarter than that, or at least willing to do the quick Google search required to figure out that a lot of her interpretations have no historical basis.

The anti-Gregory backlash amongst viewers of *The White Queen* extends past the shipping wars to her depiction of her third protagonist Margaret Beaufort and, to a lesser extent, Queen Margaret of Anjou, who is a minor character in several episodes. While Elizabeth's witchcraft is generally portrayed in the series as a source of empowerment, Margaret's religious fervor would, were it not for Amanda Hale's compelling performance, probably come off as cartoonish. Margaret is a character who wanted to devote herself to the church as a child, but was instead pushed into an early marriage and forced to give birth at age thirteen. Although none of this is presented onscreen and the series begins some years later, Margaret wears this trauma as part of the brittle persona she shows the world. Her piety structures her life and gives it meaning as she desperately tries to bring her exiled son Henry home to England. While Elizabeth deals in curses, Margaret calls upon God's will that the house of Lancaster will eventually triumph in the wars that have defined her life. The tension between her genuine piety and the actions she undertakes for her son is fascinating to watch, but the series only rarely invites the viewer to sympathize with her. Furthermore, the apparently requisite romance with Jasper Tudor, her late first husband's brother and uncle to her son Henry, has no basis in the historical record and, even within the series' universe, is underdeveloped to a fault. Margaret of Anjou, in the meantime, is introduced early on as 'The Bad Queen' and does little to move beyond that black-and-white characterization, particularly in her indulgence of her apparently sadistic son—at least based on his treatment of Anne—and the disturbing hints of yet *another* incestuous relationship.

## Conclusions

There are some things that *The White Queen* did well. It is rare, for instance, to see a period drama that devotes as much attention to women's relationships and to childbirth, other than—for obvious reasons—*Call the Midwife*. Unfortunately, most of these relationships fall into predictable patterns of rivalry, resolving only when the plot requires them to. While the series was billed as women plotting and conspiring and ruling England behind the scenes, most of the plotlines revolved around romance, sex, and women fighting over men. And, of course, there was the fact that most of the power exercised by the titular White

Queen emerged from her magical bloodline and her ability to successfully curse her enemies.

Philippa Gregory and *The White Queen*'s producers all hail the series as a groundbreaking feminist historical drama, and none of them acknowledge that their specific brand of dramatic license in fact serves to undermine precisely the empowering message they were trying to deliver. This has not been lost on the viewers. Instead of simply accepting the depiction of female agency that Misty Urban describes in her chapter as 'full of enormous destructive power,' the series' audience is talking back, arguing, and calling upon both earlier interpretations and the historical record to suggest more nuanced approaches to the battles women *did* fight in the medieval period—ones that do not in any way involve magic, incest, or inexplicable conversations with bodies of water.

## Notes

1. Jason Mittell, *Complex TV: The Poetics of Contemporary Television Storytelling* (New York: New York University Press, 2015), 7.
2. Mittell, *Complex TV*, 8.
3. While I will not address transformative fanworks here for reasons of space, they are also part of these critical conversations and I discuss them at length in my forthcoming book *Premodern Women in Television Drama: Representation, Realism, and Response.*
4. Since Starz is a subscription network like HBO and Showtime, the Starz version of *The White Queen* contains additional nudity and sexual content. I specify any scenes that only appear in the Starz version.
5. lareinenoire, "I don't know if this qualifies as a book review," *The Mirror in My Mind* (blog), *Dreamwidth*, last modified October 24, 2009. The post references the following exchange in Shakespeare's *Henry IV, Part I* between Owen Glendower and Harry Hotspur.
   GLENDOWER:I can call spirits from the vasty deep.
   HOTSPUR:Why, so can I, or so can any man;
   But will they come when you do call for them? (3.1.52–54)
6. Jean d'Arras, *Mélusine; or, the Noble History of Lusignan*, ed. and trans. Donald Maddox and Sara Sturm-Maddox (University Park: Penn State University Press, 2012), 25. The French text repeats the word 'natural' three times; "tu vivras cours naturel comme femme naturelle et mourras naturelment." In Jean d'Arras, *Mélusine ou La Noble Histoire de Lusignan*, ed. Jean-Jacques Vincensini (Paris: Lettres gothiques, 2006), 136.

7. For the print history of both Jean d'Arras' *Roman de Melusine* and Coudrette's, see Ana Pairet, "Medieval Bestsellers in the Age of Print: *Mélusine* and *Olivier de Castille*," *The Medieval Author in Medieval French Literature*, ed. Virginie Green (New York: Palgrave, 2006), 189–204.

8. *The White Queen*, "In Love with the King," episode 1, Television Series, Directed by James Kent (BBC/Starz, 2013).

9. Gregory's novel engages more directly with the legend, as Elizabeth's first-person narration repeatedly invokes Melusina and her story, especially in times of crisis.

10. Genevieve Valentine, "The White Queen," *The Onion A.V. Club*, last modified August 9, 2013. http://www.avclub.com/tvclub/ithe-white-queeni-101440.

11. *The White Queen*, "The Storm," episode 3, Television Series, Directed by James Kent (BBC/Starz, 2013); Philippe de Commynes, *Mémoires*, ed. Joël Blanchard (Genève: Droz, 2007), 183–189 gives a sympathetic account of this incident despite his clear dislike for Warwick.

12. See Robin Hermann "Postmodern and Conservative: The King's Ministers in *The Tudors*" and "'The Dyer's Hands Are Always Stained': Religion and the Clergy in *The Tudors*," in *History, Fiction, and* The Tudors: *Sex, Politics, Power, and Artistic License in the Showtime Television Series*, ed. William B. Robison (New York: Palgrave, 2016), 167–178, 209–222.

13. Brian Lowry, review of *The White Queen*, *Variety*, last modified August 5, 2013, http://variety.com/2013/tv/reviews/the-white-queen-review-starz-1200573007/; Tom Sutcliffe, "TV review: The White Queen is less historically plausible than Game of Thrones (despite being ostensibly true)", *The Independent*, last modified June 17, 2013, http://www.independent.co.uk/arts-entertainment/tv/reviews/tv-review-the-white-queen-is-less-historically-plausible-than-game-of-thrones-despite-being-8661016.html.

14. E. J. Nielsen, "The Gay Elephant Meta in the Room: *Sherlock* and the Johnlock Conspiracy," in *Queerbaiting: Contemporary Tactics of LGBT Representation*, ed. Joseph Brennant (Iowa City: University of Iowa Press, forthcoming).

15. Personal communication with the blog's moderator conducted in February 2017.

16. Dominic Mancini, *The Usurpation of Richard the Third*, trans. C. A. J. Armstrong (Oxford: Clarendon Press, 1969), 61.

17. Antonio Cornazzano, "La Regina d'ingliterra," printed as an appendix in Conor Fahy, "The Marriage of Edward IV and Elizabeth Woodville: A New Italian Source," *The English Historical Review* 76 (1961): 660–672.

18. Thomas More, *The History of King Richard III*, ed. Richard S. Sylvester, in *The Complete Works of Sir Thomas More*, vol. 2 (New Haven: Yale University Press, 1967), 61. Although it is unlikely that Shakespeare had read Mancini, he includes a reversal of this trope in Act 1, Scene 2 of *Richard III*, where Richard of Gloucester threatens to kill himself if Lady Anne refuses to marry him.

19. thewhitequeenconfessions.tumblr.com, last modified June 20, 2013. Any misspellings or peculiarities in punctuation come from the original posts.

20. Louisa Mellor, "The White Queen episode 1 review," *Den of Geek*, June 16, 2013. http://www.denofgeek.com/tv/the-white-queen/25997/the-white-queen-episode-1-review.

21. More, *The History of King Richard III*, 57. For the literary history of Mistress Shore, see Richard Danson Brown, "Mistress Shore and Elizabethan Complaint," *Review of English Studies* 49 (1998): 398–415; Richard Helgerson, "Weeping for Jane Shore," *South Atlantic Quarterly* 98, vol. 3 (1999): 451–476; Mary Steible, "Jane Shore and the Politics of Cursing," *Studies in English Literature 1500–1900* 43, no. 1 (2003): 1–17; Maria Margaret Scott, *Re-presenting "Jane" Shore: Harlot and Heroine* (Aldershot: Ashgate, 2005).

22. *The White Queen*, "Love and Death," Episode 6, Television Series, Directed by Jamie Payne (BBC/Starz, 2013).

23. thewhitequeenconfessions.tumblr.com, last modified October 3, 2013.

24. thewhitequeenconfessions.tumblr.com, last modified October 17, 2014.

25. Anon., *The True Tragedie of Richard the third* (London; Thomas Creede, 1595), sig. E2r; W. W. Greg (ed.), *The True Tragedy of Richard III* (Oxford: Malone Society, 1929), TLN 1077–1078; Thomas Heywood, *The First and Second Parts of King Edward IV*, ed. Richard Rowland (Manchester: Revels, 2005).

26. *The White Queen*, "The Bad Queen," episode 4, Television Series, Directed by Jamie Payne (BBC/Starz, 2013).

27. "Episode 4: Women are pawns, except when they're witches," *Woodville Women Don't Talk to Rivers*, July 11, 2013. http://melusineloriginale.tumblr.com/post/55224002396/episode-4-women-are-pawns-except-when-theyre.

28. Melanie Piper, "Real body, fake person: Recontextualizing celebrity bodies in fandom and film," *Transformative Works and Cultures* 20 (2015): 4.4.

29. thewhitequeenconfessions.tumblr.com, last modified September 14, 2013.

30. Sir George Buck, *The History of the Life and Reigne of Richard the Third. Composed in five Bookes By Geo: Buck Esquire* (London: W. Wilson, 1646), 128–129 (sigs. R4v–S1r).

31. See Arlene Okerlund, *Elizabeth of York* (New York: Palgrave, 2009) and Thomas Penn, *Winter King: Henry VII and the Dawn of Tudor England* (New York: Simon & Schuster, 2011).

# BIBLIOGRAPHY

## Published Works

Anon. *The true Tragedie of Richard the third: Wherein is showne the death of Edward the fourth, with the smothering of the two young Princes in the Tower: With a lamentable ende of Shores wife, an example for all wicked women. And lastly, the coniunction and ioyning of the two noble Houses, Lancaster and Yorke. As it was played by the Queenes Maiesties Players.* London: Thomas Creede, 1594.

———. *The True Tragedy of Richard III.* Ed. W.W. Greg. Oxford: Malone Society, 1929.

Arras, Jean d'. *Mélusine ou La Noble Histoire de Lusignan.* Edited by Jean-Jacques Vincensini. Paris: Lettres gothiques, 2006.

———. *Mélusine; or, the Noble History of Lusignan.* Edited and translated by Donald Maddox and Sara Sturm-Maddox. University Park: Penn State University Press, 2012.

Brown, Richard Danson. "Mistress Shore and Elizabethan Complaint." *Review of English Studies* 49 (1998): 398–415.

Buck, Sir George. *The History of the Life and Reigne of Richard the Third. Composed in five Bookes by Geo: Buck Esquire.* London: W. Wilson, 1646.

Fahy, Conor. "The Marriage of Edward IV and Elizabeth Woodville: A New Italian Source." *The English Historical Review* 76 (1961): 660–672.

Gregory, Philippa. *The White Queen.* Simon & Schuster, 2009.

Helgerson, Richard. "Weeping for Jane Shore." *South Atlantic Quarterly* 98, no. 3 (1999): 451–476.

Heywood, Thomas. *The First and Second Parts of Edward IV.* Manchester: Revels, 2005.

Mancini, Dominic. *The Usurpation of Richard the Third.* Translated by C.A.J. Armstrong. Oxford: Clarendon Press, 1969.

McGee, Lisa. "The Bad Queen." *The White Queen.* Episode 4. Directed by Jamie Payne. Written by Lisa McGee. BBC1/Starz, July 7, 2013.

Mittell, Jason. *Complex TV: The Poetics of Contemporary Television Storytelling.* New York: New York University Press, 2015.

More, Sir Thomas. *The History of King Richard III.* Edited by Richard S. Sylvester. In *The complete Works of St. Thomas More,* vol. 2. New Haven: Yale University Press, 1963.

Nielsen, E.J. "The Gay Elephant Meta in the Room: *Sherlock* and the Johnlock Conspiracy." In *Queerbaiting: Contemporary tactics of LGBT Representation.* Edited by Joseph Brennant. Iowa City: University of Iowa Press, forthcoming.

Okerlund, Arlene. *Elizabeth of York.* New York: Palgrave Macmillan, 2009.

Pairet, Ana. "Medieval Bestsellers in the Age of Print: *Mélusine* and *Olivier de Castille.*" In *The Medieval Author in Medieval French Literature.* Edited by Virginie Green. New York: Palgrave, 2006. 189–204.

Penn, Thomas. *Winter King: Henry VII and the Dawn of Tudor England.* New York: Simon & Schuster, 2011.

Piper, Melanie. "Real Body, Fake Person: Recontextualising Celebrity Bodies in Fandom and Film." *Transformative Works & Cultures* 20 (2015). http://journal.transformativeworks.org/index.php/twc/article/view/664.

Robison, William B., ed. *History, Fiction, and The Tudors: Sex, Politics, Power, and Artistic License in the Showtime Television Series.* New York: Palgrave Macmillan, 2016.

Scott, Maria Margaret. *Re-presenting 'Jane' Shore: Harlot and Heroine.* Aldershot: Ashgate, 2005.

Shakespeare, William. *Henry IV,* Part I. Edited by David Bevington. *The Riverside Shakespeare: The Complete Works,* 2nd ed. Boston: Houghton Mifflin, 1997.

Steible, Mary. "Jane Shore and the Politics of Cursing." *Studies in English Literature, 1500–1900* 43, no. 1 (2003): 1–17.

*The White Queen.* Television Series. Directed by James Kent. BBC1/Starz, 2013.

### Online

lareinenoire. "I don't know if this qualifies as a book review." *The Mirror in my Mind.* Dreamwidth Blog. Last modified October 24, 2009. http://lareine-noire.dreamwidth.org/265025.html.

Lowry, Brian. Review of The White Queen. *Variety,* Last modified August 5, 2013. http://variety.com/2013/tv/reviews/the-white-queen-review-starz-1200573007/.

Mellor, Louisa. "The White Queen episode 1 review." *Den of Geek,* Last modified June 16, 2013. http://www.denofgeek.com/tv/the-white-queen/25997/the-white-queen-episode-1-review.

melusineloriginale. "Episode 4: Women are pawns, except when they're witches" [recap of *The White Queen*]. *Woodville Women Don't Talk to Rivers* [Tumblr], Last modified July 11, 2013. http://melusineloriginale.tumblr.com/post/55224002396/episode-4-women-are-pawns-except-when-theyre.

Sutcliffe, Tom. "TV review: The White Queen is Less Historically Plausible than Game of Thrones (despite being ostensibly true)." *The Independent,* Last modified June 17, 2013. http://www.independent.co.uk/arts-entertainment/tv/reviews/tv-review-the-white-queen-is-less-historically-plausible-than-game-of-thrones-despite-being-8661016.html.

Valentine, Genevieve. "The White Queen." *The A.V. Club,* Last modified August 9, 2013. http://www.avclub.com/tvclub/ithe-white-queeni-101440.

# PART II

# Questions of Adaptation: Bringing Premodern Queens to the Page and Screen

## INTRODUCTION

### *Janice North*

The chapters in part two address issues associated with adapting the lives of female historical figures for popular consumption, primarily from the 'telling' medium of written history into the 'showing' mediums of film and television.[1] The specific topics and historical figures under examination in each chapter, as well as the approaches taken to studying them, are varied. However, broadly speaking, these case studies encompass a consideration of the people and processes involved in the creation and consumption of these narratives. Also in play is the nature of the media studied here—these films and television shows can be classified as both adaptations and historical dramas or period pieces.[2] Adaptations are intertextual—the 'remake' exists in a dialogue with the 'original,' while historical dramas and period pieces are intertemporal—they exist in an intertemporal space where the present engages in a dialogue with the past. In both cases this dialogue involves people, as the audiences and creators bring their knowledge of history or the adapted work to the historical drama or adaptation. Since intertemporality is discussed at length in the introduction to this volume, this brief section introduction will focus on intertextuality and the role of people—creators and consumers—in the processes of adaptation.

Intertextuality—the interaction between the adapted work and the 'original'—is a primary consideration in the study of adaptation. In some of the case studies in this section, the 'original' or 'source text' is comprised of a specific work of historical fiction—a novel, play or film—while in others it points to a more nebulous body of work—written history—in which case the source is often indeterminable, unless the writers choose to share that information publically. While the politics of intertextuality is a primary consideration in this section, and indeed, the entire volume, the contributors strive to avoid a pitfall of the adaptation case-study model signaled by Linda Hutcheon: it 'tend[s] to privilege or at least give priority (and therefore, implicitly, value) to what is called the "source" text or the "original."'[3] Instead, the chapters that follow attempt to interpret meaning from the changes that occur from one version to another, one medium to another, and across the decades or centuries. The purpose of these case studies is to discover what the creative choices made in adaptation can tell us about the political valence of the 'remake,' and therefore the values of the people involved.

The politics of intertextuality (and, indeed, intertemporality) are largely determined by the people who interact with these texts.[4] In terms of television and film, there are a host of creators involved in the process of creation—writers, actors, set and costume designers, and so on—all of whom contribute to achieving the creative vision of a director or showrunner.[5] The role of the director and his/her creative vision is considered in each of the chapters in this section—from the 'politicized filmmakers' Bernard Tavernier and Mika Kaurismäki in Séverine Genieys-Kirk's chapter, to more conservative directors, such as Javier Olivares, whose television shows—analyzed by Emily S. Beck and Emily C. Francomano—might be best described as 'crowd pleasers'.

The other side of this coin is the audience. As Susan Hayward has indicated, the desire of filmmakers to attract the largest possible audience (given the expense of producing heritage films) 'has meant that the product is predominantly audience-led.'[6] In other words, the perceived desires and preferences of the audience will shape the creation of the film or TV series.[7] The role that the audience plays in the process of creation is difficult to measure, as it cannot be clearly differentiated from the creative vision of the director. On the other hand, there is more that we can learn from audience response. Thus, in the chapters that follow, the commercial success or failure of a production is used as one indicator of how well the political message of a work resonates with the viewing public.

The essays that follow analyze portrayals of well-known (and controversial) female rulers: Isabel 'the Catholic,' Juana 'the Mad,' Christina of Sweden, and Mary, Queen of Scots. Each case poses a unique set of difficulties—choices that must be made regarding how to portray these historical women, about whom the audience likely has their own preconceived notions—in addition to the difficulties inherent in adapting written history into an audiovisual format. The historical and popular legacies of these women are palimpsestic in nature; some have been obsessed over by historians, producing dozens of biographies and hundreds of focused studies; others have been portrayed multiple times in the cinema or in novels, plays, and even operas.[8] Therefore, it is expected that the target audience will be familiar with some of this material. They may have even learned about these queens in a formal setting—as part of a college course or a grammar school history lesson.

It follows that many in the audience will experience the work as an adaptation, 'oscillat[ing] between [the original] and the new adaptation [they] are experiencing'.[9] The creators, on the other hand, are pulling from these same sources and reacting to them in the process of creation—at times 'pay[ing] tribute by copying,' and other times acting on 'the urge to consume or erase the memory of the adapted text.'[10] In both cases, the people involved in these intertextual processes bring with them their personal values contemporary to the time of the adaptation, through which they filter the stories that unfold on the screen.

All of the previously mentioned topics are discussed in the first two chapters in this section, which examine recent attempts by Spanish directors to confront a difficult chapter in their nation's past: Isabel I's treatment of Jewish minorities in the late fifteenth century. Beck's essay draws attention to strategies used by the creators of the commercially successful television series *Isabel* that point to a larger trend in recent historical dramas: the downplaying of religious elements in the historical narrative in order to facilitate audience identification with or 'allegiance'[11] to historical figures. In this way, signifiers in one system—the premodern past—are traded for signifiers in another—the twenty-first century present—in order to achieve a similar effect: a narrative in which Queen Isabel is a beloved leader, rather than a religious figurehead. The same technique is observed by Armel Dubois-Nayt in her chapter on Mary Stuart, though by her estimation this strategy does not achieve the desired effect of turning an early modern queen into a postmodern heroine.

A different perspective on Isabel and her treatment of religious minorities is explored in Francomano's essay, which looks at two texts that deal with the Spanish queen's legacy on a meta level—through time travelers who seek to preserve her legacy by righting a mistake that she made, and fictional filmmakers who battle with conservative historians and the twentieth-century dictator Francisco Franco over how to portray that legacy for popular consumption. Taken together, what these case studies seem to indicate is that when it comes to the 'Catholic Queen' of Spain, a modicum of controversy, applied by a gentle and reverent hand, is marketable to Spanish audiences. However, too much political controversy, whether stirred by the subject matter or by the comments of the director, can produce a flop.

The chapters by Janice North and Séverine Genieys-Kirk explore multiple filmic and television reincarnations of one queen over time, analyzing how outside forces, along with the creative vision of a director, have resulted in divergent portrayals of the same historical woman. This diachronic approach uncovers some signs of societal progress toward the second-wave feminist ideal of gender equality. For example, Genieys-Kirk's essay demonstrates how the overt lesbian themes that were struck from the initial script of the 1933 film biopic *Queen Christina* find their way back into Christina's story in the 2015 film *The Girl King*. On the other hand, these essays also reveal an uneven progression toward equality, dotted with digressions such as the insertion of medieval stereotypes linking female sexuality with witchcraft in the film *Mad Love*.

In the last chapter in this section, Armel Dubois-Nayt's analyzes director Thomas Imbach's use of creative license in adapting written history for the cinema in *Mary, Queen of Scots* (2013). Dubois-Nayt's chapter grapples with the 'surgical' nature and loss associated with film adaptations,[12] highlighting how key events are condensed, omitted entirely, or presented out of sequence, often in ways that affect how the meaning and significance of these events are interpreted. Dubois-Nayt weighs the effect of these creative choices against the stated objectives of the director, demonstrating how the privileging of emotional effect over historical accuracy results in the undermining of Imbach's vision of Mary as a strong female character.

In conclusion, the case studies in the second part of this volume focus on the politics of intertextuality in royal biopics, meta-historical narratives, and period pieces. As such, these essays home in on the contributions of the people involved in these adaptations—in particular, the creative choices of the directors—but also the role of the audience as consumers of these narratives. With each chapter employing a particular focus on one female ruler, these studies do not seek to make sweeping generalizations about the genre of historical film, but rather attempt to untangle the meaning behind the creative choices and the audience reactions to each work. In other words, they seek to answer the question: what can these adaptations and the techniques, processes, and creative choices that they entail tell us about our relationship to the past, particularly in terms of gender and sexuality?

## NOTES

1. Linda Hutcheon, *A Theory of Adaptation* (New York: Routledge, 2006), 22–23.
2. For a discussion of the distinctions and similarities between 'historical film' and 'costume drama,' see Jonathan Stubbs, *Historical Film: A Critical Introduction* (London: Bloomsbury, 2013): 16–19.
3. Hutcheon, *Theory of Adaptation*, xii.
4. According to Hutcheon, 'Works in any medium are both created and received by people, and it is this human experiential context that allows for the study of the *politics* of intertextuality.' (xii)
5. Hutcheon, *Theory of Adaptation*, 81.
6. Susan Hayword, *Cinema Studies: The Key Concepts*, 3rd ed. (New York: Routledge, 2010), s.v. "audience." Also see "adaptation."
7. For a discussion of the audience's impact on the creation of genres and the characteristics of 'cycles' of historical film, see Stubbs, *Historical Film*, 11–13.
8. Miguel-Ángel Laredo Quesada, Ana Isabel Carrasco Manchado, María del Pilar Rábade Orbadó, and María Cruz Rubio Liniers, eds. *Los reyes católicos y su tiempo*, 2 vols. (Madrid: Centro de Información y Documentación Científica, 2004); María A. Gómez, Santiago Juan-Navarro, and Phillis Zatlin, eds. "Appendix III: Juana as Palimpsest" in *Juana of Castile: History and Myth of the Mad Queen*, (Newark, NJ: Bucknell University Press, 2008), 252–255.; "Christina of Sweden," *Queenship Studies: A comprehensive searchable database of published works on the subject of female rulers*, Accessed September 5, 2017, http://www.queenshipstudies.com/references.cfm?sortby=&id=1369&strt=101&show=50.; Jacqueline F. Johnson, "Mary Queen of Scots: an annotated bibliography," *Bull Bibliography* 53, no. 2 (1996): 152–160; Also see "Mary, Queen of Scots," in "Scottish Bibliographies Online," *National Library of Scotland*, http://sbo.nls.uk/vwebv/search?searchArg=mary+queen+of+scots&searchCode=SUBJ%2B&recCount=25&searchType=1&page.search.search.button=Search.
9. Hutcheon, *Theory of Adaptation*, xv.
10. Hutcheon, *Theory of Adaptation*, 7.

11. Murray Smith, "Altered States: Character and Emotional Response in the Cinema, *Cinema Journal* 33, no. 4 (1994): 34–56.
12. Hutcheon, Theory of Adaptation, 19, 37.

## Bibliography

"Christina of Sweden," *Queenship Studies: A comprehensive searchable database of published works on the subject of female rulers*, Accessed September 5, 2017, http://www.queenshipstudies.com/references.cfm?sortby=&id=1369&strt =101&show=50.

Laredo Quesada, Miguel-Ángel, Ana Isabel Carrasco Manchado, María del Pilar Rábade Orbadó, and María Cruz Rubio Liniers, eds. *Los reyes católicos y su tiempo*, 2 vols. Madrid: Centro de Información y Documentación Científica, 2004.

Johnson, Jacqueline F. "Mary Queen of Scots: an annotated bibliography." *Bull Bibliography* 53, no. 2 (1996): 152–160.

Gómez, María A., Santiago Juan-Navarro, and Phillis Zatlin, eds. "Appendix III: Juana as Palimpset." In *Juana of Castile: History and Myth of the Mad Queen*, 252–255. Newark, NJ: Bucknell University Press, 2008.

Hayword, Susan. "Audience." In *Cinema Studies: The Key Concepts*, 3rd ed. New York: Routledge, 2010.

Hutcheon, Linda. *A Theory of Adaptation*. New York: Routledge, 2006.

"Mary, Queen of Scots." In "Scottish Bibliographies Online," *National Library of Scotland*, http://sbo.nls.uk/vwebv/search?searchArg=mary+queen+of+scots &searchCode=SUBJ%2B&recCount=25&searchType=1&page.search.search. button=Search.

Smith, Murray. "Altered States: Character and Emotional Response in the Cinema." *Cinema Journal* 33, no. 4 (1994): 34–56.

Stubbs, Jonathan. *Historical Film: A Critical Introduction*. London: Bloomsbury, 2013.

# CHAPTER 8

# Religious Medievalisms in RTVE's *Isabel*

## Emily S. Beck

Radio-Televisión Española's hit television program *Isabel* includes a title sequence featuring an eagle soaring over a minimalist landscape in subdued colors of greys; the scene climaxes with a splash of red across the screen immediately before the eagle lands on the throne (Fig. 8.1). The twenty-two-second sequence conveys the loneliness and fierce, quasi-predatory determination required of those who attempt the climb to the top of the social hierarchy, providing a visual cue for primary thematic threads woven into the entire series. As Jordi Frades, director of the series, explains on the program website, immediately below the video clip of the title sequence:

> The eagle is a symbol identified with the shield of the Catholic Monarchs, with Isabel, or with freedom. A metaphor for Isabel's arrival to the throne. With a smooth and determined flight. Beautifully plastic. Flying through inaccessible and snowy landscapes, like her arrival to the throne, it is majestic and elegant. The score by Federico Jusid is 'Anima Mea,' lyrics that convey a double meaning: evoking what Castile means for Isabel (her soul, her family... her life) and the other dimension that we want to show: Isabel's soul.[1]

E. S. Beck (✉)
College of Charleston, Charleston, SC, USA

© The Author(s) 2018
J. North et al. (eds.), *Premodern Rulers and Postmodern Viewers*,
Queenship and Power, https://doi.org/10.1007/978-3-319-68771-1_8

**Fig. 8.1** Image from the opening sequence of *Isabel* ©RTVE

The desire to rescue the soul of the queen, reconsider her legacy, and market Queen Isabel I of Castile as a heroine for modern audiences, one who profoundly shaped the history of the Iberian Peninsula, despite well-entrenched patriarchal attitudes, are indeed admirable goals. The symbolism of the eagle perched on the arm of the throne visually reorients the collective memory of Isabel's character away from historical tendencies that emphasized her religious piety, towards more secular values of personal determination and nationalistic priorities. To make a monarch known to history for her religious zealotry palatable as an aspirational protagonist for contemporary audiences, the program strikes an intricate balance in its inclusion and depiction of religious dimensions that broadly echo ambivalent attitudes concerning religion in contemporary Spain, particularly with regard to Isabel's role in the expulsion of the Jews in 1492 and in championing a model of ideal citizenry characterized by Christian piety and the marginalization of non-Christians.

Queen Isabel I of Castile ruled from 1474 to 1504 but her legacy has endured well beyond her thirty years of political sovereignty in the Iberian Peninsula. More than five centuries after her death, she remains a figure whose name is widely recognized but about whom tradition and lore have obscured facts. Barbara Weissberger has established in several key studies that the image of Queen Isabel has been strongly influenced by a hagiographical impulse that lauds the queen for her piety, her duty, and her devotion to Christianity, as a mechanism by which to temper anxieties produced by a female monarch.[2] Lest we attribute this tendency to a historical precedent to deemphasize feminine contributions to society, it seems that a large part of this public image is one that Isabel herself helped construct. As Weissberger compellingly demonstrates, it was Isabel who initiated the campaign of misinformation and was savvy in crafting a public image that suited her political requirements. For example, Isabel commissioned her chronicler, Fernando de Pulgar, to document historical events in a manner by which to emphasize Isabel's image as pious monarch who was deferential to her husband, Fernando.[3] Peggy Liss has also fruitfully argued that the presentations of her submission to her husband's will were quite conscious ones: the queen herself ordered that when scribes drew up certain decrees they should indicate that the policies were signed by both monarchs.[4]

In addition to Isabel's strategy of presenting herself as Fernando's helpmeet, various scholars demonstrate that the Catholic Monarchs consciously used religious ideology as guiding principles for policy decisions. Elizabeth Teresa Howe, for example, explains that Isabel's confessor Fray Hernando de Talavera likened the queen to the biblical figures of Deborah and Judith, female icons of passivity and reclusion, known best in their roles as helpers to men of action.[5] David Boruchoff has demonstrated that the emphasis on her Christian piety and religious devotion was a self-fashioning crafted by the queen in letters and echoed in chronicles as a rhetorical strategy to refute criticisms of royal policies.[6] Boruchoff adds that the Catholic Monarchs were so successful in countering disapproval by couching their policies in religious imperatives that 'it is no wonder that scholars continue to grapple with the perhaps insoluble task of separating fact from fiction in [their] reign'.[7] Queen Isabel was thus quite savvy in the creation of a public image that subordinated her sovereignty to joint-rule with Fernando, in spite of the delineation of power in their marriage contract that relegated each monarch to authority of his or her own Iberian kingdoms. Theresa Earenfight fruitfully demonstrates that the very motto of their reign, 'Each as important as the other, both Isabel and Fernando' was a conscious adaptation by both monarchs to publically synthesize medieval notions of queenship and kingship into a philosophical conception of 'joint sovereignty or plural monarchy'.[8]

Even well into the twentieth century, the story of Queen Isabel continued to be influenced by religious and gender expectations that circumscribed the queen's contributions to those of her husband. Isabel's characterization as a religious subject is embedded in her sobriquet 'The Catholic Queen' (la reina católica), and from the time of the Hapsburg Monarchs well through the government of Francisco Franco, with very few exceptions, historians and cultural critics tended to affirm the idea of Queen Isabel's complex combination of exemplary religious piety with a public presentation of her relationship with her husband that suggested she was Fernando's passive supporter rather than the architect behind the policies of her reign. In those versions of her story, the expulsion of the Jews and the founding of the Inquisition can be attributed to her passionate devotion to her faith. By cloaking her political choices as interconnected with her positions as wife and earnest spiritual leader, historiography has tended to explain away her aggressive tactics against religious minorities as bad decisions and emphasize instead her sincere and pious intentions.

Given Queen Isabel's notorious acts of ethnic and religious exclusion, and her decision to exile thousands of her own citizens, policies considered distasteful to the majority in the viewing audiences, who endorse contemporary values of tolerance and respect for others, the integration of religious material in the television program is an inherently fraught enterprise. The creators were forced to tackle the thorny issue of how to depict Queen Isabel as an admirable figure for modern television audiences while still incorporating historical events of the period, such as the expulsion of the Jews in 1492. I contend that the solution they reached was to present the queen as an open-minded, tolerant, and above all, pragmatic leader; one who is clearly a firm believer in Christianity, and yet whose piety is not the primary motivator behind her actions. Like the inclusion of the flight of the eagle presented in the title sequence, which serves to distance the figure of Queen Isabel from overtly religious symbolism, the program carefully emphasizes Isabel's secular leadership traits and her unwavering commitment to her dominions. The television program ultimately depicts Isabel as the embodiment of a particular sort of twenty-first century standard of religious tolerance and open-minded acceptance of others, while the prejudices and exclusionary practices that were inherent to her reign are dismissed as the necessary by-products of her efforts to appease factional divisions among top-tier advisors and an unruly population. In exploring Isabel's treatment of religious minorities, the creators of the program ultimately fall into the same historical trap of idealizing the figure of the queen, but this time by diminishing her commitment to the aspects of her reign that remain distasteful to modern audiences. The creators include several dimensions in the program and the accompanying website to suggest that Queen Isabel's treatment of religious minorities aligns with twenty-first century norms of inclusion, thus modifying the characterization of the monarch in significant ways, and ultimately asserting a new sort of hagiography adapted to postmodern audiences: the television version of Queen Isabel is estimable to viewers in the twenty-first century precisely because she deviates from social norms of her era in her inclusion and tolerance of religious minorities.

Recent television programming tends to avoid overt depictions of organized religion. As Meriem Pagès and Karolyn Kinane explain in their introduction to *The Middle Ages on Television*:

> Especially significant in *Merlin* and other recent television medievalisms is the conspicuous absence of organized religion, specifically Christianity. The Church, whose ominous presence contributed greatly to the negative image of the Middle Ages in the popular medievalism of the 1980s and 1990s, seems to have all but vanished from today's contemporary medievalisms. What is particularly striking about this phenomenon lies in its close relationship with the medium of television ... Without the looming 'threat' of the medieval Church as it was imagined in the last quarter of the 20th century, viewers may allow themselves to form an attachment not simply with the characters of medieval-themed show but also with the world they inhabit. Through its representation on commercial television, the medieval is thus slowly reclaiming its function as a site of popular escape and fantasy.[9]

Pagès and Kinane observe the tendency to modify the role of the Church with magic and to pare down the presentation of religion in television programming as much as possible. There are likely many reasons behind the general omission of religion on the small screen but chief among them is the desire not to offend audiences or sponsors. Contemporary audiences tend to avoid overt discussions about religion and are uneasy about the role Christianity played in much of European history. According to the most recent report produced by the Center for Sociological Research, although some 70% of present-day Spaniards identify as Catholic, they currently have among the lowest church participation in history; only a quarter of those polled attended church services with any regularity.[10] The surprising thing, therefore, is not that RTVE's *Isabel* avoids discussions of religion, but rather the hesitant inclusion of religious material in the program, even a particularly ugly chapter in Iberian history characterized by anti-Semitism and discrimination against religious minorities. Furthermore, the inclusion of religious dimensions did not deter public interest, as the show was a hit with Spanish audiences; season one garnered an average of approximately 17% of the total Spanish viewing public and several episodes boasted higher than 20%.[11] *Isabel*'s popularity has led to interest abroad as well; the show has been widely acquired by broadcasters internationally, and is available free through the streaming service on RTVE's official website and with English subtitles through *DramaFever*.[12] In spite of the regular inclusion of religious themes in the program, including the presence of an unruly Castilian populace that attacks Jews and *conversos* (converts to Christianity) with impunity, and consistent diplomatic exchanges between the monarchy and the papacy, the show ultimately resorts to fantasy in the presentation of Queen Isabel as a character who is open-minded about religion and who recognizes that spirituality can come in different shapes and forms.

In addition to the association with the eagle in the title sequence, the series makes an effort to steer audiences' attention toward the secular traits that led to Isabel's successes. Although the costume choices in the first season consistently present Isabel dressed in virginal white, with natural hair that is demurely clipped back, often with a crucifix around her neck, and the impression of no makeup, there is a conscious effort to emphasize the queen's instinctive ability to lead others, and thus limit the number of scenes in which the queen is shown praying or committed to her religious training. The first episode flashes back to a scene in which Isabel plays chess with her mentor, establishing that, even as a child, Isabel demonstrated a strong knack for strategy; the creators do not include a similar scene to demonstrate her strong religious inclination or precocious spiritualism from an early age. This lack in the series can even feel surprising, given the general association of Isabel as the Catholic Queen, for there are relatively few moments that demonstrate her religious devotion. There are a few brief moments scattered throughout the first season, such as at the beginning of episode five, following the untimely death of her little brother Alfonso, in which her advisors complain to each other that her mourning period interferes with the necessity of continuing to manage the war of succession against King Enrique IV. This scene is brief and her dedication to her prayers for her brother is over within a one-minute-and-forty-second scene that also jumps to a discussion among her advisors. Furthermore, although the scene presents Isabel praying, it is not primarily aimed at developing Isabel's pious character or presenting her as a devout practitioner of Christianity; rather, the focus is her sadness at the loss of her treasured brother, and the solitude she experiences given her separation from her mother. The historical record tells us that Isabel was privately and publically sincere in her earnest religious devotion, spending significant portions of every single day at prayer.[13] One could watch several hours of the first season of the television program with little indication of this fact. Instead there are frequent scenes that establish Isabel's perceptive ability to grasp complex political relationships. For example, in episode two, her mentor, Gonzalo de Chacón, is surprised, given her young age, that she has discerned the rationale behind the interest in marrying her off to the Portuguese king. The consistent emphasis on young Isabel's astute political expertise allows the program creators to carefully downplay Isabel's religious devotion to make her sympathies with religious minorities more believable and her religious inclinations more in line with those of twenty-first century Spanish audiences.

Throughout the first season, several narrative threads emphasize Isabel's commitment to all of her Castilian subjects and depict her clear disgust of the unfair treatment of converts to Christianity at the hands of Castilian mobs. In episode four, for example, Isabel's younger brother Alfonso, heir to the Crown, defended the conversos who were attacked while praying in churches in Toledo and Isabel affirms that the fair treatment and protection of all Christians, including recent converts, is important to her. She tells her advisor, Gonzalo de Chacón, that it is right and just to protect all Christians; but Chacón patiently explains to young Isabel that the noblemen who took the city and attacked the conversos are supporters of Prince Alfonso and if Isabel and Alfonso do not allow their supporters to attack conversos with impunity, the Trastámara heirs will lose the support of that faction, they will lose the recently gained city of Toledo, and they will probably lose the war of succession against Enrique IV. Chacón explains that Isabel and Alfonso need to appease the anti-Semitic and religiously intolerant noblemen who have led the charge in Toledo, because they are key supporters of the Trastámara heirs' rights to the throne:

CHACÓN.    In Toledo the Jews support Enrique, and these noblemen
took the city for us. Alfonso must rectify [the decision to
punish them] or we will lose the city [...]
ISABEL.    But God's law says that...
CHACÓN.    God rules in churches but in wartime we must support our
allies. Sometimes being just is not the correct choice.[14]

The program posits that Isabel and Alfonso (and even their half-brother,
King Enrique IV, although he is not shown in this scene) are horrified by the actions of the Castilian mobs who threaten conversos and
Jews. Isabel, in particular, argues for the importance of recognizing all
Christians, including more recent converts, as faithful believers deserv-
ing of royal protection. It is her advisor Chacón who recommends the
discriminatory strategy as a mechanism by which their side may gain the
political advantage. In the scene following this exchange, Isabel demonstrates her acceptance of Chacón's advice and her pragmatic approach to
governance when she reminds her brother Alfonso that the priority for
the moment is to win the war of succession against Enrique IV, at which
point they may use the power of the royal office to affect social change
in the treatment of conversos: '[Alfonso], when you get the power, then
you can reinstate order.'[15] The first season of *Isabel* follows the political
rise of a heroine who did not seek out the highest office for herself but
rises to the challenge when her kingdom needs her. She is Christian and
moral in her actions but her religious characterization is decidedly subordinate to her secular values of determination, political savvy, and her
strong affinity for leadership.

The end of season one presents Isabel's coronation and marriage to
Fernando and the first several episodes of the second season depict her
transition to her new roles as wife and queen, while fighting a civil war
against her rival for the throne, her half-niece Juana. Season two includes
the events leading up to 1492 and includes the expulsion of the Jews but
continues to emphasize Isabel's acceptance of cultural hybridity and religious diversity. In episode 16, for example, the third episode of season
two, Isabel gratefully accepts the financial support of the Iberian Jewish
community rather than wait for papal support of her war against her rival
for the throne. The interaction between the three characters in the scene
illustrates a series of subtle ways that the program shapes the audience's
perception of Isabel's tolerance and friendly relations with religious
minorities. Queen Isabel speaks with two of her advisors, Andrés Cabrera

and Fray Hernando de Talavera. Talavera is her religious advisor and confessor while Cabrera has been in her entourage since she was a child and is one of her most trusted mentors. Through the first season of the program, audiences learn repeatedly of Cabrera's origins as a converso, indicating that, at some point in the past, one of his relatives converted to Christianity; in this scene, his status as a religious minority is repeated when Talavera reacts with surprise that Cabrera is related to a rabbi. As the scene unfolds, there is happy, hopeful music that plays when Cabrera mentions his background. The scene ends with Isabel's friendly smile and assurance that she trusts completely in Cabrera and his ability to get the funds:

CABRERA.  Your Highness, there may be another way to procure the funds. If you authorize me to do so, I will speak with my relative Abraham Senior.
TALAVERA.  The high rabbi of Castile is a relation of yours?
CABRERA.  Indeed. Though my family has been Christian for a long while now, there remain Jewish relatives among our family members. (*music*)
ISABEL.  Do you think he might give us a loan?
TALAVERA.  Without waiting to see the fruits of the cardinal's dealings [with Rome]? It may not be necessary.
ISABEL.  We are at war; no amount of money will be enough. Do it immediately; **I trust in you and your discretion** (*smile*).

(emphasis added)[16]

The episode explains that Isabel's ability to get the money from Iberian Jews is vital to the success of her claims and that she cannot depend on Rome since the papacy has not yet determined whether to support her ascension to the throne of Castile. The Church is thus presented as an abstract power fraught with political complications that impede the queen's supposedly legitimate progress. She is not only represented here as a pragmatic ruler ('We are at war, no amount of money will be enough') but an additional emphasis in this scene is on Isabel's tolerance toward different religions and her close relationship with Cabrera, in spite of his converso background.

In a following scene, Cabrera goes to the Rabbi Abraham Senior to seek the funds and here the episode establishes the negative characterization of Isabel's enemies:

CABRERA.    [Isabel] will win. She has to win. If she does not, let me tell
you what will happen: Alfonso de Portugal will leave Castile
in the hands of Pacheco and Carrillo. Do you remember
how Jews were treated when Pacheco was the governor? Do
you think it will be better for you under his son?[17]

Cabrera emphasizes Queen Isabel's fair treatment of her subjects and her
trustworthiness as a monarch, but the Rabbi's support of Isabel's cause
also hinges on Cabrera's insistence that Isabel's enemies are known anti-
Semites who will made the lives of Iberia's Jews miserable. Cabrera convinces the Rabbi by insisting that ultimately there is no real choice for
the Iberian-Jewish community as Isabel represents their only hope for
compassionate treatment and a tolerant ruler. Contemporary audiences
know that Isabel will ultimately decide to exile the Jews, and the fore-
knowledge adds tension and suspense to the exchange: what will make
Isabel change her mind? Yet these two exchanges solidify the presentation of Queen Isabel as a compassionate ruler who opposes the accepted
discriminatory practices of her rivals.

Episode 26, the final episode of season two, presents the momentous
events of 1492: the conquest of Granada and Boabdil's surrender of
the city to the Catholic Monarchs, negotiations related to Christopher
Columbus' travels, and the expulsion of Jews. In addition to each of
those pivotal events, the story line focuses on the financial interests that
divide Isabel and Fernando: she secured a papal bull to wage a crusade
against Granada and to evangelize converts and, now that the conquest
is complete, she plans to use the funds to support Columbus's explora-
tory voyage to the Indies. Meanwhile, Fernando desperately needs the
remaining funds to secure Aragonese interests against the French for
sovereignty over Roussillon and Sardinia. He insists that he has consistently backed Castilian priorities and now Isabel needs to reciprocate and support his realms, 'When will it be my kingdom's turn?'[18]
Isabel's religious advisors are likewise at odds about how to best spend
the remaining money. High Inquisitor Fray Tomás de Torquemada
demands the papal bull be used toward establishing an inquisitorial presence in the newly conquered kingdom of Granada. Isabel's confessor
Fray Talavera disagrees and urges the queen to give the recent converts
time to embrace their new Christian faith; he also implores her to limit
Torquemada's zealous ambitions: 'Those people deserve an opportunity that Torquemada will not grant them.'[19] Ultimately, the program

presents the expulsion of the Jews as an intricate negotiation of spousal
and political interests, with little development of the religious motivations that led to the policy. According to the presentation of events in
the episode, it is Fernando who suggests the idea of expelling the Jews,
much to Isabel's surprise and initial reluctance. She is eventually convinced, in spite of her arguments on behalf of the Jews, as a means of
marital compromise and as a strategy by which to limit Torquemada's
reckless ambitions. The discussion of the expulsion arises suddenly,
with little narrative development: it begins with a brief scene in which
Fernando and Torquemada meet to discuss Fernando's desire to use
the money to assist Aragon while Torquemada insists that the monarchs
use the funds to expand the Inquisition into Granada. The conversation
between the two men is left pending and there is an abrupt scene change
in which Isabel reacts to Fernando's suggestion to expel the Jews:

ISABEL.     Expel the Jews? Why? They have lived in our kingdoms for
            centuries ... The loans from the Jewish community have
            financed many of our ventures ... And they have handled
            many of our business transactions as well. Are we going to
            cast out those who have been favorable to us? [...]
FERNANDO.   By instituting a single faith in our realms, we will gain the
            unity we have long desired ... And we need Rome's favor.
ISABEL.     We have just carried out the biggest and most expensive
            crusade ever waged against infidels. Why would Rome
            deny us its support now?
FERNANDO.   Rome may have doubts now that you have kept some of
            the money left over from the papal bull. The expulsion will
            assuage Torquemada...
ISABEL.     I insist on putting forth one condition ... That I be the
            one to decide the terms of the expulsion. I will not permit
            Torquemada free reign on this issue.[20]

The scene suggests that the expulsion of the Jews was a political strategy
on the part of Isabel to limit Torquemada's ambitions to establish inquisitorial control in the newly won territory of Granada; he manages to
convince Fernando that exiling the Jews will convince Rome of the monarchs' devotion to the Christian cause, which will help Fernando secure
papal assistance against the French. Fernando, in turn, approaches Isabel
to institute the expulsion of the Jews and she agrees, not because of any

overtly religious reason, but primarily to placate Fernando's bruised ego, reestablish matrimonial accord, and to halt Torquemada's ruthless campaign against Christian converts. As the episode presents it, Isabel is surprised, even somewhat bewildered by the idea of expelling her loyal Jewish citizens. She agrees to the scheme, against her true desires for religious tolerance and acceptance, in order to have the opportunity to limit Torquemada's zealotry and bring peace to her realms. The scene suggests that the expulsion of the Jews was a policy that Isabel begrudgingly accepted as a political strategy to appease her inner circle and that she was a lone voice in favor of tolerant policies toward religious minorities.

The emphasis given to Isabel as the ruler whose treatment of religious minorities is more sympathetic and accepting than that of her rivals is further promoted on the RTVE website. There is even an article titled: 'Why did Isabel and Fernando expel the Jews?' in which the historians consulted emphasize that her decision was in line with the general anti-Semitic policies insisted upon by the papacy and in effect throughout European courts of the time:

> 'It must not have been to Isabel's liking.' Teresa Cunillera, historical advisor for the series, surprises us with this declaration and advises that **before we judge the edict of expulsion of the Jews, we should be aware of the history**. Cunillera affirms that the queen was obliged to resort to this difficult step due to the pressures that the Church imposed: 'It was an extreme measure that wasn't only done here. It was something that occurred throughout Europe and was expanding.'—Paloma G. Quirós, 'Historical Curiosities'[21]

Isabel is thus presented as an almost progressive leader who saw her hand forced from all angles: from the Church itself, from her political rivals, from European-wide expectations, and from nameless, faceless Castilian mobs who demanded the expulsion of all non-Christian others.

The characterization of Isabel as friendly toward religious minorities and open-minded about creating a unified peninsula in which all religions will coexist in peace is a case where the program establishes a new medievalism that rests on an idealized presentation of the story of the queen to exaggerate her commitment to religious tolerance for contemporary audiences. The possibility that Isabel, at least initially, was not bigoted against Jews or conversos is not strictly incorrect, nor entirely at odds with the historical record; Henry Kamen highlights the numerous friendly and professional relationships that monarchs shared with both Jews and conversos, both in their personal entourage and more broadly at court.[22] His findings about those relationships, and the apparent contradiction as demonstrated through the decision to expel the Jews, led Kamen to assert that the 'monarchs were never personally anti-Semitic,' but that 'the decision to expel, however, was the crown's alone, and it appears to have been taken exclusively for religious reasons'.[23] Joseph Pérez weighs the evidence and comes to a similar conclusion: 'The rationale of ensuring religious orthodoxy given in the preamble to the Edicts of Expulsion is undoubtedly genuine: Isabel and Fernando wished to create a situation that could not be undone; by eliminating Judaism, they hoped to discourage those who might Judaize.'[24]

In the television program, the religious rationale for the expulsion is largely absent. Instead, throughout seasons one and two, Queen Isabel is a champion of conversos' and Jewish rights, and only agrees to the drastic step of expelling the Jews as a way to reassert power over her avaricious spiritual advisor and to placate her husband. The depiction of the expulsion of the Jews as a policy decision in which Isabel is deferential to Fernando's needs and accommodating of her husband's will is a representation that entirely aligns with historiographical accounts that subsume her autonomy to the will of her husband. The suggestion that unruly Castilian mobs can only be appeased by the drastic step of expulsion profoundly reorients the policies of the queen in the historical record. The representation here undermines the autonomy that Isabel has boasted until this episode, and implies that she was merely a pawn unable to curb the violence of her realms, rather than an active policymaker who believed that insincere conversions had resulted in a threat to Christianity. In addition, the concluding moments of the episode, which close season two, suggest that the monarchs' unity and happiness in their marriage rests on the compromise they have reached by agreeing to expel the Jews, which now allows them to use the funds toward increasing Iberian hegemony worldwide. Thus, as the episode presents it, expelling the Jews was a tragic event, but it led to the creation of the Castilian Empire with a global footprint.

On the homepage for the program, one can see that the producers have taken pains to market the show with a focus on Isabel's characteristics as an independent, female monarch who shaped her country during a time of social crisis and, in focusing on those dimensions, they have chosen to subordinate her characterization as a religious queen. One of the first aspects viewers see is an image of the entire series broken down into five segments as a short introduction to capture new viewer interest and to stimulate reflection for devotees of the show (Fig. 8.2).

The show's creators and marketing team have decided that the five moments that best summarize the television program are the marriage of Fernando and Isabel (which was the most watched episode of the entire series),[25] Isabel's self-proclamation as queen, the surrender of Granada, Columbus's arrival in America, and Isabel's death. One of the most glaring omissions from this introductory pentaptych is that of the history of Iberia's religious minorities, the establishment of the Inquisition, and the expulsion of the Jews. As Martha W. Driver and Sid Ray assert, 'The anachronism of medieval film alone has much to teach us about how we see the Middle Ages and how our understanding of it is mediated by the culture we inhabit.'[26] The presentation of these five key events of Isabel's life on the homepage of the program glosses over the legacy she left regarding Jews and conversos, suggesting that postmodern audiences are disturbed by religious intolerance and are hesitant to embrace a protagonist whose policies run counter to the values held by mainstream viewers of the twenty-first century. In episode 26, the creative suggestion that the expulsion of the Jews was a decision Isabel made in the interests of marital compromise and submission to her husband's needs, undermines the independent vision and leadership skills the queen demonstrated through the rest of seasons one and two.

**ISABEL EN CINCO MOMENTOS**

La boda de Isabel y Fernando    Isabel se autoproclama Reina    La rendición de Granada    Colón llega a América    La muerte de Isabel la reina

**#TANTOMONTA**

**Fig. 8.2**  Screen shot of homepage of *Isabel* website ©RTVE 2017. "Portada," *RTVE*, http://www.rtve.es/television/isabel-la-catolica/

Religion remains a divisive issue that contemporary audiences are hesitant to confront. In the case of the Catholic Monarchs, the discriminatory practices infamous to their reign force the inclusion of a distasteful subject. Nevertheless, the television program ultimately shies away from asking hard questions about Isabel's policies, reflecting on what Spain lost through the expulsion of non-Christians, or seriously reexamining the process by which Isabel's policies guided Iberia's transition from the most multicultural region of any European kingdom of the day—with significant numbers of Jewish and Muslim citizens at all levels of the social strata—to a territory whose notorious inquisitorial practices would make it known to the world as among the least tolerant of religious and ethnic difference. Instead, the program suggests that Queen Isabel I of Castile was but one voice unable to challenge the nameless, faceless mobs whose intolerance was distasteful to her and yet whose support she relied upon.

The ambivalent treatment of religion in the television program echoes a similar tendency occurring in contemporary Spain. On June 24, 2015, the Spanish Parliament passed law 12/2015, granting Spanish nationality to the Sephardic Jews who had been exiled under the policies of the Catholic Monarchs.[27] There was strong support for the bill, suggesting broad public interest in efforts to make reparations for exiled Jews. Nevertheless, the law has been criticized for the challenge required in submitting the required documentation. Applicants must demonstrate proof of Sephardic heritage and a 'special connection to Spain'.[28] The documentation required is complex and requires a significant investment of money and time; in addition, presence in Spain is required for part of the process, as well as official examinations to demonstrate familiarity with the Spanish language, and legal and cultural aspects of Spain. The significant burden placed on applicants significantly limits the number who will be granted citizenship, thus suggesting that Parliament did not intend to admit large percentages of the Sephardic descendants in the world. According to the Spanish newspaper, *El País*, as of August 27, 2016, only one person out of 2424 applicants from varied countries had been granted Spanish nationality as a result of the law, though many of the cases remained in various stages of processing.[29] Given these numbers, the author of the article declares that the law 'runs the risk of becoming known as a fiasco'.[30] While the symbolic gesture to make amends for human rights violations that occurred five hundred years ago is an important one, the decision to make process relatively onerous for applicants will dissuade all but the most eager.

While we should absolutely not dismiss the television program *Isabel* and the opportunities it provides to complement historical presentations of the queen that focus entirely on her religious characterization, it is important to recognize that, despite the impression of historical accuracy, the television program makes choices to appeal to twenty-first century television audiences that do not necessarily conform to historical accuracy. In this television program, the representation of Isabel relies on an assumption that her practice of Christianity aligns with the secular trends of present-day Spaniards: Catholic in name, but rarely participatory in practice. In so doing, the creators of the show rewrite recent cultural memory to present Queen Isabel I of Castile as a model of tolerance and compassion and they distance their protagonist from any hint of religious zealotry or ardent commitment to religion at the cost of others. Ultimately, their presentation continues to fall into the same historical trap of a hagiographical presentation of the queen, though this time the depiction suggests an idealized version of Christianity that appeals to twenty-first-century viewers' beliefs in religious tolerance and acceptance of others' beliefs. Given that the collapse of *convivencia* ('living together,' or religious diversity of the three monotheistic religions in the Iberian Peninsula over centuries) was and remains one of the most puzzling and significant aspects of Queen Isabel's legacy, the treatment of religious minorities in the program merits additional critical scrutiny. In particular, the television program fictionalizes the injustices that were integral parts of her dynastic program merely because they are inconvenient truths for the present age.

## NOTES

1. "El águila es un símbolo que se identifica con el escudo de los Reyes Católicos, con Isabel o con la libertad. Una metáfora de Isabel llegando al trono. Con un vuelo suave pero contundente. Plásticamente precioso. Volando por unos paisajes nevados, inaccesibles, como su llegada al trono, que es majestuosa y elegante. La música de Federico Jusid es 'Anima Mea,' letra que tiene un doble sentido: lo que significa Castilla para Isabel (su alma, su familia... su vida) y lo que queremos mostrar de Isabel: Su Alma." "Cabecera de la serie," Isabel-la serie, RTVE, accessed January 28, 2017. http://www.rtve.es/alacarta/videos/isabel/isabel-cabecera-serie/1559206/. This and all translations from the RTVE website are my own.

2. Barbara Weissberger, *Isabel Rules: Constructing* Queenship, *Wielding Power* (Minneapolis: University of Minnesota Press, 2004). See especially the introduction to the study, xi–xxvii, and Chap. 1, "Anxious Masculinity," 1–27.
3. Weissberger, *Isabel Rules*, 84–85.
4. 'pongase rey e reyna,' quoted in Peggy Liss, "Isabel, Myth and History," in *Isabel la Católica, Queen of Castile: Critical Essays*, ed. David A. Boruchoff (New York: Palgrave Macmillan, 2003), 60. See also Liss's biographical study of Queen Isabel, *Isabel the Queen: Life and Times*, 2nd ed. (Oxford, UK: Oxford University Press, 2004).
5. Elizabeth Teresa Howe. "Zenobia or Penelope? Isabel la Católica as Literary Archetype," in David A. Boruchoff, *Isabel la Católica, Queen of Castile*, 95.
6. David A. Boruchoff, "Instructions for Sainthood and Other Feminine Wiles in the Historiography of Isabel I," in David A. Boruchoff, *Isabel la Católica, Queen of Castile*, 5.
7. Boruchoff, "Instructions," 13.
8. The motto of Isabel and Fernando was 'Tanto monta, monta tanto, Isabel como Fernando;' quoted in Theresa Earenfight, "Two Bodies, One Spirit: Isabel and Fernando's Construction of Monarchical Partnership," in *Queen Isabel I of Castile: Power, Patronage, Persona*, ed. Barbara Weissberger (Woodbridge, Suffolk, UK: Tamesis, 2008), 3–18.
9. Meriem Pagès and Karolyn Kinane, eds. *The Middle Ages on Television: Critical Essays* (Jefferson, NC: McFarland, 2015), 7.
10. Cited from the Centro de Investigaciones Sociológicas (CIS), Study #3162, "Barómetro de Diciembre 2016," a sociological poll given to 2466 Spaniards to measure current beliefs about their situation, much like a Gallup Poll, 70% of Spaniards identify as Catholic, but 73.1% rarely or almost never attend religious services. See page 23, Question 31, '¿Cómo se define Ud. en materia religiosa: católico/a, creyente de otra religión, no creyente o ateo/a?' (With what religion do you identify? Catholic, believer of another religion, non-believer, or atheist?) 70% of respondents identified as Catholic. In Question 31a, those who identified as Catholic or believers in another religion were asked how often they attended mass or other religious services, not counting social ceremonies, like weddings, communions, or funerals. 58.6% of respondents answered that they 'casi nunca' (almost never) attend religious services, and another 14.5% attend 'varias veces al año' (occasionally throughout the year). The study is published online: http://datos.cis.es/webFtp/fileGetter.jsp?dwld=Es3162mar_A.pdf. Accessed February 27, 2017. See also Robert Manchin's *Gallup Report* of the decline in church attendance across Europe.

11. Santiago Aparicio, "'Isabel' cierra su segunda temporada con un 16.8% y pierde tres puntos respecto a la primera," *FormulaTV.com*, December 3, 2013. http://www.formulatv.com/noticias/34477/isabel-cierra-segunda-temporada-pierde-tres-puntos-respecto-primera/. The final episode of season one, "Capítulo 13," was one of the most-watched episodes for Spanish television in 2012, with 4,651,000 viewers, or 22.6% of the viewing public, according to "Vertele: Noticias *Isabel*," a division of the newspaper *El Diario*. http://vertele.eldiario.es/noticias/Isabel_0_1634236561.html. Accessed February 2, 2017.

12. "Isabel—Season 1," *Dramafever*. https://www.dramafever.com/drama/4221/1/Isabel_-_Season_1/.

13. One of the first points presented in the documentation for her canonization as saint is the evidence of Isabel's daily devotion to prayer: 'In an era when it was usual for good Christians to attend Mass only a few times each year and confession annually, Isabel attended Mass every day. This had been her habit since her childhood with her mother.' See http://www.queenisabel.org/RelatedResources/IsabelProtector-2.html.

14. My translation from "Capítulo 4," *Isabel*, television series, season 1, episode 4, RTVE/Diagonal TV, aired October 1, 2012. http://www.rtve.es/alacarta/videos/isabel/isabel-capitulo-4/1538906/.

15. 'Cuando tengáis el poder, podréis poner orden.' "Capítulo 4."

16. My translation from "Capítulo 16," *Isabel*, season 2, episode 3, RTVE/Diagonal TV, aired September 23, 2013. http://www.rtve.es/television/isabel-la-catolica/capitulo-16/.

17. '[Isabel] ganará, debe ganar. De lo contrario, os diré lo que sucederá: Alfonso de Portugal dejará Castilla en manos de Pacheco y Carrillo. ¿Recordáis cómo se trataban a los judíos cuando era Pacheco quien gobernaba? ¿Creéis que con su hijo os va a ir mejor?' "Capítulo 16."

18. '¿Y cuándo mi reino?' "Capítulo 26," *Isabel*, season 2, episode 13, RTVE/Diagonal TV, aired December 2, 2013. http://www.rtve.es/television/isabel-la-catolica/capitulo-26/.

19. 'Esas gentes merecen una oportunidad que Torquemada no les concederá.' "Capítulo 26."

20. My translation from "Capítulo 26."

21. Translation is my own; the emphasis is included in the original essay, "Curiosidades históricas del capítulo 26 de '*Isabel*' ¿Por qué Isabel y Fernando expulsaron a los judíos?" *Isabel-la serie*, RTVE. http://www.rtve.es/television/20131202/isabel-fernando-expulsaron-judios/807521.shtml.

22. Henry Kamen, *The Spanish Inquisition* (New Haven: Yale University Press, 1997), 11–16.

23. Kamen, 16, 19–20.

24. Joseph Pérez, "Isabel la Católica and the Jews," in David A. Boruchoff, *Isabel la Católica, Queen of Castile*, 163.
25. This was the most watched episode of the show with 4,025,000 viewers, which represents 19.8% of the viewing public (*FormulaTV*).
26. Driver, Martha W. and Sid Ray, eds. *The Medieval Hero on Screen: Representations from Beowulf to Buffy* (Jefferson, NC: McFarland, 2004), 5.
27. "Normativa," Ministerio de Justicia de España, accessed February 1, 2017. http://www.mjusticia.gob.es/cs/Satellite/Portal/es/areas-tematicas/nacionalidad/concesion-nacionalidad/normativa.
28. The law reads: 'Pueden acogerse al procedimiento previsto en esta Ley todos aquellos sefardíes que prueben dicha condición y una especial vinculación con España.' "Normativa."
29. González, Miguel. "Sólo 2.424 sefardíes han pedido la nacionalidad española," *El País*, August 27, 2016. http://politica.elpais.com/politica/2016/08/27/actualidad/1472323420_545660.html. See also Janis Siegel, "500 Years after expulsion, Jewish American claims Spanish citizenship," *The Times of Israel*. February 23, 2016. http://www.timesofisrael.com/500-years-after-expulsion-jewish-american-claims-spanish-citizenship/.
30. 'La ley de concesión de la nacionalidad española a los sefardíes, presentada como la reparación histórica a los judíos expulsados de Sefarad (España) hace 524 años, corre el riesgo de saldarse con un fiasco.' "Sólo 2.424 sefardíes han pedido la nacionalidad española."

## BIBLIOGRAPHY

Aparicio, Santiago. "'Isabel' cierra su segunda temporada con un 16.8% y pierde tres puntos respecto a la primera." FormulaTV.com, December 3, 2013. http://www.formulatv.com/noticias/34477/isabel-cierra-segunda-temporada-pierde-tres-puntos-respecto-primera/.

"Barómetro de Diciembre 2016: Avance de Resultados," *CIS—Centro de Investigaciones Sociológicas*. Estudio n° 3162, December 2016. http://datos.cis.es/webFtp/fileGetter.jsp?dwld=Es3162mar_A.pdf.

Boruchoff, David A. "Instructions for Sainthood and Other Feminine Wiles in the Historiography of Isabel I." In *Isabel la Católica, Queen of Castile: Critical Essays*, edited by David. A. Boruchoff, 1–23. New York: Palgrave Macmillan, 2003.

"The Case for Isabel's Canonisation." 2010. http://www.queenisabel.org/Canonisation.html.

Driver, Martha W. and Sid Ray, eds. *The Medieval Hero on Screen: Representations from Beowulf to Buffy*. Jefferson, NC: McFarland, 2004.

Earenfight, Theresa. "Two Bodies, One Spirit: Isabel and Fernando's Construction of Monarchical Partnership." In *Queen Isabel I of Castile: Power, Patronage, Persona*, edited by Barbara Weissberger, 3–18. Woodbridge (Suffolk): Tamesis, 2008.

González, Miguel. "Sólo 2.424 sefardíes han pedido la nacionalidad española," *El País*, August 27, 2016. http://politica.elpais.com/politica/2016/08/27/actualidad/1472323420_545660.html.

Howe, Elizabeth Teresa. "Zenobia or Penelope? Isabel la Católica as Literary Archetype." In *Isabel la Católica, Queen of Castile: Critical Essays*, edited by David A. Boruchoff, 91–102. New York: Palgrave Macmillan, 2003.

*Isabel*. Television Series. RTVE/Diagonal TV. Seasons 1–3 (2012–2014). All episodes are available online: http://www.rtve.es/television/isabel-la-catolica/capitulos-completos/.

Kamen, Henry. *The Spanish Inquisition: A Historical Revision*. New Haven: Yale University Press, 1997.

Liss, Peggy. "Isabel, Myth and History." In *Isabel la Católica, Queen of Castile: Critical Essays*, edited by David A. Boruchoff, 57–78. New York: Palgrave Macmillan, 2003.

———. *Isabel the Queen: Life and Times*, 2nd ed. Oxford, UK: Oxford University Press, 2004.

Manchin, Robert. "Religion in Europe: Trust Not Filling the Pews." *Gallup*, September 21, 2004. http://www.gallup.com/poll/13117/religion-europe-trustfilling-pews.aspx.

Pagès, Meriem, and Karolyn Kinane, eds. *The Middle Ages on Television: Critical Essays*. Jefferson, NC: McFarland, 2015.

Pérez, Joseph. "Isabel la Católica and the Jews." In *Isabel la Católica, Queen of Castile: Critical Essays*, edited by David A. Boruchoff, 155–169. New York: Palgrave Macmillan, 2003.

Quirós, Paloma G. "Curiosidades históricas del capítulo 26 de 'Isabel': ¿Por qué Isabel y Fernando expulsaron a los judíos?" *RTVE*, December 2, 2013. http://www.rtve.es/television/20131202/isabel-fernando-expulsaron-judios/807521.shtml.

Siegel, Janis. "500 Years after expulsion, Jewish American claims Spanish citizenship," *The Times of Israel*, February 23, 2016. http://www.timesofisrael.com/500-years-after-expulsion-jewish-american-claims-spanish-citizenship/.

"Vertele: Noticias *Isabel*," *El Diario*, December 1, 2015. http://vertele.eldiario.es/noticias/Isabel_0_1634236561.html.

Weissberger, Barbara F. *Isabel Rules: Constructing Queenship, Wielding Power*. Minneapolis: University of Minnesota, 2004.

———, ed. *Queen Isabel I of Castile: Power, Patronage, Persona*. Woodbridge (Suffolk): Tamesis, 2008.

# CHAPTER 9

# 'The Queen of Time': Isabel I in *The Ministry of Time* (2015) and *The Queen of Spain* (2016)

## Emily C. Francomano

Isabel I, queen of Castile (1474–1504) is highly visible in popular culture in Spain, and particularly so at the time of this writing. *Isabel*, the critically acclaimed and much-watched RTVE miniseries (September 2012–December 2014), which is discussed in several of the other essays in this volume, has brought the historically and mythically important Isabel into full view, reaffirming her centrality in Spanish national identity and recovering her as an emblematic and positive figure for twenty-first century Spain. The noted Isabelline scholar Barbara F. Weissberger neatly sums up the show's handling of its legendary protagonist:

> [The] portrayal of Isabel conforms closely to the dominant historiography given initial shape by the queen's own court chroniclers … despite constant attempts by both allies and opponents to manipulate her for their own gain, she remains the self-contained, modest, pious, and resolute young woman idealized over the last five hundred years.[1]

E. C. Francomano (✉)
Georgetown University, Washington, D.C., USA

© The Author(s) 2018
J. North et al. (eds.), *Premodern Rulers and Postmodern Viewers*,
Queenship and Power, https://doi.org/10.1007/978-3-319-68771-1_9

179

The enduring appeal of this portrait stems in part from the association of Isabel's reign with the inauguration of a 'golden age' and the emergence of Spain as a modern state.[2] Moreover, as Emily S. Beck argues in this volume, *Isabel* depicts the Queen as the 'embodiment of a particular sort of twenty-first century standard of religious tolerance and open-minded acceptance of others,' while shifting the responsibility for the violence of the Inquisition and the Expulsion onto her advisor, her husband, and her anti-Semitic subjects.[3]

There are some counter-histories that challenge the apparently seamless trajectory of quasi-hagiographic Isabelline image-making. If, during the Franco Regime, Isabel was venerated as a national Catholic icon, and as a figure that wedded totalitarian twentieth-century Spain to its medieval roots, in the years leading up to and following the transition to democracy, Isabel's saintly image was frequently deconstructed, demythologized, and lampooned. Juan Goytisolo and Salman Rushdie, among others, caricatured Isabel in fiction, and pseudohistorical comedy films of the 1980s, such as *Christopher Columbus, Professional Discoverer*, also took parodic aim at the crowning events of Spanish national history associated with Isabel I.[4] Parodies, however, are confirmations of canonicity as well as ironic inversions, and the transition's caricatures contributed to the stability of Isabel's centrality in narratives of Spanish history.[5] Two recent productions, the television series *The Ministry of Time* (February 2015–present) and the 2016 film *The Queen of Spain*, once again bring twenty-first century audiences into contact with Isabel.[6] Unlike *Isabel*, however, these two re-creations are equivocal in their handling of the iconic queen. *The Ministry of Time*, has been met with almost unqualified acclaim by media critics.[7] *The Queen of Spain*, on the other hand, flopped spectacularly. This essay explores the two productions as historiographic metafictions that combine the representation of history with self-reflexive commentaries on historical revisionism that call attention to Isabel's ambivalent legacy as well as their contrasting reception.[8]

## THE MINISTRY OF TIME

*The Ministry of Time* imagines the existence of a clandestine government agency dedicated to traveling back in time to make sure that the past matches up with the received narrative of Spain's national history. The Ministry is staffed with civil servants from multiple temporalities who meet in the present—as the Ministry does not send agents into the future—and have all been given clearance to know the state secrets that necessitate time travel. Their missions are to return to pivotal moments in Spain's history that are in danger of becoming counter-histories because of 'alterations in time,' generally caused by misuses of time-travel by non-state actors or Spain's historical enemies. Examples include the French under Napoleon, who attempt to prevent Spain from gaining its independence in 1814 by traveling to Madrid in 2015 or the directors of the Museum of Modern Art in New York, who decide not to return *Guernica* to Spain in 1981.

In the context of Spain's current acrimonious debates about historical memory, the Civil War, and Franco's dictatorship, *The Ministry of Time* enters into turbulent political waters by simultaneously affirming the existence of a unified national narrative and portraying that same narrative as in constant danger of dissolution. Yet the show's entrance is a toe-dipping rather than a deep dive into political commentary, because *The Ministry of Time* generally prefers to go back to moments in time that it would seem are easy to agree upon. Moreover, the Ministry takes its directions from the Prime Minister's office, insinuating that cultural memory is—rightly—under direct state control. This fictional situation is reminiscent of both the Franco dictatorship's management of the national image and the aims of the so-called 'Law of historical memory,' passed in 2007.[9]

At first glance, the view of Isabel in *The Ministry of Time* is largely aligned with *Isabel*. The similarities are compounded by the facts that both shows were created by Javier Olivares for RTVE, in collaboration with Pablo Olivares in the case of the newer series, and that Michelle Jenner plays the role of the Catholic Queen in both shows, though she has only a cameo appearance in *The Ministry of Time*. Isabel's importance to the Ministry goes beyond her brief appearance in a single episode: in *The Ministry of Time*, she is credited with founding the secret time-traveling directorate, whose origins date back to the eve of 1492, the *annus mirabilis* that saw the birth of the modern nation state, the publication of the first Spanish grammar, the conquest of Granada, and the Expulsion of the Jews. For many, of course, 1492 was an *annus horribilis*, but that is not how it has been traditionally enshrined in Spanish national cultural memory.

In the first episode, "Time Is What It Is," new recruits to the agency are told the history of the Ministry: in 1491, Isabel obtained *The Book of*

*Doors in Time* and, with it, the power to become 'the Queen of Time,' in exchange for her promise to spare Abraham Levi, a rabbi, from expulsion.[10] However, as Salvador Martí, the Ministry's top functionary, explains, 'It's not an inspiring story.'[11] Isabel did not keep her promise, and though Levi was not expelled, he was eventually burned at the stake by the Inquisition, an institution established in Castile by the historical Isabel and her husband Fernando II of Aragon in 1478. In episode four of the first season, *A Timely Negotiation*, the Ministry's agents return to 1491 in order to correct Isabel's apparently less-than-merciful behavior towards Levi and save him from Torquemada's judgment.[12] While the queen is only part of the Ministry's oral history in episode one, in episode four she appears in the flesh portrayed by the same actress (Michelle Jenner) audiences know from the series *Isabel*. The reason for the return to the fifteenth-century origins of the Ministry is an inconvenient reminder of Isabel's less savory historical achievements. Levi's present-day descendants have sent one Aaron Stein, a lawyer from New York, to Madrid to demand $100,000,000 and the return of the book as reparation for Levi's torture and death. Stein threatens Salvador that if the Ministry cannot come up with the money, the Ministry and all its manipulations of history will be exposed.

Three agents, born over the course of the 500 years that have passed since the Catholic Monarchs' campaigns of religious and imperial control, are sent back to save the rabbi and safeguard the Ministry's future: Julián, a twenty-first century paramedic played by Rodolfo Sancho, who also played the role of Isabel's husband Fernando in *Isabel*; Amelia Folch, a bluestocking from Barcelona in the 1880s; and Alonso de Entrerríos, a soldier from the sixteenth century. The time-traveling agents' direct encounter with Isabel is an ironic revisitation of twenty-first century audiences' reception of *Isabel* and a rehearsal of many of the clichés used to describe powerful historical women. The meeting begins with an intertextual jibe about Rodolfo Sancho's previous role as Fernando in *Isabel*: Julián sees the queen, and says to Amelia, 'I could swear I've seen her somewhere before.'[13] Then, when the agents describe the danger that Levi is in, Isabel responds with surprise and anger—'Abraham Levi is under my protection!'[14]—and asks Cardinal Cisneros, who is by her side, if he knows anything about the situation. When Cisneros denies any knowledge of Levi's plight, she asks, 'And my husband?' and the Cardinal bows his head in assent.[15] After

Isabel promises to write a letter ordering Levi's release and dismisses the agents, she is heard off screen berating Cisneros 'How many times have I said that nothing may be done without my permission? *I* am the ruler of Castile, not my husband!' and Julián, overhearing, remarks, 'What a temper that woman has!'[16] Amelia, a feminist *manquée* of her era, responds, 'A woman needs that and more to get to the throne. And even more so in the fifteenth century.'[17] Alonso, a traditionalist and monarchist, says, 'It's none of our business. She's the queen.'[18] In the next scene, Amelia also reaffirms the traditional view of Isabel, shared in the official cultural memory of the multiple temporalities the agents represent: 'Isabel was always a woman of her word.'[19]

Like so many heroines in neomedieval fantasies, Isabel is portrayed in both *Isabel* and *The Ministry of Time* as an extraordinary individual who rises above the expectations of the patriarchal system that produced her and to which she contributes.[20] Amelia's observation that a woman in Isabel's position and time needed to be of strong character recalls the supposed exceptionalism of medieval heroines and serves as a neomedieval evaluation of the enormous changes in gender roles between the fifteenth and twenty-first centuries. On the other hand, Julián's stereotypically misogynist response, while clearly another comic and intertextual reference to *Isabel*, shows that the twenty-first century has not exactly progressed as much as Amelia might have imagined back in her nineteenth-century home. If for Amelia, and perhaps some viewers of *Isabel*, Isabel is a 'mother to think back through' to tell a feminist history, for the modern man, Julián, she fits the stereotype of the virago.[21]

As in all of the other episodes, the agents' mission succeeds. Levi is saved from the flames, Isabel will now always be the honorable woman of her word that has gone down in history, and the Ministry will remain hidden to do the important work of historical memory and revision that the Catholic queen founded it for. Moreover, as in *Isabel*, the founder of the modern nation and iconic 'exceptional' medieval woman is distanced from the Inquisition's activities, even though they formed part of a concerted political and ideological program supported by both of the Catholic Monarchs. In this way, *The Ministry of Time* allegorizes historical revisionism, while simultaneously championing the importance of an exemplary icon. The series balances metafictional historiographic reflexivity with the love, ever-tempered by gender politics, of the historical fiction that is Isabel.

## THE QUEEN OF SPAIN

Fernando Trueba's *The Queen of Spain* debuted on November 25, 2016 after months of the kind of marketing that is familiar to lavish productions directed by and starring Oscar winners, yet the theater in central Madrid where I saw the film the following day was nearly empty.[22] While the self-proclaimed '*ministéricos*' were sharing their love and fandom of *The Ministry of Time* on social media, Trueba's critics took to the internet to call for a boycott of *The Queen of Spain* in reaction to the director's declaration that 'never, not even for five minutes of my life, have I felt Spanish' in his acceptance speech for the Spanish national prize for cinematography in September 2015, a statement he explained later as a critique of nationalisms.[23] The wrath that he incurred, followed by reviews that were critical of the film's representations of Isabel I, serve to ironically highlight how images of the queen are still bound up closely with feelings of national identity.[24] Trueba's *The Queen of Spain* takes the impossibility of separating images of Isabel from politics as a given. Set in 1956, the film portrays the making of a film about Isabel I and the conquest of Granada, against the backdrop of Franco's totalitarian regime, censorship in Spain and the USA, the building of The Valley of the Fallen, and Hollywood's use of an economically depressed Spain as a convenient place for making movies, such as those known as 'paella westerns'.

*The Queen of Spain* is a sequel to Trueba's 1998 *The Girl of Your Dreams*, the story of a Spanish–German film production set in 1938, featuring Penélope Cruz as diva Macarena Granada, Antonio Resines as the film director Fontiveros, as well as Rosa María Sardá, Loles León, and Jorge Sanz, among others.[25] *The Girl of Your Dreams* pitted the artists against both the Nazis and the Spanish Fascists. In one scene, Joseph Goebbels, Reich Minister of Propaganda, tries to seduce Macarena Granada by promising to give her the best and biggest roles in German film, including the part of 'Isabel of Spain, who expelled the Jews from Spain'.[26] Goebbels's vision of Macarena as Isabel comes to fruition in *The Queen of Spain*, but thanks to Hollywood's cooperation with the Franco regime rather than with the Nazis. The production, a colossal epic supported by Franco, clearly recalls the making of another epic about a national medieval hero that, like Isabel, held a special place in Francoist ideology, *El Cid* directed by Anthony Mann in 1961.

In *The Queen of Spain*, the actors and crew of the Hispano-Nazi production portrayed in *The Girl of Your Dreams* are joined by a famous but catatonic American director, John Scott, who sports a John Fordesque eyepatch (Clive Revill), Jordan Berman, a black-listed American screenwriter (Mandy Patinkin), and Gary Jones, a Hollywood heartthrob (Carey Elwes). In addition to the constant palimpsestic presence of *The Girl of Your Dreams*, *The Queen of Spain* recalls *The Princess Bride* by reuniting Patinkin and Elwes, and visually echoes a host of other movies, including *The Seven Year Itch* and *Sabrina*. *The Queen of Spain* is a film-lovers film.

*The Queen of Spain* pokes fun at Hollywood medievalism and at the custom of white actors performing in blackface, but also lovingly recreates 1950s special effects, showing us, for example, the creation of a detailed model of Granada and the optical effects created by hand-painted hanging miniatures and matte shots to create the illusion of a vast panorama or a cathedral interior draped with flags.

Ironically, the filming of the film-within-a film 'The Queen of Spain' stages a symbolic return of the Jews to Spain, in the form of Berman and the American producer, Sam Spiegelman (Arturo Ripstein). This return is figured as simultaneously post-expulsion and post-Holocaust, in its intertextual references to both *The Girl of Your Dreams'* portrayals of Jews in Berlin in 1938 and multi-temporal evocations of 1492 and post-war Europe. Macarena is also returning to Spain after becoming an American citizen and Hollywood sensation in order to star in 'The Queen of Spain,' even though she is fiercely anti-Franco. The cast and crew use the filming of battles from the War of Granada as a ruse for rescuing Fontiveros, a non-Jewish survivor of the concentration camps, from the Valley of the Fallen where he has been imprisoned and condemned to forced labor working on the monument to Franco's victory.

Dense and conflictive historical memories are piled high in *The Queen of Spain*, where the historical film-within-a-film setting goes beyond cinematic metafiction to historiographic metafiction. Like *The Ministry of Time*, in *The Queen of Spain*, the remaking of the past within and *for* the present reveals the work of interpretation necessary for creating a historical film, and the powerful impact of mediatization on historical memory. However, *The Queen of Spain's* layering of its diegetic present, 1956, with the twenty-first century present of its audience creates an ironic distance that *The Ministry of Time* only hints at as its twenty-first century time-travelers visit Spain's past.

Penélope Cruz, who looks more like Sophia Loren in the role of Jimena in *The Cid* than Michelle Jenner in *Isabel*, is possibly the least likely of actors to be typecast as Isabel I. And, in the hands of the film producers, both fictional and real, Isabel as portrayed by Macarena (as played by Cruz) is an anachronistic travesty.[27] Heavily made-up, long dark hair flowing, and decked out in low-cut velvet and gold brocade, the Isabel of 'The Queen of Spain' is as sexy as Elizabeth Taylor's Cleopatra and as tuneful as Julie Andrews's Queen Guinevere; in short, she is nothing like traditional images of Isabel. As the crew is filming a scene in which Isabel and Fernando run towards each other, passionately embrace and kiss deeply, the historical consultant on set, Doña Matilde Velorracho (Ana Alonso), begins to complain vociferously about the scene's immorality and ahistoricism. Doña Matilde, upright historian and biographer of the Catholic queen, simultaneously represents the Franco Regime's images of a pious and saintly Isabel and the historian's habitual dissatisfaction with anachronisms in medieval films.[28]

As both April Harper and Janice North show in their essays in this volume, historical fiction in film and television has not distinguished itself by nuanced, politically progressive representations of medieval women, regardless of a particular production's approach to the past. *The Queen of Spain* is particularly clumsy in its handling of gender issues and sexuality; the gay characters in the story are either limp-wristed stereotypes or sexual predators, and Macarena is sexually voracious and uncomplicated in her earthy lust, depicted as part of the demo-cratic freedoms she enjoys as a Spanish-born American citizen, uncon-strained by the national Catholic mores imposed by the Franco regime. Unlike *Isabel*, *Juana la Loca*, *La Corona Partida*, and *1492: Conquest of Paradise*, however, *The Queen of Spain* does not attempt to represent the Middle Ages accurately, but rather to portray Spain in the 1950s, where filmmaking could, on the one hand, whitewash the political repression the of present, but on the other, be a force for liberation. This is much the case for *El Cid*, which lends itself to a traditional national Catholic reading, but also portrays the Cid as a classically liberal hero positioned between two equally repressive regimes, the Almoravids and the Castilian rule of Alfonso VI.[29]

How can the historical record and Isabelline hagiographic historiog-raphy be reconciled? In one brief sequence, *The Queen of Spain* sums up the problem Isabel I presents to cultural memory and the challenge faced by Spanish directors and actors attempting to make the medi-eval queen appeal to contemporary audiences, a challenge that Emily

S. Beck explores in her essay on *Isabel* in this volume. Some forty-five minutes into the film, we see Macarena sitting at her mirror, made up as Isabel, and peering over the cover of Doña Matilde's biography *Isabel the Catholic* to ogle one of the film crew. The scene presents us with a triptych of three divas reflected in the make-up mirror, each suggestive of the mediatization and historical revisions that have molded cultural memory of Isabel I: Macarena-Isabel the Hollywood queen, a traditional portrait of Isabel, the saintly queen, and a photograph of Doña Matilde, the Francoist official biographer Fig. 9.1.

The book has completely changed Macarena's image of Isabel: 'I'm beginning to hate this Isabel, what a bitch, she's really getting on my nerves,' she says, and then approaches the director, John Scott, for advice on how to play her role.[30] Speaking in English, Macarena explains,

> I had the idea that this woman was a saint, when she was anything but. She threw the Jews out of Spain. She did the same thing with the Muslims. She organized the Inquisition. And on top of that she was a pig who swore never to wash until she won Granada back. Anyway, none of this appears in the script.

**Fig. 9.1**   Film, History, and Film-History meet in *The Queen of Spain*

When she finishes her short historical revision of Isabel, Macarena finds that the director has fallen asleep. Macarena, as the artist, shares the conundrum of how to play Isabel with the producers of *Isabel*, but Hollywood could not care less about the historical Queen Isabel or the saintly ideogram of cultural memory.

*The Queen of Spain* and the film-within-a film, 'The Queen of Spain' conclude with an iris-in shot of Cruz-Macarena-Isabel crowned upon her throne. This triumphant finale is filmed just after Trueba brings Franco (Carlos Areces) face to face with Hollywood's version of his legendary Catholic queen. In their confrontation, the power of the Hollywood star combined with the privilege of an American passport deflates the coercive power of the dictator, who—though he can remind Macarena of how her father died imprisoned by his regime—cannot control her. Macarena, in full Isabelline regalia, blows smoke into Franco's face and swears at him with an idiomatic phrase that loosely translates to 'I couldn't give a flying fuck,' and is, like Macarena herself, the antithesis of Isabelline decorum.[31] In this remake of Isabel, Franco has met his match. History, personified by Cruz-Macarena-Isabel will not be managed by the state, though the state may finance a film that Doña Matilde complains 'is indecent, intolerable, an ahistorical absurdity'.[32]

There is little that is straightforward about Trueba's characterization of cinematic medievalism. *The Queen of Spain* rejects both the national Catholic revision of Isabel and the academic's desire for historical accuracy, in the defense of the freedom of artistic expression when representing the Middle Ages and the power, if not the responsibility, of creative art to oppose totalitarianism, a stance shared by *The Girl of Your Dreams*.

## CONCLUSION

Remaking Isabel I, the Catholic Queen, on screen is sure to provoke strong feelings, particularly at moments when national identity and historical memory are the subjects of fierce public debates. In *The Ministry of Time*, as in *Isabel*, Isabel represents a medieval past that the present celebrates, but also one that it must at least seem to have outgrown in the pursuit of twenty-first century religious tolerance. If *The Ministry of Time's* Isabel is familiar, recognizably crafted from traditional historiography, and bolstered by *Isabel*, Trueba's queen is aggressively cast against type. In *The Queen of Spain*, Isabel is wrested from Francoist ideology in order to become an ahistorical Hollywood fantasy for the 1950s, while twenty-first century audiences, unlike Macarena and an entire generation of Spaniards, have access to Isabel as rewritten by post-Franco and post-modern historiography, which allows us to see 'The Queen of Spain' as movie medievalism.

In both *The Ministry of Time* and *The Queen of Spain*, the reflexivity of historiographic metafiction counters the power that historical television and film can have to impose simplified narratives onto complex histories, and draws attention to how 'to re-write or to re-present the past in fiction and in history is, in both cases, to open it up to the present, to prevent it from being conclusive and teleological,' underlining 'the ideological implications of writing about history, among others'.[33] The creation of ironic distance suggestively, if only implicitly in the case of *The Ministry of Time*, encourages audiences to reevaluate how we imagine Isabel and how she is portrayed in popular culture. *The Ministry of Time* and *The Queen of Spain* remind us that 'The Queen of Time' is a queen for all seasons, a figure from the past upon which the desires and anxieties of multiple pasts and presents are projected, and whose actions and words are molded by the successive medievalisms of official history, popular culture, and cultural memory.

## NOTES

1. Barbara F. Weissberger, "Isabel on TV: Politics Past and Present," *Early Modern Women, An Interdisciplinary Journal* 8 (2013): 352.
2. J. N. Hilgarth, "Spanish Historiography and Iberian Reality," *History and Theory* 24.1 (1985): 23–43.
3. Emily S. Beck, "Religious Medievalisms in RTVE's *Isabel*," in *Premodern Rulers and Postmodern Viewers: Gender, Sex, and Power in Popular Culture*, eds. Janice North, Karl Alvestad, and Elena Woodacre (Palgrave Macmillan, 2018), 159–178: 162.
4. *Cristóbal Colón, de oficio descubridor*, directed by Mariano Ozores (Constan Films, 1982); Nancy F. Marino, "Inventing the Catholic Queen: Images of Isabel I in History and Fiction" in *Queen Isabel I of Castile: Power, Patronage, Persona*, ed. Barbara Weissberger (Woodbridge, UK: Tamesis 2008), 186–199, and Weissberger *Isabel Rules: Constructing Queenship, Wielding Power* (Minneapolis: Minnesota University Press, 2004).
5. On parodies and canonicity, see Linda Hutcheon, *A Theory of Parody: The Teachings of Twentieth-Century Art Forms* (New York: Methuen, 1985), esp. 106–107.

6. Original titles: *El Ministerio del Tiempo* and *La reina de España*. All translations are my own.
7. For an anthology of reviews and essays, see *Dentro de* El Ministerio del Tiempo, ed. Concepción Cascajosa (Alcalá de Hernares: Léeme, 2015).
8. I take the term and definition of historiographic metafiction from Linda Hutcheon, *A Poetics of Postmodernism* (London-New York: Routledge, 1988), 106–118.
9. "Law 52/2007, December 26, by which the rights of those who suffered persecution or violence during the civil war and the dictatorship are recognized and increased and corrective measures are instituted." ("Ley 52/2007, de 26 de diciembre, por la que se reconocen y amplían derechos y se establecen medidas en favor de quienes padecieron persecución o violencia durante la guerra civil y la dictadura"), *Boletín oficial del estado*, 301 (2007). Accessed May 1, 2017. http://www.boe.es/boe/dias/2007/12/27/. The law, passed under the socialist government led by José Luis Rodríguez Zapatero, was opposed by the Popular Party, in power when *The Ministry of Time's* first season was produced. Consequently, *The Ministry of Time*, produced by state television, imagines a ministry under the directorate of the current Prime Minister, Mariano Rajoy. The complex and divisive politics of the Law of Historical Memory lie beyond the scope of this short essay. For an overview, see Jo Labanyi.
10. Javier Olivares and Pablo Olivares, "Capítulo 1: El tiempo es el que es" *El Ministerio del Tiempo*, season 1, episode 1, directed by Marc Vigill, aired February 24, 2015. The Spanish title of the book is *El libro de las puertas del tiempo*. Levi tells Isabel that she will be 'la reina del Tiempo'.
11. 'No es una historia edificante.' Scripts for all episodes are available on http://www.rtve.es/television/ministerio-del-tiempo/la-serie/.
12. José Ramón Fernández, Javier Olivares, and Pablo Olivares, "Capítulo 4: Una negociación a tiempo," *El Ministerio del Tiempo*, season 1, episode 4, directed by Jorge Dorado, aired March 16, 2015.
13. 'Juraría que la conozco de algo.'
14. '¡Abraham Levi está bajo mi protección!'
15. '¿Y mi marido?'
16. '¿Cuántas veces he dicho que no se haga nada sin mi consentimiento?... ¡La reina de Castilla soy yo, no mi esposo!' and '¡Vaya carácter tiene esta mujer!'
17. 'Una mujer necesita eso y más para llegar al trono. Y más en el siglo XV.'
18. 'No es nuestro asunto. Es la reina.'
19. 'Isabel siempre fue mujer de palabra.'
20. Jane Tolmie, "Medievalism and the Fantasy Heroine," *Journal of Gender Studies* 15.2 (2006): 145–158.
21. The desire to rehabilitate Isabel's image for the twenty-first century is akin to the search for 'mothers to think back through,' as Sheila Delany, via Virginia Woolf, characterizes the recuperation of medieval women

writers, at times taken up naively as unambiguous 'feminist' models for the present day. Shelia Delany, "'Mothers to Think Back Through': Who Are They? The Ambiguous Example of Christine de Pizan," in *Medieval Texts and Conteporary Readers*, ed. Laurie A. Finke and Martin B. Shichtman (Ithaca: Cornell University Press, 1987): 177–197.

22. Trueba's *Belle Époque* won the Oscar for best foreign film in 1994. Other films have won Goyas and prizes at the Berlin International Film Festival.

23. 'Nunca me he sentido español. Ni cinco minutos de mi vida,' D. Prieto and C. Pastor, "Fernando Trueba: 'Nunca me he sentido español'" *El mundo*, September 9, 2015. http://www.elmundo.es/cultura/2015/09/19/55fd5984ca47417c128b4578.html.

24. *The Queen of Spain* received few good reviews. Although many critics were predisposed to pan the film due to the scandal, *The Queen of Spain* also elicited a great deal of well-deserved negative criticism regarding its quality. It is a lengthy, gimmicky movie that recurs frequently to stereotypes. This writer is in agreement with most of the negative reviews regarding the film's artistic virtues. However, as an avid historical film-goer interested in medievalisms and historical memory, she also freely admits that she loved it. For a range of critical reactions, see Juan Saguino, "No, el boicot a Trueba no tiene la culpa del fracaso de 'La reina de España'," *Vanity Fair*, November 30, 2016. http://www.revistavanityfair.es/actualidad/cine/articulos/boicot-a-trueba-no-tiene-culpa-fracaso-la-reina-de-espana/23163. See also, Javier Ocaña, "Sombras en los ojos de la niña," *El País*, November 24, 2016. http://cultura.elpais.com/cultura/2016/11/24/actualidad/1479943642_150688.html, and Oti Rodríguez Marchante "'La reina de España' (✱✱): El valle de los alicaídos," *ABC*, November 24, 2016. Accessed May 13, 2017. http://www.abc.es/play/cine/criticas/abci-reina-espana-valle-alicaidos-201611242128_noticia.html. Luis Martínez "La última columna: Fernando Trueba," *El mundo*, November 25, 2016. Accessed May 18, 2017. http://www.elmundo.es/opinion/2016/11/25/58373d5146163ff2468b45f5.html.

25. Rafael Azcona, Manuel Àngel Egea, Carlos López, David Trueba and Fernando Trueba, *La niña de tus ojos*, directed by Fernando Trueba (1998; Lolafilms, 1998), DVD.

26. 'Usted interpretará a Isabel la Católica que expulsó a los judíos de España.' As Polly Hodge points out, Trueba portrays Goebbels as attempting to capitalize on fifteenth-century Spain and the Nazi regime's shared antisemitism in his failed seduction. "Maestros de la manipulación," *Hispania* 98, no. 3 (2015): 434–435.

27. Oti Rodríguez Marchante, writing for the right-leaning *ABC* took particular offence at Trueba's 'vision of history' ('vision de la historia'), taking the film-within-a-film's recreation of Isabel for Trueba's own image of fifteenth-century history. "'La reina de España' (✱✱): El valle de los alicaídos."

28. I believe that the character Doña Matilde Velorracho is based upon Ángeles Villarta, author of *Isabel the Catholic, the Queen of the Spaniards* (Isabel la Católica, la Reina de los españoles), published in 1950. In 2012, Villarta was named 'dama de honor' by the Fundación Nacional Francisco Franco. Accessed May 17, 2017. http://www.fnff.es/M_Angeles_Villarta_Tunon_414_c.htm.
29. Mark Jankovich, "The Purest Knight of All': Nation, History, and Representation in El Cid (1960), " *Cinema Journal* 40, no. 1 (Autumn, 2000): 79–103.
30. 'Le estoy cogiendo una tirria a la Isabel esta, menuda tiparraca la tía, me está atravesando.'
31. 'Me las paso por el coño.'
32. '¡indecente, es intolerable, esto es un complete disparate histórico!'
33. Hutcheon, *A Poetics*, 110; 117.

## Bibliography

### Films and Television Series Cited

*Cristóbal Colón, de oficio descubridor*. Feature Film. Directed by Mariano Ozores. Constan Films, 1982.

*El Cid*. Feature Film. Directed by Anthony Mann. Samuel Bronston Productions, 1961.

*El Ministerio del Tiempo*. Television Series. RTVE. Season 1 (2015). Episodes are available online: http://www.rtve.es/television/ministerio-del-tiempo/capitulos-completos/temporada1/.

*Isabel*. Television Series. RTVE/Diagonal TV. Seasons 1–3 (2012–14). Episodes are available online: http://www.rtve.es/television/isabel-la-catolica/capitulos-completos/.

*La niña de tus ojos*. Feature Film. Directed by Fernando Trueba. Lolafilms, 1998.

*La reina de España*. Feature Film. Directed by Fernando Trueba. Lolafilms, 2016.

### Film reviews

Martínez, Luis. "La última columna: Fernando Trueba," *El mundo*, November 25, 2016. http://www.elmundo.es/opinion/2016/11/25/58373d514616 3ff2468b45f5.html.

Ocaña, Javier. "Sombras en los ojos de la niña." El País. November 24, 2016. http://cultura.elpais.com/cultura/2016/11/24/actualidad/1479943642_150688.html.

Rodríguez Marchante, Oti. "'La reina de España' (**): El valle de los alicaídos." *ABC*, November 24, 2016. http://www.abc.es/play/cine/criticas/abci-reina-espana-valle-alicaidos-201611242128_noticia.html.

Juan Saguino, "No, el boicot a Trueba no tiene la culpa del fracaso de 'La reina de España'," *Vanity Fair*, November 30, 2016. http://www.revistavanityfair.es/actualidad/cine/articulos/boicot-a-trueba-no-tiene-culpa-fracaso-la-reina-de-espana/23163.

## Works and References Cited

Beck, Emily S. "Religious Medievalisms in RTVE's *Isabel*." In *Premodern Rulers and Postmodern Viewers: Gender, Sex, and Power in Popular Culture*, edited by Janice North, Karl Alvestad, and Elena Woodacre, 159–178. New York: Palgrave Macmillan, 2018.

Cascajosa, Concepción, ed. *Dentro de* El Ministerio del Tiempo. Alcalá de Hernares: Léeme, 2015.

Delaney, Sheila. "'Mothers to think back through': Who are They? The Ambiguous Example of Christine de Pizan." In *Medieval Texts and Conteporary Readers*, edited by Laurie A. Finke and Martin B. Shichtman, 177–197. Ithaca: Cornell University Press, 1987.

Fundación Nacional Francisco Franco. "María Ángeles Villarta Tuñón." Undated. http://www.fnff.es/M_Angeles_Villarta_Tunon_414_c.htm.

Harper, April. "Silencing Queens: The Dominated Discourse of Historical Queens in Film." In *Premodern Rulers and Postmodern Viewers: Gender, Sex, and Power in Popular Culture*, edited by Janice North, Karl Alvestad, and Elena Woodacre, 51–68. New York: Palgrave Macmillan, 2018.

Hilgarth, J. N. "Spanish Historiography and Iberian Reality." *History and Theory* 24, no. 1 (1985): 23–43. http://www.jstor.org/stable/2504941.

Hodge, Polly. "Maestros de la manipulación: Titiriteros de la memoria histórica en *No* de Pablo Larraín y *La niña de tus ojos* de Fernando Trueba." *Hispania* 98, no. 3 (2015): 431–441.

Hutcheon, Linda. *A Theory of Parody: The Teachings of Twentieth-Century Art Forms*. New York: Methuen, 1985.

Jankovich, Mark. "'The Purest Knight of All': Nation, History, and Representation in El Cid (1960)." *Cinema Journal* 40, no. 1 (Autumn, 2000): 79–103.

Labanyi, Jo. "Memory and Modernity in Democratic Spain: The Difficulty of Coming to Terms with the Spanish Civil War." *Poetics Today* 28, no. 1 (Spring 2007): 89–116. https://doi.org/10.1215/03335372-2006-016.

———. "Historias de víctimas: la memoria histórica y el testimonio en la España contemporánea." *Iberoamericana* 6, no. 24 (2006): 87–98. http://www.jstor.org/stable/41661175.

"Ley 52/2007, de 26 de diciembre, por la que se reconocen y amplían derechos y se establecen medidas en favor de quienes padecieron persecución o violencia durante la guerra civil y la dictadura." *Boletín oficial del estado*, 301 (2007). http://www.boe.es/boe/dias/2007/12/27/.

Marino, Nancy. "Inventing the Catholic Queen: Images of Isabel I in History and Fiction." In *Queen Isabel I of Castile: Power, Patronage, Persona*, edited by Barbara F. Weissberger, 186–199. Woodbridge, UK: Tamesis, 2008.

North, Janice. "From Mad Love to Mad Lust: The Dangers of Female Desire in Twenty-first Century Representations of Juana I of Castile in Film and Television." In *Premodern Rulers and Postmodern Viewers: Gender, Sex, and Power in Popular Culture*, edited by Janice North, Karl Alvestad, and Elena Woodacre, 195–214. New York: Palgrave Macmillan, 2018.

Weissberger, Barbara F. "Isabel on TV: Politics Past and Present." *Early Modern Women, An Interdisciplinary Journal* 8 (2013): 349–359. http://www.jstor.org/stable/23617861.

# CHAPTER 10

# From Mad Love to Mad Lust: The Dangers of Female Desire in Twenty-First Century Representations of Juana I of Castile in Film and Television

*Janice North*

Juana I of Castile (1479–1555) spent the last 46 years of her life—almost her entire reign as queen—cloistered in a castle in the remote town of Tordesillas. Her father, Fernando II of Aragon, and her husband, Philip, Lord of the Netherlands and Duke of Burgundy, tried to have her declared incompetent due to insanity, and except for the period from September 1506 to July 1507, she was queen in name only. After Philip's death, her father ruled as regent in Castile until his death in 1516, after which her son Carlos became king of both Castile and Aragon. Juana's father and her son kept her isolated, closely controlling her contact with the outside world in order to avoid potential challenges to their authority. No chronicles were written for Juana, and for a time it seemed that she might be forgotten. In spite of this obscurity, today the myth of the 'Mad Queen' Juana is fairly well known. The version that is currently

J. North (✉)
Independent Scholar, Altoona, PA, USA

© The Author(s) 2018
J. North et al. (eds.), *Premodern Rulers and Postmodern Viewers*,
Queenship and Power, https://doi.org/10.1007/978-3-319-68771-1_10

so familiar is a product of nineteenth-century Romanticism. During that century, painters, playwrights, and historians were drawn to her story, which appealed to their Romantic sensibilities: a 'medieval' tale of a woman driven mad by an obsessive love for her unfaithful husband. A number of histories, paintings, an opera, and a play were dedicated to telling that story, which continued to draw artists and historians in the centuries that followed.[1]

The topic of Juana's supposed madness continues to be a point of controversy to this day. Nineteenth-century historians, such as Gustav A. Bergenroth and Antonio Rodríguez Villa, considered her to be either heretical or the victim of an obsessive fixation on her husband and his corpse.[2] In the twentieth century, Ludwig Phfandl and Amarie Dénnis diagnosed Juana as a schizophrenic in order to explain her 'moments of lucidity,' a diagnosis that continues to be championed in the twenty-first century by Miguel Ángel Zalama,[3] while the popular biography by Manuel Fernández Álvarez portrays Juana as a victim of the political battles waged between her family members.[4] Most recently, Bethany Aram has put forth a thesis that Juana's fits of rage were attempts to use *ira regis*—or royal displays of anger—in order to invoke fear in her servants and to achieve some level of control over her household, which was invariably governed by other members of her family. Aram also suggests that Juana's 'retirement' in Tordesillas and her devotion to Philip's corpse were strategies designed to put off a second marriage, thereby ensuring the succession of her son Carlos to the Castilian and Aragonese thrones.[5] Part of the problem with determining Juana's relative madness or sanity is the reliability of contemporary accounts. In short, it is hard to separate historical fact from politically motivated fiction.

This essay does not seek to answer the question of whether or not Juana was 'mad,' nor the roots of her purported mental disturbance. Rather, it examines how the queen has been portrayed in popular media—the driving force perpetuating her memory—and in particular how the myth of the 'Mad Queen' has evolved from the original Romantic tale of a love-sick woman to the most recent television and film portrayals.[6] The analysis will focus on two twenty-first century depictions, Vicente Aranda's 2001 film *Juana la Loca* (*Mad Love*), and the version offered by RTVE in the television series *Isabel* (2014) and the 2016 film *La corona partida* (*The Broken Crown*).[7]

These portrayals will be compared against their antecedents: Juan de Orduña's 1948 film *Locura de amor* (*Madness for Love*) and the nineteenth-century play that inspired that film, Manuel Tamayo y Baus's *La locura de amor* (*The Madness of Love*).[8] As this analysis will show, Juana's story has been reinvented in the twenty-first century, and yet one thing has not changed; namely, Juana's tragic fate continues to be attributed to the failings of a passionate and weak femininity.

## THE MADNESS OF LOVE FROM THE THEATER TO THE SCREEN

Among the number of famous paintings and literary works that depicted Juana's love-madness in the nineteenth century, arguably the most influential has been Manuel Tamayo y Baus's *La locura de amor*. This play, which was a commercial and international success at the time, has been adapted into a feature film not once, but four times in the past two centuries.[9] In the play, Philip's counselors, who hope to separate Juana from her husband and from the governance of her kingdom, accuse her of being insane with jealousy. At the outset, the queen appears to be quite sane, though she suffers because she expects her philandering husband to be faithful to her. As Philip courts a Moorish princess named Aldara, eventually sneaking her into the court to be one of Juana's handmaidens, Juana chooses love over duty. She offends the dignity of her station and ignores her responsibilities in favor of discovering the identity of Philip's lover. Eventually, Juana confronts Aldara and challenges her to a duel, convincing everyone around her that the queen is indeed crazy. Then, in an abrupt turn of events in the fourth act, Juana changes. She redeems herself, if only momentarily, by disrupting a *Cortes* that her husband has called in order to declare her incompetent. Juana defends herself ably, proving not only her sanity, but also her capability as a queen. She promises that she will now put her duty as queen before her personal happiness and compares herself to her worthy mother, Isabel *la Católica* (the Catholic):

> From now on, I will no longer lament licentious offenses. To love a man is to love as all women; but a Queen must love like God, loving an entire people ... Do not think, sirs, to again overstep the bounds of the law, with which the powerful hand of the Catholic Isabel contained you. Tremble before the daughter, as you trembled before the mother.[10]

In spite of this momentary redemption that puts her on a par with her idealized mother, Juana loses her resolve when Philip falls ill, confesses his love for her, and begs for her forgiveness. Upon her husband's death, Juana finally loses her mind, declaring that Philip is not dead, but merely sleeping.

In Tamayo y Baus's play, Juana is torn between her political and personal selves. On one hand, she wants to be a worthy heir to her mother's legacy, but this desire is superseded by another, more powerful desire: a desire for domestic bliss. As she explains to her handmaiden Elvira:

> Often the revered shadow of my mother Isabel appears before my eyes ... And I hear the voice of Queen Isabel say to me: Think of your sacred duties ... love your people ... conserve my legacy, give Spain new glories and blessings; and my heart only answers: I love in each one of its beats, and I want to cry like a repentant queen, but I cry like a woman in love.[11]

David R. George argues that rather than a censure of Juana's weakness, the play contains a criticism of a society that is losing its moral compass. Juana seeks marital fidelity and happiness in her role as a wife, and yet the world treats her if she were crazy. George interprets Juana's 'madness' in the *denouement* as the protagonist's decision to give up fighting against the degenerate world that she lives in, opting to be considered insane rather than to conform to society's expectations.[12] It is true that Juana is treated sympathetically, as is reflected in the words and actions of the loyal Castilians who adore Juana and blame Philip. Nevertheless, Juana's debility is clearly gendered feminine. Her *raison d'être* is her love for a man, and she shows little inclination or ability to assume her political responsibilities. Whether it is censure or praise of the historical woman, Juana chooses the role of wife over of that of queen, and she is characterized by an excess of feminine passion and weakness that ultimately keep her out of the political sphere.

Considered within its historical-political context, there are additional reasons to interpret Tamayo y Baus's play as circumscribing female action to the domestic realm. The play debuted in 1855, toward the end of the reign of Isabel II of Spain (1833–1868), who—as María Elena Soliño explains—used historical paintings of Isabel I to draw parallels between her rule and that of the Catholic queen. However, as Soliño points out, in the last years of her reign depictions of Isabel I tended toward the domestic rather than the regnant.[13] Soliño also signals that during the reign of Isabel's son, Alfonso XII, depictions of Juana 'filled the need to erase the memories of unruly female sovereignty left behind by the ousted Isabel II, and replace them with a visual landscape of female passivity and helplessness more in accordance with the values of the Restoration of a Spanish monarchy still firmly rooted in traditional patterns'.[14]

While Tamayo y Baus's play predates Isabel's ouster, given its depiction of Juana as incapable of governance and in need of male support, it seems reasonable to conclude that something similar is occurring here. In a discussion between Don Álvar and the Admiral at the beginning of the fifth act, these two patriots agree that the queen will not be able to carry on after her husband's death, and yet they do not criticize her. Don Álvar declares that, 'if she has to lose her husband, it would be best if Doña Juana should also die' since, only in heaven 'will she be able to find the rest and happiness that she deserves'.[15] The scene ends with the Admiral's affirmation that the only solution is for King Fernando to return to Castile to take Juana's place. Thus, while the reign of Isabel the Catholic merits respect, it is an anomaly, and Juana—and by extension, nineteenth-century royal women—should not be expected to participate in governance.

Juan de Orduña's 1948 adaption of Tamayo y Baus's play is a mostly faithful imitation of the original, though with the addition of a political allegory in support of Francisco Franco.[16] The film is an account of how the queen lost her mind, told in a series of flashbacks by Captain Álvar to the young King Carlos upon his arrival in Spain. In this version, Juana is 'harassed and driven mad by foreigners who, in their boundless ambition, employ intrigue and deception and put the unity of Spain in danger'.[17] The principal foreign threat comes from Philip's counselor Philibert de Veyre and the Moorish princess Aldara, whom he enlists in a plot to drive the queen crazy with jealousy. Aldara is motivated by a desire for revenge against the Catholic queen who conquered her father's kingdom of Granada, and Philibert by his ambition, which poses a threat not just to the unity of the kingdom, but also to the Catholic hegemony of Spain, since he seeks to promote a 'marriage between Flanders and Granada' via Philip's relationship with Aldara.[18]

In the film, Juana and Aldara serve as foils for one another, and their characters are adapted in ways that speak to Juana's gendered representation. Orduña's Juana is virginal, passive, and honorable, while Aldara is characterized by lust, aggression, and deceit. This juxtaposition is made clear by a reversal of roles in the scene where the women confront one another. In the third act of Tamayo y Baus's play, Juana laments her condition as a woman, since men can kill their rivals. When Aldara claims she also wants physical vengeance, Juana promptly fetches two swords, throwing one at Aldara's feet and demanding that she defend herself. Aldara calls for help, and the queen is made to look as if she has lost her senses. In Orduña's film, however, it is Aldara who attacks the queen, this time with a less honorable weapon—a dagger concealed on her person. A frightened Juana calls for help, but Aldara cunningly tosses the dagger at the queen's feet and convinces everyone that Juana attacked her in a fit of jealousy. With these alterations, Juana loses her virility, becoming a helpless victim of the dishonest Moorish amazon.

Another change that contributes to Juana's characterization as weakly feminine surrounds the *Cortes* in Burgos. Notably absent from this adaptation is Juana's temporary recuperation, wherein she decides to give up her obsession with Philip and to set her sights on being a good queen. Instead, as the men gather at the *Cortes*, a resigned Juana refuses to intervene. Captain Álvar only manages to rouse her to action by appealing to her domestic sensibilities, suggesting that Philip plans to make Aldara his wife and queen. Moreover, Juana is not successful in defending herself at this gathering. She attempts to vindicate her jealousy by delivering into the hands of her principal defender, the Admiral, proof of her husband's infidelity in the form of a letter that Aldara wrote to Philip. However, Philibert has replaced the letter with a blank piece of parchment, and when the Admiral confesses that there is nothing written there, Juana pulls a horrified face and grabs her head between her hands—apparently convinced of her own madness—and then slumps, disgraced, from the room.

Orduña's Juana is a hopelessly tragic and passive figure who—like the motherland—is in need of masculine protection. She is victimized by foreigners, including a crafty and aggressive Muslim woman who threatens Spain's unity and its Catholic heritage, values symbolized by the memory of the virile and virginal Queen Isabel. Eventually, these threats are neutralized by Álvar, the military caretaker who delivers Juana's kingdom to Carlos, and by Divine Providence, which Álvar claims killed the king.[19] For Orduña, female sexuality—embodied in the Moorish seductress—is as dangerous and as Other to Spain as are the ambitious Flemish foreigners who plot to destroy the legacy of the Catholic queen.

## REDEMPTION OR THE DANGERS OF FEMALE DESIRE?
## VICENTE ARANDA'S *JUANA LA LOCA*

The second half of Vicente Aranda's 2001 film *Juana la Loca* is essentially an adaptation of Tamayo y Baus's play, while the first half chronicles Juana's marriage and life in the Low Countries. As the original Spanish title (*Juana the Mad*) suggests, Aranda's film is a deeply personal narrative that strips the original story (entitled *The Madness of Love*) of its political import and refocuses it on the experience of the protagonist. The film seemingly aligns with a popular biography by Fernández Álvarez that came out the year before, in which the historian asserts that Juana suffered from a voracious sexual appetite that led to her instability and the volatility of her marriage.[20] However, instead of blaming Juana for her passions, Aranda sets out to redeem Juana and her sexuality:

> With this film ... I want to explain why Juana the Mad was considered crazy at the time. Or rather, I want to explain precisely why, from a current perspective, she was not crazy ... For me, [Juana] was a woman who did not want to be queen [because] that took her away from her true desires, which were to be with her husband.[21]

Aranda's title is ironic in that his Juana is not mad, but rather modern, in a post-sexual-revolution sense. According to María Asunción Gómez, 'Aranda deconstructs the romantic myth of Juana's madness of love in order to relay his own modernized version of it ... Overflowing romantic passion now becomes a sort of sexual addiction in which the woman becomes an active agent, but within an unfortunate relationship of dependence on the man that jeopardizes her emotional stability.'[22]

In Aranda's film, Philip's relationship with Juana contributes to the redemption of her character through the normalization of her sexual addiction. In contrast to the narrative set forth by Fernández Álvarez, Philip is not the victim of his wife's sexual voracity, but rather a willing participant. As Asunción Gómez suggests, Philip seems to enjoy his wife's vehement displays of jealousy. For example, we glimpse a small smile on Philip's face as he comforts his lover, whose hair Juana has shorn in a fit of jealousy. When he confronts his wife over this incident, she holds a knife to his throat and declares that she wants to be everything to him: 'your wife, your woman, and your whore'.[23]

Philip frees himself, knocking Juana to the ground and heading toward the door. However, he is drawn back by Juana's moans of pleasure as she writhes on the ground, and the scene ends with him joining her on the floor for make-up sex that takes place off screen. In regards to this scene, Asunción Gómez affirms that Philip 'feels a special attraction to the actions that his wife carries out due to her jealousy' and that when 'Juana succumbs to the loss of her dignity because of her overwhelming desire … [Philip] feels a kind of sadomasochistic attraction toward her'.[24] Philip also clearly harbors doubts about his wife's alleged madness. In Aranda's film, Philip is largely a pawn in the plans of those who want to separate the couple and he vacillates, even as his father-in-law and closest advisors urge him to declare his wife insane.

By shifting from a naïve love-obsession to a more self-aware fixation on lust, Aranda breaks the mold with this version of Juana. Indeed, Juana's sexual pleasure is used in this film to disrupt the eroticism of the male gaze. Asunción Gómez explains how this occurs in a scene in which Juana takes pleasure from breastfeeding her infant child and her husband criticizes her for the practice of breastfeeding:

> In this scene two very different stances in regards to female sexuality are presented. Felipe's attitude reflects the dichotomous definitions of sexuality that mark an incompatibility between the maternal and erotic functions of woman's breasts. On the contrary, to Juana, reproductive practices are a source of eroticism. By portraying breasts in their erotic function—yet not to provide pleasure for the male viewer, but rather for the mother—Aranda deviates from the patriarchal point of view that opposes the two functions of the female organ.[25]

While it is true that Aranda's film explores, and even celebrates, women's sexual pleasure with Juana, it continues to objectify the female body, most notably in scenes that feature the Moor Aixa, a character that replaces the Granadan princess, Aldara, from previous versions of the story.

Aixa is introduced into the narrative in a voyeuristic fashion. Her identity is made known to Philip by her lover and 'protector,' Captain Corrales, as the king watches her perform an erotic belly dance at an inn in Castile. Afterwards, Corrales offers the king a closer look at her 'very beautiful body,' leading him backstage to watch Aixa undress through a small window hidden behind a curtain.[26] The next time we see Aixa she is preparing herself to be prostituted to the king. In this scene, the audience learns that she is a witch and witnesses her invoking Satan and the demon Asmodeus to cast a spell on a coin. When the king arrives, Aixa is lying on the bed, naked but for an elaborate webbing of jewelry. The audience is again engaged in voyeurism, as they watch Philip enter the room and see Aixa. As they make love, Aixa holds the coin over Philip's back and makes him promise to bring her to court as one of the queen's ladies before he 'spills forth,' so that she is effectively using both sex and witchcraft to bring him under her spell. In these scenes, a naked or nearly naked woman is gazed upon and lusted after by both the king and the camera. Aixa's face is often left out, as the camera focuses on the feminine curves of her body. So, while Juana (Pilar López de Ayala)'s breasts are cleverly used to disrupt the voyeuristic male gaze, the film falls back into traditional patterns of objectifying the female body with Aixa.

Aixa's role is significantly reduced in Aranda's film. In comparison with Aldara, who is a prominent character in both the original play and in the 1948 film, Aixa has little dialogue and her motivations are not clearly explained. No longer a princess (despite Corrales's claim to the contrary) Aixa is simply a Moor, a whore, and a witch, whose only stated motivation in taking Philip as a lover is to secure protection from the townspeople who might denounce her to the Inquisition. The only reason Aixa is included in the narrative is to serve as the object of Juana's jealousy and Philip's lust. With her backstory goes the religious confrontation between Spanish Catholics and Muslims Others, as is demonstrated by the stripping of religious references from the dialogue of her confrontation with the queen. In the end, this film is not about politics or religion, but rather about sex, and Aixa is a stereotyped character that conflates female seduction with witchcraft and religious and ethnic outsiders, even as she brings about Juana's perdition and slide into madness.

While Aranda set out to vindicate Juana's alleged sexual voracity in a celebration of post-sexual-revolution, female *jouissance*, one can read this depiction of the queen in a different fashion. Like other historical queens whose lives are adapted repeatedly for the screen, Juana's story revolves around her turbulent romantic relationship with a man. This depiction continues to obscure Juana's political self, further perpetuating the myth of the 'Mad Queen' who went crazy for love.

## In the Shadow of Her Mother: RTVE's Juana

What is arguably the most innovative aspect of RTVE's version of Juana's story is that it endeavors to inform its audience of Juana's attempts to exercise queenship. Director Jordi Frades said that with *La corona partida*, he and screenwriter José Martín set out to tell a story that was different from that told by Aranda or Orduña:

> We wanted to show other aspects [of the story] so that the viewer didn't have the sensation that we were telling the same story again ... I believe that our Juana shows the more political side, more of the queen's side ... more of the power struggle with her in the middle.[27]

Both the series and the film expand on Juana's story to include her political involvement. For example, the series includes Juana and Philip's sojourn in France on their way to be sworn as heirs to the Castilian and Aragonese thrones.[28] This episode depicts Juana as a strong woman with an acute sense of political ceremony, as she conducts herself with the dignity befitting her rank as princess of Asturias.

In contrast to Aranda's film, RTVE's version of Juana's story is told within the larger context of her mother's story. In both Tamayo y Baus's play and Orduña's adaptation, the reign of Queen Isabel is held up as a benchmark of greatness, against which Juana's lack of will to rule is compared—while in Aranda's film, Isabel only makes a brief appearance in order to emphasize the impersonal and unnatural way in which Juana was raised and married off to a foreigner.[29] RTVE brings the story full circle: Isabel is the true protagonist of the television series in which Juana plays a part, and it is Isabel's life story that provides a context in which Juana's actions are to be viewed. The placement of Juana's story within the context of Isabel's invites the audience to compare these two queens, a comparison that does not favor Juana. While Isabel is an analytical, sane, and dedicated queen, Juana is emotional, insane, and utterly selfish, with the possible exception of her enduring love and respect for her parents, especially her mother, whom she claims to want to emulate.[30] The key to this contrast between mother and daughter is the dichotomy of analytical / emotional, which genders Isabel as masculine and Juana as feminine.

Initially, Juana is presented to us as very much her mother's daughter. In the same way that season one offers us an Isabel who exceeds her younger brother in intelligence and political acumen,[31] Juana's brother Juan marvels at his sister's perspicacity and tells her that 'you ought to be the queen of Castile and Aragon ... You are more intelligent than I am.'[32] Like her mother, Juana is an independent young woman who chafes at being ordered by her fiancé not to ride horses or being told that, as a woman, she will be expected to turn a blind eye to her husband's infidelity. Despite these similarities, the differences in Isabel and Juana's characters soon become apparent. For example, while conversing with Beatriz de Bobadilla on the subject of extramarital love, Juana scandalizes Beatriz with her curiosity about 'women who have not turned away from [extramarital] love when it presents itself to them'.[33] In contrast, the youthful and prudish Isabel was terrified by the prospect of consummating her marriage.[34] This is significant because Juana's interest in romance and sexual pleasure are connected to her hyperemotionality, which leaves her open to her husband's manipulation.

In order to fully appreciate how sex plays a role in Juana's story, we need to return to the first and second seasons of *Isabel*, before Juana became a primary character. Sex is at times a dangerous force that is used to malign the characters of RTVE's historical television series. Such is the case with Juana de Avis, Isabel's sister-in-law and primary antagonist in the first season. This Juana is presented as a *mujer brava* (bad-tempered woman) who torments Isabel with sexual acts and innuendos, and whose extramarital relationship casts doubt on her daughter's legitimacy.[35] In the second season, the treatment of Fernando's extramarital affairs goes beyond questioning gendered double standards, as they eventually put his family's lives in danger. The king begins an affair with Beatriz de Osorio, one of Isabel's ladies. In Chapter 19, a jealous Beatriz attempts to murder Prince Juan by opening a window and removing the infant's blankets, bringing about a serious fever. In the following episode, she slowly poisons the queen until Fernando realizes what is happening and asks his wife to find Beatriz a suitable marriage that will take her away from court. This is the context in which Juana's conduct must be read— a context in which characters who allow themselves to be ruled by lust do harm to themselves and to those whom they love.

Once she arrives in Flanders, Juana's interest in sexual pleasure develops into a dangerous lust. It does not take long—about one and a half episodes—for Juana to start to show signs of an unhealthy attachment to Philip. In one scene she greets him with desperate kisses, complaining that one day apart is too long for 'your captive, who values your life more than her own,' and tries to initiate sex with him despite the doctor's orders to abstain in order to protect the child she is carrying.[36] After she gives birth to their first child—a daughter—Juana worries that Philip is angry with her and begs his forgiveness as she desperately removes her clothes, urging him to 'impregnate me again. Impregnate me now. This time it will be a boy, I swear it!'[37] He shoves her away, disgusted. While RTVE's Juana does not approach the eroticism of Aranda's, she is nevertheless characterized as irrational, lacking in self-control, and with little regard for her dignity.

In the television series, the principal problem with Juana's infatuation is that it prevents her from acting in her best interests. For example, her marital bliss leads her to overlook her husband's misdeeds, such as his refusal to give her access to her dowry or his attempts to impede her communication with her parents. Though initially Philip professes his love to Juana, the audience knows that it is all an act, as from the very first they are made privy to his true intentions—to control Juana and to gain her allegiance against her parents. As time passes, Juana becomes aware of Philip's true nature and tries to oppose him, which leads Philip to become abusive. He threatens Juana with abandonment, imprisons her, and even uses physical force, pushing, striking, and even choking her when she refuses to cooperate with him. And yet she is still drawn him, professing at one point, 'He is God to me.'[38] All of this only serves to fuel her madness, which culminates in the penultimate episode, where she threatens to kill her own son out of jealousy and keeps the castle awake at night, screaming curses at her husband. Afterward, Juana lapses into a catatonic state, refusing to eat, dress, or even speak, and those around her fear that she may die. Philip's sister, Marguerite, articulates what the showrunners have made apparent: 'The wife that you have is the one that you yourself have created.'[39]

The follow-up film, *The Broken Crown*, on the other hand, privileges the portrayal of Juana as a political victim over that of a love-sick woman. In contrast to the television series, in the film, Juana has no illusions about Philip's falseness and she plays the loving wife only to spare herself the torture of isolation and imprisonment. Her rages become less frequent and she is shown attempting to gain control over her situation in a more measured fashion. While she makes love to Philip and contains her angry outbursts, she also meets in secret with the Spanish ambassador to give him a letter authorizing her father to rule in her name.

One could argue that RTVE's depiction of Juana follows the thesis set forth by historian Bethany Aram about Juana's (mis)use of *ira regis*. Instead of trying to reason with or persuade her husband when they are in disagreement, Juana takes the more aggressive route of insulting him, throwing things at him, and even striking or spitting on him. These confrontations are typically illustrated by Juana's disheveled hair and the dramatic swirl of her skirts, and they often end with Juana making a mad gesture in which she grabs her head with both of her hands and then sinks to the floor in anguished sobs.

When held up in contrast to Isabel, who carefully controls her emotions in some cases and uses *ira regis* effectively in others, it is clear that Juana is not a competent political player. She overplays her hand in her confrontations with Philip, since at first she is merely the consort of an archduke, and later his captive in a realm that she does not rule. Juana attempts this tactic again in *The Broken Crown*, when she arrives in Spain and demands to be allowed to see her father. When her servants make no move to help her, she runs to a window where she shakes herself with fury and screams repeatedly, 'I want to see my father!'[40] Her shrieks continue into the night, disrupting the sleep of the entire court. While on one hand, this scene makes Juana seem imbalanced, on the other it is effective in demonstrating Juana's historical lack of control over her household, even when she was queen of Castile.

In the end, although Juana shows an interest in wresting the government of Castile from her husband, she seems to agree with those who think her unfit to rule. In the famous 1506 *Cortes* that she interrupts, Juana acts with confidence until Philip informs her that her father will not be coming to meet her, as she had hoped. She wavers visibly, and although she protests that she does not believe it is proper for her foreigner husband to govern Castile, she refuses to take the responsibility for herself. When Philip dies, the only action Juana is willing to take is to revoke the privileges that he has granted and to restore her parents' royal council, 'the rest,' she says, 'when my father returns'.[41] When Fernando does return, Juana makes her intentions clear to him: he can rule in her stead, but he should not expect her to help him. In *The Broken Crown*, Juana chooses to stay out of the government of her realms. Even her dedication to the obsequies for her husband's corpse are explained in the film by Cardinal Cisneros as a strategy to escape her responsibilities as queen; although arguably the inclusion of these scenes perpetuate, rather than challenge, the myth of her obsession with Philip.[42]

The series and the subsequent film place great emphasis on demonstrating how Juana is 'the broken crown' of the title. As heir, she is the embodiment of that crown, and she is torn between loyalty to her parents and obedience to her husband. Her parents encourage her to support them, but when she does, she endangers more than just her relationship to her husband—she also jeopardizes her wellbeing. When Fernando bids farewell to his daughter on her way to Tordesillas, Juana's last words to him are words of reproach: 'In order to be a good king, it is not necessary to be a bad father.'[43] Juana's great tragedy in *The Broken Crown* is that her political body is more important than her personal body. The latter is abused by her husband—and even her father—to such an extreme that it 'breaks' her mind, and thus she ends up incapable of ruling.

The double meaning of the film's title merits mention, as it demonstrates how even in a film that was intended to tell her story, Juana is eclipsed by her mother. While the title refers to the battle that Philip and Fernando waged over Juana's political body, it also refers to Fernando's attempt to deny Philip the Aragonese throne by engendering a son, a move that could have split up the realms that he and Isabel had united with their marriage. The film opens with Isabel's funeral and ends with Fernando's death. On his deathbed Fernando experiences a hallucination in which he sees Isabel and asks for her forgiveness: 'Forgive me, because I tried to break the promise that I made to you. And God in his infinite wisdom has not permitted me to do so.'[44] The crown is more than Juana, as it truly belongs to Isabel and Fernando, who dreamed of creating a great kingdom ruled by one monarch.

## CONCLUSION

Twenty-first century audiovisual portrayals of Juana appear to take their cue from recent shifts in historiography. Aranda's film challenges historians' assertions about Juana's heightened sexual drive and the effects that it had on her relationship with her husband, at the same time that it echoes the depiction of Juana as a victim of her circumstances, a narrative that became more popular in historiography at the end of the twentieth century.[45] The recent rise in queenship studies seems to have influenced director Jordi Frades's desire to tell more 'more of the queen's side' of the story—that is, Juana's attempts to exercise power—rather than stick to the original love story narrative.

Indisputably, Juana's story has changed in the twenty-first century, and yet it appears that it cannot escape the antifeminist past in which it was forged. Aranda's film continues to privilege Juana the lover over Juana the queen, and to present us with the dangers of female sexuality. For RTVE's Juana, female sexuality is also dangerous, as it is tied to a passionate (that is, hyperemotional and confrontational) nature that is ill-suited to positions of power. Juana's inability to control her lustful urges lead to her inability to control herself, ultimately making her a failed queen and reinforcing the myth of the 'Mad Queen' Juana.

## NOTES

1. See María Asunción Gómez, Santiago Juan-Navarro, and Phyllis Zatlin, "Introduction: Juana of Castile: From Romanticism to the Twenty-First Century," in *Juana of Castile: History and Myth of the Mad Queen*, ed. María A. Gómez, Santiago Juan-Navarro, and Phillis Zatlin (Newark, NJ: Bucknell University Press, 2008), 9–28; David R. George, Jr, "Necrophilia, Madness, and Degeneration in Manuel Tamayo y Baus's *La locura de amor* (1855)," in *Juana of Castile: History and Myth*, 63–64; and "Appendix III: Juana as Palimpset" in *Juana of Castile: History and Myth*, 252–255.
2. Gustav A. Bergenroth, "Jeanne la Folle," *Revue de Belgique* 1 (1869): 81–112; Antonio Rodríguez Villa, *La Reina doña Juana la loca Juana la Loca*: Estudio histórico (Madrid: Librería de M. Murillo, 1892).
3. Ludwig Phandl, *Juana la loca: Su vida, su tiempo, su culpa*, trans. Felipe Villaverde (Madrid: Espasa Calpe, 1943); Amarie Dénnis, *Seek the Darkness: The Story of Juana la loca Juana la Loca* (Madrid: Sucesores de Rivadeneyra, 1969); Miguel Ángel Zalama, *Vida cotidiana y arte en el palacio de la Reina Juana I en Tordesillas* (Valladolid: Universidad de Valladolid, 2000).
4. Manuel Fernández Álvarez, *Juana la Loca: La cautiva de Tordesillas*, Espasa Calpe, 2000.
5. Bethany Aram, *Juana the Mad: Sovereignty and Dynasty in Renaissance Europe* (Baltimore, MD: The John Hopkins University Press, 2005), 65–90, 97–104.
6. 'Although the dynamic exchange between history and literature is common in the fictionalization of any historical personality or event, the case of Juana is especially remarkable. Instead of fiction mirroring history, here historiography seems to have mirrored fiction.' María Asunción Gómez, Santiago Juan-Navarro, and Phyllis Zatlin, "Introduction," 10.
7. Vicente Aranda and Antonio Larreta, *Juana la Loca Juana la Loca* (*Mad Love*), feature film, directed by Vicente Aranda (Sony Pictures Classics, 2001); Season 3, *Isabel*, television show (RTVE/ Diagonal TV2014). All

episodes are available online at: http://www.rtve.es/television/isabel-la-catolica/capitulos-completos/; *La corona partida*, feature film, directed by Jordi Frades (A Contracorriente Films, 2016).

8. *Locura de amor*, feature film, directed by Juan de Orduña (CIFESA, 1948); Manuel Tamayo y Baus, *La locura de amor* (1947; Alicante: Biblioteca Virtual Miguel de Cervantes, 2000). http://www.cervantesvirtual.com/obra/la-locura-de-amor--0/.

9. In addition to Orduña's film, there were two silent films that previously adapted the play, directed by Ricardo Baños (1909) and Miguel Villar Toldán (1926).

10. 'De hoy más no lloraré torpes ingratitudes. Amar como todas las mujeres, es amar a un hombre; a semejanza de Dios debe amar una Reina, amando a un pueblo entero …Ni penséis vosotros romper de nuevo el freno de las leyes, con que os sujetó la mano poderosa de la católica Isabel. Temblad ante la hija, como temblabais ante la madre' (act iv, scene v). All translations are my own unless otherwise noted.

11. 'Muchas veces se presenta a mis ojos la venerada sombra de mi madre Isabel … Y oigo que la voz de la Reina Isabel me dice: Piensa en tus sagrados deberes … ama a tu pueblo … conserva mi herencia, débate España nuevas glorias y dichas; y mi corazón sólo responde: amo en cada uno de sus latidos, y quiero llorar como Reina arrepentida, y lloro como mujer enamorada' (act i, vii).

12. George, "Necrophilia," 67–75.

13. María Elena Soliño, "Madness as Nationalistic Spectacle: Juana and the Myths of Nineteenth-Century History Painting," in *Juana of Castile: History and Myth*, 186–187.

14. Soliño, "Madness as Nationalistic Spectacle," 193.

15. 'Si ha de perder su esposo, preferible es que Doña Juana también se muera…allí sólo puede encontrar los justos reposo y ventura' (act v, scene ii).

16. See Santiago Juan-Navarro, "Political Madness: Juan de Orduña's *Locura de amor* as a National Allegory," in *Juana of Castile: History and Myth*, 210–227.

17. María Asunción Gómez, "Woman, Nation, and Desire in Orduña's *Locura de amor* and Vicente Aranda's *Juana la Loca Juana la Loca*," in *Juana of Castile: History and Myth*, 228–229

18. Philibert makes the comment 'Buena union, ¿no os parece?' early in the film, when speaking to a Castilian nobleman about Philip's infatuation with Aldara.

19. 'Fue la mano de Dios.'

20. Fernández Álvarez, *La cautiva de Tordesillas*, 79, 108; As this book was released only a year before the film premiered, Aranda may have been

influenced by an earlier version, Manuel Fernández Álvarez, *Juana "la Loca"*, *1479–1555* (Palencia: Diputación Provincial, 1994), 34, 62.

21. 'Con esta película ... quiero explicar por qué Juana la Loca estaba para aquella época loca. O sea, quiero explicar por qué precisamente, desde una perspectiva actual, no lo estaba ... Para mí [Juana] era una mujer que no quería ser reina ...que eso le alejó de sus verdaderos deseos, que eran estar cerca de su marido.' Elsa Fernández-Santos, "Vicente Aranda recrea los engaños y los celos que enloquecieron a Juana de Castilla: El cineasta rueda en Portugal una nueva versión de la obra de teatro 'Locura de amor,'" *El país*, November 22, 2000. http://elpais.com/diario/2000/11/22/cultura/974847605_850215.html.

22. Asunción Gómez, "Woman, Nation, and Desire," 233–234.

23. 'Quiero ser tu mujer, tu hembra y tu puta.'

24. Asunción Gómez, "Woman, Nation, and Desire," 236.

25. Asunción Gómez, "Woman, Nation, and Desire," 238.

26. 'Es un cuerpo muy bello.'

27. 'Queríamos dar otros matices para que el espectador no tuviera la sensación de que volvíamos a contar la mismas historia ... Yo creo que nuestra Juana muestra la parte más política, más de reina ... más la lucha de poder con ella en medio.' Andrea Fuentes, "Jordi Frades: 'El argumento de la película es perfectamente entendible para quienes no hayan visto Isabel,'" *Ecarletera*, February 19, 2016. http://www.ecartelera.com/noticias/29058/entrevista-jordi-frades-la-corona-partida/.

28. "Capítulo 35: Felipe y Juana llegan a sus reinos," *Isabel*, television series, season 3, episode 9, RTVE/Diagonal TV, aired November 3, 2014; Aram, *Juana the Mad*, 58–60.

29. In an interview, Aranda defended his position that Juana was not mad by turning the accusation against her mother: 'The real madwoman ... was her mother, Isabel the Catholic, a woman blinded by megalomania.' ('La verdadera loca ... era su madre, Isabel la Católica, una mujer presa de megalomania.') Elsa Fernández-Santos, "Vicente Aranda."

30. 'My ambition will be to be as good a wife and ruler as you.' ('Mi afán será ser tan buena esposa y soberana como vos.') "Capítulo 30; Atracción fatal," *Isabel*, season 3, episode 4, RTVE/Diagonal TV, aired September 29, 2014.

31. See Emily Beck's chapter in this volume and Janice North, "Three Queens for the Same Throne: Politics, Sex, and Disorder in TVE's *Isabel*," *Bulletin of Spanish Studies* (forthcoming).

32. 'Vos deberías de ser reina de Castilla y Aragón ... Sois más inteligente que yo.' "Capítulo 29: Nacidos para gobernar," *Isabel*, season 3, episode 3, RTVE/Diagonal TV, aired September 22, 2014.

33. 'Pero ... ¿no es cierto que hay mujeres que no han vuelto el rostro cuando el amor se ha presentado ante ellas?... ¿No conocéis la historia de Helena y Paris, o la reina Ginebra y Lanzarote?' "Atracción fatal."

34. "Capítulo 8," *Isabel*, season 1, episode 8, RTVE/Diagonal TV, aired October 29, 2012.
35. See North, "Three Queens"; For a description of the popular concept of the *mujer brava* in the fifteenth century, see Fray Luis de León, *La perfecta casada*, ed. Joaquín Antonio Peñalosa (Mexico City: Editorial Porrúa, 1999), 64–65.
36. '…vuestra cautiva, la que estima más vuestra vida que la suya misma.' "Capítulo 32: Reina de toda la península," *Isabel*, season 3, episode 6, RTVE/Diagonal TV, aired October 13, 2014.
37. 'Preñadme de nuevo. Preñadme ahora. ¡Esta vez será varón, os lo juro!' "Reina de toda la península."
38. 'Es Dios para mí.' "Capítulo 37: La llamaban Juana la Loca *Juana la Loca*," season 3, episode 11, RTVE/Diagonal TV, aired November 17, 2014.
39. 'La mujer que tenéis es la que vos mismo habéis modelado.' "Capítulo 38: ¿Conservarán el legado de Isabel?," season 3, episode 12, RTVE/Diagonal TV, aired November 24, 2014.
40. '¡Quiero ver a mi padre!'
41. 'Lo demás, cuando vuelva mi padre.'
42. 'Creo que doña Juana se refugió en el culto al cadáver de vuestro padre con un solo fin: librarse del apremio de todos para que tomara decisiones.'
43. 'Para ser un buen rey, no es necesario ser un mal padre.'
44. 'Perdonadme, pues quise romper la promesa que os hice. Y Dios con buen juicio no lo ha permitido.' This scene is followed by a single shot of a blank-faced Juana, dressed in a habit, alone in a barren room near a window in Tordesillas, followed by captions that explain how she spent the rest of her life, and how her son came to power and converted the 'respected and strong state' into an empire. (My translation.)
45. In addition to Fernández Álvarez's biography, see Isabel Altayó and Paloma Nogués, *Juana I: La reina cautiva* (Madrid: Silex, 1985).

# Bibliography

## Plays and Filmography

*Isabel*. Television Series. RTVE/Diagonal TV. Seasons 1–3 (2012–2014). All episodes are available online at: http://www.rtve.es/television/isabel-la-catolica/capitulos-completos/.
*Juana la Loca* (*Mad Love*). Feature Film. Directed by Vicente Aranda. Sony Pictures Classics, 2001.
*La corona partida*. Feature Film. Directed by Jordi Frades. A Contracorriente Films, 2016.

*Locura de amor.* Feature Film. Directed by Juan de Orduña. CIFESA, 1948.

Tamayo y Baus, Manuel. *La locura de amor* (1947; Alicante: Biblioteca Virtual Miguel de Cervantes, 2000). http://www.cervantesvirtual.com/obra/la-locura-de-amor-0/.

## Published works

Altayó, Isabel and Paloma Nogués, *Juana I: La reina cautiva.* Madrid: Silex, 1985.

Ángel Zalama, Miguel. *Vida cotidiana y arte en el palacio de la Reina Juana I en Tordesillas.* Valladolid: Universidad de Valladolid, 2000.

Aram, Bethany. *Juana the Mad: Sovereignty and Dynasty in Renaissance Europe.* Baltimore, MD: The John Hopkins University Press, 2005.

———. "Queen Juana: Legend and History." In Asunción Gómez et al. 2008, 33–46.

Asunción Gómez, María. "Woman, Nation, and Desire in Orduña's *Locura de amor* and Vicente Aranda's *Juana la Loca.*" In Asunción Gómez et al. 2008, 228–229.

Asunción Gómez, María, Santiago Juan-Navarro, and Phillis Zatlin, eds. *Juana of Castile: History and Myth of the Mad Queen.* Newark, NJ: Bucknell University Press, 2008.

———. "Introduction: Juana of Castile: From Romanticism to the Twenty-First Century." In Asunción Gómez et al. 2008, 9–28.

Beck, Emily S. "Religious Medievalisms in RTVE's *Isabel.*" In *Premodern Rulers and Postmodern Viewers: Gender, Sex, and Power in Popular Culture*, edited by Janice North, Karl Alvestad, and Elena Woodacre, 159–178. Palgrave Macmillan, 2018.

Bergenroth, Gustav A. "Jeanne la Folle." *Revue de Belgique* 1 (1869): 81–112.

Dénnis, Amarie. *Seek the Darkness: The Story of Juana la Loca.* Madrid: Sucesores de Rivadeneyra, 1969.

Fernández Álvarez, Manuel. *Juana "la Loca", 1479–1555.* Palencia: Diputación Provincial, 1994.

———. *Juana la Loca: La cautiva de Tordesillas.* Madrid: Espasa Calpe, 2000.

George, David R. Jr. "Necrophilia, Madness, and Degeneration in Manuel Tamayo y Baus's *La locura de amor* (1855)." In Asunción Gómez et al. 2008, 61–76.

Juan-Navarro, Santiago. "Political Madness: Juan de Orduña's *Locura de amor* as a National Allegory." In Asunción Gómez et al., 2008, 210–227.

Leon, Fray Luis de. *La perfecta casada.* Edited by Joaquín Antonio Peñalosa. Mexico City: Editorial Porrúa, 1999.

North, Janice. "Three Queens for the Same Throne: Politics, Sex, and Disorder in TVE's *Isabel.*" *Bulletin of Spanish Studies* (forthcoming).

Pfandl, Ludwig. *Juana la loca: Su vida, su tiempo, su culpa.* Translated by Felipe Villaverde. Madrid: Espasa Calpe, 1943.

Rodríguez Villa, Antonio. *La Reina doña Juana la loca: Estudio histórico.* Madrid: Librería de M. Murillo, 1892.
Soliño, María Elena. "Madness as Nationalistic Spectacle: Juana and the Myths of Nineteenth-Century History Painting." In Asunción Gómez et al. 2008, 186–187.

### News Stories/Internet Sources

Fernández-Santos, Elsa. "Vicente Aranda recrea los engaños y los celos que enloquecieron a Juana de Castilla: El cineasta rueda en Portugal una nueva versión de la obra de teatro 'Locura de amor.'" *El país*, November 22, 2000. http://elpais.com/diario/2000/11/22/cultura/974847605_850215.html.
Fuentes, Andrea. "Jordi Frades: 'El argumento de la película es perfectamente entendible para quienes no hayan visto Isabel.'" *Ecartlera*, February 19, 2016. http://www.ecartelera.com/noticias/29058/entrevista-jordi-frades-la-corona-partida/.

CHAPTER 11

# The Filmic Legacy of 'Queen Christina': Mika Kaurismäki's *Girl King* (2015) and Bernard Tavernier's Cinematic 'Amazons' in *D'Artagnan's Daughter* (1994) and *The Princess of Monpensier* (2010)

*Séverine Genieys-Kirk*

When Hollywood star Greta Garbo chose to play Queen Christina of Sweden (1626–1689) in the puritan climate of the 1930s, she shocked her audience used to seeing her play vulnerable heroines: it was a personal statement that tainted her career at the time; yet it turned her into a new archetype of femininity and an icon of mystical beauty that was to have a far-reaching influence on the creative world of filmmakers.[1]

Queen Christina is a prime example of how historical truth has been compromised by patriarchal ideology in the portrayal of powerful women, but also of how the mainstream representation of women has

S. Genieys-Kirk (✉)
University of Edinburgh, Edinburgh, UK

© The Author(s) 2018   215
J. North et al. (eds.), *Premodern Rulers and Postmodern Viewers*,
Queenship and Power, https://doi.org/10.1007/978-3-319-68771-1_11

been challenged since the advent of cinema. Bernard Tavernier and Mika Kaurismäki, as *'cinéastes engagés'* ('politicized filmmakers') and 'citizens of cinema' in the respective landscapes of French and Finnish film-making culture,[2] seem to have ventured on a similar cinematic journey, as they delve into the early modern world of court intrigues, violence, and torture. Kaurismäki's historical drama, *The Girl King* (2015)[3] and Tavernier's two films, *D'Artagnan's Daughter* (1994) and *The Princess of Montpensier* (2010), propose revisionist adaptations of women's life-stories. Although Kaurismäki deals with a historical subject (Queen Christina of Sweden), and Tavernier with fictitious characters in screenplays adapted from Riccardo Freda's film *The Son of D'Artagnan* (1950) and from Madame de La Fayette's pseudo-historical novel *La Princesse de Montpensier* (1662), what is striking are the ways in which they negotiate with their cinematic heritage. While Kaurismäki's biopic ingeniously dialogues with its predecessors, Rouben Mamoulian's *Queen Christina* (1933) and Anthony Harvey's *The Abdication* (1974),[4] Tavernier's cinematic amazons further attest to the impact of the legendary aura of the Garbo movie. Through the lens of feminist historiography, this essay examines the extent to which Kaurismäki and Tavernier exhibit a feminist take on their filmic representation of female agency as they revisit their classics. In other words, what does 'feminism' mean to postmodern filmmakers who set out to tell the lives of 'unconventional' women, and how does that guide their respective Pygmalionesque quests in re-casting women's life-stories, whether these stories are based on history or a novel?

## From *Queen Christina* (1933) to *The Girl King* (2015)

With a timeline stretching from 1933 to 2015, the cinematic life of Queen Christina carries with it the feminist seeds of ideological change: Mamoulian's, Harvey's, and Kaurismäki's biopics on the Swedish queen highlight distinct shifts in the ways in which the film industry has engaged with the literary, historical, and 'official' narratives of women's pasts.[5] There has been no shortage of documentary evidence on Queen Christina's life. Contemporary testimonies emphasize her overtly masculine behavior, her unfeminine voice, often turning her into some burlesque character from a quixotic anti-novel. Jocular accounts of her hermaphroditic appearance as 'a sort of half man, half woman,'[6] as well as the circumstances of her birth, have led to anatomical speculations on her biological sex. Her attraction for pastimes considered as the prerogative of men (military games, fencing, pistol-shooting), her ease in a male entourage, and her erudition astonished the world. She was a curiosity, not least because she behaved, thought, and spoke like a man, but because she was a paradox—a queen who was 'born' a prince, and educated like one, who called herself the 'king' of her people (*Rex Sueciae*),[7] who was known for her misogynistic comments on women in her *Maxims*, and yet who loved women, formulated feminist statements on marriage, and positioned herself against the Establishment. She pushed the boundaries of knowledge, she was revolutionary, and she welcomed innovative thinking, embraced modernity, and questioned the principles of Lutheranism, Sweden's state religion. She shocked the world when she abdicated. Soon after, she converted to Catholicism; but her intentions for converting and her impiety baffled those who crossed her path. Although none of the films venture beyond the episode of her abdication and conversion, they have crystallized the extraordinary 'politico-erotic fascination' she has exerted on her contemporaries and her biographers across time.[8]

Most notable is *Queen Christina*: Mamoulian's romanticized biopic of the Swedish queen portrayed by Garbo. Due to its then-controversial lesbian theme, the original screenplay by Salka Viertel, a close friend of Garbo's, underwent significant revisions.[9] In the process, the queen's life story was re-invented. Christina falls in love with the handsome Spanish envoy, Don Antonio—which provides a plausible narrative for her abdication. However, her dream to be united with the man she loves shatters into pieces. The denouement, which is shot 'in a purely visual climax unburdened by the falsity of words,'[10] highlights how fragile and untenable the Western woman's emancipation dream was in the traditionalist context of the 1930s.[11] The once outspoken queen is now expressionless, as Antonio breathes his last in her arms. Yet, even in this statuesque final moment, her gaze is to be decoded as the exquisite embodiment of female fortitude. In Mamoulian's words, she was 'to make [her] face into a mask,' to 'let [the audience] write: sadness, inspiration, courage, whatever they choose, whatever they prefer'.[12] In 1974, Harvey followed the lead by revisiting the Hollywood classic in *The Abdication* starring Liv Ullmann. The film focuses on the months following her abdication and on the speculative anecdote of her romance with Cardinal Azzolini.[13] The latter is entrusted with the task of cross-examining her intention but gives in to her charm and wit. The film transforms the reputedly masculine queen into a stereotypical victim of social constraints, revealing 'the private woman' in her utmost frailty and vulnerability.[14] How to deal with the subject of the queen's sexuality and subversion of society's patriarchal rules constituted a more radical challenge in the conservative climate of Hollywood's cinema production in the 1930s than it did in the revolutionary, emancipatory atmosphere of the 1970s, which saw the advent of queer studies. The latter's impact on society has only begun to be more visible at the turn of the twenty-first century and, as we shall see, Kaurismäki's film, *The Girl King*, encapsulates this paradigm shift in popular culture.

Mamoulian's, Harvey's, and Kaurismäki's films return to the early childhood of Christina, who became queen of Sweden at the age of six upon the death of her father, King Gustav II of Sweden. A strong-willed child in Mamoulian's version, she is presented in Harvey's film through two contradictory flashbacks, as a perfectly groomed little princess, and then as a perfectly groomed little prince—thus highlighting Christina's troubled sense of her own identity. While in Mamoulian's film the plot swiftly progresses from her childhood to her adulthood, Harvey resorts to a long flashback to relate Christina's awakening sexual desires as a teenager. Kaurismäki, however, dwells much longer on the early stages of her life, such as the anecdotal confusion over her sex at her birth; her childhood with her neurotic, unloving mother forcing her to kiss the corpse of her dead father; and the routine medical checks she undergoes until she comes of age. Through these sequences, Kaurismäki convincingly suggests how the queen as Malin Buska may have come to develop a sense of self as she grew into an adult.

When compared with Ullmann and Buska, Garbo radiates a blend of *sprezzatura* and unsurpassed elegance even in her blatant manifestation of virility. The low pitch of her voice, of her laughter, and her brusque walk are all temporary, and most of the time are associated with light-hearted scenes, thus deflecting the potential threat to the conservative ideology of the 1930s, which this cinematic model of female emancipation might have conveyed. No such sense of light-heartedness prevails in either of the remakes. Ullmann and Buska undeniably offer a more realistic image of the reported roughness of their historical model: the language of Ullman's and Buska's Christina can be crude, even irreverent and impious. This contrast is further enhanced by the way Kaurismäki intellectualizes the portrait of the queen as a serious scholar. In Harvey's film, although the queen is shown to be excelling in the art of rhetoric, her scholarly personality is cursorily alluded to in a flashback scene set in a large study room with her books randomly scattered on a table. This scene, in which she sings a bawdy ballad on her mandolin about her monstrous, unbearable self, reaches a climax as she loses control of herself, smashes her instrument, and throws her books. The sequence draws upon a misogyny commonplace in early modern representations of femininity that stigmatized reading as demonizing and sullying women's souls. In the process, the queen's extensive and eclectic knowledge is therefore instantly associated with her idiosyncratic behavior, madness, and self-hatred.

Conversely, the queen in the 1933 and 2015 biopics is primarily presented as an assertive, knowledgeable individual with a mind and 'room of her own'. Christina/Garbo is depicted as a bookworm who rises early to catch up with her reading. Interestingly, the screenplay emphasizes Christina's familiarity with one specific aspect of French culture: romance literature. The work she is seen reading is by this 'good Molière'; and from the conversation she has with her servant, we can infer that the play is *Les Précieuses ridicules* (1659). She jocularly admits to her servant Aage that she agrees with the titular characters. Molière's 'affected ladies' speak strongly against the institution of marriage, basing their worldview on their own readings of Madeleine de Scudéry's early feminist novels. This conversation with Aage creates a comical *mise en abyme* of a Molière play, evoking the well-trodden assumption that novel reading distracts women from their social and domestic duties—namely, being good wives and producing heirs. In the inn scene, when the cross-dressed queen meets Antonio for the second time, she learns from him that in Spain she is seen as a 'bluestocking' who 'cares more for running than for love'.[15] Christina laughs back and answers with a rhetorical question, thereby evading Antonio's statement. When the enamored Antonio discovers her real identity, he realizes that Christina is anything but prudish and certainly not ridiculous.

Instead, the focal point of Kaurismäki's biopic is the thorough rendering of Christina's relationship with Descartes. He emphasizes her scholarly education, firstly as a young girl displaying a precocious inclination for philosophical and theological debates during her lessons with her male mentor. He shows her as actively building Sweden's cultural heritage by bringing knowledge from all over Europe to Sweden and making plans for the finest library. Clearly, he projects a more forceful image of women as epistemic subjects in an androcentric domain of study—in this case, philosophy and science. Free of the constraints that were imposed on the production of *Queen Christina*, Kaurismäki transforms Mamoulian's screenplay: in the latter, the reference to Molière's comedic portrayal of early feminism allows the viewers to engage humorously with the queen's subversive ideas about the institution of marriage, and prepares them for her critique of the hegemonic structure of society, as the scene swiftly moves to the subtle evocation of Christina's homosexuality where she tenderly kisses her lady-in-waiting Ebba Sparre.[16]

In Kaurismäki's version, Christina's intellectual encounter with Cartesian precepts on love serves as a pivotal moment in the film in her legitimization of her feelings for Ebba. The subdued kiss scene in the Garbo movie, which is revisited by Harvey through the device of voyeuristic scenes,[17] is explored further by Kaurismäki through several instances of intensely intimate moments filled with the savoring of Descartes's words. Throughout the 2015 biopic, Christina progresses on the ladder of love (sight, sound, touch, taste)[18]—as she furtively gazes at Ebba on their first encounter; as they hide on the porch of a townhouse, giggling over Descartes's manuscript, *Les Passions de l'âme*, which the French ambassador Chanut has just given her; when she teaches Ebba how to shoot; and then in the chalet scene where, against the rules of courtly etiquette, the queen has dinner with Chanut and Ebba.

This chalet scene provides us with a significant instance of dialogic creativity as the inn scene alluded to earlier in Mamoulian's biopic is re-explored by Harvey. In the 1933 and 1974 biopics, the upper and lower floors serve as metaphors for the divide between the private and the public, the sensual and the rough, the sublime and the grotesque. In Mamoulian's celebrated yet controversial sequence in which the cross-dressed queen and Antonio are forced to sleep together, due to a shortage of accommodation, the bedroom scene turns into a bower of bliss.[19] In Harvey's version, the bedroom is a secret retreat where Christina comes and confesses her lustful sins to a Catholic priest in hiding. As Christina (Ullmann) recalls her regular visits and goes into a trance, the past and the present collide: the dark mantle of the priest that she is holding on to in her vision morphs into the crimson robe of the Cardinal, whom she is about to kiss. As he abruptly stops her from doing so, she comes back to her senses. This brutal return to reality is heightened by the overwhelmingly inquisitive presence of the Cardinal's peers: the nascent romance between the queen and the Cardinal is under constant watch, and at once the inner space of their shared emotions recedes.

Quite distinctly, the memory of Mamoulian's beautifully shot scene with its erotic undertones through the presence of exotic fruits 'warmed and ripened in the Spanish sun', and with its suggestive atmosphere of amorous embraces, lingers in Kaurismäki's chalet scene. The latter too is suffused with erotic exoticism, as Christina marvels over a bowl of cherry tomatoes, and flirtatiously gives one to Ebba for her to taste. Thus, the scene displaces the conventional narrative of heterosexual love, as we find it in Mamoulian's and Harvey's romanticized versions, to that of homo-eroticism in Kaurismäki's version. Likewise, just as the idyllic retreat of Christina/Garbo is unsustainable, and just as Christina/Ullmann's earthly desire for the Cardinal is illusory, so this moment of happiness between Christina/Buska and Ebba is disrupted by the arrival of the stern chancellor, Axel Oxenstierna, reminding the queen of her duty and rank. The chalet scene is a sensual prelude to one of the bedroom scenes, which recasts Harvey's love-making scene from a different vantage point.[20] As Christina/Buska asks her lady-in-waiting to unclothe herself to try on the 'luminous' dress she has given her, she wants to know from Ebba how her fiancé looks at and touches her:

CHRISTINA.   How does he look at you?
EBBA.        Sometimes he touches his chest like you right now, and he places his hands on his chin, like you.

In her sensual description of her fiancé's gaze and lovemaking, Ebba semantically plays with subject positioning whereby the queen acts as a mirror of the desiring male. Crucially, the scene sparks off an intensely intimate relationship between the two women. The doomed destiny of Christina's love for Ebba reaches a climax when they are taken by surprise, half-naked, in the castle's crypt where newly arrived books, including the *Codex Giga*, have been stored. The lavishly illuminated bible of the devil is the focal point of this lovemaking scene. We witness a queen who is enraptured by her recent acquisition, revealing the other side of her protean, impious personality: just as the book embodies the forbidden fruit of knowledge, so does her physical possession of Ebba. There is no limit to her love; propriety is forgotten. Kaurismäki has explicitly expanded on the elliptical subtext of the bawdy song in Harvey's flashback of the queen's hysterical fit. Both versions visually link female learning to lust and perdition: Christina's ostentatious subversion of ascribed gender roles leads to her isolation, madness, and alienation. In Mamoulian's film, Christina is more controlled and dignified; yet the climactic scenes in which her confidant Axel Oxensternia reminds her of her royal duties provide her cinematic successors with a powerful template for the expression of their frustration at their lack of agency. Christina/Garbo repeatedly dismantles the fallacy of patriarchal ideology and public state discourse: 'I am to have no voice. It is intolerable! There is a freedom which is mine, and which the state cannot take away. For the unreasonable tyranny of the mob and to the malicious tyranny of palace intrigue, I shall not submit!' Although a symbol of power, she realizes the limits of her prerogatives: she is a woman. Objecting to the commodification of women's future, she universalizes women's call for freedom—their call for owning a voice of their own. Her 'lack of voice,' a predicament with which female viewers of the 1930s would have possibly identified, is a recurring theme in the film, and is associated with a world of shadows, self-doubt, and inner struggle, as the queen reaches her final decision to abdicate: 'I have grown up in a great man's shadow. All my life I have been assumable ... an abstraction. A human being is mortal and changeable ... I am tired of being assumable, Chancellor, I long to be a human being. This longing I cannot suppress.'[21] Certainly, even though Garbo 'present[s] an airbrushed, romanticized portrait of the real woman,'[22] her formulation of her character's rebellion against the patriarchal codification of her emotional life paved the way for Harvey's and Kaurismäki's explorations of the psychological dilemmas with which the independent-minded queen is faced.

With their emphasis on the complex issue of gender conventions, Harvey's and Kaurismäki's films can be read as extended metaphors for that very 'long[ing] to be a human being'.[23] This is evidenced from Kaurismäki's negotiation with both Mamoulian's and Harvey's screenplays. Strikingly, *The Girl King* ends where *The Abdication* begins—that is with Christina/Ullmann, walking away from the stage of politics, leaving behind a world of constraints. The movement of her feet is smoothly captured through a tracking shot, casting off the soft shades of the silky creamy fabric of her dainty shoes as she takes each step forward. This tracking shot works as a metonymy for Christina's newly acquired freedom, guiding the viewer's gaze into a luminous, translucent space that has a dream-like quality. Christina twirls round in a green field, her long hair loose in the wind. Finally, she can renounce the societal codes of femininity artificially imposed on her. The next scene, which stages her arrival in Rome, shows the queen in her male garment. The somber colors of her outfit and the low-key light foreshadow her inner fight with her past into and out of which she steps seamlessly through flashbacks. In the abdication scene, Kaurismäki uses similar backlighting effects to those employed by Harvey, which soften the sharp edges of her masculine silhouette slowly disappearing into the distance with Descartes's voice filling the space of the screen: 'To attain the truth in life, we must discard all the ideas we work on and reconstruct the entire system of our knowledge.'[24] Ending with the oft-cited Cartesian motto of wisdom paraphrased from Descartes's opening statement in *Metaphysical Meditations*, the film brings a holistic sense of closure to the queen's chaotic world. Although the second part of her eventful life remains untold in this film, the voice-over points to the next milestone in the queen's quest for self-fulfillment, as portrayed in Harvey's film.[25] However, even for those who have not seen Harvey's film, Kaurismäki's citation has us reflect on our own ontological make-up and question our preconceived ideas about selfhood. Kaurismäki's voice-over is therefore an evocative reminder of the existential quest that lies ahead of us all, namely, in Garbo's words, of that 'longing' that is within us 'to be a human being'.

Throughout her cinematic journey from Mamoulian's to Kaurismäki's biopics, the protean treatment of the Swedish queen reflects the modern woman's battle for carving out a space and voice of her own in a traditionalist society. Each interpretation of the queen has its own psychological depth. While Garbo's impersonation is estheticized, Ullmann and Buska create an earthlier version of the Swedish queen—under their lead she is no more an 'abstraction'; her speech is not as poeticized, she is all body and flesh. Yet, over their impersonation of Christina hovers the memory of the iconic Garbo: her performance offered a script teeming with new possibilities for others to seize upon. Undeniably, *Queen Christina* has left a durable imprint on our cinematic female imaginary, showing the way forward not solely to actresses like Ullmann and Buska but also beyond the generic confines of biopics. As we shall see in the following discussion, Mamoulian's 'Queen Christina' serves as a blue-print for Tavernier's enhanced and modernized characterization of his sixteenth- and seventeenth-century heroines.

## Queen Christina (1933) and Bertrand Tavernier's Cinematic Amazons

On the surface, *D'Artagnan's Daughter* (1994) and *The Princess of Montpensier* (2010) offer antithetic images of cinematic amazons. Here the term 'amazon' is to be understood in its seventeenth-century sense in the context of French politics and salon culture, when a new cultural trend emerged, heralding examples of female fortitude and female wit under the banner of *femmes fortes*.[26] Female-authored fiction of that period teems with examples of women as intellectualized metaphors of 'triumphant women,' speaking their mind, outwitting their male counterparts, and voicing an early feminist discourse.[27] It was in this context that Madame de La Fayette created her more domesticated, but nonetheless strong-minded female characters in her pseudo-historical novels. As we shall see, with his 'Proustian sensibility' and own touch as a 'cinéaste de l'émotion,'[28] Tavernier transforms these once iconic images of female heroism into a postmodern script that suggestively dialogues with its literary and cinematic pasts.

As an adaptation of Riccardo Freda's film *The Son of D'Artagnan* (1950), *D'Artagnan's Daughter* is a perfect example of Tavernier's dialogic creativity paired with a sense of subversion.[29] As Tavernier's title indicates, he presents a reversal of gender roles. The two characters, Raoul in Freda's film and Eloïse in Tavernier's version, live in a religious retreat, but not for the same reasons. Raoul, son of D'Artagnan, has decided not to follow in the heroic and flamboyant steps of his father; instead, he has taken up a monastic lifestyle. As for Eloïse, upon her mother's death, she was entrusted to the good care of nuns in a remote convent. However, after witnessing carnage in their respective retreats, they are both animated by a law-spirited urge to punish the murderers of the king's courier in Freda's film and of the Mother Superior in Tavernier's film. Eloïse's sense of righteousness is also nurtured by the strong desire to meet her father after many years of separation.[30]

Tavernier's cinematic interplay with Mamoulian's *Queen Christina* is striking in *D'Artagnan's Daughter*, starring the dashing and iconic French star Sophie Marceau as Eloïse. Both films have a spectacular and violent start. Mamoulian's film begins with a battle scene in which Christina's father dies, and Tavernier's begins with the chasing of a slave finding refuge in the convent where Eloïse lives, followed by the murder of a nun. While these two *in-media-res* openings are characteristic of period dramas, they do not merely function as the backdrop for the plot but also symbolically mark Christina's and Eloïse's entry into the public sphere, the male-owned dominion of politics. Like Christina, who rebukes her opportunistic and despicable suitor, Count Magnus, when she declares, 'I am not an idle woman, Magnus, I have a world in my hands,' Eloïse takes on the moral and political mission to restore order in the seventeenth-century world of intrigues and conspiracies. She refuses the passiveness prescribed to women of her station. Tavernier creates a heroine with the bravura of a seventeenth-century *Frondeuse*: not born 'a prince' like Christina, Eloïse comes close to the Amazonian panache of the Swedish queen: as the daughter of the celebrated musketeer, she spent her early childhood in a male environment. Her education at the convent hardly smothered her tomboy taste for fighting and fencing. She did not receive the princely education of her female contemporary, and is not explicitly shown to be harboring intellectual aspirations the way Christina does. However, like her, she nurtures pacifist ideals.

Common to both films is the theme of cross-dressing as a means to escape from a world of constraints in the case of Christina, and for Eloïse as a means to find her way into the rough world of ruffians in order to find her aged father and bring the criminals to justice. As Eloïse dons her male garment, helped by two nuns, the three women feel hilarious at her extravagant idea:

ELOISE.    It feels nice. We should start a new fashion!
NUN 1.     Women in trousers! In public! [How shocking!]
NUN 2.     God [will never stand such an indecent sight!]
ELOISE.    Leave God out of this! Did he give us legs to hide them? I rather like mine!
NUN 1.     And mine!
NUN 2.     I can show mine too![31]

Seventeenth-century tales of cross-dressed women are the sites of burlesque situations, giving rise to comical misunderstandings, which both Mamoulian and Tavernier explore in the scene where the two women meet their lover-to-be. Tavernier has chosen a similar setting for this first encounter: the inn, a predominantly male environment characterized by its roughness and rowdiness, and therefore an unlikely place for a young lady or queen to stop. Tavernier has created a pastiche of Mamoulian's famous scene, where the cross-dressed queen puts a stop to the quarrel of her peasants over her numerous love affairs: as they disagree on the number of lovers she has accumulated over the years, she jumps onto a table, shoots her pistols in the air, and declares that, 'the queen has had twelve lovers this past year!' The matter being settled, Christina and Antonio (still thinking he is speaking to a young courtier) resume their gallant conversation.

In Tavernier's scene, young poet Quentin de la Misère is seen observing Eloïse who is eating roast lamb. He notices straight away she is a woman, and writes a love message, which he asks the innkeeper to bring over to her. The message is intercepted and read aloud; bawdy jokes about the poet's love for boys are made, and a fight breaks out. Eloïse heroically joins in, but her pretender is a poor fighter mesmerized by his intrepid damsel in distress. The young pair eventually escape. In this comical pastiche of Mamoulian's inn scene, gender roles are further reversed: the timorous young man, who is filled with ecstatic love, is afraid of horse-riding and stunned by his lady's equestrian skills.

Throughout the scene, Tavernier further emphasizes his dialogic interplay by modelling Eloïse's apparel and demeanor on that of Christina: her hat, her amused gaze, and her mocking laughter are all reminiscent of Garbo's portrayal of the cross-dressed queen. Although Eloïse is not presented as an intellectual and is mainly shown as a fearless swashbuckler, Eloïse's witty remarks on the superficiality of prescribed gender roles recall Christina's own audacity and readiness to challenge the official ideology of seventeenth-century patriarchal society.

Significantly, however, the two films give weight to father–daughter relationships. Although Christina's father is dead, he plays an important role as a driving force in Christina's desire to achieve princely knowledge and ensure stability, justice, and peace in her kingdom, until the shadow of the dead man, in the form of duty, weighs too much on her shoulders, and she decides to abdicate. Yet, the memory she has of him is one of tenderness and love—a positive depiction of fatherhood. Tavernier too proceeds to explore the father–daughter relationship in a tender light, while tracing the journey of a father's deep emotions for his daughter and of his laborious acceptance of her brashness and masculine ways, especially in a society that requires women to behave demurely, and be 'chaste, silent and obedient'. In Tavernier's film, the reunion between a daughter and a father who are nearly strangers to each other thus generates several scenes suffused with both emotion and amusement.

The film is as much about saving the king from a conspiracy as about D'Artagnan's progressive acknowledgement of his daughter's physical and strategic abilities. Lynn Anthony Higgins argues that once the conspirators are defeated and brought to justice, patriarchal order is restored, meaning that Eloïse must re-integrate the domestic space society has carved out for women.[32] However, the final scene implies otherwise; as D'Artagnan nostalgically reminisces on her heroic act of prowess, he tenderly rebukes her for her masculine fashion: 'You were so lovely against the light, so dazzling, so alive! You know what? I'd like to see you in a dress.'[33] But Eloïse's facial expression shows surprise and disapproval; and with her usual humor, she subtly overturns her father's plea for her donning feminine apparel by announcing she is planning to be enrolled as the king's spy. The film ends with a fencing match of jovial ripostes between father and daughter:

| | |
|---|---|
| ELOISE. | [Only I can foil plots better than anyone else.] |
| D'ARTAGNAN. | You invent them! |
| ELOISE. | [I don't invent them]; I uncover them! |
| D'ARTAGNAN. | You hatch them! |
| ELOISE. | [I don't hatch them], I find them! |
| D'ARTAGNAN. | You imagine them! |
| ELOISE. | I unmask them! |
| D'ARTAGNAN. | You dream them! |
| ELOISE. | I spy them, I subdue them, I smother them![34] |

Eloïse has the last word in this highly humoristic final counter-parry: she may not be able to 'sew, cook, embroider' or 'make jam in the old way,' but '[she] can fight' both with her sword and wit, as it turns out. Just as her cinematic predecessor, Queen Christina, embodies the 'new woman' of the 1930s, Eloïse embodies in the 1990s the vibrancy of a new generation of Western women, who do not just aspire to break away from conventional standards of femininity, but actively seek to fulfill their aspirations.

Her father's rhetorical attempts to bring her back to a more domesticated lifestyle suggests there still is a long way before the deeply ingrained perceptions of what femininity and masculinity entail start fading away. Ironically, however, as with Queen Christina in Mamoulian's film, the juvenal beauty of Eloïse, despite her masculine ways, is for us spectators to marvel at: subtly eroticized, her body, once divested of its male apparel, first figuratively in her fiancé's poetry, and then literally in a scene where she undresses in front of her lover who is fast asleep, is a reminder that visual representations of iconic women, even in their most war-like demeanor, are guided by the artistic principle of esthetic enjoyment. However, Tavernier does not dwell on the scene. The bedroom scene is kept short, suggestively erotic. Eloïse's fiancé does not wake up! Eloïse takes it humorously; and the next day, the Venusian beauty who has slipped back into her Minervan outfit tells him he has missed some 'spectacle'. A far cry from the highly sexualized body of Queen Margot in Patrick Chéreau's film released in the same year,[35] Eloïse provides a prototype of femininity that has the appeal of 'the ink-stained amazons and cinematic warriors' of the modern constellation of superhero girls.[36]

## QUEEN CHRISTINA (1933) AND THE PRINCESS OF MONTPENSIER (2010)

The Princess of Montpensier, starring Mélanie Thierry, deeply contrasts with Tavernier's earlier foray into the world of female heroism: swashbuckling remains the prerogative of men; and the doomed, carnage-like atmosphere of the sixteenth-century religious wars takes us away from the lighter, comedic tones that suffuse D'Artagnan's Daughter (despite its violent beginning).[37] In this adventure film, the exploration of the father–daughter relationship allowed Tavernier to inject Molièresque humor whereby the precepts of patriarchal ideology are shown to be flawed, excessive, and illegitimate. The result is amusement, laughter and, for the female viewer, a certain enjoyment at Eloïse's physical prowess and verbal jousts. On the contrary, in The Princess of Montpensier tragedy predominates, although some instances lighten up the oppressive environment into which the heroine is propelled.

La Fayette's novel is the story of a young woman, Mlle de Mézières, whose hopes to marry her childhood lover, Henri (the historical Duke of Guise, Henry I), are dashed all at once when her father marries her off to the young prince of Montpensier, who is then sent to war, leaving his former mentor, count of Chabannes, to take care of his wife's education.[38] Chabannes becomes her confidant but falls in love with her, as does the duke of Anjou, the future king of France, who is enthralled by her beauty. In an elliptical and concise style, the narrative goes on to explore the princess's inner fight between her duty and her love for Henri, causing her to be led astray, and to be subject to her jealous husband's accusations, eventually resulting in their separation. The pace of the novel quickens: news of Henri's marriage reaches the princess; distraught and weakened by her melancholia, she dies. The novel ends abruptly and conventionally with a warning against the dangers of passion.

Tavernier's film adaptation is faithful. Fleshing out the silences and ellipses of the text, he 'consistently add[s] elements that elucidate historical facets and factors ... mak[ing] them more realistically plausible' for his modern audience.[39] His explicating approach reveals the audacity of La Fayette's text beneath its euphemistic depiction of primal emotions and adulterous passions.

As critics have remarked, Tavernier's 2010 film conjures up striking parallels with the macabre atmosphere of Chéreau's biopic, *Queen Margot*, based on Alexandre Dumas's 1845 novel and starring another iconic actress Isabelle Adjani.[40] With the religious wars in the background, the film's texture recalls the somber and tragic destiny of Queen Margot molested by the vagaries of fate. Set in the same period, the two films share their most infamous characters, Catherine de Medici, the duke of Guise, and Queen Margot herself. Like Queen Margot in Chéreau's film, the princess is idolized for her rare beauty, but unlike Dumas's eponymous heroine who embodies lust, La Fayette's female protagonist is presented as an unattainable object of desire and symbolizes purity. This is enhanced through Tavernier's christening of the princess as Marie and as Mariette in the more intimate scenes. Thereby, Tavernier makes La Fayette's heroine more tangible, as her Christian name is used by the male characters to express their closeness to her.

Tavernier's adaptation puts emphasis on the education of the princess by elaborating La Fayette's short statement: 'He quickly made her into one of the most accomplished ladies of her time.'[41] Although Marie strikes us as naive and has a childishness about her (features that are absent from La Fayette's text), she comes across as determined and witty. Her rhetoric is simple and yet incisive, often disarming her mentor, Chabannes, who gradually falls in love with her. She is unafraid of calling into question the validity of societal diktats. For example, while Chabannes insists on her reading Latin, she insists on learning how to write. She argues that through her practicing writing she will then be able to improve her Latin. First showing some resistance, Chabannes gives in; and soon the art of calligraphy becomes Marie's favored activity.

She excels to such an extent that her husband mistakes her handwriting for Chabannes's own. Although the film does not dwell on her achievements, her repartees indicate she has intellectually matured and developed critical sharpness when she comments on the teachings of Chabannes who has carefully selected the subjects of study in accordance with gender rules. She teases him for not introducing her to 'military' talk, which precludes her from joining in at the impromptu dinner table with the duke of Anjou and his men.[42] This is only an aside, but it serves nonetheless as a forceful statement whereby the rationality of the epistemic divide between the two sexes is challenged. To be sure, when imagining this scene, Tavernier must have had his own cinematic creation in mind, namely Eloïse—if not historical examples of queens and noblewomen who distinguished themselves as well versed in the rhetoric of warfare, such as the historical and cinematic Queen Christina.

A major twist to La Fayette's novel is Tavernier's revision of the denouement. La Fayette's novel reaches its climax when the Prince of Montpensier discovers his wife lying nearly lifeless on her bedroom floor in the presence of Chabannes, who has facilitated an encounter between her and Henri. The latter has a narrow escape; Chabannes is banished by the prince and must leave; and the ill princess is left in the care of her lady-in-waiting. In his adaptation, Tavernier opts for a theatrical *mise-en-scène*: when the prince discovers Chabannes in Marie's bedroom, and threatens him with his sword, she is standing at the far end, looking pale and terrified. Chabannes calmly leaves the castle, and the next screenshot takes the viewer back to Henri who re-emerges from his hiding place. Marie initiates their lovemaking. Tavernier's authorial intention to create an image of female emancipation is clearly indicated in his screenplay: 'Marie knows intuitively that by giving herself to him she loses herself.'[43] This marks a new turning point in Marie's emotional life.

Henri disappears at the break of dawn. The film could have ended here, leaving it up to the viewers to draw their own conclusions, but it does not. There remain a few climactic scenes before the final resolution of the plot. The first of these scenes shows Marie in 'her riding habit, full of energy and determined not to change her mind'.[44] We learn that the couple has been discussing their marital future, and Marie has arrived to announce her decision to 'inaugurate the liberty which [he] impose[s] upon her. To live alone'.[45]

The camera then shifts back and forth between the galloping princess towards her place of exile and Chabannes who is writing a farewell letter to her. Her newly acquired liberty has a transformative effect on her. Although it is not all that obvious from the long panoramic shot in the film, which shows the princess galloping into the distance at breakneck speed, the screenplay indicates that she 'has changed her horse and saddle, and is now riding like a man'[46]—an image within which her newly found liberty is metaphorically encapsulated. The camera returns to Chabannes who is trapped in the middle of a fierce crowd animated by their hatred of Huguenots. The next morning, Montpensier arrives on the carnage scene and finds his old friend lying dead. He discovers Chabannes's farewell letter. This ignites his jealousy; and he decides to bring the letter over to Marie, only to tell her that Henri is about to sign a marriage contract in Blois. Upon hearing this, she is determined to prevent Henri from it, despite her husband's threat that if she does so, this means 'divorce'.[47]

Throughout the film, Marie is often reminded of her station as a princess by her husband—that is, of her social duty. Her title fashions how she must act and think in public. But like Queen Christina, she too is animated by an inner voice. In relinquishing her title lies her belief that this will allow her to fulfill her dream of happiness. To some extent, Marie's determination reminds us of Christina/Garbo's reason for abdicating: 'There is a voice in our soul that tells us what to do, and we obey, and I have no choice.' As with Mamoulian's Christina, nothing holds Marie back: she rides to Blois but discovers Henri is unfaithful to her, as her old friend Chabannes had predicted.[48] She rides away with Chabannes's voice in her head. Each word of Chabannes's farewell letter rhythmically punctuates the sound of her horse hooves, until she suddenly gallops off into a snowscape. She arrives at the chapel where Chabannes is buried. She has come to recollect on the tomb of the man whose unvalued friendship and dedication to her have shaped her own sense of selfhood, and will guide her final steps towards a life of exile. The film ends with a poignant voice-over: the princess does not die as in La Fayette's denouement, but her words have the wintry whiteness of the snowy landscape that surrounds her. In an eloquently suggestive close-up, Tavernier's craft as a *cinéaste* revives the forlorn memory of a cinematic icon: 'the face of Garbo' which, as famously captured in Roland Barthes's words, 'participates in that same realm of courtly love, when the flesh develops certain mystical sentiments of perdition'.[49] As the camera closes in on Marie's face, her aborted dream radiates the distillated essence of Garbo as Christina, 'reveal[ing] the same countenance of snow and solitude'.[50]

To conclude, Kaurismäki's and Tavernier's creative negotiations with their cinematic models of the seventeenth-century *femme forte* reveals how powerful an art form cinema has been in shaping a multifaceted female genealogy. Their films act as conscious 'feminist interventions' in the landscape of international cinema, in that 'they are important in creating awareness of the socially constructed nature of representations of women in films, and in offering an impetus towards the creation of alternative representations'.[51] Most evidently, through the postmodernist prism of gender and feminist politics, Kaurismäki's biopic epitomizes cultural change in a way that engages twenty-first century viewers as agents in the gender revolution.[52] Likewise, Tavernier's authorial agenda is inflected by a feminist impulse to raise important issues on gender, domestic violence, and women's right to self-fulfillment.[53] In both cases, the result is a gripping tale of love, passion, and friendship, which, against the Caravaggesque backdrop of political and religious tensions, reflects twenty-first century preoccupations with women's assumed roles in society. Thus, from their own vantage point, Tavernier's and Kaurismäki's retelling of the past signals a new turn in the pluralistic histories of cinema and feminism.

## Notes

1. See Mark A. Vieira, *Greta Garbo: A Cinematic Legacy* (New York: Harry N. Abrams, 2005), 171–191; Elizabeth A. Ford and Deborah C. Mitchell, *Royal Portraits in Hollywood: Filming the Lives of Queens* (Lexington: The University of Kentucky Press, 2009), 8–33; David Luhrssen, *Mamoulian Life on Stage and Screen* (Lexington: The University of Kentucky Press), 67–75.
2. On these two cinéastes, see Lynn Anthony Higgins, *Bertrand Tavernier* (Manchester: Manchester University Press, 2011), and Pietari Käpää, *The Cinema of Mika Kaurismäki: transvergent cinescapes, Emerging Identities* (Chicago: Chicago University Press, 2011).
3. The screenplay is by Michel Marc Bouchard, and adapted from his play, *Christine, La Reine-Garçon* (2012) translated into English by Linda Gaboriau.
4. The screenplay is based on Ruth Wolff's 1972 play. On how Harvey engages with the play, see Ford and Mitchell, *Royal Portraits*, 23–33.
5. References to these films will be to the following versions: *Queen Christina*, feature film, directed by Rouben Mamoulian Metro-Goldwyn-Mayer, 1933 (Burbank, CA: Warner Home Video, 2005), DVD; *The Abdication*, feature film, directed by Anthony Harvey, Warner

Bros., 1974 (Burbank, CA: Warner Home Video, 2002, 2009), DVD; *The Girl King*, feature film, translated by Linda Gaboriau, directed by Mika Kaurismäki, Marianna Films/Triptych Media, 2015 (New Almaden, CA: Wolfe Video, 2015), DVD.

6. See Jean-Pierre Cavaillé, "Masculinité et libertinage dans la figure et les écrits de Christine de Suède," *Les Dossiers du Grihl 6* (2010). https://doi.org/10.4000/dossiersgrihl.3965.

7. See Jean-François Raymond, *Christine de Suède: Apologies* (Paris: Cerf Editions, 1994), 136, fn. 16 quoted in Cavaillé.

8. Cavaillé, "Masculinité et libertinage," 1.

9. See Vieira, *Greta Garbo*, 171–190.

10. Luhrssen, *Mamoulian*, 72.

11. Luhrssen, *Mamoulian*, 74.

12. James Silke, *Rouben Mamoulian: Style is the man* (New York: American Film Institute, 1971), quoted in Lurhrsen, *Mamoulian*, 24.

13. On her relationship with Azzolini, which is likely to have remained platonic, see Veronica Buckley, *Queen of Sweden, The Restless Life of a European Eccentric* (New York: Harper Collins, 2004), 192–198.

14. Ford and Mitchell, *Royal Portraits*, 23.

15. The term 'bluestocking' is anachronistic, since it was coined in the eighteenth century. Furthermore, Antonio's definition of the term implying such a woman is some type of muscular athlete that is deprived of feminine attributes reveals the long-lasting misogynistic misconception of the female intellectual. As a concept, the bluestockings' movement was inspired by seventeenth-century French salon culture, and the so-called constellation of the *Précieuses*. The *Précieuses* did not actually exist and are the progenies of a fictional construct, which was used to mock women writers as pedantic. On this aspect, see Faith Beasley, *Salons, History and the Creation of Seventeenth-Century France* (Aldershot: Ashgate, 2006).

16. On the recommendation of head producer Irving Thalberg, the scene had to be 'handled with taste'. Vieira, *Greta Garbo*, 176.

17. See Ford and Mitchell, *Royal Portraits*, 29–30.

18. On the neo-Platonic interpretations and shifting definitions of the ladder of love, see Jill Kraye, "Ficino in the Firing Line: A Renaissance Neoplatonist and his Critics," in *Marsilio Ficino 1433–1499: His Sources, His Circle, His Legacy* (Leiden: Brill, 2001), ed. M. J. B. Allen and V. Rees, 377–397 and "The Transformation of Platonic Love in the Italian Renaissance," in *Platonism and the English Imagination*, ed. A. Baldwin and S. Hutton (Cambridge: Cambridge University Press, 1994), 76–85.

19. On the controversy over this scene, see Vieira, 171–190.

20. See Ford and Mitchell, *Royal Portraits*, 29–30.

21. *Queen Christina* (my ellipses).

22. Ford and Mitchell, *Royal Portraits*, 23.

23. Harwood and Viertel, *Queen Christina*, scene 22 (my ellipses).

24. Descartes's statement in the original French translation of "Méditation I" in his *Méditations Métaphysiques* reads as follows: 'il me fallait entreprendre serieusement une fois en ma vie de me defaire de toutes les opinions que j'avois recuës jusques alors en ma creance et commencer de nouveau dés les fondemens, si je voulois establir quelque chose de ferme, & de constant dans les sciences' (Paris: Vve Jean Camusat and Jean Petit, 1647), 8. Descartes's famous incipit as we know it today was popularized in nineteenth-century sources, most notably in Pierre-François Tissot's textbook, *Leçons et modèles de littérature ancienne et moderne depuis Ville-Hardouin jusqu'à M. de Chateaubriand*: 'pour atteindre la vérité: il faut, une fois dans sa vie, se défaire de toutes les opinions que l'on a reçues et reconstruire de nouveau, et dès le fondement, tout le système de ses connaissances' (Paris: J. L'Henry, 1835), 309.

25. For an in-depth analysis of Harvey's psychological portrait of the queen, see Ford and Mitchell, *Royal Portraits*, 23–33.

26. Ian Maclean, *Woman Triumphant: Feminism in French Literature (1610–1652)* (Oxford: Clarendon Press, 1977).

27. See Joan De Jean, *Tender Geographies: Women and the Origins of the Novel in France* (New York, University of Columbia Press, 1991).

28. Higgins, *Bertrand Tavernier*, 21 and 119. This characterization of Tavernier as 'cinéaste de l'émotion' became a set phrase to describe the French filmmaker after the publication of Danièle Bion's monograph: *Bernard Tavernier: cinéaste de l'émotion* (Paris: Hatier, 1984); the concept is used in French to emphasize a filmmaker's valorization of the visual production of emotion.

29. *La Fille de D'Artagnan d'après une idée originale de Riccardo Freda et Eric Poindron* (UK: *D'Artagnan's Daughter from an original idea by Riccardo Freda and Eric Poindron*), feature film, directed by Bertrand Tavernier, subtitles by Lenny Borger and Nina Bogin, CiBy 2000/Little Bear/TF1 Films, Canal+, 1994 (Second Sight Films, 2010), DVD. Unless otherwise stated, English citations are from the UK DVD version; where brackets are used, the translation is mine.

30. On the sources and for an analytical summary of the film, see Higgins, *Bertrand Tavernier*, 134–137.

31. Where brackets are used, the translation is mine.

32. Higgins, *Bertrand Tavernier*, 137.

33. 'Tu étais si belle contre le soleil, si éclatante, si vivante. Tu sais ce qui me ferait plaisir? […] Si tu mettais une robe…'.

34. Where brackets are used, the translation is mine.

35. On this film see Julianne Pidduck, *La Reine Margot* (Champaign: University of Illinois Press, 2005).

36. The phrase is borrowed from Jennifer K. Stuller's monograph *Ink-stained and Cinematic Warriors: Superwomen in Modern Mythology* (New York: I.B. Tauris, 2010).

37. *La Princesse de Montpensier (UK/USA: The Princess of Montpensier)*, feature film, directed by Bernard Tavernier, Pardis Films, 2010 (Studio Canal, 2011), DVD.

38. La Fayette, Marie-Madeleine Pioche de La Vergne. *Histoire de la Princesse de Montpensier*, edited by Marc Escola in *Nouvelles Galantes du XVIIe siècle* (Paris: Gallimard-Flammarion, 2004), reprinted in the edition of the screenplay by Jean Cosmos, Jean-François Rousseau and Bernard Tavernier, *La Princesse de Montpensier. Suivi de la nouvelle de Madame de La Fayette* (Paris: Flammarion, 2010): 190–237. References to the screenplay will be indicated as follows: Tavernier, followed by page number.

39. Joan M. West, "The Princess of Monpensier," *Cinéaste* 36, no. 3 (Summer 2011): 44, 44–45.

40. See Pidduck, *La Reine Margot*. Also see Higgins, *Bertrand Tavernier*, 257–259.

41. La Fayette, *Histoire*, 174. "Il la rendit en peu de temps une des personnes du monde la plus achevée." (my translation).

42. Tavernier, "Salle à manger", scene 79, 109.

43. Tavernier, "Chambre Marie", 162. "Marie sent instinctivement qu'en se donnant elle se perd."

44. Tavernier, "Hôtel Montpensier/Galerie Cour," 163. "En tenue d'amazone, enérgique et butée."

45. Tavernier, "Hôtel Montpensier/Galerie Cour," 163. "J'inaugure la liberté que vous m'imposez. Seule de mon côté."

46. Tavernier, "Rivière," 165. "Elle a changé de monture et de selle et chevauche à califourchon comme un homme."

47. Tavernier, "Salle à manger," 176–179.

48. Tavernier, "Château de Blois," 182–185.

49. Roland Barthes, *Mythologies*, trans. Richard Howard (New York: Hill and Wang, 2012), 73.

50. Barthes, *Mythologies*, 74.

51. Annette Kuhn, *Women's Pictures: Feminism and Cinema* (London: Routledge, 1982, 1994), 6.

52. See his interview with the Cinephiliac. http://movieboozer.com/featured/interview-girl-king-2015-director-mika-kaurismaki, December 15, 2015.

53. See his preface to the screenplay: 7–22, 21; he reiterates this view in an interview with Philippe Rouyer and Yann Tobin, "Entretien avec Bertrand Tavernier: Un film 'biologique', pas numérique", *Positif: Revue Mensuelle* 597 (November 2010), 9–13. See also John Esther, "Cinema can open windows: an interview with Bertrand Tavernier," *Cinéaste* 36, no. 3 (Summer 2011): 46.

# Bibliography

Barthes, Roland. *Mythologies*. Translated by Richard Howard. New York: Hill and Wang, 2012.

Beasley, Faith. *Salons, History and the Creation of Seventeenth-Century France*. Aldershot: Ashgate, 2006.

Buckley, Veronica. *Queen of Sweden, The Restless Life of a European Eccentric*. New York: Harper Collins, 2004.

Cavaillé, Jean-Pierre. "Masculinité et libertinage dans la figure et les écrits de Christine de Suède," *Les Dossiers du Grihl* 6 (2010). https://doi.org/10.4000/dossiersgrihl.3965.

Cosmos, Jean, Jean-François Rousseau and Bertrand Tavernier. *La Princesse de Montpensier: un film de Bertrand Tavernier*. Paris: Flammarion, 2010.

De Jean, Joan. *Tender Geographies: Women and the Origins of the Novel in France*. New York: University of Columbia Press, 1991.

Descartes, René. *Méditations Métaphysiques traduites du latin de l'auteur par M.D.D.L.N.S.* Translated by Charles D'Albert Duc de Luynes. Paris: Vve Jean Camusat and Jean Petit, 1647.

Esther, John. "Cinema can open windows: An interview with Bertrand Tavernier." *Cinéaste* 36, no. 3 (Summer 2011): 46.

Ford, Elizabeth A. and Mitchell, Deborah C. *Royal Portraits in Hollywood: Filming the Lives of Queens*. Lexington: The University of Kentucky Press, 2009.

Higgins, Lynn Anthony. *Bertrand Tavernier*. Manchester: Manchester University Press, 2011.

Käpää, Pietari. *The Cinema of Mika Kaurismäki: transvergent cinescapes, Emerging Identities*. Chicago: Chicago University Press, 2011.

Kaurismäki, Mika. "Interview with the Cinephiliac." *Movie Boozer*, December 15, 2015. http://movieboozer.com/featured/interview-girl-king-2015-director-mika-kaurismaki.

Kraye, Jill. "The Transformation of Platonic Love in the Italian Renaissance." In *Platonism and the English Imagination*, edited by Anna Baldwin and Sarah Hutton, 76–85. Cambridge: Cambridge University Press, 1994.

Kraye, Jill. "Ficino in the Firing Line: A Renaissance Neoplatonist and his Critics." In *Marsilio Ficino 1433–1499: His Sources, His Circle, His Legacy*, edited by M. J. B. Allen and V. Rees, 377–397. Leiden: Brill, 2001.

Kuhn, Annette. *Women's Pictures: Feminism and Cinema*. 2nd ed. London: Routledge, 1994.

La Fayette, Marie-Madeleine Pioche de La Vergne. "Histoire de La Princesse de Montpensier." In *La Princesse de Montpensier: un film de Bertrand Tavernier*, edited by Jean Cosmos, Jean-François Rousseau, and Bernard Tavernier, 189–237. Paris: Flammarion, 2010.

Luhrssen, David. *Mamoulian: Life on Stage and Screen*. Lexington: The University of Kentucky Press, 2013.

Maclean, Ian. *Woman Triumphant: Feminism in French Literature (1610–1652)*. Oxford: Clarendon Press, 1977.

Pidduck, Julianne. *La Reine Margot*. Champaign: University of Illinois Press, 2005.

Rouyer, Philippe and Tobin Yann. "Entretien avec Bertrand Tavernier: Un film 'biologique', pas numérique." *Positif: Revue Mensuelle* 597 (November 2010): 9–13.

Silke, James. *Rouben Mamoulian: Style is the man*. New York: American Film Institute, 1971.

Stuller, Jennifer K. *Ink-Stained Amazons and Cinematic Warriors: Superwomen in Modern Mythology*. New York: I.B. Tauris, 2010.

Tissot, Pierre-François. *Leçons et modèles de littérature ancienne et moderne depuis Ville-Hardouin jusqu'à M. de Chateaubriand*. Paris: J. L'Henry, 1835.

Vieira Mark A. *Greta Garbo: A Cinematic Legacy*. New York: Harry N. Abrams, 2005.

West, Joan M. "Review of *The Princess of Monpensier* by Bernard Tavernier." *Cinéaste* 36, no. 3 (Summer 2011): 44–45.

## Filmography

*The Abdication*. Feature Film. Directed by Anthony Harvey. Warner Bros., 1974 (Burbank, CA: Warner Home Video, 2002, 2009). DVD.

*The Girl King*. Feature Film. Directed by Mika Kaurismäki. Marianna Films/ Triptych Media, 2015 (New Almaden, CA: Wolfe Video, 2015). DVD.

*La Fille de D'Artagnan d'après une idée originale de Riccardo Freda et Eric Poindron* (UK: *D'Artagnan's Daughter from an original idea by Riccardo Freda and Eric Poindron*). Feature Film. Directed by Bertrand Tavernier. CiBy 2000/ Little Bear/TF1 Films, Canal+, 1994 (Second Sight Films, 2010). DVD.

*La Princesse de Montpensier* (UK/USA: *The Princess of Montpensier*). Feature Film. Directed by Bernard Tavernier. Pardis Films, 2010 (Studio Canal, 2011). DVD.

*La Reine Margot* (UK: *Queen Margot*). Feature Film. Directed by Patrick Chéreau. AMLF, 1994 (Paris: Pathé, 2015). DVD.

*Queen Christina*. Feature Film. Directed by Rouben Mamoulian. Metro-Goldwyn-Mayer, 1933 (Burbank, CA: Warner Home Video, 2005). DVD.

# CHAPTER 12

# Thomas Imbach's Marian Biopic: Postmodern Period Drama or Old-Fashioned Psychogram?

*Armel Dubois-Nayt*

It may seem to be stating the obvious to say that the tragic life of Mary Queen of Scots combines all the visual elements and the narrative twists needed to make a grand film epic: the lavishness of the French court where she was brought up, her royal weddings, the joyous entertainments she introduced in Scotland, the glamour of her vast wardrobe, the physical attributes of the six-foot-tall enigmatic royal, her chaotic love life, along with the love and hatred that she inspired in many but also all the blood that was shed for her before her own beheading. These are few of the many appeals that should make her bankable and attractive to the film industry. Yet, amongst the many fights Mary lost against Elizabeth, the filmic one is the most recent.

While there have been many films on Elizabeth in the past two decades, Mary's story has not been on the big screen since Jarrott's 1971 biopic.[1] Several movies have been announced in recent years, including an aborted attempt starring Scarlett Johansson that was to be directed by Alexander

A. Dubois-Nayt (✉)
University of Versailles-Saint-Quentin, Versailles, France

© The Author(s) 2018
J. North et al. (eds.), *Premodern Rulers and Postmodern Viewers*,
Queenship and Power, https://doi.org/10.1007/978-3-319-68771-1_12

Mackendrich[2] and another promised adaptation based on a screenplay by Michael Hirst with Irish actress Saoirse Ronan.[3] So far, the only project that has managed to reach the silver screen is the 2013 drama directed by Thomas Imbach with Camille Rutherford as the eponymous protagonist.

This paper focuses exclusively on Imbach's film in order to complement Scott Culpepper's study of Mary in popular media that mentions Imbach's biopic, but focuses more specifically on the CW Network television Series *Reign* (premiered October 17, 2013) to demonstrate that popular interpreters adapt Mary Stuart's complex and controversial history to meet the needs and tastes of each generation.[4] Culpepper does not consider the consequences of these artistic or commercial choices on the mindsets of viewers, nor on their mental construction of gender roles, an iterative process in which popular culture plays a crucial part.[5]

The aim of this paper is to demonstrate that Imbach's approach to the character of Mary Queen of Scots may not have resulted in what he set out to achieve. Imbach embarked on his project with a double goal: portraying the young queen as a 'European heroine caught between Catholic France and Protestant Scotland' and making the genre of the period drama 'move forward,' which he felt had not been the case for thirty years.[6] The first part of this study will describe Imbach's post-modern artistic vision, what he called his 'pre-industrial narrative style,' as well as his understanding of his eponymous character whom he regarded as a 'model for the modern viewer who is not interested in getting a return on investments' and who 'throws herself into life with a passion'.[7] This analysis will then turn to the ambiguity of the film, which tries to make something new out of something old while working within the framework of a well-known story that has generated many controversies.[8] The question here is not whether the film deserves to be classified as a historical film, but whether a film about such a high-profile historical character can indulge in 'capacious invention' and ignore 'the findings and assertions of what we already know' about Mary Queen of Scots, particularly if, in the process, it repeats historical fabrications used against her in real life and in historiography.[9] It will be demonstrated that the film, although partly informed, still conveys die-hard myths surrounding the Scottish queen and gets bogged down in both early modern and modern interpretations of her life, as its screenplay relies heavily on Stephan Zweig's biography of Mary Stuart.[10] This will lead to a final question about this postmodern production that claims to inspire the audience with a female role model but disempowers Mary as a political player.

## Imbach's Artistic Vision

Imbach's film is clearly a period drama, in so far as he 'decided to stick to the time in which the story takes place' after considering 'an African Mary or a Paris Hilton Character'.[11] It does not retell the whole story of the Scottish monarch and leaves out her 19 years of captivity in England. However, the story spans her whole life from womb to tomb, suggesting, through its ellipse and the image of a twenty-five-year-old face on the block, that Mary's life actually ended with her abdication.

This biopic replays the following key events: her birth in a country torn by war; the rough wooing that led to her departure for France; her encounter with Francis, the dauphin, their wedding, and his death; Mary's return to an impoverished and unwelcoming Scotland; her first meeting with Scottish reformer John Knox; her controversial marriage to Henry Lord Darnley and its bloody aftermath, including the murder of her Italian secretary David Rizzio and the king of Scots' assassination; the birth of the future James VI; her ruinous third marriage with James Hepburn; and the resulting rebellion against the royal couple and her surrender at Carberry Hill. In the final scene, the film rewinds to where it started on the day of her execution, echoing the motto she adopted: 'In my end is my beginning'.[12]

Imbach is clearly not exhaustive and he had no intention to be, for he was only interested in the events that could be treated 'like earthquakes that start out being barely susceptible and then suddenly erupt'.[13] This minimalist plot is propped up by an anti-spectacular visual stance, which manifests itself through the use of few horses, a limited wardrobe, and a preference for outdoor sets and historic buildings. It is both the result of a limited budget and an assumed decision to 'work with reduction and generate a cinematographic feel for the era'.[14]

From a narrative point of view, the story is told on three levels, which is probably its most striking singularity. There is a succession of action scenes and dialogues filmed in a reductive way but meant to put some flesh on the historical figures. Concurrently, the film is related as a series of voice-over monologues that are supposed to be unsent letters that Mary wrote to her trusted confident, her cousin Elizabeth. These intimate letters are meant to convey Mary Queen of Scots's inner thoughts—her emotions and deepest urges—and to add to the pathos they are regularly read out whilst the camera moves at eye level through deserted and bleak landscapes. This imaginary correspondence, however, does not borrow from Mary's historical letters to the English queen. Still, in the movie, the fictitious letters are one portion of her unhappy emotional life as imagined by Imbach and convey her longing for a friendly sisterhood mixed with a sexual fantasy that draws out to its limit the possibility of dynastic union made in real life impossible by the two queens being of the same sex.

The antagonistic relationship of the Scottish and English queens is not left out, however. It is the focus of the puppet shows that punctuate the film until the end and give it its tempo. Mary's Italian secretary, David Rizzio—who is clearly one of the most political characters in the film—plays the part of the puppeteer. The two papier-mâché dolls of the queens are clearly not intended to render a truthful account of the complex relationship of the two cousins and are here to contrast the two queens as good and evil in their power struggle. In that respect, as in Ford and Jarrott's earlier biopics, the film does not abstain from taking sides and uses the puppet shows to contrast the two women. Its only advantage from an historical point of view is that it enables Imbach to resist the temptation to dramatize a meeting that never took place between Elizabeth and Mary, unlike Ford and Jarrott who preferred creating a spectacular ahistorical rendezvous in the vein of Schiller's theatre play or Donizetti's opera *Maria Stuarda*. Yet fidelity to fact is not Imbach's main concern, as evinced by his choice to base his screenplay on Stefan Zweig's 1935 romanticized biography that, in Imbach's own terms, 'put more emphasis on psychology than on history'.[15] Imbach explained that he was drawn to the character of Mary Queen of Scots because he could relate to her, '[He] could see traits in her that [he] also sees in himself and that aren't terribly in vogue today. She is looking for something unconditional.'[16] In that respect, Imbach's endeavor fits perfectly with the idea that historical films say more about the period in which they were shot than about the period that they portray. Imbach viewed Elizabeth 'like a modern manager who has sacrificed her personal life for the greater good' while Mary was the 'more modern woman' of the two, for she wanted to have it all: love, career, and motherhood.[17] Imbach chose to depict the two sixteenth-century queens as having the same beliefs and opinions as the filmgoers with the risk, as we will see later, of misinterpreting and misrepresenting major issues of the time.

This approach is bound to make his film challenging to history and its specialists. As Thomas S. Freeman clear-sightedly noted, it is not captious to judge historical films by the standards of academic history, for whatever some film historians and directors might contend, 'Audiences expect historical films to be accurate and they want to believe that they are.'[18] As Imbach's biopic engages in the political tragedy of Mary Queen of Scots, it is bound to deal with the issues raised by her rule as a woman, who was brought up in France, and as a Catholic presiding over a Protestant kingdom. In real life, her authority was challenged by Republican theorists such as Knox and Buchanan, and she was surrounded by men from across the political and religious spectrum who considered gynecocracy at best as an oddity.

The way Imbach chose to depict Mary's years in power determined his place in the long list of supporters and detractors of Mary Queen of Scots as a sovereign. The Swiss director might have had good intentions but the controversy between those who have tarnished her image and those who have embellished it has gone on for too long and is still too vivid for him to decide if he can escape it. As Freeman contends, 'film is the primary medium by which people learn about the past', and this is why, when it comes to gender order, cinema is one of the institutions that 'anchors masculine domination in our social practices and our unconscious' by 'transforming history into nature and eternalizing the arbitrary' as Bourdieu explained.[19] Imbach claimed that he viewed Mary as more modern than her English cousin but has he managed to convey that feeling and turn the Scottish queen into a postmodern heroine?

## DRAMATIC LICENSE OR AMBIGUOUS FALLACIES?

To answer this question, one needs to examine the accuracy of the film in dealing with the story of Mary Queen of Scots being open minded towards dramatic license, which seems hardly avoidable when condensing 45 years into two hours. This is the natural tendency of any historical drama, but it is clearly intensified in Imbach's film that squeezes together events to achieve the earthquake effect he was looking for. This is how, for instance, Mary Queen of Scots learns on her wedding night to Francis, which took place on 24 April 1558, that Mary Tudor has died and Elizabeth succeeded her—which actually happened six months later on 15 November 1558. What is more problematic in that scene is that Mary rejoiced at the succession of her Protestant cousin as if she did not care about religious issues and had no deep attachment to the Catholic Church, something to which I will return later.

To introduce the key characters of the plot and build up dramatic tension along with characterization, the film manipulates the facts of history. In Imbach's version, Mary meets Rizzio in France in an ahistorical balcony scene where he sings to the four Maries—the four girls from the Scottish nobility who had accompanied her to France and become her closest friends. At the time Mary was in France, Rizzio was actually in Savoy, and not only did he arrive in Scotland after her in the train of the Savoyard Ambassador, but he did not become her secretary until 1562.[20] With the same intent, Imbach's screenplay moves up Mary's encounter with Bothwell so that later on in the film she can be 'hit with the sudden realization that he has always been right by [her] side.' Bothwell thus takes the place of Nicolas de Villegagnon as the captain of the galley that brought her back to Scotland and on hearing the gunshots of the English—another distortion of the truth—he forcibly throws her over his shoulder and takes her down in her cabin. The historical Mary on the other hand refused to go down when the captain suggested it after seeing one ship of her flotilla sink and sailors drown in front of her eyes. As for the historic Bothwell, he was not far from her but he was not on board her galley, for, as Lord Admiral, his role was confined to escorting her baggage.

Such anticipations can be acceptable compromises granted by historians to filmmakers. And if one can be surprised to see the young Mary walking under the scrutiny of her mother with a book on her head, as if she was attending a Georgian finishing school, one can admit that at least it is a modest attempt at hinting at Mary's impressive French education. A book in her hand would, however, have been more effective to acknowledge royal women's access to education at the time, and a more accurate picture of the value attached to an item as expensive as a book, which was often, in the case of early modern girls, a Bible or a book of Psalms.

Next to anticipation, contraction is also one of the narrative techniques used by Thomas Imbach in his dramatic sequence of events. Rizzio's murder is quickly dealt with and directly followed by Mary's escape from Holyrood with Darnley, to whom she hands—on the spot—an act of pardon for him and the rest of the murderers. The truth is badly distorted in Imbach's haste; Mary never granted these acts of pardon, and the images of her physical sickness at the murder do not manage to convey the intensity of the fear she must have experienced during the hours she spent fearing for her own life and trying to sway Darnley back to her.

The christening of infant James diverges even more seriously from undisputed facts as it shows the notoriously absent king, his father, expressing his frustration and jealousy at the ceremony. 'I see only Bothwell,' Darnley complains to his wife. The historical truth is that the guests only saw Bothwell because Darnley was sulking.[21] Imbach's screenplay also takes Bothwell straight to Mary's bed on the eve of the baptism, and turns the day into the starting point of their alleged affair. The chronology of Bothwell and Mary's affair is not a historical detail. It is of paramount importance, for over the centuries it has been used, by her opponents, as proof of her complicity and guilt in her second husband's murder. Modern historians, starting with John Guy, have disproved that they were lovers before Darnley's murder and, *a fortiori*, before her son's baptism.[22] Imbach is therefore clearly ignoring recent historical research. The film also leaves little doubt about her complicity in Darnley's murder. On the night it takes place, she is portrayed dancing with an unclear conscience at the wedding of Bastian Pagez and falling on her knees when she hears the blast that blew down the house in Kirk o'Field where Darnley was staying. Instead, Mary was actually in bed when she heard it at two o'clock in the morning and she initially did not know what happened, believing that she had been the target. In the film, she confides to her imaginary correspondent Elizabeth: 'I am filled with horror at my own actions,' admitting to a crime of which many historians have exonerated her. But the ghost of Rizzio, and through him the filmmaker, continue to repeat one of the tritest arguments of her opponents: 'Some deeds get done by doing nothing.'[23]

The film then gets sketchier, going directly from the death of Darnley to her marriage to Bothwell, skipping, amongst many things, her abduction by Bothwell to Dunbar and his historic mock trial.[24] While the film here has clearly reached a point of no return and slipped into fantasy, it does not mean that from this point on everything is false. The drama rightly shows her isolated from her former allies with all her friends turning their backs on her, including Mar and his wife, to whom she had entrusted her son and who now refused to give him back to her, and Du Croc, the French ambassador, who had advised her to choose 'the right gardener for her little tree'. The final scene at Carberry Hill is also accurate, although economical with the truth. Most of the elements of that dramatic day have been reunited on screen, even if they do not appear in the accepted order of things, and the film clearly fits in with Guy's description of Mary at Carberry Hill.[25]

This scene is Imbach's last opportunity to picture Mary in charge. The royal couple is shown completely isolated, facing an invisible army of rebels hidden on the other side of the hill. Mary is definitely in control of herself and of the men around her. She first turns down Bothwell's idea to avoid battle and challenge the Lords in a single combat—an idea that historically came from the Lords. She then rides back and forth to negotiate with them raising her white blouse over her head, while history has it that it was Kirkcaldy of Grange who came to Mary under a white flag to convince her to give in. Finally, in a grand gesture, she decides to surrender and sacrifice herself for Bothwell's freedom. Here, the film clearly takes on what was put out for public consumption at the time of the events and includes a last passionate kiss between the two lovers that was given in full sight of both armies according to Sir James Melville. There is, however, a contending version of events written by the Captain of Inchkeith, one of Bothwell's men, which claims that Mary refused to surrender and was ready for a fight. As John Guy concluded, 'it is impossible to judge between these versions' and Imbach simply chose the one that enabled him to empower the queen in his own terms.[26]

Imbach, however, does not break free from the dynamic of retribution that sustains the accounts of Mary's life since John Knox' *History of the Reformation*.[27] The last image of Mary at Carberry Hill is that of the blood from her miscarriage running down her leg. Bad queens in sixteenth-century historiography were punished by God through the death of their children. According to John Knox, this was the fate of Mary's mother who had lost the two sons she had had with James V before Mary was born and it seems that the modern audience watching Imbach's tragic version of Mary's story is left, if not on a similar moral judgment, at least on a climax that concludes theatrically her fall in the abyss of passion.[28]

Imbach's narrative clearly follows the fatalistic structure of all the tragedies of passion, without which his portrayal of Mary cannot be understood, which again can be explained by the main source on which he relied: Stephan Zweig's biographic work. The latter viewed Mary as an Atreidian and Shakespearian figure, a mixture of Clytemnestra and Lady Macbeth, consumed with what he viewed as typically female passion. He wrote: 'Mary Stuart was a supreme example of this kind of love ... that allows passion to have its fullest range and to exhaust the emotions even should this lead to self destruction.'[29]

Zweig himself was deeply influenced by Freud's understanding of passion as a form of alienation.[30] In Imbach's film, the character of Mary repeatedly refers to the forces that overwhelm her and that she does not understand. Yet, this Freudian psychological approach of the historical figure necessarily raises the question of its compatibility with Imbach's intent to portray Mary as a post-modern heroine. It can be contended that by relying on a source imbued with Freudianism, Imbach indeed took up an impossible challenge, for in Freud's theory there are clear misogynistic undertones that have offended feminists for a long time.

As Freud himself suggested, the supposed female moral inferiority was a *topos* of misogynist thinking since time immemorial but it was reactivated during Mary's reign, first by John Knox and later by Buchanan, who opposed female government on the ground that women ruled from the heart and not the head, set reason aside and gave into sexual lust.[31] This made gynecocracy synonymous with tyranny. Imbach therefore enters shady waters when basing his interpretation of the historical character of Mary Queen of Scots on her sexuality. If the object of her passion turns out to be Bothwell in the film, what triggers it is clearly and uniquely her sex drive. Zweig had described Mary's sexual encounter with Bothwell as a volcanic explosion that followed intercourse with men who 'had lacked virility, they had been weaklings' and as finally satisfying a woman 'who had long been in a vacillating and irritable state of mind, whose passionate nature had been aroused by her foolish fondness for Darnley—aroused but not assuaged'.[32] Imbach's Mary put into words this frustration mingled with longing and the film clearly illustrates Freud's theory. At first, when confronted with the impotence of her first spouse, Francis II, who pathetically prefers playing with a pistol hidden under his pillow than succumbing to his lovemaking bride, Imbach's character manages to sublimate her inner drive by displacing it by political challenges, such as inheriting the English crown and ruling over Scotland. Then after her second marriage and disappointing sexual experience with Darnley, she initially achieves satisfaction through the birth of her son but that does not last for long. In Imbach's Freudian reconstruction of the past, Mary is one 'who, in consequence of [her] unyielding constitution, cannot fall in with this suppression of instinct' and who is bound to oppose society and become an outlaw.[33] Imbach's character building is clearly a textbook case iterating Freud's assumptions about femininity:

But experience shows as well that women, who being the actual vehicle of the sexual interests of mankind, are only endowed in a small measure with the gift of sublimating their instincts, and who, though they may find a sufficient substitute for the sexual object in an infant at the breast, do not find one in a growing child — experience shows, I repeat that women, when they are subjected to the disillusionments of marriage, fall ill of severe neuroses which permanently darken their lives.[34]

In the last scene of the film, Mary has clearly lost her senses. She hallucinates and sees her hands covered with blood. She is a psychological wreck who views her execution as a relief. She is not a religious martyr but a martyr of a society entirely built on the repression of impulses. This is where Imbach is closer to Freud than to the Protestant historiographers he sometimes follows, for his intent is clearly not to pass moral judgment. Freud deplored the 'double sexual standard' and questioned the worth of our civilized morality.[35] Imbach's postmodernist film does not condemn the outlaw Mary became and even glorifies the freedom with which the character chose her destiny. Is this, however, enough to consider that he has managed to build a character that 'represents values that we need to defend,' as Imbach contends, or from a viewer's perspective, one that can inspire the audience?

By focusing on what he regarded as 'fundamental human qualities,' namely 'profound and unconditional commitment,' Imbach has completely lost sight of the fundamental female qualities and abilities that are at the core of the historical, literary, and artistic debate surrounding the Scottish queen. By presenting her as 'a modern woman' but as 'an old-fashioned queen,' Imbach pandered to gender prejudices that have prevented him from moving the Marian biopic forward and offering a genuinely postmodern filmic representation of the Scottish queen.

## No Postmodernism Without Historicism

In fact, Imbach's representation of Mary as an old-fashioned queen turns out to be an old-fashioned representation of the queen, clad in postmodern inventions that disempower her as a ruler, a Catholic, and even as a lover. This is where the historical inaccuracies are the most detrimental to the postmodern narrative, for they clearly limit the inspiring potential of the heroine for the audience who can neither understand her in her sixteenth-century context nor easily identify with her in the twenty-first century. This last section will demonstrate how the audience is misled about the challenges the historical Mary had to face and argue that as a role model Imbach's Mary is, like most female characters around her, a rather weak, light-headed young woman who does not take her politics or her religion seriously and is systematically outdone by her male contenders.

In the first place, by focusing exclusively on her in psychoanalytic terms, the film fails to show the cultural elements that framed the psychology of the historic Mary, and as the narrative is set in the historic context of sixteenth-century Europe, the audience is never given the context necessary to understand her successive moves. For instance, it shows a naïve young woman announcing to her English cousin that she has been told that she is the legitimate heir to the crown of England and that she has decided to 'add the English coat of arms on her royal portraits,' a gesture that in real life was a declaration of dynastic war. Nothing is said or shown of the pressure under which her Guise uncles or the French king Henry II put her. The latter only appears in the film to caution her not to be 'a victim of her own instincts and of her kindness which could cloud her intelligence'.[36] To understand Mary's strong sense of queenship, one must take into account how it was shaped in France by a king and a court that treated her as a pawn in the French imperial game and in the Guise family ambitions.

The same can be said about the negotiations for her second marriage, which, according to the film, were limited to Elizabeth sending her cousin a cortege of young suitors, among whom was Henry Darnley. This is gross historic counterfeiting since it misses the opportunity to show Mary taking charge of her own marital destiny by negotiating independently from her French and English relatives a marriage to Don Carlos, Philip II's son. It also suggests that Elizabeth was pleased when Mary set her heart on Darnley, which is historically inaccurate.

As for the Scottish context in which she evolves, it is hardly understandable by the novice. The audience can easily understand that, in Scotland, Mary was surrounded by ambitious men who did not take her authority seriously and looked for any opportunity to take control. In the film, her Puritan half-brother James Moray, who criticizes her tyrannical rule before it even starts, takes her round a kingdom killed by taxes 'so that [she] may continue to wear pretty clothes'. He mocks her for believing that she can succeed where strong men have failed, a reference to the aborted reigns of many Stuart kings before her. He is exasperated at her clemency during a Justice Ayre and makes it clear that she does not know how to handle her subjects. Finally, he belittles James's baptism as 'a pretentious little party,' while, historically, it was a crucial occasion for Mary to reconcile herself with the Lords who had turned against her after her marriage with Darnley and Rizzio's murder—an expensive occasion, no doubt, which the real Moray attended in the suit of green Mary had given him.[37]

Another ambitious man surrounding Mary was obviously her second husband, Henry Darnley, who is presented as a Catholic ideologue ready to destroy the Protestants and the heretical queen with the help of God and the pope. The film quickly moves to Mary's terror at Darnley's religious fanaticism. Here the film does not render a truthful account of the king's religious plots that were stirred up behind the queen's back at a time when Mary was refusing him the right to bear the royal arms of Scotland or to grant him the crown matrimonial. Imbach's screenplay decides to focus on Darnley's emotional despair, his romantic jealousy, and sexual misery but in so doing it makes it impossible for Darnley to appear as the political contender that Mary had to face on a daily basis in real life.

Finally, in the case of her third husband, the film again departs from historical accounts. Imbach's Mary self-critically admits to her political incompetence before surrendering part of her authority, if not all, to Bothwell: 'I have always felt so lonely when making my decisions that I only relied on my instincts to guide me.'[38] It is true that Mary's historic letter to her cousin justifies her decision to marry the Earl of Bothwell by 'the factions and conspiracies that of long time have continued therein' and the demand from her people that she should marry a native-born Scot who was 'acquainted with their traditions and the laws and customs of [her] realm,' but there is a long way between the explanation of a political move and the relief expressed by Imbach's character.[39]

Bothwell's manly initiative is enlarged and beautified in a manner that may not be consciously gender-prejudiced but contradicts the historical facts and fails to highlight some of the political qualities of Mary Queen of Scots. Once Bothwell has taken charge in the movie and gets ready for war, he is filmed in the mint melting her jewels and other valuables to turn them into coins. Mary enters the room and grabs the font of solid gold that Elizabeth had presented to her for James's baptism, rescuing it from the heat. Bothwell immediately shouts at her as if she was utterly deprived of political acumen: 'For heaven's sake woman, there is a war coming.'

Such a distortion of historical information shows how gender prejudices are kept alive despite the efforts of serious historians, such as John Guy in the case of Mary Queen of Scots, to put women's history right. In the wake of her marriage to Bothwell, Mary tried to raise an army and made sure that they were paid. To do so, 'she—not Bothwell—stripped her cupboard bare and sent large quantities of gold and silver plate to the mint. Even the font of solid gold that Elizabeth had presented for the baptism was to be melted down and turned into coins worth £3 each in contrast to Imbach's account.'[40] So much for the thoughtless woman mawkishly attached to material things, so much also for the war leader eager to meet the demands of his soldiers portrayed by Imbach.

Any specialist on Mary Queen of Scots will be astounded by the prospect of taking her faith and religious beliefs away as if the psychology of an early modern woman at the time of the Reformation, and the inner conflicts it triggered, could be understood without taking into account this core element. There is no doubt here that Imbach's biopic flattens the difference between past and present and applies the post-Enlightenment republican ideal of religious tolerance to a monarch of divine right and her Protestant subjects, which is obviously utter historical nonsense. The defense of Catholicism—to which Mary's unconditional personal loyalty is clearly established in the historical record—is left to her Italian secretary David Rizzio who is, along with Darnley, one of the few ideological Catholics in the film to contend that 'tolerance can be dangerous'.

The film is not wrong in picturing Mary accepting 'a compromise based on the religious status quo and the inroads made by the Protestant Reformation'[41] but by turning John Knox into an ally it again downplays the verbal and physical violence to which she and her Catholic priest were exposed. Instead, Knox is portrayed as a congenial family man who comes to meet her for the first time with his wife and children. The scene, which is inspired by the first historical meeting between the queen and the Scottish Reformer on 4 September 1561, obliterates its religious motives. In the picture, Mary is supposed to have been offended by his sermons against female rule, which repeated the theory he developed in the *First Blast*, while in real life she had summoned him to account for his campaign against idolatry and the attack of her private chapel where she was hearing Mass. Imbach's Mary does not mention the right of resistance on which Knox's pamphlet concluded and which loomed large over her head throughout her reign in Scotland. Instead, Mary takes an ecumenical stand and asks Knox, while offering her hands to him: 'Do not we have the same God?' We all know what Knox would have answered, had he been asked, but the scene suggests otherwise, and he is shown attending events that the historical character condemned.

For example, Knox is present at James's christening in the film, which is ludicrous considering that the baptism was performed according to the Catholic rites and that Knox later rebuked the countess of Argyll, who was acting as Elizabeth's proxy as godmother, for taking part. Even more abhorrent historically is Knox's conducting the marriage of Mary and Bothwell and rejoicing in the following terms: 'This is a historical occasion. Before me kneel a Protestant and a Catholic joined as one before God. This embodies the very essence of tolerance. The people, the country should rejoice.' More than an historical occasion it is a historical misunderstanding. Not only was Knox away from Edinburgh when the marriage took place but his assistant at St. Giles Kirk made it clear that he 'abhorred and detested the proposed marriage' and initially refused to proclaim the banns.[42]

In his introduction to *Tudors and Stuarts on Film*, Thomas S. Freeman noted 'No aspect of the past resonates less with modern audiences than the religious views and zeal of the past and no aspect of the past has been treated so carelessly by filmmakers.'[43] This is clearly an understatement in the case of Imbach's Marian biopic and it seems that by dulling the religious convictions of one of Mary's fiercest opponents, the screenplay again misses the possibility to show the political challenges she had to face, and consequently her political worth. In a film where all religious-minded protagonists are resolutely tolerant, with the exception of Darnley and to a lesser extent Rizzio, Mary's moderation cannot be accurately depicted for what it was—namely, political pragmatism. From a feminist perspective, this is frustrating, since once more the audience is offered female sensitivity where political acumen was at stake.

To conclude, Thomas Imbach's benevolent attitude towards his eponymous character does not seem to bear the fruit the postmodern viewer was entitled to expect from someone who posited that he wanted to renew the period drama as a genre. His creative filmic techniques do not make up for the gender-prejudiced *topoi*, characterization, and plotline of the movie. Claiming to make a period drama as opposed to an historical film could justify, to some extent, limited involvement with historical discourses but the choice of Mary Queen of Scots to attempt to modernize the genre may not have been the wisest. She is too popular and too controversial a character for new elements of her story to be fabricated. Mary's prosecution was based on forged evidence and, for generations of historians, unraveling the mystery around her has primarily consisted in disentangling what is false from what is true. Clothing her story on the silver screen in more falsehood is treating this long-term undertaking flippantly, to say the least.

## NOTES

1. Until 2013, only four films had depicted the life of Mary Queen of Scots or in the case of the first one just her beheading: *The Execution of Mary, Queen of Scots* (1895); John Ford's *Mary of Scotland* (1936) with Katharine Hepburn; *Das Herz der Königin* ("The Heart of the Queen", 1940) directed by Carl Froelich and starring the Swedish-German actress from the Nazi period Zarah Leander; and, finally, Charles Jarrott's *Mary Queen of Scots* (1971) with Vanessa Redgrave. The filmography of Elizabeth Tudor is much longer, chronologically: *Les Amours de la reine Élisabeth* (*Queen Elizabeth*, 1912) directed by Henry Desfontaines and Louis Mercanton with Sarah Bernhardt as Elizabeth; *The Virgin Queen* (1923) a silent movie directed by J. Stuart Blackton, *Fire over England* (1937) by William K. Howard with Flora Robson as Elizabeth I; *The Private Lives of Elizabeth and Essex* (1939) directed by Michael Curtiz with Bette Davis and Errol Flynn; *The Sea Hawk* (1940) by the same director and with this time Flora Robson as Elizabeth and Errol Flynn as her buccaneer; *Young Bess* (1953) by George Sidney with Jean Simmons; *The Virgin Queen* by Henry Koster with Bette Davis; *Elizabeth R* (1971) by Roderick Graham and Richard Martin with Glenda Jacson; *Elizabeth* (1998) and *The Golden Age* (2007) by Shekhar Kapur with Cate Blanchett; *The Virgin Queen* and *Elizabeth I* (2005) by Tom Hooper with Anne-Marie Duff and Helen Mirren as Elizabeth.

2. Andrew Gumbel, "Scarlett Johnsson set to play Mary Queen of Scots," *Independent*, September 29, 2006. http://www.independent.co.uk/arts-entertainment/films/news/scarlett-johansson-set-to-play-mary-queen-of-scots-418011.html.

3. Baz Bamigboye, "Sex, politics and a royal role to relish for Ronan: Actress Saoirse to star as Mary, Queen of Scots in new film," *Daily Mail*, December 9, 2016. http://www.dailymail.co.uk/tvshowbiz/article-4015558/Sex-politics-royal-role-relish-Ronan-Actress-Saoirse-star-Mary-Queen-Scots-new-film.html.

4. Scott Culpepper, "Long May She Reign: Portrayals and Interpretations of Mary, Queen of Scots, in Popular Media" Paper presented at the Annual

Center for Medieval and Renaissance Studies Conference, St. Louis University, MO, June 2014. *Faculty Work: Comprehensive List*. http://digitalcollections.dordt.edu/faculty_work/25.

5. David Gauntlett, *Media, Gender and Identity: An Introduction* (London and New York: Routledge), 2nd ed., 2008.
6. "Interview with Thomas Imbach," Picture Tree International presents Mary Queen of Scots—Press Kit, 4, accessed January 23, 2017. http://www.maryqueenofscots-movie.com/press/text/MARY_press_kit_E.pdf.
7. "Interview with Thomas Imbach," 4.
8. Robert Rosenstone. *History on Film/Film on History* (Harlow: Pearson Education, 2006), 45.
9. Thomas S. Freeman, "Introduction: It's Only a Movie," in Doran and Freeman, *Tudors and Stuarts*, 3.
10. Stefan Zweig, *Mary Stuart* (London: Puskin Press, 2011).
11. "Interview with Thomas Imbach," 4.
12. 'En ma fin git mon commencement' was the motto she adopted and embroidered on her cloth of estate during her captivity in England.
13. "Interview with Thomas Imbach," 5.
14. "Interview with Thomas Imbach," 4.
15. "Interview with Thomas Imbach," 4.
16. "Interview with Thomas Imbach," 4.
17. "Interview with Thomas Imbach," 5.
18. Freeman, "It's Only a Movie," 5.
19. Pierre Bourdieu, *Masculine Domination*, trans. Richard Nice (Cambridge: Polity Press, 2001), vii, 2.
20. John Guy, "Mary Queen of Scots," 142. Imbach repeats the historical license of Jarrott in *Mary Queen of Scots* (1971).
21. John Guy, *The True Life of Mary Stuart* (Boston and New York: Mariner Books, 2005), 273.
22. Guy, *The True Life*, 384–404.
23. 'Certains actes s'accomplissent en ne faisant rien.' All translations are mine.
24. Guy, *The True Life*, 321.
25. Guy, *The True Life*, 331.
26. Guy, *The True Life*, 335.
27. John Knox, *The Historie of the Reformation of the Church of Scotland* (London, printed by John Raworth, 1644).
28. Roger A. Mason, ed. *Knox on Rebellion* (Cambridge: Cambridge University Press, 2004), 67.
29. Zweig, *Mary Stuart*, 198.
30. Marie-José Grihom and Pascal-Henri Keller, "La passion: entre aliénation et creation." *Revue française de psychanalyse* 74, no. 4 (2010): 165.

31. John Knox, *The First Blast of the Trumpet Against the Monstruous Regiment of Women* (Genève, J. Poullain and A. Reboul, 1558); George Buchanan, *The History of Scotland* (Glasgow, 1845), vol. 2, Book 12.
32. Zweig, *Mary Stuart*, 206.
33. Sigmund Freud, *"Civilized" Sexual Morality and Modern Nervous Illness*, Read Books Ltd, 2013, 11. https://qiugranatinve.files.wordpress.com/2016/11/sudok.pdf.
34. Freud, *"Civilized" Sexual Morality*, 22–23.
35. Freud, *"Civilized" Sexual Morality*, 34.
36. 'victime de ses instincts féminins et de ta gentillesse qui pourrait obscurcir ton intelligence.'
37. Guy, *The True Life*, 274.
38. 'J'ai toujours été si seule en prenant mes décisions en me laissant simplement guider par mes instincts.'
39. Alexander Labanoff, *Lettres, Instructions et Mémoires de Marie Stuart Reine d'Écosse* (London: Charles Dolman, 1844), II, 45.
40. Guy, *The True Life*, 328.
41. Guy, *The True Life*, 6.
42. Guy, *The True Life*, 319.
43. Freeman, "It's Only a Movie," 18.

## BIBLIOGRAPHY

Bamigboye, Baz. "Sex, politics and a royal role to relish for Ronan: Actress Saoirse to star as Mary, Queen of Scots in new film," *Dailymail*, Last amended December 9, 2016. http://www.dailymail.co.uk/tvshowbiz/article-4015558/Sex-politics-royal-role-relish-Ronan-Actress-Saoirse-star-Mary-Queen-Scots-new-film.html.

Bourdieu, Pierre. *Masculine Domination*. Translated by Richard Nice. Cambridge: Polity Press, 2001.

Buchanan, George. *The History of Scotland*. 2 vols. Glasgow, 1845.

Capp, Bernard. *When Gossips Meet: Women, Family and Neighborhood in Early Modern England*. Oxford: Oxford University Press, 2004.

Culpepper, Scott. "Long May She Reign: Portrayals and Interpretations of Mary, Queen of Scots, in Popular Media" Paper presented at the Annual Center for Medieval and Renaissance Studies Conference, St. Louis University, MO, June 2014. *Faculty Work: Comprehensive List*. http://digitalcollections.dordt.edu/faculty_work/25.

Doran, Susan and Thomas S. Freeman. *Tudors and Stuarts on Film*. New York: Palgrave Macmillan, 2009.

Dubois-Nayt, Armel. "Les représentations filmiques de Marie Stuart: Une femme de pouvoir dans l'air du temps." *Caliban* 27 (2010): 273–284.

Ford, Elizabeth A. and Deborah Michell. *Royal Portraits in Hollywood*. Lexington: University Press of Kentucky, 2009.

Freud, Sigmund. *"Civilized" Sexual Morality and Modern Nervous Illness*. Read Books Ltd, 2013. https://qiugranatinve.files.wordpress.com/2016/11/sudok.pdf.

———. "Some Psychological Consequences of the Anatomical Distinction between the Sexes." August 1925. Aquestionofexistence/Problems_of_Gender/Entries/2011/8/28_Sigmund_Freud_files/FreudSomePsychological ConsequencesoftheAnatomicalDistinctionbetweentheSexes.pdf.

Gauntlett, David. *Media, Gender and Identity: An Introduction*, 2nd ed. London and New York: Routledge, 2008.

Grihom, Marie-José and Pascal-Henri Keller. "La passion: entre aliénation et creation." *Revue française de psychanalyse* 74, no. 4 (2010): 1161–1175.

Gumbel, Andrew. "Scarlett Johnsson set to play Mary Queen of Scots," *Independent*, September 29, 2006. http://www.independent.co.uk/arts-entertainment/films/news/scarlett-johansson-set-to-play-mary-queen-of-scots-418011.html.

Guy, John. "Mary Queen of Scots." In *Tudors and Stuarts on Film*, edited by Susan Doran and Thomas S. Freeman, 136–149. New York: Palgrave Macmillan, 2009.

———. *The True Life of Mary Stuart*. Boston and New York: Mariner Books, 2005.

Imbach, Thomas, Andréa Staka, Eduard Habsburg and Catherine Schedlbert. *Mary Queen of Scots*. Directed by Thomas Imbach. 2013. Metrodome, 2014. DVD.

"Interview with Thomas Imbach," Picture Tree International presents Mary Queen of Scots—Press Kit, accessed January 23, 2017. http://www.maryqueenofscots-movie.com/press/text/MARY_press_kit_E.pdf.

Knox, John. *The First Blast of the Trumpet against the Monstruous Regiment of Women*. Genève, J. Poullain and A. Reboul, 1558.

———. *The Historie of the Reformation of the Church of Scotland*. London: John Raworth, 1644.

Labanoff, Alexander. *Lettres Instructions et Mémoires de Marie Stuart Reine d'Écosse*. Vol. 2. London: Charles Dolman, 1844.

Mason, Roger A., ed. *Knox on Rebellion*. Cambridge: Cambridge University Press, 2004.

Rosenstone, Robert. *History on Film/Film on History*. Harlow: Pearson Education, 2006.

Zweig, Stefan. *Mary Stuart*. London: Puskin Press, 2011.

# PART III

# Undermining Authority: Rulers with Conflicted Gender and Sexual Identities

## INTRODUCTION

### Karl C. Alvestad

The depiction of premodern rulers and manifestations of their gender have reached a point where film and TV producers have been able to explore and adapt the past to their own modern ideas and societal values. Sometimes these depictions are rooted in the past and at other times they are more reflective of the modern milieu in which these works have been produced. Within Western culture, heterosexual masculinity is often presented and expected as the gender norm, and it is the baseline by which dissenting expressions of gender are measured. Gender identities that transgress the boundary by displaying effeminate men or masculine women are often met with anxiety and societal discomfort.[1] Depictions of rulers whose gender and sexual identity distort the normative boundaries are both windows to contemporary societal attitudes and a gateway to understanding the cultural influences on the audiences' interaction with the past. In such depictions, gender expression and sexual identity can be seen as performative, as suggested by Judith Butler; furthermore, these performances are presented to add to or detract from the legitimacy and strength of a ruler.[2] Niall Richardson and Sadie Wearing suggested in 2014, on the basis of Butler's argument, that gender expressions that do not fit neatly within the binary, male/female, are seen as conflicting with the binary and thus queer, and deliberate gender-bending results in queering of one's gender.[3] Key to their argument is the idea that gender expression is in part performative. As such, they claim that a gender expression and performance defines the gender identity of an individual.[4] Richardson and Wearing also observe how expressions of queered gender and sexuality in modern media can result in reactions of distaste or discomfort for members of the audience who adhere to the gender binary, whilst also demonstrating that female masculinity or male femininity in this context is seen as queer and thus other.[5] They note that society finds these expressions challenging, and that these expressions can identify how fragile societal ideas of gender norms are. Judith Halberstam supports these sentiments, and takes it further by highlighting that expressions of male masculinity are intrinsically linked to power, whilst female masculinity and male femininity is dangerous to the patriarchal heteronormative power balance since it undermines its core foundation in the male–female/masculine–feminine binary.[6]

In this part of the volume, the chapters will explore how the depiction of gender and sexual identities influence the presentation of rulers and their perceived power and ability to rule. Key to this exploration is the depiction and re-interpretation of medieval and early modern individuals whose gender and sexual identities conflict with a heteronormative modern perception of the past. By breaking the binary between femininity and masculinity, the depictions of Elizabeth I and Boabdil—examined by Aidan Norrie and Elizabeth Drayson—challenge perceptions of historical heteronormativity, and their narratives question the established gender politics whilst also justifying the strength of Elizabeth and the failures of Boabdil. Boabdil's ethnic background can further be seen as challenging his masculinity, particularly as he, as a non-white character, is depicted through the gaze of a Western narration in the television series *Isabel*. The orientalism embedded in the depiction of Boabdil further queers his masculinity and reflects the many ways in which non-white characters are presented and depicted in historical films.[7] Additionally, the chapters by Drayson and Karl C. Alvestad in this section explore the question of what happens to the depiction of rulers when gender expression and gender politics divert from the modern binary. They, alongside Michael R. Evans observe that when a ruler's masculinity is questioned, his legitimacy is also questioned. Such observations offer valuable insights into ideas of masculinity and gender identity at the time of the productions. These depictions are more closely linked to the societal concerns at the time of production than to those contemporary with the time of the rulers.

The changes in societal values and concerns are reflected in popular media through challenges to, or maintenance of, the heteronormative hegemony. Chris Holmlund observed in 2002 that films and TV series 'shape and express how we see' the body and the self.[8] Holmlund's observation highlights that the depictions of masculinity and femininity found in films—whether historical or contemporary—reflect the ideas of the time of the production. As such, depictions of masculinity and femininity as discussed in these chapters are mirrors of concerns and ideals contemporary with the productions, rather than the rulers depicted. Taking this forward and linking the expression of gender with that of power, it is apparent that the depiction of power and authority reflects modern anticipations and anxieties regarding contemporary power. In the context of Holmlund's observation, Elizabeth and Edward's sexuality take on a new meaning; they highlight the danger of a conflation of public and private life. Expressions of deviant sexuality and passion are presented as undermining power and authority in premodern and modern Western societies. In this, a conflation of the bedroom and the throne room changes the way that the audience perceives and interacts with premodern rulers. Elizabeth and Edward have both become LGBT heroes, whilst also being shunned for their non-heteronormative' sexual preferences in these modern depictions. These depictions thus illustrate how modern societal values and concerns are reflected in and shaped by what the audience encounters in films and television shows. Similarly, the continued perception of the queerness of these relationships perpetuates a norm based on the public performance of power and heteronormativity.

In the same way, expressions of masculinity in female rulers and femininity in male rulers question the 'natural' order and heteronormative binary of the Western world. Boabdil's tears and Olaf II Haraldsson's controlling wife are in their respective productions presented as abnormal and undermine the ideas of the modern expression of masculinity. These subversions of masculine power are not unlike Elizabeth I's masculinity discussed by Norrie, which in her very nature of being a woman is seen as undermining the 'natural' balance of male power. Female masculinity and female authority are explicitly linked in the modern depictions of ruling queens and the concerns about such power, but they are also linked to social change as Halberstam points out.[9] Halberstam suggests female masculinity illustrates concern about societal change as well as the changes themselves, implying that the queering of the feminine masculine binary is a commentary on the time of the production rather than the time depicted in these productions. As such, these performances raise questions about authority, power, and the nature of rulership, which is a central theme of this collection.

This part of the volume will explore these questions of how the depictions of rulers change over time, and how their gender and sexual identity is part of these changes. They question how modern social and cultural concerns about power, gender, and sexuality influence the depictions of the rulers. As a result, the papers in this section take a wide geographic and cultural approach in their case studies, allowing for greater comparisons and conclusions. Even though the rulers discussed in this section of the volume, Isabella Capet, Olaf II Haraldsson, Boabdil, and Elizabeth I of England, have little in common at first glance, they are all remembered for the challenges they faced during their reigns. The section has been structured to allow dialogue between the case studies: the first and the second paper demonstrate how Isabella Capet and Olaf II Haraldsson's gender expressions are framed and defined by other characters around them; whereas the third and fourth paper focus on how Boabdil and Elizabeth I are defined and framed by their own gender expression.

Evans' chapter explores how Isabella Capet is presented in films and TV series in relation to her husband, Edward II of England. His paper focuses on how the depictions of this relationship in films and TV series such as *Braveheart* (1995) and *World Without End* (2012) fit with Christine Ekholst's thesis about overly powerful queens and weak kings. In doing so, he highlights how concerns about female power and male femininity is translated through the ages and reproduced for a modern audience. Evans' paper is followed by Alvestad's chapter on Olaf II Haraldsson, where Alvestad explores the gender politics of the Norwegian court in the early eleventh century as imagined in late twentieth-century texts and films. In his paper, Alvestad demonstrates that the questions raised through the modern depictions of Olaf II question Olaf's traditional heroic status and query his power and authority in relation to his wife. Key to this assessment is the comparison between Vera Henriksen's depiction of Olaf and that produced by Prima Vera, both of which undermine the traditional image of Olaf's authority and his masculinity. Additionally, Evans' and Alvestad's papers demonstrate how male authority in popular culture is dependent on unchallenged masculinity and strength, whilst they also show how even the hint of female masculinity is equated with male femininity.

Drayson's chapter about Boabdil, the last ruler of Granada, compares and contrasts the historical Boabdil with that of two modern depictions. Her essay focuses on the development of Boabdil's image in the modern world, and how his gender and otherness is manifested and interpreted as manifestations of strength or weakness. Through her discussion of the surrender of Granada, Drayson stresses how Boabdil's tears for the loss of the city, as well as his status as an ethnic/religious Other, are presented as a symbol of the Sultan's femininity, weakness, and illegitimacy to the land. She further draws attention to how events contemporary to the productions, such as the terror attack in Madrid 2004, can influence how a culture and a ruler is presented and viewed in historical films and TV series.

Finally, Norrie's chapter explores some of the many film depictions of Elizabeth I of England, and in doing so, he explores how her gender and perceived masculinity influence her depictions through time. Norrie's chapter brings to the foreground how modern depictions of premodern rulers break the gender binary through presenting and adding to the mythos developed about the rulers during and after their lifetimes. In exploring the queering of Elizabeth, Norrie demonstrates how her image and myth as a strong female ruler can be adapted through the actions of modern producers into a woman familiar and attainable to modern audiences. His paper reveals that breaking or bending the gender binary for a female ruler is not as detrimental as it is for a male ruler. The female king is thus an authority even when her gender and sexual identity break the mold.

Combined, these chapters provide an in-depth analysis of how rulers are presented to a modern audience familiar with the normative gender binary. The papers in this part of the book demonstrate how film directors and showrunners adapt and amend their presentations of these rulers to reflect and inform the social norms contemporary to the time of their productions. Furthermore, their analyses show that authority sits best when not faced with a queer ruler, for an effeminate king is, in the worldview of the films, worse than a female king. On the basis of these papers it could be argued that the contemporary representation of rulers whose gender and sexual identities are seen as deviating from the male–female binary experience an undermining of their authority. These representations highlight and problematize our own contemporary anxieties with similar non-heteronormative identities and behaviors, whilst also shedding light on our relationship with power and authority today.

## NOTES

1. Maurice Berger, Brian Wallis, and Simon Watson, "Introduction." In *Constructing Masculinity*, ed. Maurice Berger, Brian Wallis, and Simon Watson (London and New York: Routledge, 1995), 3.
2. Niall Richardson and Sadie Wearing, *Gender in Media* (Basingstoke and New York: Palgrave Macmillan, 2014), 51.
3. Richardson and Wearing, *Gender in Media*, 49.
4. Richardson and Wearing, *Gender in Media*, 51.
5. Richardson and Wearing, *Gender in Media*, 56.
6. Judith Halberstam, *Female Masculinity* (Durham and London: Duke University Press, 1998), 3.
7. Moises Park, "The Latin Dragon: Remasculinization of the 'Oriental' Male in Marko Zaror's Films." In *Transnational Orientalisms in Contemporary Spanish and Latin American Cinema*, ed. Michele C. Dávila Gonçalves (Newcastle upon Tyne: Cambridge Scholars Publishing: 2016), 14.
8. Chris Holmlund, *Impossible bodies* (London and New York: Routledge, 2002), 3.
9. Halberstam, *Female Masculinity*, 3.

## BIBLIOGRAPHY

Berger, Maurice, Wallis, Brian, and Watson, Simon, "Introduction." In *Constructing Masculinity*, edited by Maurice Berger, Brian Wallis, and Simon Watson, 1–7. London and New York: Routledge, 1995.

Halberstam, Judith, *Female Masculinity*. Durham and London: Duke University Press, 1998.

Holmlund, Chris, *Impossible bodies*. London and New York: Routledge, 2002.

Park, Moises, "The Latin Dragon: Remasculinization of the 'Oriental' Male in Marko Zaror's Films." In *Transnational Orientalisms in Contemporary Spanish and Latin American Cinema*, edited by Michele C. Dávila Gonçalves 9–32. Newcastle upon Tyne: Cambridge Scholars Publishing: 2016.

Richardson, Niall, and Wearing, Sadie, *Gender in the Media*. Basingstoke and New York: Palgrave Macmillan, 2014.

# CHAPTER 13

# Queering Isabella: The 'She-Wolf of France' in Film and Television

*Michael R. Evans*

Isabella Capet, daughter of Philip IV of France, wife of Edward II of England, is one of the most notorious medieval queens. By overthrowing her husband, Edward, and becoming de facto ruler of England alongside her lover, Roger Mortimer, Isabella rebelled against her husband, her king, and prescribed gender roles, earning the post-medieval sobriquet 'the She-Wolf of France'. Isabella has also frequently attracted attention as the consort of another scandalous figure, Edward II, whose probable homosexuality has fascinated post-medieval audiences, even though the consensus among historians is that Edward provoked opposition more for the political elevation of his 'favorites' than for his sexuality *per se*. In the words of J. S. Hamilton, a biographer of Edward's favorite Piers Gaveston, 'such a sober commentator as the author of the *Vita Edwardi Secundi* compared Edward's love for Piers to that of David for Jonathan, but the comparison indicates a sympathetic understanding rather than condemnation. Other chroniclers make reference to Edward's inappropriate behavior in loving Piers too much, not in loving him.'[1] The pairing of

M. R. Evans (✉)
Delta College, Bay City, MI, USA

© The Author(s) 2018
J. North et al. (eds.), *Premodern Rulers and Postmodern Viewers*,
Queenship and Power, https://doi.org/10.1007/978-3-319-68771-1_13

Edward and Isabella has been identified by Christine Ekholst as an example of a type of overly powerful queen who rebels against a homosexual husband and king, attracting censure from the chroniclers for both king and queen: 'Kings might be accused of sodomy and sexual relationships with other men … Because of the stereotypes, this marked the king as weak and effeminate and not able to rule. Queens would be accused of adultery and having too much of a sexual appetite. These behaviors were often linked with the idea that she'd be influenced by the other man, and might become unruly, ambitious and too interested in national affairs.'[2]

This chapter will explore how Isabella is portrayed in films and television shows from the 1970s to the present, in light of the stereotyped pairing that Ekholst outlines. The films and television shows I will discuss are: the two French television adaptations of Maurice Druon's *Les Rois maudits* (*The Accursed Kings*, 1972–1973, 2005); Derek Jarman's film adaptation of Christopher Marlowe's *Edward II* (1991); Mel Gibson's *Braveheart* (1995); and the TV miniseries *World Without End* (2012), based on the novel by Ken Follett. These film and television adaptations will be analyzed to assess whether modern popular culture continues to see Isabella only as one part of the stereotyped pairing of homosexual king and controlling queen. In particular, I will consider what her portrayal, in relation to that of Edward, reveals about attitudes toward masculinity, femininity, sexuality, and power. Isabella may be viewed sympathetically as a woman trapped in a loveless marriage, or unsympathetically as a murderous and over-mighty woman. Likewise, Edward can be portrayed positively as a martyr for his sexuality, or in a condemnatory way as an effeminate homosexual. In most screen portrayals, the respective images of Edward and Isabella are directly linked; a positive presentation of the one usually appears at the expense of the other. Despite their both being victims of prevailing gender and sexual norms, it seems that neither can be defined except in opposition to the other.

## LES ROIS MAUDITS

Two television series were based on the novels of Maurice Druon,[3] chronicling the disasters that befell France from the execution of the Templars in 1314 to the early years of the Hundred Years' War. The first was broadcast in 1972–1973; the second adaption was shown in 2005. The source novels occupy an important place in French historical fiction, and anecdotal evidence suggests that many readers were first drawn to medieval history through Druon's work. Druon was a *résistant* during the Nazi occupation, a long-serving member of the *Académie Française*, and minister of culture in a Gaullist government in the early 1970s. Both series credit 'Maurice Druon *de l'Académie Française*' (my emphasis) in their opening credits, reflecting the esteem in which he is held in France (in the 1972–1973 version, these are the first words that appear on the screen). Although less well known in the Anglophone world than in France, Druon's novels have enjoyed a revival of interest following George R. R. Martin's revelation that they were an inspiration for *A Song of Ice and Fire*; in Martin's own words, 'The Starks and the Lannisters have nothing on the Capets and Plantagenets. It is the original *Game of Thrones*.'[4]

The series' title—the *Accursed Kings* in English—alludes to the curse proclaimed by the last Templar Grand Master, Jacques de Molay, on the day of his execution by Philip IV; within a year, Philip, Pope Clement V, and Philip's minister Guillaume de Nogaret would all perish, following de Molay's curse / prophecy. However, it is Isabella's marriage to Edward of England that is the original sin leading to the collapse of the Capetian dynasty. The first novel and first episode of the TV series centers on the *Tour de Nesle* affair, when two of Philip IV's daughters-in-law were imprisoned for adultery, and a third condemned for enabling the affairs. In Druon's version, Isabella (Geneviève Casile in the 1972–1973 adaptation; Julie Gayet in 2005) sets these events in motion by entrapping her sisters-in-law; she sends them (via her co-conspirator Robert of Artois) distinctive purses as gifts, which they give in turn to their lovers, revealing their identities. The meeting between the queen and Robert of Artois forms the opening chapter of the first novel, and the first significant scene in the 1972–1973 TV series (after a tableau introducing the characters and a title sequence depicting Artois on a galloping horse).

Although Isabella features less prominently until later in the series and the sequence of novels, she is central to the longer story arc; her Capetian blood in the veins of her son, Edward III of England, is the cause of the Hundred Years' War. We meet Isabella again in the fifth and sixth books (episodes five and six of the 1972–1973 series; four and five of the 2005 adaptation) titled *La Louve de France* (*The She Wolf*) and *Le Lys et le Lion* (*The Lily and the Lion*), respectively. These cover the overthrow of Edward II by Isabella and Mortimer, and the outbreak of the Hundred Years' War.

Isabella is, however, not the central female character in the cycle; this role is played by Mahaut, countess of Artois, who is portrayed as the stereotypical female manipulator behind the scenes. Aided by Béatrice d'Hirson, the niece of her chancellor, she poisons her way through the Capetian line in a manner reminiscent of the Empress Livia in Robert Graves's *I, Claudius*. Mahaut's enmity with her nephew Robert over the inheritance of Artois drives the wider action as the whole kingdom is pulled into their quarrel.

Women, whether manipulative, power-hungry, or over-sexed, are therefore central to the fate of the Capetians. In the words of Sarah Hanley:

> Onto this teetering dynasty—royal daughters but no sons—springs the vicious, manic, sex-crazed sister of the three dead Capetian rulers, Isabella, queen of England, direct descendant of Philip IV and Louis IX. The 'she-wolf' with noticeably sharp teeth, Isabella deposes her feckless husband, Edward II, lets sexual passion overrule reason by coupling with Roger Mortimer, Earl of March, who engineered the brutal murder of Edward, leaving her regent for her son, Edward III. Isabella claims the French throne on his behalf.

> In Druon's telling, the women are beautiful and narcissistic, lustful and naïve ... They are either sluts or downright murderous. They are also the snarling she-wolf whose sharp little teeth go for the jugular, the blood-stained whore Isabella, more animal than human. They have no recognizable brains: fodder to convince that women—brainless purveyors of vice—are indeed unfit to wear the crown.[5]

A fear of subversive female influence pervades the narrative. The opening scene of episode one, featuring Isabella and Robert of Artois (Isabella's co-conspirator in the Tour de Nesle affair), in the 1972–1973 TV series begins with Artois bluntly announcing to her, 'Your sisters-in-law are whores.' He is presented as a hypermasculine figure. He has a focused energy that contrasts with both the undirected raving of Edward and with Isabella's immobility. He is described as a 'giant' in the books, and always wears scarlet.[6] In the 1972–1973 version he is played with wonderful scenery-chewing vigor by Jean Piat, while in the 2005 series, whose bigger budget allows for more action, he is often shown atop a galloping horse. He constantly directs (sexual) invective against women, whom he calls *putain* (whore), *garce* (harlot), *catin* (bitch), *gueuze* (tramp), and so on.

While Hanley is correct to criticize Druon's depiction of women, his Isabella is a little more complex than a 'sex crazed' whore. In fact, she evolves from being an asexual figure to a woman who falls under the spell of romantic love when she meets Mortimer. When we first meet her at court in England, she is portrayed in the 1972–1973 series as authoritative, cold even—the stereotypical ice-queen. She sits immobile on her throne, and in one scene avoids eye contact with King Edward as he walks around the room raging about his misfortunes (Fig. 13.1).

Her hair is elaborately tied and constricted beneath a headdress in both TV adaptations; it contrasts with the free-flowing hair of her more sexual sisters-in-law, seen as they meet with their lovers. She flirts with Artois at their first meeting, before deciding she must place duty before love. When her actions condemn her sisters-in-law to imprisonment, Jeanne (wife of the future Louis X) taunts Isabella that at least she (Jeanne) has known love, something that Isabella will never experience.

**Fig. 13.1**   Isabella (Geneviève Casile) and Edward II (Michel Beaune); *Les Rois maudits* (1972)

At the height of her authority, Isabella is masculinized, and in episode 5 of the 1972–1973 version, we see her in armor as she rallies her forces to invade England. She has ceased to be the immobile ice-queen, but her clothing still renders her asexual.

Despite being a key agent in earlier events, Isabella becomes curiously passive following her overthrow of Edward II. When she is with Mortimer, she loses agency; although she is now re-sexualized, it is in a clichéd romantic way, as she professes her love for him in *amour courtois* terms, making reference to the *Lais* of Marie de France. The respective section in Druon's novel is titled 'Isabella in love' ('Isabel aux amours' in the original).[7] Mortimer is almost literally the stereotypical knight in shining armor sweeping the heroine off her feet. The models in romance that she compares him to are ironic; the 1972–1973 series emphasizes the comparison of Mortimer to Graëlent, a knight who is loved by a queen. However, Marie de France's Graëlent rejects the queen's advances out of loyalty to his lord the king, the complete opposite to Mortimer's actions.

Isabella then literally lets her hair down; the lovers swear an oath to one another, and 'exchange our blood' in the 1972–1973 adaptation— 'mingle our blood' in the 2005 version. (The English translation of Druon's novel uses the expression 'blood-brotherhood,' adding an interesting, gendered, sense of equality that is absent in the 'échanger nos sangs' of the original French novel.)[8] They prick their breasts and mix their blood. In the source novel,[9] Mortimer uses his dagger, and Isabella her hairpin, letting her hair flow free; in the 1972–1973 series, we only see Mortimer cut himself with his dagger, allowing Isabella even less agency in the scene. Interestingly, the 2005 version—perhaps reflecting a twenty-first century audience's expectation of a more assertive female character—reverses this, with Isabella's hairpin being used to prick both their breasts. The blood-alliance implies equality, but as in much of the action involving Isabella and Mortimer, it is the latter who takes the initiative and suggests the sharing of their blood.

Subsequently, Mortimer, not Isabella, becomes the active party in the overthrow and killing of Edward. She prevaricates over the decision to kill the king; it is Mortimer who acts. The weakening of Isabella's role reflects an overall theme of the cycle: the removal of women from the inheritance, as Philip V invokes the Salic Law (*La Loi des mâles*) to ensure his succession, with unintended consequences leading to the Hundred Years' War. This precedent removes Philip's own daughters from the inheritance, leaving the crown to pass ultimately to his cousin Philip VI. It is the reassertion of the right of inheritance through the female line—that is, via his mother Isabella—by Edward III of England that leads to the outbreak of the Hundred Years' War.

Edward II does not figure prominently in the first novel / episode of the cycle, *Le Roi de fer* (*The Iron King*), but his homosexuality is mentioned when we first encounter Isabella in the novels and the 1972–1973 series; Edward is in conversation with some stone masons working on the Palace of Westminster (playfully wrestling with them when we see him in the 1972–1973 TV show; gazing longingly into the eyes of one of them in the 2005 version). 'It's not masonry he likes,' remarks Isabella, 'it's his masons'.[10] He figures very prominently in the fifth novel (the fifth episode in the 1972–1973 series; the fourth and fifth in the 2005 adaptation, which compresses the Mortimer–Isabella story line, omitting scenes in England in favor of retaining the focus on events in France), but is fairly peripheral to the overall story arc at the French court. He is condemned as a weak king more than for his sexuality; in neither TV series is he presented as a stereotypically effeminate gay man. However, his sexuality is central to Isabella's actions; she views him as 'a monster,' and is presented as a spurned lover who repeatedly says that she seeks 'vengeance'. Sarah Hanley's remark that Druon portrays women as 'brainless' may be an exaggeration, but Isabella's motives are certainly personal, not political, and she matches the stereotype of a woman driven by emotion, not reason.

For Druon and his adaptors, therefore, Isabella is not an entirely unsympathetic character. She is, at times, strong and resourceful, and is the victim of a loveless marriage to a homosexual king. However, she is also presented as manipulative and sexually jealous, oscillating between being cold and sexless, and a foolish, lovesick girl. She and Edward closely match Elkhorst's binary of power-hungry queen and weak, homosexual king, except Isabella loses her agency under the spell of Roger Mortimer.

## Derek Jarman's *Edward II*

Like *Les Rois maudits*, Derek Jarman's *Edward II* is a work of adaptation; unlike the French TV series, its source material—Christopher Marlowe's play of 1593—predates modern constructs of sexuality. In Marlowe's text, Edward's love for Piers Gaveston is suspect because it is immoderate, not because same-sex love itself is wrong.[11] However, Jarman makes Edward's sexuality central to his film. The director was a campaigner for LGBT rights and a fierce critic of the British political establishment, and his *Edward II* was made in the context of the Conservative government's ban on public funds for 'promoting homosexuality' in Section 28 of the Local Government Act of 1988, and perceived official inaction in the early years of the AIDS pandemic. Jarman was himself HIV-positive, and would die three years after the release of *Edward II*. Jarman dedicated *Queer Edward II*, the published version of his script of *Edward II*, to 'the repeal of all anti-gay laws, particularly Section 28'.[12] Jarman identified personally with Edward, and Pascale Aebischer sees his *Edward II* as 'an activist intervention in late 1980s / early 1990s British politics, and, focalized through the figure of Edward II, an autobiographical account of Jarman's experiences as a queer artist in a homophobic society'.[13]

The contemporary political message of the film is made explicit by the use (uniquely among the five works under discussion) of modern clothing—although that decision was partly dictated by the small budget.[14] Edward's supporters are represented by (real life) placard-holding protestors from the LGBT rights organization OutRage,[15] while the forces of Mortimer and Isabella are clad in military or riot-police uniforms. Jarman stated explicitly that the battle was meant to be reminiscent of the poll tax riot of 1990, a key moment in resistance to the Thatcher government.[16] The king's aristocratic opponents wear business suits, and gather around a long table. Jarman originally envisaged this as round, 'invoking the male fellowship of King Arthur's round table'[17]; the eventual use of a long table may (as suggested by Bette Talvacchia)[18] represent the boardroom of a multinational, but more likely alludes to the 'coffin-shaped table' around which British government cabinet meetings take place, as we see Mortimer opening a red box (the traditional container for British government documents). The decision to seat female 'barons' at the same table as Mortimer implicates women in the patriarchal and homophobic power structure, whereas associating him in the homosociality of a 'male fellowship' might have blurred the distinction between Mortimer as a symbol of heteronormativity and Edward as a symbol of queerness.

In this context, Isabella (Tilda Swinton) is a representative of heteronormative patriarchy: 'The collaboration of individual women with the dominant ideological structure can cause some who are gendered female to speak with the voice of male power.'[19] An audience watching the film (as I did) in 1991 would inevitably have been reminded of Margaret Thatcher, who had been Prime Minister until the previous year, and whose government was responsible for the anti-gay Section 28 legislation. In *Pansy*, an unmade project based on Marlowe's *Edward II*, set in a dystopian fascist Britain, the dictator 'Margaret Reaper' is overthrown and crucified, and the hero Pansy is crowned 'king of a realm now dedicated to "sexual freedom"'.[20]

Whenever she appears in a public, political role, Isabella is clad in elaborate gowns and jewelry, and wears carefully coifed hair. The obvious parallel is Evita Peron; or maybe Imelda Marcos, as Jarman remarks in *Queer Edward II* that on one occasion Isabella 'had 36 pairs of shoes made and the workmen sewed day and night'.[21] In the same set of notes, the director refers to Isabella's fondness for jewels and the (discredited) story that the breach between her and Edward began when he gave her jewels to Gaveston. In these comments, and in some aspects of the screen portrayal of Isabella, Jarman comes close to a presenting Isabella as the sexist stereotype of the greedy, vain woman obsessed with money and adornment: 'We've all met Isabellas, there are hundreds of them in Knightsbridge [a high-end shopping district of London's West End]. Tilda [Swinton] spent a fortune shopping with them for her earings [sic].'[22] Significantly, Swinton was concerned that a scene in which Isabella attempts—unsuccessfully—to initiate sex with an indifferent Edward 'might be misogynist'.[23] Like her counterparts in *Les Rois maudits*, Swinton's Isabella literally lets down her constricted hair and becomes emotionally vulnerable in moments of (heterosexual) love; rebuffed by her husband, 'the queen' (in Jarman's stage directions) 'distraught with jealousy, hangs over the edge of the bed.' However, Jarman tells us that Swinton 'cut the lines ["I love him more / than he can Gaveston"][24] ... She lay with her hair over the edge of the bed.'[25] This scene is the closest we are given to a glimpse of the traumatic situation into which she has been placed; a bride from an arranged political marriage to a man who cannot love her. However, this aspect of Isabella is not shown to us again, as she asserts herself through her alliance with Mortimer. The casting of Swinton, a British actor, denies us the opportunity to reflect that Isabella is a Frenchwoman, a foreigner trapped by a loveless marriage in a strange land.

Paradoxically, however, the heteronormative hyper-femininity of her appearance also marks her as part of the patriarchal establishment that oppresses Edward and Gaveston (and, by extension, all LGBT people); she frequently appears alongside her lover, Mortimer, who wears military fatigues or dress uniform. In one scene where we see them together, she wields a crossbow and takes potshots at a deer carcass; despite the contrast in their manners of dress, she shares in his violent militarism (Fig. 13.2).

It is noteworthy that Swinton often plays androgynous characters, such as the immortal and gender-bending Elizabethan courtier in *Orlando* (1992); Ella Gericke, the widow of a dockworker in Weimar Germany who takes on her dead husband's identity, in *Man to Man* (1992); the angel Gabriel in *Constantine* (2005); and the Ancient One (a man in the source material) in *Doctor Strange* (2016). Furthermore, Margaret Thatcher was frequently portrayed as masculine by both supporters and detractors, most notably in the satirical TV show *Spitting Image* in which she appeared wearing a man's business suit.

The representation of Isabella is problematic in a film that challenges normative sexual and gender roles. Jarman understands that Edward is 'forced by the demands of kingship into the heterosexual marriage bed'.[26] However, in the words of Bette Talvacchia:

**Fig. 13.2** Isabella (Tilda Swinton) and Mortimer (Nigel Terry); Derek Jarman's *Edward II* (1991)

Isabella is produced as a villain because she upholds the institutional oppression of homosexual love ... Jarman never explores a contingent aspect of the story: that Isabella's villainy was largely formed by the same destructive forces of the institution of marriage, and the subjugation of women within its structure. It is instructive to consider the many points of contact between sexism and homophobia in the ideology of institutionalized marriage ... This in part accounts for the blind hatred of the patriarchy against the male homosexual, who becomes a threat to stability through the presumed renunciation of his 'natural' position of privilege.[27]

Isabella herself delivers a line that reminds us of the homophobic nature of the opposition to Edward. Jarman altered Marlowe's line 'is it not strange that he is thus bewitched?' to: 'is it not queer that he is thus bewitched'[28] Jarman noted: 'Tilda Swinton gives the word a striking emphasis which replicates aurally the arrows pointing to the emendation in the script.'[29]

The film ends on a suggestion of queerness reasserting itself over the heteronormative order. Whether Edward II dies in Berkeley castle is left ambiguous, a nod toward the 'Fieschi Letter' that claimed he had survived and gone into exile.[30] A young Edward III, wearing his mother's jewels, shoes, and make up, dances on top of a cage in which Isabella and Mortimer are imprisoned. (Jarman had also considered having the young prince wear his mother's dress.)[31] Isabella's feminine trappings, which had been used to render her part of the patriarchy that oppressed Edward II, are now turned against the power structure that she maintained.

Jarman's treatment of Isabella is therefore contradictory; we are reminded in the scene where she attempts, unsuccessfully, to have sex with Edward that she is herself a victim of circumstance, and of the heterosexual institution of marriage. However, for the bulk of the film she cuts a dictatorial figure symbolic of the Thatcher government's persecution of LGBT people, and of the homophobic power structure in general.

## BRAVEHEART

Mel Gibson's 1995 blockbuster was widely criticized both for its historical inaccuracy and its gender politics. For example, a review in the *American Historical Review* complained that 'the historical inaccuracies draw on the worst myths of "tartanism,"' the nineteenth-century romanticization of the Highlands, and the extension of this Highland image to represent the whole nation. Hence Wallace's Lowlanders wear

Highlanders' kilts.[32] A prime example of this historical inaccuracy and stereotypical gender politics for the purposes of this paper is the presence of Isabella (in reality, still a young girl in France) at the court of Edward I, the portrayal of the future Edward II as a stereotypical effeminate homosexual, and the casual violence with which the elder Edward kills his son's lover by throwing him out of a window. *Braveheart* presents one of the few positive images of Isabella on screen, but at the expense of promoting a hypermasculine, heteronormative worldview. In the words of Elizabeth Ewan, 'Drawing on stereotypical images of homosexuals as impotent and weak, the film implies that the prince is unable to consummate his marriage to the French princess Isabella. It invents a fictional tryst between Wallace and Isabella in which the virile Wallace impregnates the virgin wife with a son, the future English king Edward III.'[33]

Fragile male sexual anxiety runs through the film. Edward I encourages English lords to settle Scotland by reviving the (mythical) *jus primae noctis*; Wallace joins the rebellion against the occupier only after his wife dies resisting rape at the hands of an English soldier. Scottish masculinity is challenged by the English threat to Scottish women, but vindicated by the hypermasculinity of Wallace (much as D. W. Griffith's *Birth of a Nation* played on white racist fears of black men and celebrated the Klan as defenders of the honor of white womanhood). Conversely, England is feminized by the homosexuality of the heir to its throne. To quote Laurie Finke and Martin Schichtman, 'In juxtapositon to the sexual deviancy of England's aristocracy, Scotland stands as a shining example of healthy, monogamous heteronormativity.'[34]

The presentation of both Edward I's hypermasculine violence and his son's effeminacy as aspects of the English court's corruption is in marked contrast to Jarman's treatment. In his notes in *Queer Edward II*, Jarman—while sharing Gibson's view of Longshanks as prone to extreme casual violence—presents the younger Edward as the scapegoat for problems brought about by his father's (heterosexual) bellicosity: 'Straight Edward I, Longshanks, the father, obstinate and very cruel. At sixteen he cheerfully cut the nose and ears from a passer-by for sport. As we shall see, his charming son gets all the blame, and by many historians isn't even allowed his sexuality. Queer Edward II.'[35] In contrast to Gibson, Jarman firmly rejected the stereotype that Edward and Gaveston were 'the limp-wristed lisping fags so beloved of the tabloids. Edward swam in the winter, hedged and ditched the fields of his house at Langley. Gaveston was the finest horseman of his age.'[36]

In Gibson's film, Isabella becomes a foil for Wallace's masculinity and the effeminacy of the younger Edward; the implication that her child—the future king Edward III—is Wallace's son demonstrates the superior masculinity and fecundity of Scotland. In contrast to Jarman's *Edward II*, the future Edward III promises the restoration rather than the disruption of heteronormativity. His paternity threatens the Plantagenet dynasty, where his maternity threatened the Capetians in *Les Rois maudits*. By impregnating Isabella, Wallace has also avenged and negated Edward I's plan to reinstitute the *jus prime noctis* to outbreed the native Scots: 'The trouble with Scotland is that it's full of Scots. Perhaps the time has come to re-institute an old custom. Grant them [the English barons] *prima nocte*! If we can't get them out, we can breed them out!' Unlike in Jarman's *Edward II*, Isabella is played by a French actress (Sophie Marceau), and her Frenchness is represented positively, in contrast to the sexually repressed nature of the English court (Isabella's maid complains that Englishmen talk too much in bed because they do not know how better to use their tongues).

Ultimately, Isabella not only stands in contrast to Prince Edward, she supplants him as the older king Edward's deputy, and even denies him an heir. In an early scene, Prince Edward sends Isabella in his place to the king's council, leading the king to tell her, 'If he wants his queen to rule after I am gone, then by all means stay.' Later, King Edward sends her instead of his son to negotiate with Wallace: 'The mere sight of him [Prince Edward] would encourage the enemy to take over the whole country.' Isabella taunts her husband for his lack of masculinity: he is 'not man enough to face' Wallace. By the end of the film, she has robbed the younger Edward of his place at court, his masculine agency, his heir (as she reveals she is carrying Wallace's child), and will later rob him of his crown; in the same scene where she reveals her pregnancy to a dying Edward I, she tells him that 'your son will not sit long on the throne, I swear it!'

However, in such a gender-binary movie as *Braveheart*, Isabella cannot be allowed to be fully masculinized. Despite the 'strength' that Wallace sees in her, she remains in many ways the stereotypical female love interest; long before meeting Wallace, she is impressed by tales that 'he fights to avenge a woman' and for love, something that she does not know in her own marriage (a parallel to her portrayal in *Les Rois maudits*). She always appears in court dresses, and often wearing a wimple that seems to constrain her ('literally hemmed in' to borrow Finke and Schichtman's description of the women in the film adaptation of *Becket*) (Fig. 13.3).[37]

In this, Marceau's Isabella resembles the portrayals in the two *Les Rois maudits* series and in *World Without End* (discussed below). Isabella's strength is a device for exposing the effeminacy of Edward; she is not, however, allowed full agency of her own. When Edward I dispatches her to negotiate with Wallace, it is a ruse to buy time while the English king assembles an army to invade Scotland. Isabella's revenge over the Plantagenets comes in the form of her pregnancy, in which she is merely the vessel for Wallace's child.

## WORLD WITHOUT END

*World Without End* was a miniseries broadcast in 2012 on Channel 4 in the UK, based on the 2007 novel of the same name by Ken Follett; both the novel and TV series cover the period from the overthrow of Edward II to the aftermath of the Black Death (c. 1350, although the dates shown on the title cards of the TV show place events a few years earlier than is historically the case, condensing the action somewhat). Historian of the Black Death Samuel K. Cohn praised the novel as a 'page-turner … with a well-woven plot fuelled by thirsting from one chapter to the next to uncover the drama of his characters before and after the Black Death'.[38]

Isabella does not appear in Follett's novel, but is a prominent character in the TV series. Whereas in reality her political power was eclipsed after 1330, she is shown as a malign influence on her son, King Edward III, drawing England into war with France, and oppressing the people with taxes to pay for it.

**Fig. 13.3**   Isabella (Sophie Marceau); *Braveheart* (1995)

Edward II appears in disguise in the person of Thomas Langley, a monk who reveals in the final episode that he is in fact the king, who has escaped Berkeley Castle. He is presented in positive counterpoint to the portrayal of his former queen. He is a strong leader, who rallies the people of Kingsbridge against the forces of the crown, making the obligatory stirring speech before battle (the analogue to Wallace's famous 'they can take our lives but they can never take our freedom' speech in *Braveheart*), thereby becoming re-masculinized. His sexuality is treated sympathetically, as is a kiss shared between two female characters, the healer-turned-nun Caris and another nun. 'God forgive anyone who misjudges you,' Caris tells 'Thomas Langley' as he mourns a dead monk whom he had loved.

Ken Follett was an enthusiastic supporter of the 'New Labour' project in British politics in the 1990s and early twenty-first century, which sought to make the Labor Party electable by adopting more moderate policies and abandoning old socialist articles of faith. His political views clearly shape his perception of the Middle Ages; speaking of *Pillars of the Earth*, he talked about his interest in the role of the medieval church in 'the struggle to create a more decent society'.[39] The politics of *World Without End* reflect those of turn-of-the-millennium liberalism and the show displays a somewhat superficial feminism, with several positive female authority figures. Women are treated sympathetically as they struggle to assert their autonomy; the wisdom of female traditional healers such as Caris is preferable to the ignorant 'medicine' of male clerics, who burn healers as witches and seem to prescribe dung as a cure-all; peasants deserve freedom and land, which the aristocracy and male clerics try to deny them; same-sex love is to be celebrated; and peasant and urban revolts are justified, but freedom is only guaranteed by intervention from above, when Langley reveals himself to be Edward II, affixes his seal to a town charter for Kingsbridge, and leads the people against royal forces. This limited radicalism, with reform delivered from above by benevolent rulers, seems to fit the politics of Tony Blair, of whom Follett was a key early supporter before turning against him in 2000.[40] In Follett's Middle Ages, characters are sympathetic if they possess 'modern' attitudes, while villains are bad insofar as they are stereotypically 'medieval' in behavior and outlook, such the greedy and ambitious prior Godwin, who corresponds to the post-Enlightenment stereotype of the medieval church as hypocritical, misogynist, and superstitious.

Isabella is a notable exception in a series where most female authority figures are sympathetic (Caris, the abbess, and the healer Mattie Wise who is hanged as a witch). Isabella's political authority is suspect, however, as it leads to unjust taxation and war with France. She is the stereotypical figure of the woman who wields power through her influence on a man, her son Edward III. Yet she is also rendered masculine by her agency; like Isabella in *Les Rois maudits*, she appears in armor in the opening sequence of the first episode, in which she takes the crown from the head of Edward II in a scene that is framed as a reverse coronation (Fig. 13.4).

Isabella is the analogue of the Sheriff of Nottingham in Robin Hood movies—the cruel oppressor who taxes the people and deprives them of their liberty until a royal *deus ex machina* appears at the end of the film. As in *Braveheart*, but this time with negative connotations, Isabella is presented as very definitely French (played by French actor Aure Atika). She stands against rugged Anglo-Saxon liberty, and draws England into an unnecessary war with France in support of a dynastic claim that is hers more than her son's. She is also, as in *Les Rois maudits*, threatening in her sexuality, which is incompatible with her role as Queen Mother. In the first episode, Edward III tells her 'You're a whore. And my mother. I suggest you choose which you want to be. I will not have both.'

*World Without End* is unusual in presenting a thoroughly supportive view of Edward II that is sympathetic to his sexuality, but also presents him as a just ruler (even Jarman does not suggest that Edward fulfilled the duties of kingship well). However, this is at the expense of reinstating the negative view of Isabella, this time in a different context, pushing her reluctant son into a war with France.

## CONCLUSION

All five screen representations of Isabella are problematic from a feminist or queer perspective. In each case, Isabella can only appear sympathetic to the extent that she is pitied as the abandoned wife of a homosexual man, and Edward to the extent that he is victim of an adulterous and power-hungry queen. In the two adaptations of *Les Rois maudits*, her agency is destabilizing and limited by her sex; for all her ruthlessness, she becomes a lovesick girl in the presence of powerful masculine fig-ures such as Mortimer. In *Braveheart* she is strong and intelligent, but only to emphasize the weakness of a stereotypically effeminate Edward. In Jarman's *Edward II*, which passionately advocates for the rights and

**Fig. 13.4**  Isabella (Aure Atika) takes the crown from the head of Edward II; *World Without End* (2012)

dignity of LGBT people, Isabella is a symbol of the heteronormative patriarchy that oppresses her husband. Finally, *World Without End* reinforces the idea of Isabella as the She-Wolf of France, murderer of her husband. None of the representations of Isabella successfully escape stereotyped gender binaries, or are able to represent sympathetically both a woman and a gay man without the authority and agency of one coming at the expense of the other.

## NOTES

1. J. S. Hamilton, *Piers Gaveston, Earl of Cornwall, 1307–1312. Politics and Patronage in the Reign of Edward II* (Detroit: Wayne State UP, 1988), 110.
2. "Historian Explores Gender Differences in Legal System," *University of Guelph*, May 30, 2012. http://news.uoguelph.ca//2012/05/historian-explores-gender-differences-in-legal-system/.
3. Maurice Druon, *Le Roi de fer* (Paris: Del Duca, 1955); *La Reine étranglée* (Paris: Del Duca, 1955); *Les Poisons de la couronne* (Paris: Del Duca, 1956); *La Loi des mâles* (Paris: Del Duca, 1957); *La Louve de France* (Paris: Del Duca, 1959); *Le Lys et le lion* (Paris: Del Duca, 1960). A seventh volume, *Quand un roi perd la France* (Geneva: Édito-service, 1977) was published seventeen years after the sixth, and after the broadcast of

the first television adaptation. It was not included in the 2005 television series, and should really be viewed as a stand-alone volume; while it follows chronologically from *Le Lys et le Lion*, it features different characters from the previous six novels and is told from a different, first-person, point of view.

4. Maurice Druon, *The Iron King*, trans. Humphrey Hare (London: Harper, 2013), vii–viii.

5. Sarah Hanley, "Imagining the Last Capetians," *Fiction and Film for French Historians: A Cultural Bulletin*, accessed July 3, 2015. http://h-france.net/fffh/classics/imagining-the-last-capetians-maurice-druon-the-accursed-kings/.

6. For example, Druon, *The Iron King*, 6, 8.

7. Maurice Druon, *The She Wolf*, trans. Humphrey Hare (London: Harper, 2014), 129–221.

8. Druon, *La Louve de France* (Paris: Livres de Poche, 1970), 166.

9. Druon, *The She Wolf*, 184–185.

10. Druon, *The Iron King*, 16. The line is quoted in both the 1972 and 2005 adaptations: 'ce n'est pas le maçonnerie qu'aime le roi; ce sont les maçons' (1972); 'ce n'est pas le maçonnerie qu'il aime; ce sont les maçons' (2005).

11. 'The intrigue in Edward's court had, according to Marlowe, as much to do with Gaveston's class and nationality as it had to do with gender … Edward's dalliance becomes a threat because he allows it to distract him from the business of sovereign rule, not because it is perceived as a moral lapse.' Bette Talvacchia, "Historical Phallicy: Derek Jarman's 'Edward II', " *Oxford Art Journal* 16, no. 1 (1993): 113.

12. Derek Jarman, *Queer Edward II* (London: British Film Institute, 1991), i; Pascale Aebischer, "'To the Future': Derek Jarman's *Edward II* in the Archive," *Shakespeare Bulletin* 32, no. 3 (2014): 433.

13. Aebischer, "'To the Future,'" 430.

14. Talvacchia, "Historical Phallicy," 114.

15. Jarman, *Queer Edward II*, 122.

16. Talvacchia, "Historical Phallicy," 118.

17. Aebischer, "'To the Future,'" 435.

18. Talvacchia, "Historical Phallicy," 119.

19. Talvacchia, "Historical Phallicy," 119.

20. Aebischer, "'To the Future,'" 447.

21. Jarman, *Queer Edward II*, 20.

22. Jarman, *Queer Edward II*, 20.

23. Jarman, *Queer Edward II*, 20.

24. Marlowe, *Edward II*, I. iv, lines 304–305.

25. Jarman, *Queer Edward II*, 24.

26. Jarman, *Queer Edward II*, 22.
27. Talvacchia, "Historical Phallicy," 123–124.
28. Marlowe, Edward II, I. ii, line 55.
29. Aebischer, "'To the Future,'" 443.
30. Jarman, *Queer Edward II*, 158.
31. Jarman, *Queer Edward II*, 164.
32. Elizabeth Ewan, Review of *Braveheart*, *The American Historical Review* 100, no. 4 (1995): 1220.
33. Ewan, Review of *Braveheart*, 1220.
34. Laurie A. Finke and Martin B. Schichtman, *Cinematic Illuminations* (Baltimore: Johns Hopkins University Press, 2010), 189.
35. Jarman, *Queer Edward II*, 2. The reference to Edward I seems to derive from a reference in Mathew Paris, who claimed that the young Edward had his followers gratuitously cut off the ears and gouge out the eye of a young man. Michael Prestwich, *Edward I* (Berkeley: University of California Press, 1988), 1.
36. Jarman, *Queer Edward II*, 30.
37. Finke and Schichtman, 98–99.
38. Samuel K. Cohn, Review of John Hatcher, *The Black Death: An Intimate History*, *The English Historical Review* 124, no. 509 (2009): 942.
39. Carlos Ramet, *Ken Follett: The Transformation of a Writer* (Bowling Green, KY: Bowling Green State University Press, 1999), 113.
40. Kamal Ahmed, "Key Labour Backer Turns on 'Cowardly' Blair," *The Guardian*, July 1, 2000. https://www.theguardian.com/politics/2000/jul/02/uk.labour1.

## BIBLIOGRAPHY

Aebischer, Pascale. "'To the Future': Derek Jarman's Edward II in the Archive." *Shakespeare Bulletin* 32, no. 3 (2014): 429–450.

Cohn, Samuel K. Review of *The Black Death: An Intimate History*, by John Hatcher. *The English Historical Review* 124, no. 509 (2009): 940–942.

Druon, Maurice. *The Iron King*. Translated by Humphrey Hare. London: Harper, 2013.

———. *The She Wolf*. Translated by Humphrey Hare. London: Harper, 2014.

———. *La Louve de France*. Paris: Livres de Poche, 1970.

Ewan, Elizabeth. Review of *Braveheart*. *The American Historical Review* 100, no. 4 (1995): 1219–1221.

Finke, Laurie A. and Martin B. Schichtman. *Cinematic Illuminations*. Baltimore: Johns Hopkins University Press, 2010.

Hamilton, J. S. *Piers Gaveston, Earl of Cornwall, 1307–1312. Politics and Patronage in the Reign of Edward II*. Detroit: Wayne State University Press, 1988.

Hanley, Sarah. "Imagining the Last Capetians." *Fiction and Film for French Historians: A Cultural Bulletin.* Accessed July 3, 2015. http://h-france. net/fffh/classics/imagining-the-last-capetians-maurice-druon-the-accursed-kings/.

"Historian Explores Gender Differences in Legal System." *University of Guelph.* May 30, 2012. http://news.uoguelph.ca//2012/05/ historian-explores-gender-differences-in-legal-system/.

Jarman, Derek. *Queer Edward II.* London: British Film Institute, 1991.

Prestwich, Michael. *Edward I.* Berkeley: University of California Press, 1988.

Ramet, Carlos. *Ken Follett: The Transformation of a Writer.* Bowling Green, KY: Bowling Green State University Press, 1999.

Talvacchia, Bette. "Historical Phallicy: Derek Jarman's 'Edward II'." *Oxford Art Journal* 16, no. 1 (1993): 112–128.

## Filmography

*Braveheart.* Feature Film. Directed by Mel Gibson. Los Angeles: Icon Productions / The Ladd Company / Paramount, 1995.

*Edward II.* Feature Film. Directed by Derek Jarman. London: BBC Films / Working Title, 1992.

*Les Rois maudits.* Television Series. Directed by Claude Barma. Paris: ORTF, 1972–1973.

*Les Rois maudits.* Television Series. Directed by Josée Dayan. Paris: France 2, 2005.

*World Without End.* Television Miniseries. Directed by Michael Caton-Jones. Munich: Scott Free / Tandem Communications.

# CHAPTER 14

# Seeing Him for What He Was: Reimagining King Olaf II Haraldsson in Post-War Popular Culture

*Karl C. Alvestad*

## INTRODUCTION

Of the premodern kings in Scandinavia, few have been depicted more in text, art, and on the silver screen than Olaf II 'the saint' Haraldsson of Norway (d. 1030). Only Queen Christina of Sweden, as discussed in Séverine Genieys-Kirk's chapter, has been commented on and depicted more often than Olaf since her death, and the modern royals have been the most popular on the silver screen. Olav II's image as king and saint has evolved over the almost one thousand years since his elevation to sainthood in 1031, and most recently he has appeared on the big screen, in *Sagaen om Olav den Hellige* (*The Saga of Saint Olaf*, 1983) and *Olav* (*Olaf*, 2012). The centuries that lay between the modern audiences and the historical life of Olaf II have contributed to the allure of the king and his life, as well as his pivotal role in the emergence of the Norwegian kingdom at the end of the Viking Age. It could be argued that Olaf II in many ways is fundamental to the idea of Norway. As a result, it

K. C. Alvestad (✉)
University of Winchester, Winchester, UK

© The Author(s) 2018
J. North et al. (eds.), *Premodern Rulers and Postmodern Viewers*,
Queenship and Power, https://doi.org/10.1007/978-3-319-68771-1_14

is interesting to explore how Olaf has been presented throughout the centuries, and an inaugural study of the depictions of Olaf in pictorial art was published in 2016 under the name of *Helgenkongen St Olav I kunsten* (*Saint Olaf's Image in Art*).[1] Yet, the images of Olaf in pictorial art do not exist in isolation, for as I have previously argued the expressions of Olaf need to be seen through the context of cultural and political ideas at the time of the production of these expressions.[2] The Olavian traditions in pictorial art are quite fixed to the hagiographic norms surrounding Olaf, with minor adaptations throughout the centuries. This trend is to some extent also reflected in literature, and especially in plays, although recent years have seen significant revisions of the Olavian image in plays and especially in films. This chapter will demonstrate that in the post-1945 canon of Olavian literature and films, the audience is confronted by a more nuanced Olavian image, an image that may help the audience better understand the king and see him for what he really was: a man and not a saint.

The image of Olaf found in medieval sources and in the pre-war literature and art is that of the heroic warrior-king who converts to Christianity and is martyred for his faith and kingdom, awarding Olaf the title *Rex Perpetuus Norvegiae* 'the eternal king of Norway'.[3] This image was embedded in both folklore and art and became absorbed into the pre-1940 historical narratives about Olaf. Historical knowledge about Olaf II is scarce, but what can be established is that he was born in the mid-990s and grew up in the southeast of Norway before following the contemporary fashion and going a-Viking in the Baltic and North Sea regions at the age of 12.[4] Olaf seems to have been involved in the political conflicts in England in the early 1010s and is famed for allegedly pulling down London Bridge in defense against a Danish attack on the city. Whilst abroad, Olaf converted to Christianity before returning to Norway in around 1015–1016 and reuniting the Norwegian kingdom under his rule as the sole king of Norway. During his reign, Olaf introduced a number of religious and legal reforms that created conflict between him and members of the traditional elites. These elites came under the influence of Knut the Great of England and Denmark in the 1020s, resulting in Olaf losing his throne and going into exile in 1028–1029.[5] Olaf returned in 1030 with an army of loyalists and foreign supporters to try to oust the Danish occupation and their collaborators, but he died in the battle of Stiklestad in the same year. Much of what is known about Olaf II comes from *Heimskringla*, penned generations after Olaf's death, making it likely that some elements of the narrative might not be fully accurate.

The nineteenth-century popularity of Olaf II was tied to two key trends: the rise of Norwegian nationalism and the rise of medievalism in Norway.[6] The new national interest in Olaf focused on presenting Olaf as a heroic and saintly king,[7] who saved and restored the Norwegian kingdom from internal and external threats. This is to some extent still the official narrative surrounding Olaf, and Olaf's image has been a focal point of the Norwegian national revival; a revival that sought to restore the medieval state of Norway to its rightful place as a nation-state. It has therefore been natural for Norwegian authors, playwrights, and filmmakers to explore Olaf, but this fame and the official narrative has also limited the possible interpretations of Olaf as discussed below.

However, this official narrative saw some revisionism in the post-war era led by Vera Henriksen's historical novels *The Sigrid trilogy* (1961– 1963), which in part was a reaction against the depictions in Olav Gullvåg and Paul Okkenhaug's musical play *Spelet om Hellig Olav* (*The Play About Saint Olaf*) (1954), and in turn, influenced *Prima Vera's Sagaen om Olav den hellige* (*The Saga of Saint Olaf*) (1983) before the narrative reverted back to its traditional form in *Olav: A Documentary on the Viking King Olav and His Legacy* (2012).[8] Some of the key changes in the post-war representation of Olaf are related to his masculinity and his personal relationships with the women around him. This chapter will, therefore, explore how these relationships are presented in the texts and films above. It will also explore what these changes suggest and imply about Olaf's masculinity. Through these lenses, it is possible to assess Olaf's journey and presentation through the last 60 years and to comprehend the post-war understanding and imagination of the 'true' Olaf.

In 2012, Stian Hansen released, on behalf of *Olavsfestdagene* (the St. Olaf Festival in Trondheim, Norway), a short film about Olaf and the Olavian legacy titled *Olav* staring Kristofer Hivju as Olaf II.[9] Hivju, who is better known for playing Tormund Giantsbane in *Game of Thrones*, embodies in many ways the essence of Olaf through his height and strength and conventional ideals of Viking masculinity. In this film, Olaf is presented as a brutal, yet religiously motivated, warrior king, who united Norway and established the foundations of the later Norwegian civilization.[10] At its core, this does not diverge significantly from the image of Olaf that is present in Norwegian textbooks and history books from the late nineteenth and early twentieth century.[11] Hansen's *Olav* returns Olaf II to the early twentieth-century national and religious narrative and brings the king back to Olaf's more famous image—the saintly king who united Norway. However, between the Second World War and the release of *Olav* in 2012, the image of Olaf became more complex and the audience who received *Olav* was familiar with some of the less heroic elements of Olaf's life such as his 'convert or death' policy during his early reign or the murder of the brothers Tore and Grjotgard Olveson.[12] This complexity has been stimulated by the appearance of Olaf in a number of texts, plays, and films. Some of the most notable appearances of Olaf II can be found in Vera Henriksen's *The Sigrid trilogy*, a trilogy consisting of *Sølvhammeren* (*The Silver Hammer*, 1961), *Jærtegn* (*Signs*, 1962) and *Helgenkongen* (*The Holy King*, 1963); Henriksen's play *Sverdet* (*The Sword*, 1974); Olav Gullvåg and Paul Okkenhaug's musical/play *Spelet om Hellig Olav* (*The Play About Saint Olaf*, 1954) and Prima Vera's film *Sagaen om Hellig Olav* (*The Saga of Saint Olaf*, 1983).

These depictions of Olaf are best understood by means of a comparative analysis around the themes of this paper, but it is worth noting that the key shifts in the Olavian image are closely connected with the question of who the lead character in the historical drama is. As such, the image of Olaf II is reflective of whose story the audience follows. Furthermore, none these depictions, and especially the two newest depictions in *The Saga of Saint Olaf* and *Olav*, are historically accurate, although both Henriksen and Hansen put considerable effort into making their presentation Olaf appear authentic. With the exception of Prima Vera's film, these depictions try to make the audience 'feel' the authentic medieval experience. They allude to, draw extensively on, and contribute to the shaping of contemporary knowledge of the Middle Ages,[13] and through this, achieve a feeling of an authentic medieval setting for the depictions. As an extension of this, it might be argued that these depictions have contributed to shaping the current understanding of Olaf II and his character.

## OLAF AS VIKING OR KING

Olaf II's masculinity is most commonly depicted through his conquest of Norway and his behavior towards those opposing him in the wars of conquest and the subsequent religious conversion. Yet, in the films, plays, and novels mentioned above, Olaf fluctuates between a man seem-ingly dominating his surroundings as a manifestation of his own mascu-linity, as in *The Silver Hammer* (1961), and a man whose masculinity is questioned on the basis of his physique and inability to handle his will-ful wife, as seen in *The Saga of Saint Olaf* (1983). These two opposing images draw on elements of the Olavian sources, but the latter in par-ticular is a reflection of contemporary questions about gender roles and power.

In Henriksen's series of novels *The Sigrid Trilogy*, the reader encoun-ters an Olaf who instills fear and resentment among his cultural and political opponents. The main character in Henriksen's novels is a fic-tional adaptation of a historical aristocratic Norwegian woman, Sigrid, at the beginning of the eleventh century, and the novels focus on her relationship with the cultural and political changes in her own time. Through various circumstances, some drawn from medieval sources and others based on Henriksen's imagination, Sigrid ends up in opposition to Olaf and his political policies.

However, unlike Hansen's manifestation of Olaf in the image of Hivju, it is not Henriksen's physical description that defines Olaf's masculinity, but rather his actions towards Sigrid and her kin where he expresses his strength and ruthlessness as a monarch. An example of this ruthlessness is Sigrid's first meeting with Olaf when he condemns her husband Olve to death for taking part in a local pagan festival.[14] Olve is accused of leading the ritual, and Olaf refused to listen to Sigrid's plead-ing. Instead, he makes Sigrid a hostage of the court and gives her to one of his own men. Sigrid's resentment towards Olaf for these actions is only matched by the resentment of her's and Olve's sons, who attempt to overthrow the king. In the subsequent rebellion, Sigrid's sons and their allies challenge Olaf, and the king's ruthlessness and masculinity are both at their most visible and volatile in the whole trilogy. For example, in the second novel, *Signs* (1962), a group of rebels try to seek legal mit-igation with the king, and the king's pride and anger cause Olaf to refuse the rebels' legal rights and to kill them.[15] Through these actions, Olaf is described as throwing overboard not only the bodies of the rebels but also the respect of his men, for they start questioning how Olaf is able to be a just king if he does not conform to the traditional notions of ruler-ship and the law in late Viking age society. Olaf's ruthlessness, which in the context of Viking warfare would have been a prime manifestation of Olaf's masculinity, is in this context deemed a liability to the king, since his emotional behavior in his rage over the rebellion undermines the law he himself had created, which ironically formed the legal foundation of his own reign. Sigrid's new husband—Kalv Arnesson—implies that Olaf's actions when dealing with this rebellion would have been appropriate as a conqueror, but not as a king, and that Olaf has not managed the change from Viking warlord to Christian king, a role in which Olaf's Viking behavior is a liability for his reign.

Olaf's violent 'Viking' behavior is implied in both Hansen's *Olav* and especially in *Spelet*. Gullvåg and Okkenhaug's musical play *Spelet om Hellig Olav* (*The Play About Saint Olaf*, 1954) focuses on Olaf's religious awakening and his attempt to re-conquer Norway in 1030, leading to his death and to his sanctity. Neither the depictions in *Olav* nor in *Spelet* can completely separate Olaf from his Viking behavior of brutality and propensity to violence, which defines his masculinity. This Viking behavior is in both depictions presented as Olaf's behavior as a young man gone a-Viking, which is corrected and amended through Olaf's conversion and later religious awakening during his exile. In the case of *Spelet*, the salvation from a violent Viking past comes through a religious redemption and a nationalistic moment of salvation at the battle of Stiklestad, a moment when the skills honed during Olaf's Viking years can be used to cement both Christianity in Norway and the notion of Norwegianness in his enemies—a notion that eventually results in the overthrow of Danish rule in Norway. In *The Play About Saint Olaf*, Olaf's Viking behavior is only implied, yet it taps into the audience's pre-existing knowledge about the king derived from government-approved textbooks. This knowledge and implied Viking past contribute the success of the depictions of Olaf as an exiled, pious king returning to liberate his kingdom.

In *The Play*, Olaf's masculinity is no longer connected to his conquest, raids, or warrior 'Viking' behavior, but rather to his heroic stand against the foreign occupier and internal collaborators as well as his religiously motivated attempt to retake the kingdom. Some of the last lines in *The Play* are: 'The king fell at Stiklestad, but the country he freed'[16]; in this line, Gullvåg implies that Olaf's loss caused the liberation of the Norwegian nation from foreign aggression and internal betrayal. The narrative of Olaf's loss and the salvation of Norway is known already from *Heimskringla* but must have held special resonance in the postwar years in Norway, when the lives lost to defend the nation from the Nazis had ultimately secured it its freedom. If we view Olaf's heroic defeat in this context, Olaf in *The Play* becomes more than the religiously motivated and fundamentalist crusader found in the religious cantata *Heimferd (The Journey Home)* by Gullvåg written 25 years earlier, for now he is associated with the heroic masculinity of the Norwegian army and resistance against German occupation in 1940–1945. This nationalist masculinity commemorates not only the heroic dead but also attempts to illustrate how even in the face of utter defeat a heroic charge (or possibly a stubborn one in the case of Olaf) could lead to victory for the Norwegian cause. This underlying narrative would be recognizable to an audience in 1954, but it is likely unrecognizable today.

Olaf's masculinity as depicted in *The Play* is still linked to the acts of heroic self-sacrifice for the nation, but this idea was less popular among in left wing political communities in Norway, where Olaf's Viking and warrior nature represents the oppression, imperialism, and chauvinistic behavior from which the Norwegian Left (especially Sosialistisk Venstre Parti, SV for short) seek to distance themselves in the hope of creating a more inclusive nation. To SV politician Torgeir Knag Fylkesnes, *The Play*'s Olaf is only a reflection of the warrior Viking,[17] not of the nationalist or the martyr Olaf that the center-right of Norwegian politics favors. To some extent, Fylkesnes' criticism of the image of Olaf is correct, and his interpretation highlights a key change in Olaf's image; because his masculinity has not continued to evolve or become more nuanced, since the first staging of the play in 1954, Olaf has stagnated and fallen short of maintaining his role in Norwegian culture as *Rex Perpetuus Norvegiae*—The eternal king of Norway.[18]

Hansen's short historical documentary *Olav* (2012), made in cooperation with *Olavsfestdagene*, must be seen in the context of development of the Olavian narrative and the criticism of the manifestations of Olaf's masculinity by Torgeir Knag Fylkesnes, which will be discussed below.[19] *Olavsfestdagene (the St. Olaf Festival)* is a Norwegian organization claiming to manage the Olavian legacy in the modern world,[20] an idea that influences Hansen's documentary. Hansen's *Olav* presents an Olaf as a rugged, ruthless man whose masculinity is defined by his propensity for violence. Yet *Olav* does not present Olaf as a warrior king, but highlights instead Olaf's peaceful legacy and kingship; in this, Hansen ties Olaf back to the nation and its foundation myth. Olaf's brutality and ruthlessness is in *Olav* explained as an element of his time. However, Hivju's Olaf is also presented as an outsider in that he is a civilized king among Vikings in a barbarian world, similar to how Hivju's depiction of

Tormund Giantsbane in *Game of Thrones* presents a Tormund as a barbarian in a 'civilized' context south of the wall. Under Hansen's direction, Hivju embodies the Olavian tradition of a larger-than-life king, whose actions were brutal but inevitably benefited the kingdom by bringing political unity and Christianity to the country. *Olav* only gives a brief overview of Olaf's life, but in its commentary and depiction of the battle of Stiklestad, it highlights Olaf's heroic defeat. Hansen emphasized the idea of Olaf as a lawmaker and a pious missionary king, a *Rex Iustus*, who sought to protect the Christian values he had introduced to the kingdom,[21] a notion fairly far removed from the Vikingness Hivju embodies. Hansen's depiction of Olaf's masculinity is intrinsically linked to his legacy rather than to the man himself, and therefore Hansen blurs the line between myth and reality—between the saint and the king. In this way, Hansen returns Olaf's masculinity to how it had been presented in 1930, a missionary martyr embodying the 'crusader masculinity' and Christian national guardian. As such, Hansen reemphasizes the existing myths of Olaf and, like Gullvåg, reminds them of the national saint.[22]

Prima Vera's *The Saga of Saint Olaf* (1983) challenges both the contemporary understanding of Olaf and the conventional narrative, in that the actor cast for the role of Olaf is not a larger-than-life person, nor does the actor present Olaf as a natural leader. Instead, the actor cast for the role, Jahn Teigen, has a build best described as skinny, which would not stand out from the crowd in the same way as Hivju. Olaf in Teigen's image has many similarities with producers of *The Last Kingdom* (2015) casting of David Dawson as a somewhat sickly yet politically astute King Alfred, rather than a brave warrior king.[23] However, unlike Dawson's depiction of Alfred, which has some grounding in historical sources, Teigen's Olaf has no historical foundation, for Olaf is reported to have been exceptionally large and strong, earning the nickname 'digre' meaning 'the Stout'.[24] Yet in both cases these depictions challenge the nationalistic conventions of what Alfred and Olaf were like and cast doubt on the cultural memory of these heroes. The casting of Teigen for the role was perhaps not surprising, as all the main roles were distributed among the members of the entertainment company Prima Vera and their friends, but it adds an interesting flavor to the depiction of Olaf as the conventional image of a Viking-warrior-turned-king no longer applies. Teigen's Olaf does not present a physically hyper-masculine king or Viking, but Teigen compensates for his physique with humor and satire. The whole production is a satirical and humorous interpretation of the Olavian legend, not unlike the Monty Python adaptation of Arthurian legends in *Monty Python and the Holy Grail* (1975). Olaf's masculinity in *The Saga of Saint Olaf* is centered on his aggression and daring behavior in the conquest and unification of Norway—a conquest undertaken through song, jokes, and treachery, rather than fire and swords, as in *Heimskringla*.

The *Saga* in its Monty Python-esque depiction of Olaf's conquest is unable to explore the complexities of the conflict and focuses on humorous effect rather than historical accuracy. This is visible in the scene when Olaf first meets his court poet Sigvart Skald, who lives in a modern caravan in a site surrounded by several rubber car tires. The whole narrative is driven by Olaf, who looks out for himself first and foremost and is a happy-go-lucky kind of character. Even in his relationship with Ingegerd, the love of Olaf's life, the daughter of Olof Skötkonung king of Sweden, and sister of King Anund Jacob of Sweden, *The Saga* comments comically on historical events by showing how Olaf falls head-over-heels in love with Ingegerd and sleeps with her before she tells him: 'Igor the Gruesome ... [and I] are getting married tomorrow.'[25] Teigen's Olaf breaks down in tears until Ingegerd promises Olaf can marry her sister Astrid. Unfortunately for Olaf, this Astrid is more than he had bargained for, and the marriage is anything but happy. Astrid dominates Olaf in the second half of the film with Olaf fearing his wife, trying to run away from her instead of standing up against her, and above all allowing himself to be dominated by her in their tent. These actions by Olaf are calculated to highlight Olaf's femininity and the problems of the perceived gender norms of the Viking age, as well as the contemporary norms in 1980s Norway where a man was supposed to be the dominant member of the household and control his wife. Olaf's actions stand in contrast to the 1980s Western and Norwegian ideal man, who was a man of action, a man of dominance, and a strong man, ideally a bit rugged like Helge Jordal in *Orions Belte* (1985) or overly muscular like Arnold Schwarzenegger in *The Terminator* (1984). As a result of his fear of Astrid, Teigen's Olaf convinces Cnut, King of Denmark and England, to attack, hoping that the attack will kill Astrid; instead, Olaf dies, and Astrid survives. The dominance caused Olaf to appear as a weak man and as untrustworthy—not the hero of legends. *The Saga*'s depiction of Olaf questions the audience's ideas of Viking masculinity and gender norms in the eleventh and twentieth century through these twists, as it also questions what defines a hero. Furthermore, through this narrative, Prima Vera raised the more important question: are our narratives and myths always true, and can we trust that the heroes of the stories actually behaved the way we are told? In this, the film questions the very foundation of the Olavian myth, the heroic last stand at Stiklestad, and its role in unifying the nation, by presenting the narrative as a desperate attempt to get rid of an unwanted wife. However, *The Saga* flopped at the box office, causing the film to have an arguably minimal impact on the image of Olaf and the Olavian memory.[26] The religious and national interpretations of Olaf's masculinity have prevailed throughout the second half of the twentieth century, regardless of Prima Vera's attempts to challenge these interpretations. Olaf's historical actions were ruthless, and a 'reconstructed' masculinity on the basis of *Heimskringla* would imply that Torgeir Knag Fylkesnes' criticism of the modern Olaf presented in *The Play* as forgetting Olaf's enforcement of cultural change and political violence during his reign is well founded, particularly with regards to Olaf's relationship with women.

## WOMEN AND RELATIONSHIPS

The women of Olaf's life, Ingegerd, Astrid, and his unnamed mistress— the mother of his heir, Magnus I Olafsson—were some of his most important political relationships historically. These women play key roles, alongside Sigrid—the lead characher in the Henriksen's *Sigrid Trilogy*— in some of the post-war depictions of Olaf, and his interplay with them gives an insight into how authors and producers saw Olaf's relationships with the women and the society around him.

Olaf's historical interaction with the societies and social norms surrounding him is not as straightforward, and Henriksen's narrative through Sigrid's eyes casts light on the less honorable elements of Olaf's life. Torgeir Knag Fylkesnes' criticism of Olaf's presentation in *The Play* in 2014 was based on the notion that *The Play* prepetuated an image of Olaf that has no semblance to the historical realities of what Fylkesnes calls a 'cultural genocide' of the pre-Christian regional cultures of Norway.[27] Fylkesnes further emphasises Olaf's less-than-heroic behavior towards the people of the realm, including women and how this is in stark contrast to the hero presented in *The Play*. Fylkesnes states: 'Olaf II Haraldsson was, in reality, a mass murderer who was elevated to sainthood after his death.'[28] Fylkesnes is correct in his criticism in as much as historical research has revealed very little about Olaf's personal and political relationships with the society in which he lived. It can be inferred from *Heimskringla* that he would have been—directly or indirectly—responsible for an increased number of widows and orphans in the kingdom.

Neither Astrid nor her sister Ingegerd is included in *The Play* or in Hansen's *Olav*. It appears that *The Play*'s masculine martyr king has no need for his queen or former fiancée to present a coherent narrative. In fact, if the audience wishes to meet the women of Olaf's life they must look elsewhere, away from the official narratives and the hero worship to the works of Vera Henriksen and Prima Vera. Only there does the audience meet Astrid and Ingegerd, as well as Sigrid. Similar to Henriksen's novels in *The Sigrid Trilogy*, her play *The Sword* (1974) explores as one of its key themes Olaf's relationship with the women around him. The play also explores the Olaf's internal conflicts that cause the king's evolution from Viking warlord to saint. The majority of the narrative is set away from Olaf's court, in the settlement of Borg (modern day city of Sarpsborg, Norway) where the king's loyal bishop Grimkjell is reflecting on Olaf's development as a ruler, a man, and as a Christian.

The conflict between Olaf and Astrid in *The Sword* is over his son Magnus' status, but Astrid is presented as reasonable and in the right. Astrid's complaint is founded on Olaf's seduction of her maid (Magnus' mother) and on Magnus' presence at court.[29] Olaf's handling of his relationship with Astrid reflects his personal struggle with cultural changes following the conversion. On the one hand, Henriksen presents him as the successor to an ancient line of kings whose masculinity was defined by war and by siring many sons, but on the other, he is chastised by the church and Astrid for preserving too much of the old pagan ways in his behavior. Bishop Grimkjell wants Olaf to surrender his sword, given to him by the spirit of an ancestor; Astrid wants Olaf to stop desiring other women to become a better husband and Christian. Astrid links Olaf's fidelity with his faith and challenges Olaf to become more pious and a better Christian, whilst at the same time Olaf is trying to preserve his grip on the kingdom. Astrid goes as far as to claim that Olaf has 'only been faithful to his sword,' implying that he has cheated everyone else, including his new religion and wife.[30] Olaf responds by asking: 'Why do you not go back to Sweden and your brother?' Astrid's response implies that her status as the queen of Norway, even if her husband shares his bed with other women, is higher than that of a king's divorced sister.[31]

She also implies that he needs her to keep the peace with Sweden, more than she needs him. In this, Astrid reminds Olaf and the audience of the socio-political situation that brought about the match—the war between Olaf and Astrid's father, Olof Skötkonung king of Sweden. This reminder calms Olaf's temper, resulting in Astrid leaving the stage seeming content with this reminder, and having re-established the status quo in their marriage. Unlike Prima Vera's *The Saga*, *The Sword* presents Olaf's relationship with Astrid as one of equals, who voice and negotiate their grievances rather than trying to kill each other. But *The Sword* also shows how Olaf finds it easy to disregard Astrid's status as his wife and queen, which arguably caused the conflict in the first place; in this, Henriksen allows Astrid to take on the thoughts and feelings Henriksen herself could imagine. Henriksen's Astrid becomes relatable to the audience as she voices her worries and challenges her husband in a modern way, for which there is little early medieval historical precedence.

In *the Sword*, Olaf is able to compromise in the conflict with Astrid in a way that he never would have been able to with Sigrid, his subject in *The Sigrid Trilogy*. In this, Henriksen develops her depiction of Olaf from a king who the audience only sees from the outside to a more private person showing his thoughts and feelings as a husband and father.

When Henriksen first introduced her version of Olaf at the end of her debut novel *The Silver Hammer* (1961), the first novel in *The Sigrid Trilogy*, he is presented as an outsider who interferes in the life of Sigrid and her husband Olve. Olaf's relationship with Sigrid is that between a king and a subject where Olve's murder and Sigrid's imprisonment are punishment for breaking Olaf's new laws—laws that in Sigrid's eyes are ruthless and go against social norms, underlining Sigrid's experience of Olaf's conquest and reign.

In these interactions, Olaf treats Henriksen's Sigrid with his 'legendary' ruthlessness and showcases his inability to see others' perspectives. In this depiction, Olaf breaks almost every cultural norm both known from the Viking age and accepted in 1950s Norway, actions that he attempts to justify by arguing that Sigrid and Olve's paganism and resistance against his rule nullifies their legal status. This nullification is not necessarily historically accurate, but it is reminiscent of the emergency legislation introduced to deal with traitors and war criminals during and after the German occupation, where the normal judicial systems were superseded by situational orders.[32] The annulment of Sigrid's legal status by Olaf stands in stark contrast to the traditional narrative of Olaf 'the lawmaker,' highlighted in the 2012 documentary *Olav*. Olaf's disregard of legal tradition in *The Sigrid Trilogy* points to a personal insecurity and a fear that undermines Olaf's justness and royal authority. These insecurities are the same that are present in the 1974 Olaf found in *The Sword*, where Olaf is unable to reconcile his Viking nature with his Christian kingship. The same insecurities present Olaf as stubborn, willful, and weak, almost effeminate in the eyes of his contemporaries, jeopardizing his masculinity and his rule.

Olaf's relationship with Astrid in Prima Vera's *The Saga* also challenges his masculinity, but in a different way than we find in Henriksen's works. Astrid's dominance not only undermines Olaf's kingship but also his manliness and masculinity. Astrid's behavior is very similar to what Carey Fleiner observes that Isabella of Angouleme does to King John in *Robin and Marian* in her chapter on Isabella. But unlike Isabella's impact on John, who is already perceived as evil, Astrid in Prima Vera's narrative takes a hero and makes him appear as a weak and untrustworthy man, who is willing to try anything to get rid of his wife. By this, Astrid undermines the very foundation of the Olavian mythology and Prima Vera's Olaf is no longer the heroic national hero, but a lovesick and regretful husband trying to get free from a woman's grasp—not a story to gain sanctity for, nor a story on which to build a nation.

The relationship between Olaf and Astrid emerges more vividly in Prima Vera's and Henriksen's narratives than in *Heimskringla* where Astrid—like most women—plays a supporting role, only to be seen or heard when it adds to the narrative of the heroes and villains. In these modern representations, Henriksen and Prima Vera look beyond the primary sources and try to make sense of the interaction between Olaf and the women around him—both in his family and those opposing him, like Sigrid. In this they construct a deeper personality for Olaf, but also try to make sense of the internal behavioral changes in him—a behavior that at best can be described as a king in conflict with his new-found faith, his contemporaries, and his legacy.

## Historical Accuracy

In her initial depiction of Olaf, Henriksen saw him as a brutish Viking king with invasive policies. She stated in her later book, *The Women of the Saga Period*, that she wished originally to display how Sigrid and women of her time would have experienced and coped with Olaf and his policies.[33] To achieve this, she wanted to be as close to the historical narrative as possible and sought to reflect Olaf's life through the eyes of his contemporaries, to see the saint from the other side of the conflict. It is safe to say that Henriksen achieved this through both the trilogy and *The Sword*. Henriksen's Olaf is in many ways, Olaf thus reflects the masculine ideal of his time, as he stands between the traditional narrative of earthly and religious conflict and illustrates the real impact of Olaf's personality on those around him. Olaf's anger over the attempted rebellion by Sigrid's sons leads to them being executed in the second book of *The Sigrid Trilogy* without due judicial process. In this, Henriksen illustrates the conflict between Olaf's personal authority and the traditional legal structures of the late Viking age, namely the law and the Things (the traditional judicial and legislative assembly in the Viking World). Henriksen's Olaf puts himself above the law and the Things, dispensing justice as he sees fit. In this, Henriksen implies that through his own giving of laws, Olaf has assumed the judicial as well as the legislative power within the realm, a power that came with increased centralization of the kingdom from the eleventh century onwards. It is not unlikely that the historical Olaf exercised this power, but it is unlikely that this was a traditional part of the king's authority, which might explain part of the conflict between Olaf and the aristocracy.

In *The Sword*, Olaf is more focused on the loss of support and the conflict between symbols of traditional kingship and his new Christian faith. *The Sword* presents an Olaf who is at odds with his own time and the society that surrounded him, similar to how he is presented in *The Sigrid Trilogy*. As such, Henriksen's Olaf has not evolved much over the 20 years between the first novel and the play, but instead, the intricacies of his emotional relationships are explored further. The key shift in Henriksen's engagement with Olaf is the shift of perspective from Olaf as an outsider in *The Sigrid Trilogy* in the eyes of Sigrid, to him as the central character in *The Sword* showing Olaf's family life. Olaf in Henriksen's texts is no longer the national hero, but a man who is at odds with his contemporaries and their expectations of a king, who struggles to reconcile his Christian present with his pagan past. It is this emotional struggle that Henriksen presents as the contributing cause of Olaf's downfall—his inability to meet the expectations of his newly converted contemporaries and the expectations of the Church. Henriksen succeeds in humanizing Olaf and the audience is able to understand and rationalize both his moves and those of his opponents. The audience's pre-existing knowledge is challenged as Olaf is no longer the national hero who saved the Norwegian nation against willful chieftains and foreign aggression; instead, he is the aggressor with no respect for contemporary law and legal customs in Sigrid's struggle for survival.

Neither Gullvåg nor Henriksen agree with the conventional image of Olaf as an ideal Viking hero, whose masculinity is closely tied to military prowess. In fact, in Gullvåg's work, Olaf is a pious Christian missionary king—an image far removed from the traditional image of a Viking warrior king. Instead, he is a saint-to-be and a national hero. Similarly, Henriksen undermines—or nuances—Olaf's military masculinity through her focus on his character and his internal conflicts. Although these Olafs are more nuanced in their depiction of Olaf's masculinity and personality, they sit poorly within the historical narrative as they look away from his violence, brutality, and political instinct. Whereas Prima Vera's depiction of Olaf takes this furthest, all three creations critique the conventional image of Olaf as a hyper-masculine warrior king and stress the need for nuance in the narratives of Olaf and his masculinity. Yet, all of these depictions from beginning to end are reflections of modern national interpretations of Olaf—the patron saint who saved Norway in one way or another.

It is this modern tradition that Hansen draws on when constructing and presenting his Olaf, yet Hivju's Olaf is Gullvåg's saint and Henriksen's is a complex and troubled Viking in the body of a giant Viking. Hansen's Olaf is at least outwardly returning to the image of Olaf as an exceptionally big and strong man, whose masculinity is seemingly closely tied to his physicality. As Hivju's character lacks the depth and nuance of the post-war traditions, Olaf is once more just a warrior king and political hero. For although Hansen's narrative is simplified to fit into a 30-minute film, it presents Olaf as the foundation of all that is Norwegian, including the nation's legal tradition, religion, and independence. One of Olaf's achievements according to Hansen is the 'final' unification and conversion of Norway, an act achieved through Olaf's death at Stiklestad. In this interpretation, Olaf is presented as a king and a saint and not as a man of his time.

## CONCLUSION

Hansen's depiction of Olaf II Haraldsson in his short film *Olav* brings Olaf full circle to the pre-war depictions of the hero-king and patron saint of Norway. Both Hansen and *The Play* reproduce and perpetuate the Olavian myth for a modern audience with little appreciation of the complexities of the contextual conflicts of the early eleventh century. In *Olav* and *The Play*, the audience encounters an Olaf whose narrative and identity is defined by his Viking past and the post-conversion present, a national hero who defines Norwegianness.

Gullvåg's and Hansen's Olafs exist in contrast to Henriksen's and Prima Vera's Olafs; the latter's identities are challenged, and their personalities emerge from the legends with vast complexity and nuance. Through their narratives and storytelling, Henriksen and Prima Vera question the elements or the whole of the Olavian myth. For through his conflict with Astrid in *The Sword* and *The Saga of Saint Olaf*, Olaf emerges having lost his halo, showing him as a man and nothing else. These revisions inform the audience that Olaf the hero is no more, Olaf the saint is a legend, and what remains in the eyes of Henriksen and Prima Vera is a man and a king, who like all men are destined to fail and make mistakes. Through this, the 1983 film and Henriksen's debut novels add nuance and complexity to the post-war cannon and to the Olavian tradition as a whole. Regardless of the revisions of Olaf presented by Henriksen and Prima Vera, modern audiences frequently encounters in texts, on stages or through the silver screen Hansen and Gullvåg's Olaf who perpetuates a traditional heroic image of Olaf. In this tradition, the line between the historical Olaf and the legendary Olaf is blurred, resulting in attempts to present Olaf as a historical king influenced by Olaf the saint, and vice versa. As such, it is difficult for the audience to see the nuanced man that Olaf really was, instead of seeing what our cultural memory tells us we should see.

## NOTES

1. Øystein Ekroll, ed., *Helgenkongen St. Olav i kunsten* (Trondheim: Museumsforlaget, 2016).
2. Karl Alvestad, "Den Nasjonale Olav: Bruk og misbruk av helgenkongens bilde mellom 1920 og 1945", in *Helgenkongen St. Olav i kunsten*, ed. Øystein Ekroll (Trondheim: Museumsforlaget, 2016), 192–193.
3. Lars Roar Langslett, Knut Ødegård, *Olav den Hellige; Spor etter Helgenkongen* (Oslo: Forlaget Press, 2011), 29–34.
4. Snorri Sturluson, *Heimskringla volume II Olafr Haraldsson (The Saint)*, trans. Alisn Finlay and Anthony Faulkes (London: Viking society for Northern Research, 2014), 3–16.
5. Sverre Bagge, *From Viking Stronghold to Christian Kingdom: State formation in Norway c. 900–1350* (Copenhagen: Museum Tusculanum Press, 2010), 31.

6. Karl Alvestad, "Kings, Heroes and Ships: The Use of Historical Characters in Nineteenth- and Twentieth-Century Perceptions of the Early Medieval Scandinavian Past" (PhD diss., University of Winchester, 2016), 180–189.
7. Alvestad, "Kings, Heroes and Ships," 97–102, 156.
8. Vera Henriksen, *Sølvhammeren* (Oslo: Aschehoug Forlag, 1983); Vera Henriksen, *Jærtegn* (Oslo: Aschehoug Forlag, 1983); Vera Henriksen, *Helgenkongen* (Oslo: Aschehoug Forlag, 1983); O. Gullvåg, P. Okkenhaug, *Mus.ms.a 5967 Paul Okkenhaug: "Spelet om Heilag Olav,"* (Verdal: Stiklestadnemda, 1970); *Prima Veras saga om Olav den hellige*, directed by Herodes Falsk and Harald Gunnar Paalgard (1ste klasses film & video A/S, Mayco A/S, 1983); *Olav: En Dokumentar om Olav den Hellige og Arven han Etterlot Seg*, Documentary, directed by Stian Hansen (Olavsfestdagene, 2012); Vera Henriksen, *Sverdet: Hellig Olav I Borg* (Oslo: Aschehoug, 1974).
9. *Olav: En Dokumentar om Olav den Hellige og Arven han Etterlot Seg*, Documentary, directed by Stian Hansen (Olavsfestdagene, 2012).
10. Hansen, *Olav*.
11. Alvestad, "Kings, Heroes and Ships," 97–102.
12. Sturluson, *Heimskringla volume II Olafr Haraldsson (The Saint)*, 203.
13. Bettina Bildhauer, "Medievalism and Cinema" in *The Cambridge Companion to Medievalism*, ed. Louise D'Arcens (Cambridge: Cambridge University Press, 2016), 50.
14. Vera Henriksen, *Jærtegn* (Oslo: Aschehoug Forlag, 1983), 33.
15. Henriksen, *Jærtegn*, 198–203.
16. 'Kongen stupte på Stiklestad, men landet gjorde han fritt.' Unless otherwise noted, all translations are my own.
17. O. Gullvåg, P. Okkenhaug, *Mus.ms.a 5967 Paul Okkenhaug: "Spelet om Heilag Olav"* (Verdal: Stiklestadnemda, 1970); Sigurd Hofstad and Ugo Fermariello, "– Olav den Hellige var en massemorder," *NRK*, July 23, 2014. https://www.nrk.no/trondelag/_-olav-den-hellige-var-en-sadist-1.11844595.
18. Hofstad and Fermariello, "– Olav den Hellige."
19. Hansen, *Olav*.
20. Olavsfestdagene, "Om Festivalen," *Olavsfestdagene.no*, accessed July 19, 2017. http://www.olavsfestdagene.no/om/.
21. Hansen, *Olav*.
22. Hansen, *Olav*; Gullvåg, Okkenhaug, *Mus.ms.a 5967 Paul Okkenhaug: "Spelet om Heilag Olav,"* (Verdal: Stiklestadnemda, 1970).
23. Whitney Friedlander, "'The Last Kingdom's' David Dawson on Learning His English History," *Variety*, October 17, 2015. http://variety.com/2015/tv/news/last-kingdom-david-dawson-king-alfred-1201620614/.
24. Langslett and Ødeggård, *Olav den Hellige*, 28.
25. *Prima Veras saga om Olav den hellige*, Feature Film, directed by Herodes Falsk and Harald Gunnar Paalgard (1ste klasses film & video A/S, Mayco A/S, 1983). 'Igor den grusoma ... og vi ska gifta oss i morran.'

26. Jon Vidar Bergan, "Prima Vera," *Store Norske Leksikon*, February 19, 2014. https://snl.no/Prima_Vera.
27. Hofstad and Fermariello, "– Olav den Hellige."
28. Hofstad and Fermariello, "– Olav den Hellige." 'Olav den Hellige er i realiteten historien om en massemorder som ble gjort hellig etter sin død.'
29. Vera Henriksen, *Sverdet: Hellig Olav I Borg* (Oslo: Aschehoug, 1974), 40.
30. Henriksen, *Sverdet*, 42. 'Du har vist troskap bare mot ditt sverd.'
31. Henriksen, *Sverdet*, 44. Astrid and Ingegerd as sisters were the daughters of Olof Skötkonung king of Sweden and sisters of King Anund Jacob of Sweden.
32. Henriksen, *Jærtegn*, 33, 198–203; Arnfinn Moland, "Likvidasjoner i motstandsarbeidet," *Norgeshistorie.no*, April 9, 2016. http://www.norgeshistorie.no/andre-verdenskrig/artikler/1734-likvidasjoner-i-mot-standsarbeidet.html.
33. Vera Henriksen, *Skjebneveven: om sagaens kvinner* (Oslo: Aschehoug Forlag, 1998), 7.

## BIBLIOGRAPHY

### Films

*Olav: En Dokumentar om Olav den Hellige og Arven han Etterlot Seg.* Documentary. Directed by Stian Hansen. Olavsfestdagene, 2012.
*Prima Veras saga om Olav den hellige.* Feature Film. Directed by Herodes Falsk, and Harald Gunnar Paalgard. 1ste klasses film & video A/S, Mayco A/S, 1983.

### Published works

Alvestad, Karl. "Den Nasjonale Olav: Bruk og misbruk av helgenkongens bilde mellom 1920 og 1945." In *Helgenkongen St. Olav i kunsten*, edited by Øystein Ekroll, 191–214. Trondheim: Museumsforlaget, 2016.
———. "Kings, Heroes and Ships: The Use of Historical Characters in Nineteenth- and Twentieth-Century Perceptions of the Early Medieval Scandinavian Past." PhD diss., University of Winchester, 2016.
Bagge, Sverre. *From Viking Stronghold to Christian Kingdom: State formation in Norway c. 900–1350.* Copenhagen: Museum Tusculanum Press, 2010.
Bergan, Jon Vidar. "Prima Vera." *Store Norske Leksikon*, February 19, 2014. https://snl.no/Prima_Vera.
Bildhauer, Bettina. "Medievalism and Cinema." In *The Cambridge Companion to Medievalism*, edited by Louise D'Arcens, 45–59. Cambridge: Cambridge University Press, 2016.

Ekroll, Øystein, ed. *Helgenkongen St. Olav i kunsten*. Trondheim: Museumsforlaget, 2016.

Friedlander, Whitney. "'The Last Kingdom's' David Dawson on Learning His English History." *Variety*, October 17, 2015. http://variety.com/2015/tv/news/last-kingdom-david-dawson-king-alfred-1201620614/.

Gullvåg, Olav, and Paul Okkenhaug. *Mus.ms.a 5967 Paul Okkenhaug: 'Spelet om Heilag Olav'*. Verdal: Stiklestadnemda, 1970.

Henriksen, Vera. *Helgenkongen*. Oslo: Aschehoug Forlag, 1983.

———. *Jærtegn*. Oslo: Aschehoug Forlag, 1983.

———. *Skjebneveven: om sagaens kvinner*. Oslo: Aschehoug Forlag, 1998.

———. *Sverdet: Hellig Olav I Borg*. Oslo: Aschehoug Forlag, 1974.

———. *Sølvhammeren*. Oslo: Aschehoug Forlag, 1983.

Hofstad, Sigurd, and Ugo Fermariello. "– Olav den Hellige var en massemorder." *NRK*, July 23, 2014. https://www.nrk.no/trondelag/_-olav-den-hellige-var-en-sadist-1.11844595.

Langslett, Lars Roar, and Ødegård, Knut. *Olav den Hellige; Spor etter Helgenkongen*. Oslo: Forlaget Press, 2011.

Moland, Arnfinn. "Likvidasjoner i motstandsarbeidet." *Norgeshistorie.no*, April 9, 2016. http://www.norgeshistorie.no/andre-verdenskrig/artikler/1734-likvidasjoner-i-motstandsarbeidet.html.

Olavsfestdagene. "Om Festivalen." Accessed July 19, 2017. http://www.olavsfestdagene.no/om/.

Sturluson, Snorri. *Heimskringla volume II Olafr Haraldsson (The Saint)*. Translated by Alison Finlay and Anthony Faulkes. London: Viking society for Northern Research, 2014.

# CHAPTER 15

# Televising Boabdil, Last Muslim King of Granada

*Elizabeth Drayson*

The aim of this essay is to bring the medieval past into dialogue with two contemporary visual portrayals of Muhammad XI, known as Boabdil, the last Muslim king of Granada, who surrendered the keys of his city to the Catholic monarchs Fernando II of Aragon and Isabel I of Castile in 1492.[1] Boabdil's reign marked the end of the last Islamic, Arabic-speaking kingdom in Spain, which led to the emergence of the modern Spanish nation state under the rule of Fernando and Isabel. However, despite his status and importance, the Muslim king has been largely ignored by history, though often romanticized in art and literature. My focus is the representation of Boabdil in the twenty-first century through the medium of television, where gender, in its social and religious dimensions, and in its influence on the stereotypical characterization of male rulers on the small screen, is crucial to his depiction. The ever-increasing popularity of historical television drama in Spain produced two highly successful Spanish TV series in which the years leading up to the conquest of Granada play a vital role. Boabdil is center stage in Vicente

E. Drayson (✉)
University of Cambridge, Cambridge, UK

© The Author(s) 2018                                                                 303
J. North et al. (eds.), *Premodern Rulers and Postmodern Viewers*,
Queenship and Power, https://doi.org/10.1007/978-3-319-68771-1_15

Escrivá's *Requiem for Granada* (*Réquiem por Granada*), which aired in eight episodes in 1991, while the Moorish ruler plays a key part in *Isabel*, a three-season Televisión Española series shown between 2012 and 2014, which charts the life of the Castilian queen. Their opposing portrayals of Boabdil and the fall of Granada shed fresh light on the adaptation of medieval history for television, and on the nature and status of the last Muslim ruler in Spain, whose gendered characterization reflects the ambivalent meaning of Boabdil's life and deeds and relates to past and present debates over both Spain's Islamic legacy and the legitimacy of Christian rule after 1492.

These TV series are very recent manifestations of the enduring interest in rewriting the story of Boabdil, as if it were a tapestry whose repeated re-weaving seeks to address those unanswered questions that surround his life. The conflict between the Nasrid dynasty of Granada, to which Boabdil belonged, and the combined Castilian and Aragonese forces of Fernando and Isabel had lasted for the ten years leading up to the momentous day when Boabdil handed Granada over to the Catholic Monarchs. The Muslim seizure of the town of Zahara in December 1481 and the retaliatory Christian capture of Alhama in February 1482 began a prolonged struggle between the two sides, during which discord in the Granadan royal family would be a key factor in the final outcome. The emir Abu-l-Hasan Ali's first son, Abu Abdallah Muhammad b. Ali, known to the Christians as Boabdil, was incited to revolt against his father by the powerful Abencerraje clan, and was proclaimed Sultan Muhammad XI in 1482. His father fled to Malaga, yet the two rival factions of father and son continued to fight the Christians vigorously. Boabdil's unlucky defeat and capture at the battle of Lucena in April 1483 was a turning point in the conflict, enabling his father to recapture Granada, as well as forcing the young sultan to pay the price of his freedom by pledging his vassalage to the Catholic monarchs and promising to collaborate with them against his father.

The Christian king Fernando used the deadly antagonism between father and son to win a diplomatic victory, but Queen Isabel wanted to go further, insisting that the time was right to conquer the entire kingdom of Granada and end the centuries-old struggle to reconquer Spain. Boabdil returned to the city in 1484 but was forced to flee again when his uncle, Muhammad Ibn Sad, el Zagal, seized control and deposed his own brother, Boabdil's father, who died in 1485. El Zagal ruled from 1485–1487 as Muhammad XII, but Boabdil and this second rival for the throne decided to present a united front against the intensifying Christian campaign. Yet again, Boabdil was captured and forced to renew his vassalage to Fernando and Isabel. By 1487, the Christians had gained the upper hand over El Zagal, who withdrew to Almería, leaving Granada in his nephew's hands. Boabdil initially agreed under duress to surrender Granada, but reneged on the pact and continued to resist. In 1490, Fernando and Isabel built the military headquarters of Santa Fe west of the capital, allowing them to sever the city's communications with the outside, and facing it with the specter of starvation. Rather than suffer that fate, Boabdil opened secret negotiations, and finally agreed to the terms of the capitulation on 25 November 1491. When the Castilians entered the city on 2 January 1492, the last Nasrid sultan departed for the Alpujarra region where he was given a feudal estate under Castilian sovereignty. Shortly after, his beloved wife Moraima died, a personal tragedy that partly provoked his decision to emigrate to Morocco in 1493, where he ended his days.

Boabdil has been repeatedly evoked in literature, art, and music as a legendary figure, whose story has been adapted to confront issues relating to national identity as well as political, racial, and religious crises. In the earliest dramatic representations of the conquest of Granada, Boabdil's inevitable fall from power is converted into a lionization of Fernando and Isabel. The Christian rulers seem almost superhuman in their greatness, and Boabdil is a man bedeviled by bad luck, vacillating and alternately hopeful and despairing, but always a worthy rival of his enemies. The sultan's life story and the Granadan war were transformed into song over a period of almost 200 years, from the late 1500s to the mid-seventeenth century, in the cycles of sung poetry written in Castilian known as the frontier ballads (*romances fronterizos*). These poems told stories from popular legend or about intensely powerful episodes of human drama relating to national or local events, and were often used to send news from one town to another. The fall of Granada inspired a magnificent cycle of frontier ballads, many written by court poets to flatter the monarchs and grandees who were directly involved in the policy of reconquest. Composed by bards who were both Christian and Spanish, they reflected the perspective of the victors, idealizing the military aspects of the war and contributing to the aggrandizement of the new Spain. They were unique creations of the old Granadan frontier that still live on today, when all else passed many centuries ago. Yet religious and political issues remain in the minor key and emotion and drama in the major, as Boabdil is portrayed compassionately as a man in the grip of powerful feelings of desolation and despair. One ballad in particular fostered the myth of Boabdil's cowardice and weakness and deepened the negative perceptions stirred up by a Granadan *fatwa,* or ruling on a point of law, dated October 1483, which had strongly prejudiced the Granadans against him. He had invoked the wrath of the religious authorities who had censured him for rebelling against his father, and this hatred was seized by the master shoemaker and maurophile Ginés Pérez de Hita and woven into his remarkable and influential two-volume historical novel *Civil Wars of Granada (Guerras civiles de Granada).* Boabdil's tears of despair and grief are immortalized by Pérez de Hita in his reprise of the legend of the Moor's Last Sigh: 'And when the Moorish king reached his house, which was in the Alcazaba, he began to weep for what he had lost. Upon which his mother told him that as he had been unable to defend his kingdom like a man, he did well to weep for it like a woman.'[2] The now familiar incident of his weeping and his mother's cutting rebuke became widely known following the success of Pérez de Hita's unsentimental portrait of Boabdil as a gullible victim of deception, and came to have great resonance in future re-creations of the life of the deposed sultan. By the late eighteenth century, the last sultan of Granada was still a presence in the literary imagination, but a change was taking place. The combination of popular legend, lament, and triumphant Christian rhetoric, which had vilified Boabdil in the preceding centuries, began to give way to a more ambivalent attitude towards him, which we can see in his divergent interpretations. Soon, with the development of Romanticism and its rapt interest in medievalism and orientalism in the nineteenth century, the Muslim ruler was viewed from a different perspective altogether.

Boabdil found the most unlikely champion in the American Washington Irving, whose *Tales of the Alhambra,* published in 1832 during the era of late Romanticism, turns the disparaging misconception of Pérez de Hita and others on its head. The master shoemaker had his reasons for his portrayal of the Rey Chico (Young or Boy King), but Irving launches a direct attack on Pérez de Hita's *Civil Wars,* claiming that he, Irving, had examined all the authentic chronicles and letters written by Spanish authors contemporary with the Moorish king, as well as Arabian authorities in translation, and could find nothing to justify the accusations made in that work.[3] The misunderstood sultan found another advocate in Louis Aragon, who was born in Paris in 1897 and became a literary and political giant in France. A founding member of the Surrealist movement in 1924, along with André Breton and Philippe Soupault, and a lifelong and active member of the Communist party, Aragon presented Boabdil's surrender and the fall of Granada as the beginning of the depression of the Muslim world, which continued in the French colonization of parts of Africa, in particular Algeria and Tunisia.[4] In the last decades of the twentieth century, Boabdil took on a new stature as writers and other artists both inside and outside Spain rescued him from the opprobrium of history. Among the key figures, the Castilian playwright and poet Antonio Gala found great success with the publication of his novel *The Crimson Manuscript (El manuscrito carmesí)* in 1990, giving the most eloquent possible assertion of Muhammad XI's worth and greatness of spirit.[5] Gala wanted to show how this medieval ruler's date with destiny is a valid symbol for human lives today, while Salman Rushdie's 1995 magical realist novel *The Moor's Last Sigh*, is a tale of an unloved son, a rejected outsider whose emotional and physical exile are mapped onto the figure of Boabdil as exiled sultan.[6]

Five centuries after his death, Boabdil continues to be a potent symbol of resistance to the forces of Western Christendom, and his image endures in contemporary culture. Present-day Arab writers such as the Damascus-born poet Nizār Qabbānī and the Syrian poet Šawqī Bagdādī have returned to Boabdil and the fall of Granada to address the relationship of modern Arab literature to the West, and to its own past.[7] The figure of Boabdil has also been the focus of a number of musical works, including five nineteenth-century operas, and several shorter pieces, and he was represented visually by many nineteenth-century Spanish painters of history, as well as in twentieth-century sculpture. In the light of this interest in the visual portrayal of the last sultan of Granada, we might expect him to have caught the attention of film directors, yet to date, there has been no cinematic recreation of his life. The 1936 film *Alhambra* or *The Moor's Sigh (El suspiro del moro)* directed by Antonio Graciani sounds promising, but is in fact a romantic comedy about a young aristocrat's ill-fated love affair with a distant descendant of Boabdil, whose blossoming relationship in the beautiful surroundings of the Alhambra comes to nothing due to racial and religious prejudice. A melodrama first screened in 1950 with the same title, directed by Juan Vilá Vilamala, is just a more somber version of the earlier film. In 2008, the movie star from Málaga, Antonio Banderas, started work on a plan to produce and act in a new film about the last Muslim king of Granada.

He believed that the projected movie, to be entitled *Boabdil*, 'embraces an important field in the world of cinema, as it will be an epic, romantic film, which at the same time will allow reflection upon the current bipolarity existing between the Arab world and the west, viewed from the perspective of over five hundred years of history'.[8] Banderas has spent some years, so far in vain, seeking finance for the new film, which he insists will be in Arabic and Spanish, and which would aim to draw attention to the connection between the medieval Moorish king and current social and political concerns. His words are a good indication of the strong contemporary interest in the vexed life of the ill-fated Boabdil.

While film has so far failed to do justice to the story of the last Moorish sultan of Granada, television has stepped up to the mark. In 1978–1979, Televisión Española broadcast a thirteen-episode series *The Minstrel and the Queen (El juglar y la reina)*. Each 50-minute episode was independent and devoted to historical events in the different kingdoms of the Iberian peninsula from the thirteenth to the seventeenth century. The eleventh episode, *Boabdil the Great (Boabdil el Grande)*, was broadcast at Christmas 1978, just three years after the death of Franco and shortly before voting opened in the referendum of December 1978, which resulted in the approval of the new Spanish Constitution. It was part of a propagandistic project that set out to show Spaniards the weight and importance of their monarchy in the historical future of their country, and part of its originality lay in its basis on the common heritage of the medieval ballad tradition. The depiction in episode 11 of Spain's relationship with the Muslim Other in the form of Boabdil revealed the undeniably liberal nature of the series, which brought to light certain deeply repressed aspects of Spanish history.

As this brief survey shows, the last Muslim sultan of Granada has been a symbol of diverse political and cultural issues, which begs the question of his true status. Was Boabdil a weak yet pragmatic opportunist who acted in his own interests, or a courageous and tragic hero who saved the cultural heritage of Granada? His representation as a prominent character in the Spanish TV series under discussion encourages us to explore exactly what his portrayals in *Requiem* and *Isabel* reveal about this ambivalent monarch, and to seek the unanswered questions to which those portrayals respond. The first point to make is that both series depict historical events whose interpretation diverges widely. We might describe *Requiem* and *Isabel* as heritage TV series, akin to heritage film in so far as that both problematize history and uncover its political and esthetic ambivalence, so often caught, as Andrew Higson points out, between reactionary attitudes and transgression.[9] A familiar theme of both is the exploration of the crisis of inheritance and the meaning of national ownership. The issue of to whom Spain belongs and to whom it should belong is at the heart of these two series, which present Boabdil from opposing perspectives, a Christian one in *Isabel* and a Muslim one in *Requiem*.

*Isabel* was directed by the Catalan Jordi Frades and made for Televisión Española by Diagonal TV. As its title suggests, the three-season series, with a budget of almost €600,000 per season, charts the reign of Queen Isabel I of Castile, played by Michelle Jenner. The first season was shot in 2011 in various locations including Cáceres, Madrid, and Segovia, and was first shown in September 2012. The second season, which spans the years 1474 to 1492, and in which Boabdil appears, was filmed in early 2013. For the first time in 25 years, the Alhambra opened its doors and allowed many scenes to be shot in the palace itself. This highly successful historical drama, with audiences of over four million viewers per episode,[10] is overlaid with the exultant Christian rhetoric of reconquest embodied in Rodolfo Sancho's portrayal of King Fernando II of Aragon as a largely stereotypical male ruler, a warrior strong in mind and body—chivalrous, yet prone to extra-marital affairs resulting in illegitimate offspring. Boabdil is played by Alex Martínez, who describes the character he plays as a very valiant and important person in Spanish history. As a counterpoint to the victorious Fernando, the sultan is initially presented as the equally stereotypical opposite of the conventional medieval male ruler. For a start, he is a poet, shown on various occasions writing at his desk. His naive otherworldliness is one reason why his fierce, warlike father denies him the throne. Another reason is that the emir Abu l'Hasan, who was known to the Christians as Muley Hacén, the name used in this series, married a beautiful Christian renegade, Isabel de Solís, known as Zoraya, whom he set above his first legitimate wife, Aixa. He insisted that the son Nasr born of their union should inherit the throne, instead of Boabdil as legitimate heir. Muley Hacén tells his brother El Zagal that Boabdil would not know how to rule because his mother Aixa has converted him into her puppet. Granada needs a warrior, he says, not a poet. In making his point, Muley Hacén underlines the difference between their two characters. He orders a silver serving dish to be brought to Boabdil, who lifts the lid to find not a tasty delicacy but a severed head.

The historical accounts of Boabdil's mother Aixa as a strong, feisty woman who looks out for and supports her son are magnified in this series to convert her into a veritable virago who stands up to Queen Isabel, and advocates fighting to the death against the Christian threat. Despite Boabdil's belief in the horoscope that predicts his grim fate, the year 1482 sees Aixa plotting with the Abencerraje clan to overthrow Muley Hacén. While the emir orders his troops into battle against the Christian army at Alhama, the Abencerrajes seek revenge for Muley Hacén's legendary and savage murder of many of their clan, whose throats had just been slit at a glittering dinner in the Alhambra. They attack the palace, liberating Boabdil and his mother from the dungeon where they are imprisoned, and set the young heir on the throne. Muley Hacén and his new family manage to escape, only to learn that the Muslim city of Alhama has been vanquished by the Christians.

Boabdil insists he will go into battle to prove himself a worthy sultan, but the fighting lessons he takes beforehand reveal him to be woefully inept. At the fateful battle of Lucena—which took place in 1483—in this version, Boabdil's headstrong, foolish actions result in his immediate capture by the Christians, thereby providing Fernando and Isabel with the perfect hostage. Despite failing to capture Lucena, Isabel declares that a defeat has never been so advantageous. The heroic Christian captain Gonzalo de Córdoba arrives at the Christian court to announce that Muley Hacén is back in the Alhambra and is suing for peace, but on one condition: the release of his son, whom he views as a traitor, into his hands. The shrewd cunning of Isabel is brought to the fore when she suggests that the conflict between Boabdil and his father should be fueled. She and Fernando tell their captive that his father is back and wants his head, obliging Boabdil to form an alliance with the Catholic monarchs against Muley Hacén. He has to choose between the Alhambra and his own life.

Up to this point, Boabdil conforms to his stereotype as an unworldly poet whose abhorrence of violence and ineptitude at fighting make him unfit to rule, but then something interesting happens. The young sultan steps up to the mark. His mother travels to the enemy court accompanied by Boabdil's wife, Moraima, and their young son, Ahmed. Aixa has raised a huge sum of money to pay his ransom, but offers her grandson as a hostage for good measure. Fernando sees the power of this bargaining tool, and decrees that Ahmed will only be returned when Granada is handed over to the Christians. Compelled to agree to the future surrender of his city and kingdom, with his tiny son Ahmed taken as a prisoner of war, Boabdil vows to adopt a new way of ruling, through peace and justice. However, Muley Hacén is stricken by a fatal illness, and gives his kingdom to his brother El Zagal instead of to his legitimate heir, Boabdil. El Zagal suggests to his nephew that they split the territory between them, with the uncle ruling in Granada itself, and Boabdil, always intent on making a pact instead of fighting, is obliged to concede to his uncle's wishes. He allays the fury of the Christians, who accuse him of betraying their agreement, by asserting that he needs time to win back Granada. Fearing quite rightly that further war with the Christians would destroy the city, he seeks the path of negotiation, to avoid bloodshed and keep Islam alive. Ignoring his mother's insistence that he die fighting rather than surrender, Boabdil saves his city and people from further tragedy by relinquishing his kingdom to the Catholic Monarchs, in exchange for the return of his son.

In the TV scene of the surrender of Granada, history painting merges with history on television in a superb and exact reconstruction of the famous painting by the nineteenth-century artist Francisco Pradilla y Ortiz Fig. (15.1).

This work is an image with a strong political charge as it sought to glorify a defining moment in Spanish history, and the purpose of the commission was to represent Spanish unity and illustrate the starting point for those great future deeds done by the Catholic Monarchs and their successors. The victors show their power in their glittering apparel and armor, their strength in numbers, and the disproportionately large size of the Christian personages who dominate the right side of the picture. Christians and Muslims are separated by a muddy track, symbolic of the permanent divide between them, which is in fact the focal point of the painting. Boabdil looks diminished in stature, and also in numbers of retainers, dwarfed before the might of the royal Christian retinue. The painting was seen as an image of Christian supremacy, yet it is hard not to detect sympathy in the depiction of Boabdil, whose figure is poignantly silhouetted against the backdrop of the Alhambra and the city whose keys he holds in his hand and is about to relinquish. His followers have sad expressions and bowed heads, and his page-boy seems overcome, perhaps by the sight of the Christian monarchs, perhaps with a sense of the tragedy of the situation. The appropriation of this painting as a moving TV image chimes well with the portrayal of Boabdil in series two of *Isabel*. Although the Muslim ruler has become a courageous, wise,

**Fig. 15.1** *The Surrender of Granada (La rendición de Granada)*, Francisco Pradilla y Ortiz, 1882

and strong sultan, Boabdil's final scene in this TV drama reverts to the conventional legend in which he looks back on Granada as he leaves it forever and weeps, while his cruel mother blames him for crying like a woman for what, she says, he could not defend like a man.

In *Isabel*, the narrative of the fall of Granada is set in the context of Queen Isabel's life, so the Christian perspective dominates. In sharp contrast, director and scriptwriter Vicente Escrivá describes his *Requiem for Granada* as 'an exaltation of Arabic culture'.[11] It was a series first shown in 1990 in eight one-hour episodes, made in collaboration with Italian and German television, with a budget of over 1.3 million pesetas, a cast of 200 actors and 5000 extras, 1200 horses, 80 camels, and the expertise of over 100 special advisors. Like *Isabel*, it was filmed in a variety of locations, including the Alhambra, the Great Mosque of Cordoba, and the royal palaces of Seville. The filming was beset with problems, including the illness of some of the actors and the Andalusian regional council's decree on equine flu, which prevented the transfer of horses from Madrid to shoot the battle scenes. It was one of the most ambitious TV productions of its time, and inspired Escrivá to write a novel of the same title, published in 1991. It is a powerful requiem for Nasrid Granada in which Escrivá's Boabdil is played by Manuel Bandera. In the opening scene of the series, a camel driver comes across the deposed sultan strapped to a camel and barely alive in the deserts of North Africa. He reads aloud a scroll Boabdil is carrying with him, which describes him as a man 'as great in power as in misfortune, who is paying the terrible price of being faithful to himself, and to Islam'.[12] From the start, we see that Boabdil has chosen knowledge over wealth, and is portrayed as courteous, noble, just and lenient, generous, and compassionate. Although his desire for peace between Christians and Muslims is strong, unlike his counterpart in *Isabel*, he is a bold, brave warrior, which more accurately reflects the historical reality. A man of letters and man of war, he flouts the gender stereotype in which these qualities are mutually exclusive. The issue of gender is most important in this series in its social and religious dimensions, as the plot hinges on the conflict of ancestral lineage. Inheritance through the male ruling line is even more fundamental to Islamic dynasties than Christian ones, and through this, Boabdil is the legitimate heir to the throne as firstborn son of the emir. As in *Isabel*, this legal right clashes with the wishes of his father, who favors his son by the converted Christian Zoraya, and this creates the main internal tensions in the narrative. Yet Boabdil has an even stronger claim to rule, which inverts gender conventions. His mother Aixa, here named Fatima, was a Nasrid princess, which meant that she benefited from the link of kinship through blood relationship down the female line that had existed in the Nasrid dynasty since the fourteenth century. By virtue of this connection, women of royal blood could transmit rights to the throne, rights that she exercised as mother of the next true Nasrid sultan. Aixa/Fatima was also believed to be the descendant of the Prophet Mohammed, a claim repeated several times in the course of *Requiem*. Boabdil's father-in-law insists: 'Don't you know that this man has the blood of the Prophet in his veins?'[13] These compelling circumstances intensify the conflict of succession with the illegitimate heir, who is the son of an infidel.

Escrivá also underlines opposing models of patriarchy by contrasting the cruel and deluded Muley Hassan, who rejects his firstborn son's claim to reign and scorns him, with the strongly emphasized anxiety of Boabdil for his own small son, who is at the mercy of the enemy. This anxiety arises from a situation that demonstrates the clear opposition between the dignified, just and peaceable Boabdil and the devious cunning of King Fernando. After the sultan's capture at the battle of Lucena, the Christian king pretends to befriend Boabdil, while proffering him the document containing the secret capitulations that are part of Fernando's price for the sultan's freedom. Fray Hernando de Talavera, confessor of Queen Isabel, observes Fernando's manipulative conversation with Boabdil and becomes an unlikely sympathizer with the Muslim, admiring his resistance, decrying Fernando's trickery and contending that, since he is captive, Boabdil has no option but to accept the terms. After putting Boabdil on the back foot by dropping the bombshell that his uncle El Zagal has decapitated the sultan's younger brother that morning, Fernando makes it plain that Boabdil needs his help to regain his throne, which he will willingly give in exchange for the imprisonment of the sultan's three-year old son, Ahmed, as a hostage. Much is made of the child hostage and the great sorrow and affliction it brings to his father and mother, and all the sultan's actions during his son's captivity are mindful of the grave risk to the child's life, as Boabdil juggles peaceful diplomacy with the need to fight and defend. As he reluctantly signs the surrender document, his last act for his people is to set out terms that will enable them to continue living in Granada and to follow their religion and culture. In contrast with the scene of the departure of the Nasrid family from Granada in *Isabel*, Boabdil is not scorned by his mother, but remains sad and dignified as he leaves the city to the sound of Christian bells chiming in the background. There is no weeping.

What are the implications of these portrayals of the last sultan of Granada, in which gender is fundamental to lineage and inheritance, and to the construction of the male ruler's character? The story of the conquest of Granada has deep resonance. For the second time in almost 800 years, a strong culture collapsed, partly through its own internal conflicts and complexities, and partly because barbarians were pressing at its borders, who sought to impose their own customs, world views, and religious faith.[14] On the first occasion in 711, Iberian Peninsula was invaded by the Muslim forces perceived as barbarians, who conquered its Christian Visigothic kingdom ruled by King Roderick, and remained for nearly 800 years, creating one of the three great cultures of medieval Spain. On the second occasion in 1492, the roles were reversed and the barbarians at the borders this time were the Christians who fought to eliminate the last vestiges of Muslim power and rule in Spain. Like the heritage films discussed by Andrew Higson,[15] these two television series celebrate the pleasures of the past while responding anxiously to historical trauma. As he suggests, 'the sense of impending narrative-historical loss is ... offset by the experience of spectacular visual pleasure'.[16] The former is often progressive, as we see in *Requiem*, and stresses the conflicts at the heart of inheritance, while the latter tends to be reactionary, consoling the audience for an apparent loss of imperial power or privilege.

Yet in the case of *Isabel*, despite its insistent focus on the triumphs and challenges of the queen of Castile, the series is not unrelievedly pro-Christian. The evolution of the character of Boabdil from weakness to strength, and his depiction as a poet and thinker, hint at the idea of a new, more forgiving model of patriarchal monarch, a Muslim to boot, who was nevertheless destined to succumb to the might of Castile and Aragon. Boabdil and his ancestors of course represent the original invaders of the peninsula, the original immigrants. Shown from 2012 to 2014, at a time when the crisis of immigration loomed large in Spain, the clear message of Spain as the victor in season two of *Isabel* may be significant. However, the scene where Fernando and Isabel enter the Alhambra for the first time and are spellbound by a beauty unachievable in Spanish Christian culture of the time is equally so, since it is a visual expression of the sophistication and refinement of Nasrid culture now in the victorious hands of the less evolved Christian Catholics. It spells out the imposition of one civilization upon another.

With regard to *Requiem for Granada*, it was a bold undertaking that would have been very hard to make after the terrible al-Qaeda train bombings in Madrid in March 2004. Screened in 1990 amid a climate of rediscovery of Arab culture in Spain, its unabashed admiration for Boabdil as an important and courageous ruler, who suffers loss and exile to preserve the city that has become a symbolic site of the transfer of cultural and religious power, illustrates the ambivalent nature of a legendary man whose life still continues to pose questions. These two significant and successful TV series respond to unanswered questions that are as vital and relevant today as they were at the end of the Middle Ages, questions that address concerns about who has the right to live and rule in Spain, and also about what was lost as well as gained at that crucial historical moment when Boabdil handed over the keys of his city.

# Notes

1. This essay expands on ideas broached in Chap. 8 of my book: Elizabeth Drayson, *The Moor's Last Stand: How Seven Centuries of Muslim Rule in Spain Came to an End* (London: Profile Books, 2017).
2. 'Y ansí como el moro rey llegó a su casa, que era en el Alcazaba, comenzó a llorar lo que había perdido. Al cual llanto le dijo su madre que pues no había sido para defendella como hombre, que hacía bien de llorarla como mujer.' Ginés Pérez de Hita, *Guerras civiles de Granada, Primera parte,* ed. Shasta Bryant (Newark, Delaware: Juan de la Cuesta, 2000), 287. Unless otherwise noted, all translations are my own.
3. Washington Irving, *Tales of the Alhambra* (Granada: Ediciones Miguel Sánchez, 1994), 84.
4. Louis Aragon, *Le fou d'Elsa: poème* (1963; repr., Paris: Gallimard, 1980).
5. Antonio Gala, *El manuscrito carmesí* (1990; repr., Barcelona: Editorial Planeta, 2007).
6. Salman Rushdie, *The Moor's Last Sigh* (London: Vintage, 1996).
7. See Pedro Martínez Montávez, *Al-Andalus, España, en la literatura árabe contemporánea: La Casa del pasado* (Madrid: Editorial Mapfre, 1992).
8. 'cubre un campo importante del mundo del cine pues es una película épica, romántica y al mismo tiempo permite reflexionar sobre la bipolaridad actual que se está dando entre árabe y occidental desde la perspectiva de hace quinientos años de historia' at "Antonio Banderas realizará 'Boabdil' de la mano del mundo musulmán," *Ideal.es,* last modified October 10, 2008. http://www.ideal.es/granada/20081018/cultura/antonio-banderas-realizara-boabdil-20081018.html.
9. Andrew Higson, *English Heritage, English Cinema: Costume drama since 1980* (Oxford: Oxford University Press, 2003), 109.
10. *Formulatv.com,* "Cuota máxima para 'Isabel' (20,7%) y cuota mínima de temporada para 'La que se avecina' (22,4%)," last modified October 30, 2012. http://www.formulatv.com/noticias/27630/cuota-maxima-isabel-cuota-minima-temporada-la-que-se-avecina/.
11. Entrevista con Vicente Escrivá, *El País,* October 9, 1991.
12. 'tan alto en poder como en desventuras, paga el terrible precio de haber querido ser fiel a sí-mismo, y al Islam', *Réquiem por Granada,* Television Miniseries, directed by Vicente Escrivá. (RTVE, 1991).
13. 'Sabes que este hombre lleva la sangre del Profeta en sus venas', *Réquiem por Granada,* Television Miniseries, directed by Vicente Escrivá (RTVE, 1991).
14. See Umberto Eco, *Travels in Hyper Reality: Essays,* translated by William Weaver (London: Picador, 1987), 74, where the author describes this pattern of collapse and invasion as fundamental to what he calls a 'good Middle Ages.'

15. See Higson, *English Heritage, English Cinema*, 80.
16. Higson, *English Heritage, English Cinema*, 80.

## BIBLIOGRAPHY

Aragon, Louis. *Le fou d'Elsa: poème*. 1963. Reprint, Paris: Gallimard, 1980.
Drayson, Elizabeth. *The Moor's Last Stand: How Seven Centuries of Muslim Rule in Spain Came to an End*. London: Profile Books, 2017.
Eco, Umberto. *Travels in Hyper reality: Essays*. translated by William Weaver. London: Picador, 1987.
*Formulatv.com*. "Cuota máxima para 'Isabel' (20,7%) y cuota mínima de temporada para 'La que se avecina' (22,4%)." Last modified October 30, 2012.  http://www.formulatv.com/noticias/27630/cuota-maxima-isabel-cuota-minima-temporada-la-que-se-avecina/.
Gala, Antonio. *El manuscrito carmesí*. 1990. Reprint, Barcelona: Editorial Planeta, 2007.
Higson, Andrew. *English Heritage, English Cinema: Costume Drama since 1980*. Oxford: Oxford University Press, 2003.
*Ideal.es*. "Antonio Banderas realizará 'Boabdil' de la mano del mundo musulmán." Last modified October 10, 2008.  http://www.ideal.es/granada/20081018/cultura/antonio-banderas-realizara-boabdil-20081018.html.
Irving, Washington. *Tales of the Alhambra*. Granada: Ediciones Miguel Sánchez, 1994.
*Isabel*. Television Series. Directed by Jordi Frades. RTVE/Diagonal TV, 2012–2014.
Martín, Aurelio. "Termina el rodaje de *Réquiem por Granada*, serie producida para Televisión Española." *ElPais.com*. Last modified August 9, 1990. http://elpais.com/diario/1990/08/09/radiotv/650152801_850215.html.
Martínez Montávez, Pedro. *Al-Andalus, España, en la literatura árabe contemporánea: La Casa del pasado*. Madrid: Editorial Mapfre, 1992.
Palacio, Manuel. *La televisión durante la Transición española*. Madrid: Cátedra, 2012.
Pérez de Hita, Ginés. *Guerras civiles de Granada, Primera parte*. Edited by Shasta Bryant. Newark, Delaware: Juan de la Cuesta, 2000.
"*Réquiem por Granada*: historia grande para la pequeña pantalla", *ABC SEVILLA* (Sevilla) January 1, 1990, 83.
*Réquiem por Granada*. Television Miniseries. Directed by Vicente Escrivá. RTVE, 1991.
Rushdie, Salman. *The Moor's Last Sigh*. London: Vintage, 1996.
Smith, Paul Julian. *Spanish Visual Culture: Cinema, Television, Internet*. Manchester: Manchester University Press, 2006.

# CHAPTER 16

# A Man? A Woman? A Lesbian? A Whore?: Queen Elizabeth I and the Cinematic Subversion of Gender

*Aidan Norrie*

Queen Elizabeth I of England seems to suffer from an identity crisis in modern historical films. England's first unmarried, Protestant, female king has appeared on the silver screen for over a century. In the 55-plus films

A version of this chapter was presented in the 2016 International Medieval Congress session, 'Premodern Rulers and Postmodern Viewers: Gender and Sex in the Representation of the Medieval and Early Modern World in Film and Television.' I thank both the audience for their feedback, and Elena Woodacre for inviting me to present as part of the session. The writing of this chapter has been greatly assisted by conversations with, and comments from, Jo Oranje and Robert Norrie. Finally, I thank Professor Evelyn Tribble and the Donald Collie Fund at the University of Otago for providing a grant to purchase the images included in this chapter.

A. Norrie (✉)
Centre for the Study of the Renaissance, The University of Warwick, Coventry, UK

J. North et al. (eds.), *Premodern Rulers and Postmodern Viewers*,
Queenship and Power, https://doi.org/10.1007/978-3-319-68771-1_16

319

that have depicted the infamous Virgin Queen since 1912, filmmakers have offered their own interpretations of this enigmatic monarch.[1] While the various events of Elizabeth's life and reign are repeatedly depicted—with varying levels of respect for the details of the historical event—the films always seem to stumble on one particular point: that is, the portrayal of Elizabeth's gender.

Elizabeth's gender has always been integral to her televisual and cinematic representations. The duality of Elizabeth as a female king easily creates tension that can be used to move the film's story along without alienating audiences. As Thomas Betteridge has observed, Elizabeth on film is invariably structured around three key binary oppositions: 'duty versus womanhood, public role versus private desires, and denial versus desire'.[2] These binaries demonstrate the way that writers grapple with the incongruity of Elizabeth, because ultimately they are manifestations of Elizabeth's gendered construction.

As alluded to by my title, I argue that the various ways Elizabeth's gender has been constructed on film can broadly be characterized by one, or a combination, of four categories—that is, Elizabeth is depicted as a man, a woman, a lesbian, or a whore. These four categories not only echo arguments that have been raised by scholars and writers for centuries, but they also reflect different opinions of Elizabeth, her gender, and her authority that raged during her life.[3] Thus, modern historical films are a new medium for explaining and discussing old debates.[4] As Hayden White argues, these modern discussions are just as important as their contemporary counterparts because 'it is only the medium that differs, not the way in which the messages are produced'.[5]

In analyzing Elizabeth's public monarchical persona, Christopher Haigh described the Queen as a 'political hermaphrodite'.[6] While I am not suggesting that filmmakers informed their cinematic vision with Haigh's work, the appearance of the concept both in the historiography and on the screen demonstrates that Elizabeth herself is partly to blame for her ambiguous depiction. For instance, in the Golden Speech of 1601, Elizabeth referred to herself variously as king, prince, and queen—switching between roles and genders with ease—and making clear use of the doctrine of the king's two bodies.[7] As Carole Levin has observed, Elizabeth presented herself as 'both woman and man in one, both king and queen together, a male body politic in concept while a female body natural in practice'.[8] With this chapter, I take this gender ambiguity (which has existed since Elizabeth's reign), offer examples of the ways it is manifested in films, and demonstrate the gendered implications. Thinking about the various ways that Elizabeth is gendered on the screen is important because, according to Robert Rosenstone, 'Historical films ... intersect with, comment upon, and add something to the larger discourse of history out of which they grow and to which they speak'.[9]

Throughout this chapter, 'whore' will be treated as an inherently gendered concept that is distinct from 'woman'. While the term is almost exclusively applied to women, history also demonstrates that the people who were branded with the term—often prostitutes and other sex workers—have typically existed outside society's gender binary, and have often been excluded, existing almost as a separate, distinct gender.[10] Similarly, the word as an insult takes on explicitly gendered meanings in the Bible;[11] and the Consistory Court in London heard many cases in the early modern period that intertwined defamation, morality, sexual (mis) conduct, and gender.[12]

Space constraints prevent an entirely comprehensive discussion of the appearance of these four categories across Elizabeth's historical films. Thus, in order to create a cohesive argument, the majority of my examples will come from two films: Shekhar Kapur's 1998 film, *Elizabeth*, and its 2007 sequel, *Elizabeth: The Golden Age*. These are arguably the most well known of the major historical films, and they are both produced within the context of second-wave feminism, and the emergence of gender history. However, relevant examples will also be taken from *Shakespeare in Love* (dir. John Madden, 1998) and *Orlando* (dir. Sally Potter, 1992) to demonstrate the wider applicability of my argument.

## MAN

Elizabeth's depiction as a man is both fascinating and subversive. Almost every film that depicts Elizabeth aims to focus either on her various romances, or the stark contrast of the 'bewigged, beruffed, and bejeweled' Elizabeth with the somber and serious male councilors who always seem to be around her.[13] In spite of this, Kapur is happy to render Elizabeth's gender as masculine. As Andrew Higson has observed, 'Kapur cunningly confuses gender roles' to suit his purposes.[14]

In a short scene in *The Golden Age*, Elizabeth (played by Cate Blanchett) and Walter Raleigh (Clive Owen) are talking in the Queen's chambers. Raleigh must have invited Elizabeth to come on his ship and visit the colony in the New World, for Elizabeth says: 'Do not tease me, Mr. Raleigh. There's nothing I'd like to do more.' Raleigh replies, 'So why don't you?' From the look on Raleigh's face, Elizabeth's reply— 'All right then, I will'—is clearly unexpected: 'You see? You lie. You don't want me on your ship at all. You're a liar.' The Queen is clearly in a jovial mood, for as Bess (Bess Throckmorton, a Gentlewoman of the Privy Chamber, played by Abbie Cornish) walks in, she asks her: 'Would you like to go to sea?' Before Bess can respond, Raleigh interjects: 'I'm afraid that's not possible. Women bring bad luck on board ship.' Elizabeth is amused, 'Do they?' Raleigh elaborates: 'Lock up a hundred men in a space smaller than this room for months at a time. Men have needs. A beautiful woman would drive us all mad!' Elizabeth chuckles— probably most incredulously at the idea that only men have 'needs'— and the scene ends with Elizabeth telling her ladies that they must help her convince Raleigh to stay in England. What is easy to miss about this scene, in between the obvious flirting, is the gender problem. Why is it that Bess cannot come on the ship, but Elizabeth can? While the historical Elizabeth was at least 48 years old when she first met Raleigh, Blanchett's Elizabeth is in her early- to mid-thirties, and thus just as likely to satisfy the men's needs as the young Bess could.[15] Whether this gender issue was intentional or not, Kapur reinforces the issue he has (unsuccessfully) grappled with in both of his films: Elizabeth, the female king, is an enigma for him—neither fully a woman, nor truly a king.

Kapur's grappling with Elizabeth's gender comes to the fore later in *The Golden Age*. Most of the historical films that feature Elizabeth seek to emphasize the Queen's femininity—usually at the expense of historical accuracy. This makes the depiction of Elizabeth's speech to the troops at Tilbury all the more interesting. Elizabeth delivers the speech in the sun; her long, red hair flies behind her in the wind (despite the viewers knowing that all her hair was shaved off and that she only wears wigs). Her horse is adorned in some kind of battle garb, and most importantly, she wears shining silver armor (Fig. 16.1). She looks, in the words of one reviewer, like an early modern C-3PO.[16]

Scholars have long debated what Elizabeth actually wore at Tilbury. Answers to this question include: a white velvet gown with plumes in her hair,[17] that she was 'bare-headed and wearing a breastplate,'[18] that she wore a steel corselet,[19] or that she wore a silver cuirass and held a silver truncheon.[20] In fact, as Susan Frye has conclusively demonstrated, there is 'no contemporary evidence that she actually wore armor at all'.[21] Not

**Fig. 16.1**  An armor-clad Elizabeth (played by Cate Blanchett) addresses the troops at Tilbury. Photo by Laurie Sparham/Universal/Stu/REX/Shutterstock

only does Frye's point raise questions concerning the sources of these various answers for Elizabeth's attire, it also has implications for her gendered representation. As Frye notes, 'Although this is a small detail, it is not trivial, for her donning armor would have shown that Elizabeth was willing to go beyond the rigid, armorlike stomachers that she is shown wearing in so many portraits, to cross-dress openly.'[22] Kapur's decision to depict Elizabeth in this way, then, is not demonstrative of an established, historical fact. Instead, it shows that he either believes the audience incapable of seeing Elizabeth deliver the Tilbury speech without some kind of masculine costume, or that the woman he had previously depicted as fragile, hot-headed, and often irrational, was now suddenly the embodiment of a conquering king of old.

With her armor, and astride a militarized horse, Elizabeth prepares to deliver the famed Tilbury Speech. Except, Kapur decides that the kingly, armor-clad Elizabeth is no longer capable of having the heart and stomach of a king. By twisting the historical truth—by the time Elizabeth delivered the Tilbury speech, the immediate threat of a Spanish invasion had passed—Kapur de-kings Elizabeth, and at the same time turns her into a commanding general.[23] Below is the most famous part of the speech:

> My loving people, we have been persuaded by some, that are careful of our safety, to take heed how we commit our self to armed multitudes for fear of treachery: but I assure you, I do not desire to live to distrust my faithful, and loving people. Let Tyrants fear, I have always so behave myself, that under God I have placed my chiefest strength, and safeguard in the loyal hearts and good will of my subjects. And therefore I am come amongst you as you see, at this time, not for my recreation, and disport, but being resolved in the midst, and heat of the battle to live, or die amongst you all, to lay down for my God, and for my kingdom, and for my people, my Honour, and my blood even in the dust.

> I know I have the body, but of a weak and feeble woman, but I have the heart and stomach of a king, and of a King of England too, and think foul scorn that Parma or Spain, or any Prince of Europe should dare to invade the borders of my realm, to which rather than any dishonour should grow by me, I myself will take up arms.[24]

The speech is certainly a rousing exercise in oratorical skill. The same cannot be said, however, for the speech delivered by Blanchett's Elizabeth:

My loving people. We see the sails of the enemy approaching. We hear the Spanish guns over the water. Soon now, we will meet them face-to-face. I am resolved, in the midst and heat of the battle, to live or die amongst you all. While we stand together no invader shall pass. Let them come with the armies of Hell; they will not pass! And when this day of battle is ended, we meet again in heaven or on the field of victory.

There are few similarities between the two speeches. The only phrases that appear in both are Elizabeth's reference to her 'loving people,' and her wish to 'in the midst and heat of battle, ... live or die amongst you all'. Apart from demonstrating Kapur's discomfort with Elizabeth as a warrior-king, the speech also openly plays with Elizabeth's gender. It would not be a stretch to assume that most people who watch the film would have some sense of the historical Tilbury speech: 'the heart and stomach of a king' line is relatively ubiquitous, even if it is because of its pervasiveness in popular culture.[25] So, despite depicting Elizabeth as a conquering king, Kapur takes the line out of the speech; and to confuse his audience even more, he makes it clear that the armored Elizabeth will be joining the fight herself, even potentially leading the fight. Not only does this fly in the face of all the preparations previously depicted in the film, it also highlights the way the Kapur struggles with Elizabeth's gender. Is she a queen, encouraging her troops? Is she a queen trying (unsuccessfully) to play the part of a medieval warrior-king? Or, is she a woman who believes in her kingly authority, and is attempting to wield it at the opportune time? While one might suspect that Kapur was aiming for a mix of these three options, he does leave the issue unresolved, and therefore perpetuates the gender crisis that Elizabeth has suffered over the last century.

## WOMAN

Elizabeth is clearly a woman. This fact is not in doubt. Indeed, one of the few things that brings the various cinematic (and televisual) depictions of Elizabeth together is the fact that she seems unable to appear on screen without some mention being made to her pious chastity, or to the many male suitors she has. For this reason, my focus here on Elizabeth as a woman will be more cursory, and only specific examples will be examined.

The stereotypical depiction of Elizabeth as the pious virgin is a standard trope in films that feature Elizabeth. However, this stereotype was shattered when, in *Elizabeth*, Kapur went where no other director had gone before: he included a sex scene between Elizabeth and Robert Dudley (played by Joseph Fiennes) that unambiguously confirmed Elizabeth was not a virgin. What is perhaps most interesting about this scene is that it takes place not long after Elizabeth was crowned queen— meaning that, in Kapur's story, Elizabeth was not a virgin for almost all of her reign.

The sex scene was clearly intended to shock. Not in a graphic way, but in its blatant departure from a century of cinematic depictions. For the first time on film (and indeed, TV), Elizabeth had 'given in' to her 'womanly desires'. By engaging in a physical relationship with Dudley, Elizabeth straddles the line between woman and king far more shakily than in any other film. Elizabeth's femaleness is accentuated, but to the detriment of her monarchical authority.[26]

The sex scene in *Elizabeth* causes many of the references to Elizabeth's virginity in *The Golden Age* to take on new meaning. This was not an accident: not only was Kapur playing with the divide between Elizabeth the woman and Elizabeth the monarch; he was also highlighting the inherent frailty of Elizabeth's femininity. When Raleigh is presented to the Queen at his return from his expedition to the New World, he tells Elizabeth of the colony he founded: 'We have named it Virginia, after our Virgin Queen.' Elizabeth's response is somewhat unexpected: '"Virginia"? And when I am married, will you rename it to "Conjugia"?" With this scene, Raleigh is introduced as the man with whom Elizabeth would give into her 'womanly desires,' just as she had with Dudley in *Elizabeth*. Kapur's purpose is clear, and the 'flirtation' between Raleigh and Elizabeth continues to grow on screen, until finally the Queen and Raleigh are alone in her private chambers. She turns and says to him: 'There's something you could do for me; something I have not known for a very long time. But it's not to be spoken of afterwards. It must be forgotten. But just for now, a kiss?' The audience clearly knows what Elizabeth is talking about. Raleigh leans in and kisses Elizabeth, who responds, 'I die.' The scene trails off, and viewers are left wondering whether or not anything beyond a kiss happened. What is interesting about this scene is that Elizabeth is the one initiating the relationship. In *Elizabeth*, no details leading up to the sex scene are given, and the scene itself does not have any dialogue. In *The Golden*

*Age*, the older, and increasingly desperate-to-marry Elizabeth is seen to be taking control of her 'womanly desires'. Modern audiences can look at these scenes and ask why Elizabeth should not be allowed to engage in extra-marital sex—after all, men do it. But Kapur's purpose here is not to point out the inherent misogyny of early modern sexual attitudes, but instead to remind viewers of Elizabeth's iconographic virginity, rather than her biological virginity, and to question her ability to truly rule England in what is, for all intents and purposes, a man's world.

Elizabeth's sexual relations—both literal and implied—also color her relationship with Mary, Queen of Scots (played by Samantha Morton). Kapur depicts Mary in such a way that she initially garners the sympathy of the audience; sympathy that disintegrates into incredulity as her attempts to overthrow Elizabeth are revealed, along with the details of her backstory. After another round of restrictions are ordered for the Scottish Queen, Mary questions the need for them. Her jailer, Sir Amyas Paulet (played by Tom Hollander), tells her, 'The Queen orders these measures for your protection.' Mary responds, rather slyly, 'The Queen? I am a queen. They call her The Virgin Queen. Why is that, sir? Can it be that no man will have her?' Paulet does not respond. The audience knows that this is not the case: she has already 'had' Dudley, and the moments between Raleigh and Elizabeth demonstrate mutual affection that certainly could culminate in a sexual relationship.[27] Here, instead of showing Elizabeth succumbing to her 'womanly' desires, Kapur is highlighting the incongruous position Elizabeth holds: she is a king, who is a woman.[28] This theme resurfaces constantly in *Elizabeth* and *The Golden Age:* serving to convince the audience that Elizabeth cannot ever truly be either a woman, or a king.

* * *

1998 was a big year for Elizabeth on film. In addition to *Elizabeth*, the Queen was portrayed by Judi Dench in *Shakespeare in Love*. Elizabeth's 'big year' continued at the 1999 Academy Awards: for the first time in history, two people were nominated for Oscars for playing the same person—Cate Blanchett for Best Actress, and Judi Dench for Best Supporting Actress. While Blanchett lost out to Gwyneth Paltrow (for her role of Viola in *Shakespeare in Love*), Dench won her first Academy Award for the role. The reason I mention this is twofold. Firstly, Dench was on screen as Elizabeth for fewer than eight minutes—the shortest amount of on-screen time for any winner of an acting Oscar ever. While Dench's performance was almost universally lauded, it is not unreasonable to question whether her Oscar win merely reflects Elizabeth's allure, and the perceived challenges associated with portraying the Virgin Queen.[29] Secondly, the film—despite the short amount of time that Elizabeth is on screen—also constructs Elizabeth's gender in a fascinating way; a way that both contradicts much of Kapur's gendered construction of the Queen, and demonstrates that the subversion of Elizabeth's gender is a staple of her cinematic depictions.

*Shakespeare in Love* is essentially the story of an imaginary love affair between Viola de Lesseps (Gwyneth Paltrow) and Shakespeare (Joseph Fiennes) while he was writing *Romeo and Juliet*. Because of a (apocryphal) law that banned women from performing in the theatre, Viola dresses as a man, and successfully auditions for the role of Romeo. Viola's identity is eventually revealed; Shakespeare steps in to play Romeo, and a boy actor plays Juliet. The boy's voice cracks on opening night, and Viola comes to the company's rescue and plays Juliet. The Master of the Revels arrives at the end of the performance to arrest everyone for 'indecency', but Elizabeth, who has been secretly watching the show, reveals herself. The Queen overrides the Master of the Revels, and in doing so, highlights the duality of Elizabeth's gendering.

The Queen comes to Viola's aid—partly because, according to Elizabeth, 'the Queen of England does not attend exhibitions of public lewdness'—by declaring that while Viola's costume is indeed impressive, she is a man, and thus no law has been broken. What is curious about the scene is the way that Elizabeth delivers her judgment: she knows that Viola is not a woman because, 'I know something of a woman in a man's profession. Yes, by God, I do know about that.'

This short line reinforces the difficulty of conceptualizing Elizabeth as a female king—especially for modern audiences who do not share the same patriarchal, and almost misogynistic, worldview as did the sixteenth-century English. While there were certainly contemporaries of Elizabeth who thought female rule was unnatural, Elizabeth succeeded the throne with limited struggle; indeed, two successive female kings faced challenges from women—Mary I saw off the threat of Lady Jane Grey, and Elizabeth dealt with Mary, Queen of Scots—for the first and only time in English history.[30] However, it is the small minority of contemporary voices against female kingship that seem to always come to the fore in modern cinematic productions. Elizabeth was certainly expected to listen to male counsel; but, ultimately, God chose her to rule over England, and this right was cemented by the anointing at her coronation.[31]

Instead, Dench's Elizabeth makes it clear that she is a woman who is in the incongruous position of portraying a man. Rather than showing the Queen as being 'governed' by her feminine desires (as Kapur does), Dench's Elizabeth is constructed so that her gender is second to her role as king—a role that seems to transcend gender. The film's message is thus overly simplistic: Elizabeth may be a woman, but to survive in a man's role, she must hide from, and bury away, her gender.

## LESBIAN

At this point, a disclaimer: as far as I am aware, no film that features Elizabeth depicts her in a same-sex relationship, or engaging in same-sex sexual intercourse. This eventuality is not beyond the realms of possibility, however, as both Cleopatra and Catherine the Great have recently been the subject of lesbian adult films.[32] Nevertheless, the reason for including this category is that so much of Elizabeth's depiction in both of Kapur's films relies on a barely concealed homoerotic subtext. In some ways, this subtext is an entirely understandable, modern way of conceptualizing why Elizabeth never married: she was interested in women; and modern viewers with limited historical knowledge, and limited prompting, could easily read this subtext in Kapur's films. He ensures that his viewers are left wondering what is behind the lingering stares Elizabeth gives her ladies in waiting, and why she seems to only measure men by their political worth.

The most blatant blurring of Elizabeth's sexuality comes from a scene that does not advance the plot of *The Golden Age* in any meaningful way. The scene involves Elizabeth taking a bath, while being lovingly stroked, and sponged down, by her maid, Bess. The homoeroticism is blatant and inescapable.[33] In the scene, Elizabeth wonders aloud if she has ever been 'liked for herself'. Bess answers, 'I hope you believe I like you for yourself.' Elizabeth—who has noticed the growing affection between Bess and Raleigh, and is clearly jealous—uses the opportunity to snuff out Bess' feelings for Raleigh by telling her that he is only interested in her because she has the ear of the Queen.[34] Bess is clearly a little winded by this observation, which is probably only partly true: Bess cannot, and has not, missed the mutual affection between Elizabeth and Raleigh. Elizabeth then wraps up what has become a guilt session by saying that Raleigh wants, 'the other thing, too, of course. But then, all men want that.' To Elizabeth, then, men are only interested in Bess because she can influence the Queen, and because she is a sexual object. The scene ends with Elizabeth saying: 'Oh, I envy you, Bess. You're free to have what I cannot have.' Most literally, this refers to the fact that Bess can have sex with a man. But, on the other hand, there is nothing stopping Elizabeth having sex with a man—she has already done it, according to *Elizabeth*. The context of the line, given in a bath, while being lovingly caressed by her maid, does raise questions of what Elizabeth actually wants, and the part played by men in her desires.

## WHORE

Of all the gendered depictions of Elizabeth on film, none take their stance from the polemic tracts of Elizabeth's own reign like her depiction as a sexual deviant. 'Sexual deviant' is used here because the polemicists regularly used sexual immorality as a literary shorthand for Elizabeth's general illegitimacy for the throne.[35] Critics and historians alike have noted the anti-Catholic theme that runs through both of Kapur's films: 'Catholicism is the past, the religion of sterile old Mary; Protestantism is the future, the religion of the lively young Elizabeth and her England.'[36] Only Catholics call Elizabeth a whore in the films, and their cumulative use of the word spreads beyond the purely rhetorical.

Indeed, in *Elizabeth*, Mary I—the staunchest of all Catholics, according to Kapur—screams at her privy council when they are discussing the issue of her succession: 'My sister was born of that whore, Anne Boleyn! She was born a bastard! She will never rule England!' Not only is this acknowledgement of their relationship both overstated and ahistorical, it also tarnishes Elizabeth through her mother.[37] As this outburst occurs in the film's opening minutes, it is one of the earliest images of Elizabeth that the audience has. Not long after Elizabeth's accession, the film shows the reaction of the Pope to the Protestant queen's accession. An English Jesuit priest has come to receive instructions from the Pope, who asks the priest, 'What is the news of our [Catholic] brothers and sisters in England? Do they still support the sovereignty of that illegitimate whore?' The priest replies in the negative, setting the scene for the Northern Rebellion, which is the film's main plot complication.

Likewise, Elizabeth as a whore is (re)established in the early scenes of *The Golden Age*, when King Philip II of Spain, while overseeing the preparations of the Armada, poses the question to the non-present Elizabeth, 'why are you leading your people to hell?' In the presence of his daughter, he seemingly answers his own question by shouting, 'whore!' Again, Elizabeth's religious policy is blatantly equated with sexual deviance.

Elizabeth's own sexual deviance—perceived, rather than factual—becomes a key theme in *The Golden Age*. The best example of this can be found in the film's depiction of the Babington Plot. The Plot was another Catholic-initiated attempt to assassinate Elizabeth, and replace her with Mary, Queen of Scots, who would return England to Catholicism. The film is relatively accurate in its depiction of the Plot, including Mary's involvement. Where the film departs from the historical reality, however, is the Plot's carrying out. The real Walsingham was preemptive in his investigations, and the conspirators were arrested before they could act.[38] But, in the film, the plotters are able to put their plan into action, and Babington is given a pistol, tasked with killing Elizabeth while she is at prayers. For her part, Elizabeth glides into the chapel like some kind of angelic icon, and she takes her place at the rail next to Bess.[39] The conspirators are in the crowd that has assembled around the Queen and her litter, and they fight their way to the front. A royal servant announces, 'The Queen is at her prayers.' This seems to be the cue for Babington (played by Eddie Redmayne), and his associate Ramsey (a fictional, generic Catholic fanatic), to commence their task. The two men try to rush the chapel. Ramsey is tackled by the guards at the door, but manages to shout, 'Elizabeth is a whore! Mary Stuart is our true queen!' For the first time in the film, Elizabeth is explicitly labeled illegitimate—both literally and rhetorically—to be queen. The use of such a sexual term is not an accident, and serves to reinforce and encapsulate the way that Elizabeth's enemies—from Mary I and Philip II, to the Jesuits sent to kill her—conceive of her.

Babington, who manages to evade the guards at the door, runs to the chapel, and draws his pistol. He screams out 'Elizabeth!' For some unknown reason, Bess turns; the Queen does not. How does Babington get his target's attention? He screams out 'whore!' This is the descriptor that Elizabeth reacts to. She does not react angrily, however; instead, she turns slowly to face her would-be assassin. Babington's gun is pointed straight at her. She closes her eyes, and the gun fires. But, she is not hit. In fact, as she opens her eyes, she sees that Babington is just as surprised as she is.[40]

The gun, it turns out, was not loaded. The film implies that this was deliberate: Philip wanted Mary, Queen of Scots implicated in a plot so that Elizabeth would have no choice but to execute her; and with the only other claimant to the throne out of the way, Philip would be free to invade England and take the crown for himself.[41] This is probably hindsight mixed with blatant historical revisionism—having Mary take the throne fulfills Philip's aims, with much less personal effort and expense. The purpose of discussing this scene, however, is not to critique Kapur's reading of history; but rather to demonstrate that this scene is one of several that make value judgments based on Elizabeth's gender. Unlike in other films, Blanchett's Elizabeth has had sex: she is not a virgin. This fact brings another level to the label of 'whore'—she has had sex with a man who is not her husband. The audience is thus wedged: they know that Elizabeth is not a virgin, so she cannot claim to be sexually pure (and that is to say nothing of the barely concealed sexual desire between Elizabeth and Raleigh); but, on the other hand, the audience has seen men having sex without consequences—political or moral—so why should Elizabeth be held to a different standard?

## ORLANDO

No analysis of Elizabeth's gender on film would be complete without a discussion of Quentin Crisp's depiction of Elizabeth in the 1992 film adaptation of Virginia Woolf's classic, *Orlando*. In some ways, the depiction of Elizabeth in *Orlando* is the only one to combine the four categories of man, woman, lesbian, and whore. Elizabeth's portrayal by a man is contrasted by Tilda Swinton's depiction of Orlando (Fig. 16.2). While Orlando does change sex later in the film, he is a man when interacting with Elizabeth. Thus, the scenes between Elizabeth (a woman played by a man) and Orlando (a man played by a woman) clearly play with gender roles and assumptions. Indeed, 'to call this film gender-bending would be an understatement of monumental proportions.'[42]

To the viewer, having a man portray Elizabeth may initially be confusing, but the decision actually, in some ways, allows the historical Elizabeth to appear: as the Queen approached the end of her life, she became desperate to cling to the now politically entrenched concept of her as the Virgin Queen, and the only way she could do this was to wear flamboyant clothing, wigs, and thick makeup. In doing this, the film dares to point out the disparity between 'what is professed by those around the Queen and the reality of what the aged Queen has become.'[43]

**Fig. 16.2**  Elizabeth (Quentin Crisp, left) and Orlando (Tilda Swinton) twist gender norms as they share an intimate moment. Photo by Moviestore/REX/ShutterstockQuery

The duality of Elizabeth as a man and a woman is most visible in *Orlando* when the Queen washes her hands before dinner. They are large, man's hands, with dirty fingernails and gaudy rings on eight fingers.[44] Here, Elizabeth's hermaphroditism has its most obvious appearance on film: she has wanted to possess the 'heart and stomach of a king,' and it appears that her wish has, at least partially, been granted. This scene is a clever way of demonstrating how Elizabeth handled the duality of being a female king: she was a woman, so she needed to appear virginal and chaste, but without appearing barren and infertile; and she was ruling as a man, and thus could not appear to be governed by her feminine desires.

Nevertheless, the film does make clear Elizabeth's feminine desires. The Queen is enchanted by Orlando, and during a stroll in the garden stops to speak to him. Orlando kneels in front of the Queen, who slides a garter up his leg, and says, 'You will be the son of my old age.' Orlando is thus clearly destined to not descend into old age as his queen has.[45] After dinner, the Queen calls Orlando into her bedchamber. After being undressed to her petticoats, she lies in bed. She motions for Orlando to join her; he is visibly uncomfortable. He soon acquiesces, and ends up with his head in the Queen's lap. Given the declaration that Orlando is her 'son,' the overt sexual nature of this action is extremely unsettling. To push the point even further, Elizabeth then says, 'Ah, this is my victory,' and kisses Orlando on the forehead. Orlando's head being so close to the Queen's genitals, and the implicit sexual nature of Elizabeth's comment and kiss, leaves the viewer to think of Orlando as the Queen's whore, albeit in an asexual way.

After the 'asexual' sex, Elizabeth asks to see Orlando's 'handsome leg'. She then slides her hand up his leg, and affixes the deed to the house inside the garter. The homoeroticism of this act is obvious: whether it is the lesbian interaction of Elizabeth and the female Swinton, or the gay interaction between Orlando and the male Crisp, the viewer is forced to consider what would happen if the two characters were to actually have sex—beyond what was hinted at before. The sex never happens: instead, the Queen tells Orlando, 'For you and your heirs, Orlando, the house. But on one condition: do not fade. Do not wither. Do not grow old.' This is Elizabeth's last scene in the film, but her effect has not disappeared: somehow, by agreeing to Elizabeth's command, Orlando has become immortal—he no longer ages. In what is perhaps the most pointed reference to Elizabeth's femininity, the Queen has prevented a favorite from aging—something that Elizabeth, while desperate to, was never able to achieve herself.[46]

## CONCLUSION

As these examples demonstrate, Elizabeth suffers from a crisis of gender when she is depicted in film. Variously, she is a whore, because she had sex out of wedlock and not for the purposes of procreation; she is a lesbian, because she refused the advances of her male suitors, and she had an unusually close relationship with her maid, Bess; she is a woman, because she is weak and requires the counsel of wise men; and she is a man, because she plays the part of a conquering king, and defeats the Spanish Armada. Despite these characterizations, these same films also make it clear that she is not a whore, because she resists Raleigh's advances; that she is not a lesbian, because she never had sex with a woman; that she is not a woman, because she never married and acts too much like a man; and that she is not a man, because she uses her femininity to charm her councilors, and she keeps pretending to be interested in marrying. The duality of Elizabeth as a female king is thus rendered a gendered issue: the refusal of men, the adoption of a masculine persona, the role of the patriarchy, the issue of sexual purity, engaging in transgressive sexual activity, and 'the safety and sovereignty of the nation,' are all inelegantly and awkwardly brought together by the depictions of Elizabeth on film.[47]

So, what are audiences left with? At the most basic level, these contrasting and conflicting depictions of the Queen go some of the way to explaining the difficulty of a woman ruling a country in her own right during the sixteenth century. This is one of the great benefits of historical films: while certainly overplaying and overblowing the difficulties of female kingship, the films do convey this difficulty to their audiences. However, the danger in this is that Elizabeth's life, reign, and achievements are reduced to plot devices to perpetuate the inaccurate, romantic picture of Elizabeth's reign that exists in popular culture. We will never know whether Elizabeth truly was a virgin, or indeed what her true sexual orientation was: which is fine, because Elizabeth and her gender do not have to conform to an arbitrary gender binary, or to our vision of what the past must have been like.

It is not likely that Elizabeth's cinematic gender crisis will come to an end any time soon—it makes for far too interesting viewing. But I do hope that by analyzing and dissecting these varying, and sometimes ridiculous, depictions, Elizabeth's gender can stop being only a plot complication, and the 'bewigged, beruffed, and bejeweled' woman from a century of cinematic representations gives way to a woman who was able to clearly and publicly declare that while she may have the body of a weak and feeble woman, she certainly had the heart and stomach of a king.

## NOTES

1. For the most comprehensive study of Elizabeth I on film (and television), see: Bethany Latham, *Elizabeth I in Film and Television: A Study of the Major Portrayals* (Jefferson, NC: McFarland & Company, 2011).
2. Thomas Betteridge, "A Queen for All Seasons: Elizabeth I on Film," in *The Myth of Elizabeth*, ed. Susan Doran and Thomas S. Freeman (New York: Palgrave Macmillan, 2003), 244.

3. For example, see: Carole Levin, *The Heart and Stomach of a King: Elizabeth I and the Politics of Sex and Power* (Philadelphia: University of Philadelphia Press, 2013); Louis Montrose, *The Subject of Elizabeth: Authority, Gender, and Representation* (Chicago: University of Chicago Press, 2006); and Susan Doran, "Virginity, Divinity, and Power: The Portraits of Elizabeth I," in Doran and Freeman, *The Myth of Elizabeth*, 171–199.
4. Susan Doran, "From Hatfield to Hollywood: Elizabeth I on Film," in *Tudors and Stuarts on Film: Historical Perspectives*, ed. Susan Doran and Thomas S. Freeman (New York: Palgrave Macmillan, 2009), 102–103.
5. Hayden White, "Historiography and Historiophoty," *The American Historical Review* 93, no. 5 (December 1988): 1194.
6. Christopher Haigh, *Elizabeth I* (London: Longman, 2001), 30.
7. For the Golden Speech, see: *Elizabeth I: Collected Works*, ed. Leah S. Marcus, Janel Mueller, and Mary Beth Rose (Chicago: University of Chicago Press, 2000), 335–344. For more on the concept of the king's two bodies, see Carole Levin and Charles Beem, "*Itinerarium ad Windsor* and English Queenship," in *The Name of a Queen: William Fleetwood's Itinerarium ad Windsor*, ed. Charles Beem and Dennis Moore (New York: Palgrave Macmillan, 2013), 155–173.
8. Carole Levin, *The Heart and Stomach of a King: Elizabeth I and the Politics of Sex and Power* (Philadelphia: University of Philadelphia Press, 2013), 121.
9. Robert Rosenstone, *History on Film / Film on History* (New York: Pearson, 2006), 30.
10. The anomalous position of hetaira in Classical Athens is a clear example of this. See *The Oxford Classical Dictionary*, s.v., "hetairai."
11. Colleen M. Conway, "The Construction of Gender in the New Testament," in *The Oxford Handbook of Theology, Sexuality, and Gender*, ed. Adrian Thatcher (Oxford: Oxford University Press, 2014), 233–235.
12. Laura Gowing, "Gender and the Language of Insult in Early Modern London," *History Workshop Journal* 35 (Spring 1993): 1–3, 18–19.
13. David Starkey, "Introduction," in *Elizabeth: The Exhibition at the National Maritime Museum*, ed. Susan Doran (London: Random House, 2003), 3.
14. Andrew Higson, *English Heritage, English Cinema: Costume Drama Since 1980* (Oxford: Oxford University Press, 2003), 214.
15. Elizabeth A. Ford and Deborah C. Mitchell, *Royal Portraits in Hollywood: Filming the Lives of Queens* (Lexington: The University Press of Kentucky, 2009), 289.
16. Latham, *Elizabeth I in Film and Television*, 175. I should note, for the sake of accuracy, that Elizabeth looks more like TC-14 from *Star Wars: Episode I—The Phantom Menace*, rather than the gold-plated C-3PO.

17. Carolly Erickson, *The First Elizabeth* (1983; repr. New York: St. Martin's Press, 1997), 375.
18. Alison Plowden, *Elizabeth Regina: The Age of Triumph, 1588–1603* (New York: Times Books, 1980), 11.
19. Elizabeth Jenkins, *Elizabeth the Great* (New York: Capricorn Books, 1967), 285.
20. Garrett Mattingly, *The Armada* (Boston: Houghton Mifflin, 1959), 349.
21. Susan Frye, *Elizabeth I: The Competition for Representation* (Oxford: Oxford University Press, 1993), 3.
22. Frye, *The Competition for Representation*, 3.
23. John Guy, *Elizabeth: The Forgotten Years* (London: Viking, 2016), 105–107.
24. Anon., *Cabala, Mysteries of State, in Letters of the great Ministers of K. James and K. Charles* (London, 1654), 260. I have modernized (and regularized) the speech's spelling and grammar. For more on the Tilbury speech, and an analysis that demonstrates its authenticity, see Janet M. Green, "'I My Self': Queen Elizabeth I's Oration at Tilbury Camp," *Sixteenth Century Journal* 28 (Summer 1997): 421–445.
25. Paul E. J. Hammer, *Elizabeth's Wars: War, Government, and Society in Tudor England, 1544–1604* (New York: Palgrave Macmillan, 2003), 4.
26. Betteridge, "A Queen for All Seasons," 255.
27. Latham, *Elizabeth I in Film and Television*, 170.
28. This distinction is made clear when Elizabeth visits John Dee, the (in)famous philosopher and astrologer, for a prediction of the future: 'DEE: The alignments of the planets is most unusual this year. Mars is due to take the ascendant three days after the anniversary of Your Majesty's birth. And also on that day, there is a full moon, which governs the fortunes of all princes of the female gender. ELIZABETH: Princes of the female gender. DEE: I mean to say, a prince who is also a woman. ELIZABETH: Yes, Dr. Dee, I am following you.'
29. Latham, *Elizabeth I in Film and Television*, 186.
30. Judith M. Richards, "'To Promote a Woman to Beare Rule': Talking of Queens in Mid-Tudor England," *Sixteenth Century Journal* 28, no. 1 (Spring 1997): 101–109.
31. Susan Doran, "Elizabeth I: An Old Testament King," in *Tudor Queenship: The Reigns of Mary and Elizabeth*, ed. Alice Hunt and Anna Whitelock (New York: Palgrave Macmillan, 2010), 95–97, 107–108. For more on Elizabeth and male counsel, see: Susan Doran, "Elizabeth I and Counsel," in *The Politics of Counsel in England and Scotland, 1286–1707*, ed. Jacqueline Rose (Oxford: Oxford University Press, 2017), 151–169.

32. Catherine the Great has long been a subject of adult films. See: John T. Alexander, *Catherine the Great: Life and Legend* (Oxford: Oxford University Press, 1989), 332–341.
33. Latham, *Elizabeth I in Film and Television*, 169.
34. Latham, *Elizabeth I in Film and Television*, 170.
35. See: Peter Lake, *Bad Queen Bess? Libels, Secret Histories, and the Politics of Publicity in the Reign of Queen Elizabeth I* (Oxford: Oxford University Press, 2015); and Julia M. Walker, ed., *Dissing Elizabeth: Negative Representations of Gloriana* (Durham, NC: Duke University Press, 1998).
36. Christopher Haigh, "Kapur's *Elizabeth*," in Doran and Freeman, *Tudors and Stuarts on Film*, 133. *Elizabeth* was released in 1998—the year that the Good Friday Agreement was reached—and it has been observed that the depiction of the Catholics and Protestants is likely colored by The Troubles. See: Aidan Norrie, "The King, the Queen, the Virgin, and the Cross: Catholicism versus Protestantism in *Elizabeth*," in *From Medievalism to Early Modernism: Adapting the English Past*, ed. Marina Gerzic and Aidan Norrie (London: Routledge, forthcoming 2018).
37. Judith M. Richards, "Love and a Female Monarch: The Case of Elizabeth Tudor," *Journal of British Studies* 38, no. 2 (April 1999): 148–149.
38. Paul E. J. Hammer, "The Catholic Threat and the Military Response," in *The Elizabethan World*, ed. Susan Doran and Norman Jones (London: Routledge, 2011), 635.
39. Latham, *Elizabeth I in Film and Television*, 173.
40. Ford and Mitchell, *Royal Portraits in Hollywood*, 291.
41. Latham, *Elizabeth I in Film and Television*, 173.
42. Latham, *Elizabeth I in Film and Television*, 179.
43. Latham, *Elizabeth I in Film and Television*, 180.
44. Renee Pigeon, "'No Man's Elizabeth': The Virgin Queen in Recent Films," in *Retrovisions: Reinventing the Past in Film and Fiction*, ed. Deborah Cartmell, I. Q. Hunter, and Imelda Whelehan (London: Pluto Press, 2001), 11.
45. Latham, *Elizabeth I in Film and Television*, 182.
46. Pigeon, "No Man's Elizabeth," 13.
47. Higson, *English Heritage, English Cinema*, 214.

## Bibliography

### Films

*Elizabeth*. Feature Film. Directed by Shekhar Kapur. Universal Studios, 1998.
*Elizabeth: The Golden Age*. Feature Film. Directed by Shekhar Kapur. Universal Studios, 2007.

*Orlando.* Feature Film. Directed by Sally Potter. Adventure Pictures, 1992.
*Shakespeare in Love.* Feature Film. Directed by John Madden. Universal Studios, 1998.

### Published Works

Anon. *Cabala, Mysteries of State, in Letters of the great Ministers of K. James and K. Charles.* London, 1654.
Betteridge, Thomas. "A Queen for All Seasons: Elizabeth I on Film." In *The Myth of Elizabeth*, edited by Susan Doran and Thomas S. Freeman, 242–259. New York: Palgrave Macmillan, 2003.
Conway, Colleen M. "The Construction of Gender in the New Testament." In *The Oxford Handbook of Theology, Sexuality, and Gender*, edited by Adrian Thatcher, 222–238. Oxford: Oxford University Press, 2014.
Doran, Susan. "From Hatfield to Hollywood: Elizabeth I on Film." In *Tudors and Stuarts on Film: Historical Perspectives*, edited by Susan Doran and Thomas S. Freeman, 88–105. New York: Palgrave Macmillan, 2009.
———. "Elizabeth I: An Old Testament King." In *Tudor Queenship: The Reigns of Mary and Elizabeth*, edited by Alice Hunt and Anna Whitelock, 95–110. New York: Palgrave Macmillan, 2010.
Doran, Susan, and Thomas S. Freeman, eds. *The Myth of Elizabeth.* New York: Palgrave Macmillan, 2003.
———. *Tudors and Stuarts on Film: Historical Perspectives.* New York: Palgrave Macmillan, 2009.
Erickson, Carolly. *The First Elizabeth.* 1983. Reprint, New York: St. Martin's Press, 1997.
Ford, Elizabeth A., and Deborah C. Mitchell. *Royal Portraits in Hollywood: Filming the Lives of Queens.* Lexington: The University Press of Kentucky, 2009.
Frye, Susan. *Elizabeth I: The Competition for Representation.* Oxford: Oxford University Press, 1993.
Gowing, Laura. "Gender and the Language of Insult in Early Modern London." *History Workshop Journal* 35 (Spring 1993): 1–21.
Guy, John. *Elizabeth: The Forgotten Years.* London: Viking, 2016.
Haigh, Christopher. *Elizabeth I.* London: Longman, 2001.
———. "Kapur's *Elizabeth.*" In *Tudors and Stuarts on Film: Historical Perspectives*, edited by Susan Doran and Thomas S. Freeman, 122–134. New York: Palgrave Macmillan, 2009.
Hammer, Paul E. J. *Elizabeth's Wars: War, Government, and Society in Tudor England, 1544–1604.* New York: Palgrave Macmillan, 2003.
———. "The Catholic Threat and the Military Response." In *The Elizabethan World*, edited by Susan Doran and Norman Jones, 629–645. London: Routledge, 2011.

Higson, Andrew. *English Heritage, English Cinema: Costume Drama Since 1980.* Oxford: Oxford University Press, 2003.

Jenkins, Elizabeth. *Elizabeth the Great.* New York: Capricorn Books, 1967.

Latham, Bethany. *Elizabeth I in Film and Television: A Study of the Major Portrayals.* Jefferson, NC: McFarland & Company, 2011.

Levin, Carole. *The Heart and Stomach of a King: Elizabeth I and the Politics of Sex and Power.* Philadelphia, PA: University of Philadelphia Press, 2013.

Mattingly, Garrett. *The Armada.* Boston, MA: Houghton Mifflin, 1959.

Pigeon, Renee. "'No Man's Elizabeth': The Virgin Queen in Recent Films." In *Retrovisions: Reinventing the Past in Film and Fiction,* edited by Deborah Cartmell, I. Q. Hunter, and Imelda Whelehan, 8–24. London: Pluto Press, 2001.

Plowden, Alison. *Elizabeth Regina: The Age of Triumph, 1588–1603.* New York: Times Books, 1980.

Richards, Judith M. "'To Promote a Woman to Beare Rule': Talking of Queens in Mid-Tudor England." *Sixteenth Century Journal* 28, no. 1 (Spring 1997): 101–121.

———. "Love and a Female Monarch: The Case of Elizabeth Tudor." *Journal of British Studies* 38, no. 2 (April 1999): 133–160.

Rosenstone, Robert. *History on Film / Film on History.* New York: Pearson, 2006.

Starkey, David. "Introduction." In *Elizabeth: The Exhibition at the National Maritime Museum,* edited by Susan Doran, 3–8. London: Random House, 2003.

White, Hayden. "Historiography and Historiophoty." *The American Historical Review* 93, no. 5 (December 1988): 1193–1199.

# INDEX

Printed by Printforce, the Netherlands